SERIES

(ex•ploring)

1. Investigating in a systematic way: examining. 2. Searching
into or ranging over for the purpose of discovery.

(ex•ploring)

SERIES

1. Investigating in a systematic way: examining. 2. Searching into or ranging over for the purpose of discovery.

Microsoft® Office
Excel 2010
Introductory

Robert T. Grauer

Keith Mulbery | Mary Anne Poatsy

Prentice Hall
Upper Saddle River   London   Singapore
Toronto   Tokyo   Sydney   Hong Kong   Mexico City

Library of Congress Cataloging-in-Publication Data

Grauer, Robert T.
 Microsoft Office Excel 2010. Introductory / Robert T. Grauer, Keith Mulbery, Mary Anne Poatsy.
   p. cm.
 Includes index.
 ISBN-13: 978-0-13-509847-9
 ISBN-10: 0-13-509847-5
 1. Microsoft Excel (Computer file) 2. Business—Computer programs. 3. Electronic spreadsheets. I. Mulbery, Keith. II. Poatsy, Mary Anne. III. Title.
 HF5548.4.M523G728 2011
 005.54—dc22

                                                                                                2010020175

Editor in Chief: Michael Payne	**Marketing Coordinator:** Susan Osterlitz
Acquisitions Editor: Samantha McAfee	**Marketing Assistant:** Darshika Vyas
Product Development Manager: Eileen Bien Calabro	**Senior Managing Editor:** Cynthia Zonneveld
Editorial Project Manager: Meghan Bisi	**Associate Managing Editor:** Camille Trentacoste
Development Editors: Laura Town and Jennifer Campbell	**Production Project Manager:** Ruth Ferrera-Kargov
Editorial Assistant: Erin Clark	**Manager of Rights & Permissions:** Hessa Albader
AVP/Director of Product Development: Lisa Strite	**Senior Operations Specialist:** Diane Peirano
Editor-Digital Learning & Assessment: Paul Gentile	**Senior Art Director:** Jonathan Boylan
Product Development Manager-Media: Cathi Profitko	**Cover Design:** Jonathan Boylan
Editorial Media Project Manager: Alana Coles	**Cover Illustration/Photo:** Courtesy of Shutterstock® Images
Production Media Project Manager: John Cassar	**Composition:** PreMediaGlobal
Director of Marketing: Kate Valentine	**Full-Service Project Management:** PreMediaGlobal
Marketing Manager: Tori Olson Alves	**Typeface:** 10.5/12.5 Minion

Pearson Education Ltd., London	Pearson Education North Asia Ltd., Hong Kong
Pearson Education Singapore, Pte. Ltd.	Pearson Educación de Mexico, S.A. de C.V.
Pearson Education, Canada, Ltd.	Pearson Education Malaysia, Pte. Ltd.
Pearson Education–Japan	Pearson Education, Upper Saddle River, New Jersey
Pearson Education Australia PTY, Limited	

Prentice Hall
is an imprint of

www.pearsonhighered.com

ISBN-13: 978-0-13-509847-9
ISBN-10: 0-13-509847-5

DEDICATIONS

I dedicate this book in loving memory to Grandma Ida Lu Etta (Billie) Hort, who was a positive role model for me through her patience, caring personality, and perseverance through challenging situations. I treasure her support and encouragement throughout my personal and professional endeavors, including years of textbook writing.

Keith Mulbery

For my husband Ted, who unselfishly continues to take on more than his fair share to support me throughout this process; and for my children, Laura, Carolyn, and Teddy, whose encouragement and love have been inspiring.

Mary Anne Poatsy

ABOUT THE AUTHORS

Dr. Keith Mulbery, Consulting Series Editor and Excel Author

Dr. Keith Mulbery is the Department Chair and an Associate Professor in the Information Systems and Technology Department at Utah Valley University (UVU), where he teaches computer applications, C# programming, systems analysis and design, and MIS classes. Keith also served as Interim Associate Dean, School of Computing, in the College of Technology and Computing at UVU.

Keith received the Utah Valley State College Board of Trustees Award of Excellence in 2001, School of Technology and Computing Scholar Award in 2007, and School of Technology and Computing Teaching Award in 2008. He has authored more than 15 textbooks, served as Series Editor for the Exploring Office 2007 series, and served as developmental editor on two textbooks.

Keith received his B.S. and M.Ed. in Business Education from Southwestern Oklahoma State University and earned his Ph.D. in Education with an emphasis in Business Information Systems at Utah State University. His dissertation topic was computer-assisted instruction using Prentice Hall's Train and Assess IT program to supplement traditional instruction in basic computer proficiency courses.

Dr. Lynn Hogan, Office Fundamentals and File Management Author

Lynn Hogan has taught in the Computer Information Systems area at Calhoun Community College for 29 years. She is the author of *Practical Computing* and has contributed chapters for several computer applications textbooks. Primarily teaching in the areas of computer literacy and computer applications, she was named Calhoun's outstanding instructor in 2006. She received an M.B.A. from the University of North Alabama and a Ph.D. from the University of Alabama. Lynn resides in Alabama with her husband and two daughters.

Mary Anne Poatsy, Series Editor

Mary Anne is a senior faculty member at Montgomery County Community College, teaching various computer application and concepts courses in face-to-face and online environments. She holds a B.A. in psychology and education from Mount Holyoke College and an M.B.A. in finance from Northwestern University's Kellogg Graduate School of Management.

Mary Anne has more than 12 years of educational experience. She is currently adjunct faculty at Gwynedd-Mercy College and Montgomery County Community College. She has also taught at Bucks County Community College and Muhlenberg College, as well as conducted professional training. Before teaching, she was vice president at Shearson Lehman in the Municipal Bond Investment Banking Department.

Dr. Robert T. Grauer, Creator of the Exploring Series

Bob Grauer is an Associate Professor in the Department of Computer Information Systems at the University of Miami, where he is a multiple winner of the Outstanding Teaching Award in the School of Business, most recently in 2009. He has written numerous COBOL texts and is the vision behind the Exploring Office series, with more than three million books in print. His work has been translated into three foreign languages and is used in all aspects of higher education at both national and international levels. Bob Grauer has consulted for several major corporations including IBM and American Express. He received his Ph.D. in operations research in 1972 from the Polytechnic Institute of Brooklyn.

BRIEF CONTENTS

CONTENTS

CHAPTER TWO ➤ Formulas and Functions 129

CHAPTER THREE ➤ Charts 177

CHAPTER FOUR ➤ Datasets and Tables 229

ACKNOWLEDGMENTS

The Exploring team would like to acknowledge and thank all the reviewers who helped us prepare for the Exploring Office 2010 revision by providing us with their invaluable comments, suggestions, and constructive criticism:

Allen Alexander
Delaware Technical & Community College

Andrea Marchese
Maritime College, State University of New York

Andrew Blitz
Broward College, Edison State College

Angela Clark
University of South Alabama

Astrid Todd
Guilford Technical Community College

Audrey Gillant
Maritime College, State University of New York

Barbara Stover
Marion Technical College

Barbara Tollinger
Sinclair Community College

Ben Brahim Taha
Auburn University

Beverly Amer
Northern Arizona University

Beverly Fite
Amarillo College

Bonnie Homan
San Francisco State University

Brad West
Sinclair Community College

Brian Powell
West Virginia University

Carol Buser
Owens Community College

Carol Roberts
University of Maine

Cathy Poyner
Truman State University

Charles Hodgson
Delgado Community College

Cheryl Hinds
Norfolk State University

Cindy Herbert
Metropolitan Community College–Longview

Dana Hooper
University of Alabama

Dana Johnson
North Dakota State University

Daniela Marghitu
Auburn University

David Noel
University of Central Oklahoma

David Pulis
Maritime College, State University of New York

David Thornton
Jacksonville State University

Dawn Medlin
Appalachian State University

Debby Keen
University of Kentucky

Debra Chapman
University of South Alabama

Derrick Huang
Florida Atlantic University

Diana Baran
Henry Ford Community College

Diane Cassidy
The University of North Carolina at Charlotte

Diane Smith
Henry Ford Community College

Don Danner
San Francisco State University

Don Hoggan
Solano College

Elaine Crable
Xavier University

Erhan Uskup
Houston Community College–Northwest

Erika Nadas
Wilbur Wright College

Floyd Winters
Manatee Community College

Frank Lucente
Westmoreland County Community College

G. Jan Wilms
Union University

Gail Cope
Sinclair Community College

Gary DeLorenzo
California University of Pennsylvania

Gary Garrison
Belmont University

Gerald Braun
Xavier University

Gladys Swindler
Fort Hays State University

Heith Hennel
Valencia Community College

Irene Joos
La Roche College

Iwona Rusin
Baker College; Davenport University

J. Roberto Guzman
San Diego Mesa College

Jan Wilms
Union University

Janet Bringhurst
Utah State University

Jim Chaffee
The University of Iowa Tippie College of Business

Joanne Lazirko
University of Wisconsin–Milwaukee

Jodi Milliner
Kansas State University

John Hollenbeck
Blue Ridge Community College

John Seydel
Arkansas State University

Judith A. Scheeren
Westmoreland County Community College

Judith Brown
The University of Memphis

Karen Priestly
Northern Virginia Community College

Karen Ravan
Spartanburg Community College

Kathleen Brenan
Ashland University

Ken Busbee
Houston Community College

Kent Foster
Winthrop University

Kevin Anderson
Solano Community College

Kim Wright
The University of Alabama

Kristen Hockman
University of Missouri–Columbia

Kristi Smith
Allegany College of Maryland

Laura McManamon
University of Dayton

Leanne Chun
Leeward Community College

Lee McClain
Western Washington University

Linda D. Collins
Mesa Community College

Linda Johnsonius
Murray State University

Linda Lau
Longwood University

Linda Theus
Jackson State Community College

Lisa Miller
University of Central Oklahoma

Lister Horn
Pensacola Junior College

Lixin Tao
Pace University

Loraine Miller
Cayuga Community College

Lori Kielty
Central Florida Community College

Lorna Wells
Salt Lake Community College

Lucy Parakhovnik (Parker)
California State University, Northridge

Marcia Welch
Highline Community College

Margaret McManus
Northwest Florida State College

Margaret Warrick
Allan Hancock College

Marilyn Hibbert
Salt Lake Community College

Mark Choman
Luzerne County Community College

Mary Duncan
University of Missouri – St. Louis

Melissa Nemeth
Indiana University Purdue University
Indianapolis

Melody Alexander
Ball State University

Michael Douglas
University of Arkansas at Little Rock

Michael Dunklebarger
Alamance Community College

Michael G. Skaff
College of the Sequoias

Michele Budnovitch
Pennsylvania College of Technology

Mike Jochen
East Stroudsburg University

Mike Scroggins
Missouri State University

Nanette Lareau
University of Arkansas Community College–
Morrilton

Pam Uhlenkamp
Iowa Central Community College

Patrick Smith
Marshall Community and Technical College

Paula Ruby
Arkansas State University

Peggy Burrus
Red Rocks Community College

Peter Ross
SUNY Albany

Philip H Nielson
Salt Lake Community College

Ralph Hooper
University of Alabama

Ranette Halverson
Midwestern State University

Richard Cacace
Pensacola Junior College

Robert Dušek
Northern Virginia Community College

Robert Sindt
Johnson County Community College

Rocky Belcher
Sinclair Community College

Roger Pick
University of Missouri at Kansas City

Ronnie Creel
Troy University

Rosalie Westerberg
Clover Park Technical College

Ruth Neal
Navarro College

Sandra Thomas
Troy University

Sophie Lee
California State University, Long Beach

Steven Schwarz
Raritan Valley Community College

Sue McCrory
Missouri State University

Susan Fuschetto
Cerritos College

Susan Medlin
UNC Charlotte

Suzan Spitzberg
Oakton Community College

Sven Aelterman
Troy University

Terri Holly
Indian River State College

Thomas Rienzo
Western Michigan University

Tina Johnson
Midwestern State University

Tommy Lu
Delaware Technical and Community College

Troy S. Cash
NorthWest Arkansas Community College

Vicki Robertson
Southwest Tennessee Community College

Weifeng Chen
California University of Pennsylvania

Wes Anthony
Houston Community College

William Ayen
University of Colorado at Colorado Springs

Wilma Andrews
Virginia Commonwealth University

Yvonne Galusha
University of Iowa

We'd also like to acknowledge the reviewers of previous editions of Exploring:

Aaron Schorr
Fashion Institute of Technology

Alan Moltz
Naugatuck Valley Technical Community
College

Alicia Stonesifer
La Salle University

Allen Alexander
Delaware Tech & Community College

Alok Charturvedi
Purdue University

Amy Williams
Abraham Baldwin Agriculture College

Andrea Compton
St. Charles Community College

Annette Duvall
Central New Mexico Community College

Annie Brown
Hawaii Community College

Antonio Vargas
El Paso Community College

Barbara Cierny
Harper College

Barbara Hearn
Community College of Philadelphia

Barbara Meguro
University of Hawaii at Hilo

Barbara Sherman
Buffalo State College

Barbara Stover
Marion Technical College

Bette Pitts
South Plains College

Beverly Fite
Amarillo College

Bill Daley
University of Oregon

Bill Morse
DeVry Institute of Technology

Bill Wagner
Villanova

Bob McCloud
Sacred Heart University

Bonnie Homan
San Francisco State University

Brandi N. Guidry
University of Louisiana at Lafayette

Brian Powell
West Virginia University–Morgantown
Campus

Carl Farrell
Hawaii Pacific University

Carl M. Briggs
Indiana University School of Business

Carl Penzuil
Ithaca College

Carlotta Eaton
Radford University

Carole Bagley
University of St. Thomas

Carolyn DiLeo
Westchester Community College

Cassie Georgetti
Florida Technical College

Catherine Hain
Central New Mexico Community College

Charles Edwards
University of Texas of the Permian Basin

Cheryl Slavik
Computer Learning Services

Christine L. Moore
College of Charleston

Cody Copeland
Johnson County Community College

Connie Wells
Georgia State University

Dana Johnson
North Dakota State University

Dan Combellick
Scottsdale Community College

Daniela Marghitu
Auburn University

David B. Meinert
Southwest Missouri State University

David Barnes
Penn State Altoona

David Childress
Ashland Community College

David Douglas
University of Arkansas

David Langley
University of Oregon

David Law
Alfred State College

David Rinehard
Lansing Community College

David Weiner
University of San Francisco

Delores Pusins
Hillsborough Community College

Dennis Chalupa
Houston Baptist

Diane Stark
Phoenix College

Dianna Patterson
Texarkana College

Dianne Ross
University of Louisiana at Lafayette

Don Belle
Central Piedmont Community College

Douglas Cross
Clackamas Community College

Dr. Behrooz Saghafi
Chicago State University

Dr. Gladys Swindler
Fort Hays State University

Dr. Joe Teng
Barry University

Dr. Karen Nantz
Eastern Illinois University

Duane D. Lintner
Amarillo College

Elizabeth Edmiston
North Carolina Central University

Erhan Uskup
Houston Community College

Ernie Ivey
Polk Community College

Fred Hills
McClellan Community College

Freda Leonard
Delgado Community College

Gale E. Rand
College Misericordia

Gary R. Armstrong
Shippensburg University of Pennsylvania

Glenna Vanderhoof
Missouri State

Gregg Asher
Minnesota State University, Mankato

Hank Imus
San Diego Mesa College

Heidi Gentry-Kolen
Northwest Florida State College

Helen Stoloff
Hudson Valley Community College

Herach Safarian
College of the Canyons

Hong K. Sung
University of Central Oklahoma

Hyekyung Clark
Central New Mexico Community College

J Patrick Fenton
West Valley College

Jack Zeller
Kirkwood Community College

James Franck
College of St. Scholastica

James Gips
Boston College

Jana Carver
Amarillo College

Jane Cheng
Bloomfield College

Jane King
Everett Community College

Janis Cox
Tri-County Technical College

Janos T. Fustos
Metropolitan State College of Denver

Jean Kotsiovos
Kaplan University

Jeffrey A Hassett
University of Utah

Jennifer Pickle
Amarillo College

Jerry Chin
Southwest Missouri State University

Jerry Kolata
New England Institute of Technology

Jesse Day
South Plains College

Jill Chapnick
Florida International University

Jim Pepe
Bentley College

Jim Pruitt
Central Washington University

John Arehart
Longwood University

John Lee Reardon
University of Hawaii, Manoa

John Lesson
University of Central Florida

John Shepherd
Duquesne University

Joshua Mindel
San Francisco State University

Judith M. Fitspatrick
Gulf Coast Community College

Judith Rice
Santa Fe Community College

Judy Brown
The University of Memphis

Judy Dolan
Palomar College

Karen Tracey
Central Connecticut State University

Karen Wisniewski
County College of Morris

Karl Smart
Central Michigan University

Kathleen Brenan
Ashland University

Kathryn L. Hatch
University of Arizona

Kevin Pauli
University of Nebraska

Kim Montney
Kellogg Community College

Kimberly Chambers
Scottsdale Community College

Krista Lawrence
Delgado Community College

Krista Terry
Radford University

Lancie Anthony Affonso
College of Charleston

Larry S. Corman
Fort Lewis College

Laura McManamon
University of Dayton

Laura Reid
University of Western Ontario

Linda Johnsonius
Murray State University

Lisa Prince
Missouri State University

Lori Kelley
Madison Area Technical College

Lucy Parker
California State University, Northridge

Lynda Henrie
LDS Business College

Lynn Band
Middlesex Community College

Lynn Bowen
Valdosta Technical College

Malia Young
Utah State University

Margaret Thomas
Ohio University

Margie Martyn
Baldwin Wallace

Marguerite Nedreberg
Youngstown State University

Marianne Trudgeon
Fanshawe College

Marilyn Hibbert
Salt Lake Community College

Marilyn Salas
Scottsdale Community College

Marjean Lake
LDS Business College

Mark Olaveson
Brigham Young University

Martin Crossland
Southwest Missouri State University

Mary McKenry Percival
University of Miami

Meg McManus
Northwest Florida State College

Michael Hassett
Fort Hayes State University

Michael Stewardson
San Jacinto College–North

Midge Gerber
Southwestern Oklahoma State University

Mike Hearn
Community College of Philadelphia

Mike Kelly
Community College of Rhode Island

Mike Thomas
Indiana University School of Business

Mimi Duncan
University of Missouri–St. Louis

Minnie Proctor
Indian River Community College

Nancy Sardone
Seton Hall University

Pam Chapman
Waubonsee Community College

Patricia Joseph
Slippery Rock University

Patrick Hogan
Cape Fear Community College

Paul E. Daurelle
Western Piedmont Community
College

Paula F. Bell
Lock Haven University of Pennsylvania

Paulette Comet
Community College of Baltimore County,
Catonsville

Pratap Kotala
North Dakota State University

Ranette Halverson
Midwestern State University

Raymond Frost
Central Connecticut State University

Richard Albright
Goldey-Beacom College

Richard Blamer
John Carroll University

Richard Herschel
St. Joseph's University

Richard Hewer
Ferris State University

Robert Gordon
Hofstra University

Robert Marmelstein
East Stroudsburg University

Robert Spear
Prince George's Community College

Robert Stumbur
Northern Alberta Institute of Technology

Roberta I. Hollen
University of Central Oklahoma

Roland Moreira
South Plains College

Ron Murch
University of Calgary

Rory J. de Simone
University of Florida

Rose M. Laird
Northern Virginia Community College

Ruth Neal
Navarro College

Sally Visci
Lorain County Community College

Sandra M. Brown
Finger Lakes Community College

Sharon Mulroney
Mount Royal College

Shawna DePlonty
Sault College of Applied Arts and Technology

Stephen E. Lunce
Midwestern State University

Steve Schwarz
Raritan Valley Community College

Steven Choy
University of Calgary

Stuart P. Brian
Holy Family College

Susan Byrne
St. Clair College

Susan Fry
Boise State University

Suzan Spitzberg
Oakton Community College

Suzanne Tomlinson
Iowa State University

Thomas Setaro
Brookdale Community College

Todd McLeod
Fresno City College

Vernon Griffin
Austin Community College

Vickie Pickett
Midland College

Vipul Gupta
St. Joseph's University

Vivek Shah
Texas State University–San Marcos

Wei-Lun Chuang
Utah State University

William Dorin
Indiana University Northwest

Additionally, we'd like to thank our Instructor Resource authors:

Anci Shah
Houston Community College

Ann Rovetto
Horry-Georgetown Technical College

Arlene Eliason
Minnesota School of Business

Barbara Stover
Marion Technical College

Carol Roberts
University of Maine

David Csuha
Passaic County Community College

James Powers
University of Southern Indiana

Jayne Lowery
Jackson State Community College

Julie Boyles
Portland Community College

Kyle Stark
Macomb Community College

Linda Lau
Longwood University

Lisa Prince
Missouri State University

Lynn Bowen
Valdosta Technical College

Lynn Hogan
Calhoun Community College

Mary Lutz
Southwestern Illinois College

Meg McManus
Northwest Florida State College

Sally Baker
DeVry University

Sharon Behrens
Mid-State Technical College

Stephanie Jones
Texas Tech University

Steve Rubin
California State University, Monterey Bay

Suzan Spitzberg
Oakton Community College

Tom McKenzie
James Madison University

Finally, we'd like to extend our thanks to the Exploring 2010 technical editors:

Chad Kirsch	Janice Snyder	Lori Damanti
Cheryl Slavik	Joyce Nielsen	Sandra Swinney
Elizabeth Lockley	Julie Boyles	Sean Portnoy
Janet Pickard	Lisa Bucki	

PREFACE

The Exploring Series and You

Exploring is Pearson's Office Application series which requires students like you to think "beyond the point and click." With Office 2010, Exploring has embraced today's student learning styles to support extended learning beyond the classroom.

The goal of Exploring is, as it has always been, to go further than teaching just the steps to accomplish a task—the series provides the theoretical foundation for you to understand when and why to apply a skill. As a result, you achieve a deeper understanding of each application and can apply this critical thinking beyond Office and the classroom.

You are plugged in constantly, and Exploring has evolved to meet you half-way to work within your changing learning styles. Pearson has paid attention to the habits of students today, how you get information, how you are motivated to do well in class, and what your future goals look like. We asked you and your peers for acceptance of new tools we designed to address these points, and you responded with a resounding "YES!"

Here Is What We Learned About You

You go to college now with a different set of skills than students did five years ago. The new edition of Exploring moves you beyond the basics of the software at a faster pace, without sacrificing coverage of the fundamental skills that you need to know. This ensures that you will be engaged from page 1 to the end of the book.

You and your peers have diverse learning styles. With this in mind, we broadened our definition of "student resources" to include Compass, an online skill database; movable Visual Reference cards; relevant Set-Up Videos filmed in a familiar, commercial style; and the most powerful online homework and assessment tool around, my**it**lab. Exploring will be accessible to all students, regardless of learning style.

You read, prepare, and study differently than students used to. You use textbooks like a tool—you want to easily identify what you need to know and learn it efficiently. We have added key features that make the content accessible to you and make the text easy to use.

You are goal-oriented. You want a good grade and you want to be successful in your future career. With this in mind, we used motivating case studies and Set-Up Videos to aid in the learning now and to show the relevance of the skills to your future careers.

Moving Beyond the Point and Click and Extending Your Learning Beyond the Classroom

All of these additions will keep you more engaged, helping you to achieve a higher level of understanding and to complete this course and go on to be successful in your career. In addition to the vision and experience of the series creator, Robert T. Grauer, we have assembled a tremendously talented team of Office Applications authors who have devoted themselves to teaching you the ins and outs of Microsoft Word, Excel, Access, and PowerPoint. Led in this edition by series editor Mary Anne Poatsy, the whole team is equally dedicated to the Exploring mission of **moving you beyond the point and click, and extending your learning beyond the classroom.**

Key Features of Exploring Office 2010

- **White Pages/Yellow Pages** clearly distinguish the theory (white pages) from the skills covered in the Hands-On Exercises (yellow pages) so students always know what they are supposed to be doing.

- **Objective Mapping** enables students to skip the skills and concepts they know and quickly find those they do not know by scanning the chapter opener pages for the page numbers of the material they need.

- **Pull Quotes** entice students into the theory by highlighting the most interesting points.

- **Case Study** presents a scenario for the chapter, creating a story that ties the Hands-On Exercises together.

- **FYI Icon** indicates that an exercise step includes a skill that is common to more than one application. Students who require more information on that skill may utilize the Office Fundamentals and File Management chapter, the Visual Reference Cards, or Compass for assistance.

- **Set-Up Video** introduces the chapter's Case Study to generate student interest and attention and shows the relevance of the skills to students' future work.

- **Key Terms** are defined in the margins to ensure student comprehension.

- **End-of-Chapter Exercises** offer instructors several options for assessment. Each chapter has approximately 12–15 exercises ranging from multiple choice questions to open-ended projects.

CREATIVE CASE   DISCOVER

- **Enhanced Mid-Level Exercises** include a **Creative Case**, which allows students some flexibility and creativity, not being bound by a definitive solution, as well as **Discover Steps**, which encourage students to use Help or to problem-solve to accomplish a task.

Instructor Resources

The Instructor's Resource Center, available at www.pearsonhighered.com includes the following:

- **Annotated Solution Files with Scorecards** assist with grading the Hands-On Exercises and end-of-chapter exercises.

- **Data and Solution Files**

- **Capstone Production Tests** allow instructors to assess all skills covered in a chapter with a single project.

- **Rubrics** for Mid-Level Creative Cases and Beyond the Classroom Cases in Microsoft® Word format enable instructors to customize the assignments for their classes.

- **PowerPoint® Presentations** with notes for each chapter are included for out-of-class study or review.

- **Audio PowerPoint Presentations** provide an alternate version of the PowerPoint presentations in which all the lecture notes have been prerecorded.

- **Lesson Plans** provide a detailed blueprint to achieve chapter learning objectives and outcomes.

- **Objectives List** maps chapter objectives to Hands-On Exercises and end-of-chapter exercises.

- **Multiple Choice Answer Key**

- **Complete Test Bank**, also available in TestGen format.

- **Set-Up Video Exercises** provide companion exercises for the Set-Up Video for each chapter.

- **Syllabus templates** for 8-week, 12-week, and 16-week courses.

- **Grader projects** provide live-in-the-application assessment for each chapter's Capstone Exercise and additional capstone exercises.

- **Instructor Reference Cards**, available electronically and as printed cards, for each chapter, include:
  - **Concept Summary** outlines the KEY objectives to cover in class with tips on where students get stuck as well as how to get them unstuck.
  - **Scripted Lecture** provides instructors with a lecture outline that mirrors the Hands-On Exercises.

Online Course Cartridges

Flexible, robust, and customizable content is available for all major online course platforms that include everything instructors need in one place. Please contact your Sales Representative for information on accessing course cartridges for WebCT, Blackboard, or CourseCompass.

Student Resources

Student Data CD

- Student Data Files

- Set-Up Videos introduce the chapter's Case Study to generate student interest and attention and show the relevance of the skills to students' future work.

- Compass access via computer and mobile phone

Visual Reference Cards

A two-sided reference card for each application provides students with a visual summary of information and tips specific to each application that provide answers to the most common student questions. The cards can be easily attached to and detached from the book's spiral binding to be used as a bookmark, and all cards are clearly color-coded by application.

Compass

Compass is a searchable database of Microsoft Office 2010 skills that is available for use online on a computer or on your mobile phone. Using a keyword look-up system on your computer, the database provides multimedia instructions via videos and at-a-glance frames to remind students how to perform a skill. For students on the go, you can use your mobile phone to search and access a brief description of a skill and the click-stream instructions for how to perform the skill. This is a resource for the tech savvy student, who wants help and answers right away. Students get access to Compass through my**it**lab and/or the Student CD.

Prentice Hall's Companion Web Site

www.pearsonhighered.com/exploring offers expanded IT resources and downloadable supplements. Students can find the following self-study tools for each chapter:

- Online Study Guide

- Chapter Objectives

- Glossary

- Chapter Objectives Review

- Web Resources

- Student Data Files

my**it**lab for Office 2010 is a solution designed by professors for professors that allows easy delivery of Office courses with defensible assessment and outcomes-based training. The new *Exploring Office 2010* system will seamlessly integrate online assessment, training, and projects with my**it**lab for Microsoft Office 2010!

myitlab for Office 2010 Features. . .

- **Assessment and training built to match** *Exploring Office 2010* instructional content so that my**it**lab works with *Exploring* to move students beyond the point and click.

- **Both project-based and skill-based assessment and training** allow instructors to test and train students on complete exercises or individual Office application skills.

- **Full course management functionality** includes all instructor and student resources, a complete Gradebook, and the ability to run a variety of reports including detailed student clickstream data.

- **The most open, realistic, high-fidelity simulation** of Office 2010 so students feel like they are learning Office, not just a simulation.

- **Grader, a live-in-the-application project-grading tool**, enables instructors to assign projects taken from the end-of-chapter material and additional projects included in the instructor resources. These are graded automatically, with detailed feedback provided to both instructors and students.

OFFICE FUNDAMENTALS

1 OFFICE FUNDAMENTALS AND FILE MANAGEMENT

Taking the First Step

CASE STUDY | Rails and Trails

Watch the Set-up Video for this Case Study!

You are an administrative assistant for a local historical preservation project. The project involves creating a series of trails designed for hikers, bikers, and horseback riders. The trails generally follow the route of a historic railroad line that traversed the northwestern corner of Kentucky from the early 1900s until it was discontinued in 1991. The 78 miles of trails follow the original rail route, which passed through natural hardwood forests and open meadows. Considered a major impetus of the Kentucky Historical Preservation Society, the project has received both public and private funding through legislative appropriations and private and federal grants.

As the administrative assistant, you are responsible for overseeing the production of documents, spreadsheets, newspaper articles, and presentations that will be used to increase public awareness of the Rails and Trails project. Other clerical assistants who are familiar with Microsoft Office will prepare the promotional materials, and you will proofread, make necessary corrections, adjust page layouts, save and print documents, and identify appropriate templates to simplify tasks. Your experience with Microsoft Office 2010 is limited, but you know that certain fundamental tasks that are common to Word, Excel, and PowerPoint will help you accomplish your oversight task. You are excited to get started on the project!

Files and Folders

If you stop to consider why you use a computer, you will most likely conclude that you want to produce some type of output. That output could be games, music, or the display of digital photographs. Perhaps you use a computer at work to produce reports, financial worksheets, or schedules. All of those items are considered computer *files*. Files include electronic data such as documents, databases, slide shows, and worksheets. Even digital photographs, music, videos, and Web pages are saved as files.

> Windows 7 provides tools that enable you to create folders and to save files in ways that make locating them simple.

You use software to create and save files. For example, when you type a document on a computer, you first open a word processor such as Microsoft Word. Similarly, you could use a type of Web-authoring software to create a Web page. In order to access files later, you must save them to a computer storage medium such as a hard drive or flash drive. And just as you would probably organize a filing cabinet into a system of folders, you can organize storage media by *folders* that you name and into which you place data files. That way, you can easily retrieve the files later. Windows 7 provides tools that enable you to create folders and to save files in ways that make locating them simple. In this section, you will learn to use Windows Explorer to manage folders and files.

A **file** is a document or item of information that you create with software and to which you give a name.

A **folder** is a named storage location where you can save files.

Using Windows Explorer

Windows Explorer is a Windows component that can be used to create and manage folders.

A **subfolder** is a folder that is housed within another folder.

Windows Explorer is a component that can be used to create and manage folders. The sole purpose of a computer folder is to provide a labeled storage location for related files so that you can easily organize and retrieve items. A folder structure can occur across several levels, so you can create folders within other folders (called *subfolders*), arranged according to purpose. Windows 7 introduces the concept of libraries, which are folders that gather files from different locations and display the files as if they were all saved in a single folder, regardless of where they are physically stored. Using Windows Explorer, you can manage folders, work with libraries, and view favorites (areas or folders that are frequently accessed).

Understand and Customize the Interface

To open Windows Explorer, click Windows Explorer on the taskbar as shown in Figure 1.1. You can also right-click the Start button and click Open Windows Explorer. Figure 1.2 shows the Windows Explorer interface containing several areas. Some of those areas are described in Table 1.1.

FIGURE 1.1 Windows Explorer ➤

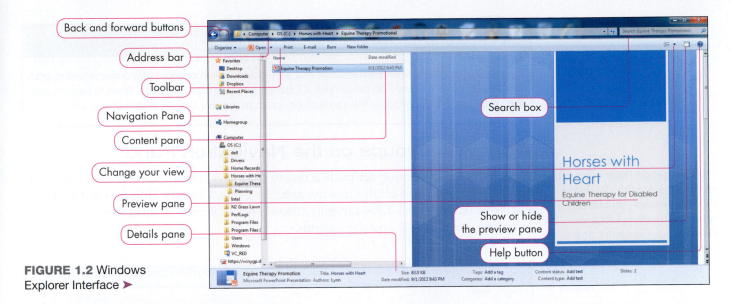

FIGURE 1.2 Windows Explorer Interface ➤

TABLE 1.1	Windows Explorer Interface
Navigation Pane	The Navigation Pane contains five areas: Favorites, Libraries, Homegroup, Computer, and Network. Click an item in the Navigation Pane to display contents and to manage files that are housed within a selected folder.
Back and Forward Buttons	Use these buttons to visit previously opened folders or libraries.
Toolbar	The Toolbar includes buttons that are relevant to the currently selected item. If you are working with a music file, the toolbar buttons might include one for burning to a CD, whereas if you have selected a document, the toolbar would enable you to open or share the file.
Address Bar	The Address bar enables you to navigate to other folders or libraries.
Content Pane	The Content pane shows the contents of the currently selected folder or library.
Search Box	Find files and folders by typing descriptive text in the Search box. Windows immediately begins a search after you type the first character, further narrowing results as you type.
Details Pane	The Details pane shows properties that are associated with a selected file. Common properties include information such as the author name and the date the file was last modified.
Preview Pane	The Preview pane provides a snapshot of a selected file's contents. You can see file contents before actually opening the file. The Preview pane does not show the contents of a selected folder.

As you work with Windows Explorer, you might find that the view is not how you would like it. The file and folder icons might be too small for ease of identification, or you might want additional details about displayed files and folders. Modifying the view is easy. To make icons larger or to provide additional detail, click the Change your view arrow (see Figure 1.2), and select from the views provided. If you want additional detail, such as file type and size, click Details. You can also change the size of icons by selecting Small, Medium, Large, or Extra Large icons. The List view shows the file names without added detail, whereas Tiles and Content views are useful to show file thumbnails (small pictures describing file contents) and varying levels of detail regarding file locations. To show or hide Windows Explorer panes, click Organize (on the Toolbar), point to Layout, and then select the pane to hide or show. You can widen or narrow panes by dragging a border when the mouse changes to a double-headed arrow. When you click Show or hide the Preview pane, you toggle—or change between— views. If the Preview pane is not shown, clicking the button shows the pane. Conversely, if the pane is already open, clicking the button will hide it.

Work with Groups on the Navigation Pane

The **Navigation Pane** is located on the left side of the Windows Explorer window, providing access to Favorites, Libraries, Homegroup, Computer, and Network areas.

The *Navigation Pane* provides ready access to computer resources, folders, files, and networked peripherals. It is divided into five areas: Favorites, Libraries, Homegroup, Computer, and Network. In Figure 1.3, the currently selected area is Libraries. Each of those components provides a unique way to organize contents.

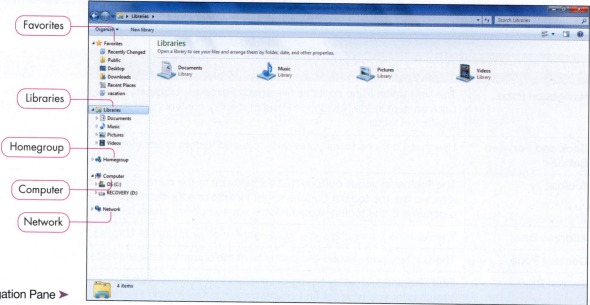

FIGURE 1.3 Navigation Pane ➤

A **library** is an organization method that collects files from different locations and displays them as one unit.

Earlier, we used the analogy of computer folders to folders in a filing cabinet. Just as you would title folders in a filing cabinet according to their contents, computer folders are also titled according to content. Folders are physically located on storage media such as a hard drive or flash drive. You can also organize folders into *libraries*, which are collections of files from different locations that are displayed as single units. For example, the Pictures library includes files from the Pictures folder and from the Public Pictures folder, both of which are physically housed on the hard drive. Although the library content comes from two separate folders, contents are displayed as a unit.

Windows 7 includes several libraries that include default folders or devices. For example, the Documents library includes the My Documents and Public Documents folders, but you can add other folders if you wish so that they are also housed within the Documents library. To add a folder to a library, right-click the folder, and then point to Include in library. Then select a library, or select Create new library and create a new one. To remove a folder from a library, open Windows Explorer, and then click the library from which you want to remove the folder. In the Library pane shown at the right side of the Windows Explorer window, click the locations link (next to the word *Includes*). The link will indicate the number of physical locations in which the folders are housed. For example, if folders in the Pictures library are drawn from two locations, the link will read *2 locations*. Click the folder that you want to remove, click Remove, and then click OK.

The Computer area provides access to specific storage locations, such as a hard drive, CD/DVD, and removable media (including a flash drive). Files and folders housed on those storage media are accessible when you click Computer. For example, click drive C, shown under Computer in the Navigation Pane, to view its contents in the Content pane on the right. If you simply want to see the subfolders of the hard drive, click the arrow to the left of drive C to expand the view, showing all subfolders. Click the arrow again to collapse the view, removing subfolder detail. It is important to understand that clicking the arrow (as opposed to clicking the folder or area name) does not actually select an area or folder. It merely displays additional levels contained within the area. Clicking the folder or area, however, does select the item. Figure 1.4 illustrates the difference between clicking the area in the Navigation Pane and clicking the arrow to the left.

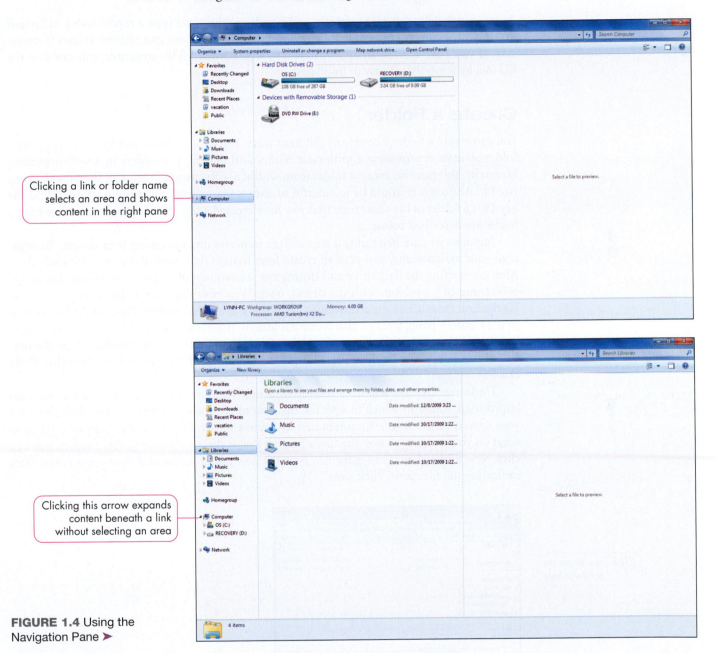

Clicking a link or folder name selects an area and shows content in the right pane

Clicking this arrow expands content beneath a link without selecting an area

FIGURE 1.4 Using the Navigation Pane ➤

Click the drive in the Navigation Pane (or double-click the drive in the Content pane). Continue navigating through the folder structure until you find the folder that you seek. Double-click the folder (in the Content pane) or single-click the folder (in the Navigation Pane) to view its contents.

The Favorites area contains frequently accessed folders and recent searches. You can drag a folder, a saved search, a library, or a disk drive to the Favorites area. To remove a favorite, simply right-click the favorite, and then click Remove. You cannot add files or Web sites as favorites.

Homegroup is a Windows 7 feature that enables you to share resources on a home network. You can easily share music, pictures, videos, and libraries with other people in your home through a homegroup. It is password protected, so you do not have to worry about privacy.

Windows 7 makes creating a home network easy, sharing access to the Internet and peripheral devices such as printers and scanners. The Network area provides quick access to those devices, enabling you to see the contents of network computers.

Working with Folders and Files

As you work with software to create a file, such as when you type a report using Microsoft Word, your primary concern will be saving the file so that you can retrieve it later if necessary. If you have created an appropriate and well-named folder structure, you can save the file in a location that is easy to find later.

Create a Folder

You can create a folder a couple of different ways. You can use Windows Explorer to create a folder structure, providing appropriate names and placing the folders in a well-organized hierarchy. You can also create a folder from within a software application at the time that you need it. Although it would be wonderful to always plan ahead, most often you will find the need for a folder at the same time that you have created a file. The two methods of creating a folder are described below.

Suppose you are beginning a new college semester and are taking four classes. To organize your assignments, you plan to create four folders on a flash drive, one for each class. After connecting the flash drive and closing any subsequent dialog box (unless the dialog box is warning of a problem with the drive), open Windows Explorer. Click Computer in the Navigation Pane. Click the removable (flash) drive in the Navigation Pane, or double-click it in the Content pane. You can also create a folder on the hard drive in the same manner, clicking drive C instead of the removable drive. Click New folder on the Toolbar. Type the new folder name, such as English 101, and press Enter. Repeat the process for the other three classes.

Undoubtedly, you will occasionally find that you have just created a file but have no appropriate folder in which to save the file. You might have just finished the slide show for your speech class but have forgotten first to create a speech folder for your assignments. Now what do you do? As you save the file, a process that is discussed later in this chapter, you can click New folder shown in Figure 1.5. Type the new folder name, and then press Enter. After indicating the file name, click Save.

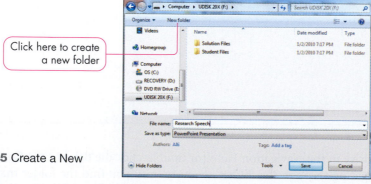

Click here to create a new folder

FIGURE 1.5 Create a New Folder ➤

Open, Rename, and Delete Folders and Files

You have learned that folders can be created in Windows Explorer but that files must be created in other ways, such as within a software package. Although Windows Explorer cannot create files, you can use it to open, rename, and delete files just as you use it for folders.

Using the Navigation Pane, you can locate and select a folder containing a file that you want to open. For example, you will want to open the speech slide show so that you can practice before giving the presentation to the class. Open Windows Explorer, and navigate to the speech folder on your removable drive (flash drive). The file will display in the right pane. Double-click the file. The program that is associated with the file will open the file. For example, if you used PowerPoint to create the slide show, then PowerPoint will open the file. To open a folder and display the contents, just single-click the folder in the Navigation Pane or double-click it in the Content pane.

At times, you may find a more suitable name for a file or folder than the one that you originally gave it. Or perhaps you made a typographical mistake when you entered the name. In these situations, you should rename the file or folder. In Windows Explorer, move through the folder structure to find the folder or file. Right-click the name, and then click Rename. Type the new name, and then press Enter. You can also rename an item when you click the name twice, but much more slowly than a double-click. Type the new name, and then press Enter. Finally, you can click a file or folder once to select it, click Organize, click Rename, type the new name, and then press Enter.

It is much easier to delete a folder or file than it is to recover it if you remove it by mistake. Therefore, be very careful when deleting items so that you are sure of your intentions before proceeding. When you delete a folder, all subfolders and all files within the folder are also removed. If you are certain you want to remove a folder or file, the process is simple. Right-click the item, click Delete, and then click Yes if asked to confirm removal to the Recycle Bin. Items are only placed in the Recycle Bin if you are deleting them from a hard drive. Files and folders deleted from a removable storage medium, such as a flash drive, are permanently deleted, with no easy method of retrieval. You can also delete an item (file or folder) when you click to select the item, click Organize, and then click Delete.

Save a File

As you create or modify a project such as a document, presentation, or worksheet, your work is placed in RAM, which is the computer's temporary memory. When you shut down the computer or inadvertently lose electrical power, the contents of RAM are erased. Even with a loss of electrical power, however, RAM on a laptop will not be erased until the battery runs down. Because you will most likely want to continue the project at another time or keep it for later reference, you need to save it to a storage medium such as a hard drive, CD, or flash drive. When you save a file, you will be working within a software package. Therefore, you must follow the procedure dictated by that software to save the file. Thankfully, most software requires that you save files in a similar fashion, so you can usually find your way through the process fairly quickly.

The first time that you save a file, you must indicate where the file should be saved, and you must assign a file name. Of course, you will want to save the file in an appropriately named folder so that you can find it easily later. Thereafter, you can quickly save the file with the same settings, or you can change one or more of those settings, perhaps saving the file to a different storage device as a backup copy. Figure 1.6 shows a typical Save As dialog box that enables you to confirm or change settings before finally saving the file.

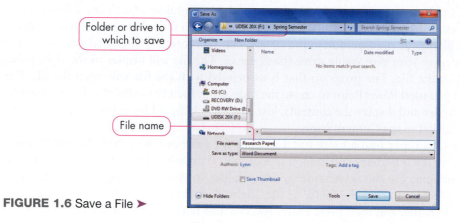

Folder or drive to which to save

File name

FIGURE 1.6 Save a File ➤

Selecting, Copying, and Moving Multiple Files and Folders

On occasion, you will want to select folders and files, such as when you need to rename, delete, copy, or paste them. You might want to open files and folders so that you can view the contents. Single-click a file or folder to *select* it; double-click a file or folder (in the Content pane) to *open* it. When you want to apply an operation to several files at once, such as deleting or moving them, you will want to select all of them. Knowing how to select several files and folders at one time makes the process of copying, or moving, items quick and simple.

Select Multiple Files and Folders

You can select several files and folders, regardless of whether they are adjacent to each other in the file list. Suppose that your digital pictures are contained in the Pictures folder. You might want to delete some of the pictures because you have already copied them to a CD and you want to clear up some hard drive space. To select certain pictures in the Pictures folder, open Windows Explorer, and then click the Pictures library. You will recall that the Pictures library groups and displays pictures from multiple folders. Navigate through any folder structure to locate the desired pictures in the Content pane. Assume that you want to select the first four pictures displayed. Because they are adjacent, you can select the first picture, hold down Shift, and click the fourth picture. All four pictures will be highlighted, indicating that they are selected. At that point, you can delete, copy, move, or rename the selected pictures. The next section of this chapter explains how to copy and move selections.

If the files or folders to be selected are not adjacent, simply click the first item. Hold down Ctrl while you click all other files or folders, one at a time, releasing Ctrl only when you have finished selecting all files or folders. All files or folders will be selected.

To select all items in a folder or disk, use Windows Explorer to navigate to the desired folder. Open the folder, then hold down Ctrl, and press A on the keyboard. You can also click Organize, and then Select All to select all items.

> ### TIP Using a Check Box to Select Items
>
> Windows 7 includes a file selection technique that makes it easy to make multiple selections, regardless of whether the items are adjacent. To activate the option, open Windows Explorer, and then change the view to Details. Click Organize, and then select Folder and search options. The Folder Options dialog box opens. Click the View tab, scroll down in the Advanced settings box, click Use check boxes to select items (see Figure 1.7), and then click OK. As you move the mouse pointer along the left side of files and folders, a check box appears. Click in the check box to select the file. In this manner, you can select multiple files and folders. If you want to quickly select all items in the folder, click the check box that appears in the Name column.

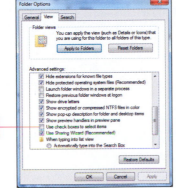

Click here to select items with check boxes

FIGURE 1.7 Use Check Boxes to Select Items ➤

Copy and Move Files and Folders

When you copy or move a folder, both the folder and any files that it contains are affected. You can move or copy a folder or file to another location on the same drive or to another drive. If your purpose is to make a *backup* copy of an important file or folder, you will probably want to copy it to another drive.

A **backup** is a copy of a file, usually on another storage medium.

Using a shortcut menu is one of the most foolproof ways to move or copy an item. In Windows Explorer, select the file or folder that you want to move or copy. If you want to copy or move multiple items, follow the directions in the previous section to select them all at once. Right-click the item, and select either Cut or Copy. Scroll through the Navigation Pane to locate the drive or folder to which you want to move or copy the selected item. Right-click the destination drive or folder, and then click Paste. If the moved or copied item is a folder, it should appear as a subfolder of the selected folder. If the moved or copied item is a file, it will be placed within the selected folder.

HANDS-ON EXERCISES

my**it**lab
HOE1 Training

1 Files and Folders

You will soon begin to collect files from volunteers who are preparing promotional and record-keeping material for the Rails and Trails project. It is important that you save the files in appropriately named folders so that you can easily access them later. Therefore, you plan to create folders. You can create folders on a flash drive or a hard drive. You will select the drive on which you plan to save your student files. As you create a short document, you will save it in one of the folders. You will then make a backup copy of the folder structure, including all files, so that you do not run the risk of losing the material if the drive is damaged or misplaced.

Skills covered: Create Folders and Subfolders • Create and Save a File • Rename and Delete a Folder • Open and Copy a File

STEP 1 ▶ CREATE FOLDERS AND SUBFOLDERS

You decide to create a folder titled *Rails and Trails Project*, and then subdivide it into subfolders that will help categorize the project files. Refer to Figure 1.8 as you complete Step 1.

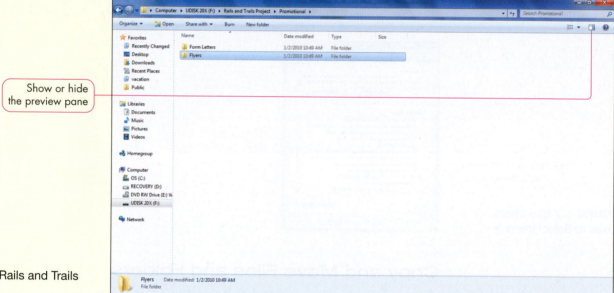

FIGURE 1.8 Rails and Trails Folders ➤

a. Insert your flash drive (if you are using a flash drive for your student files), and close any dialog box that opens (unless it is informing you of a problem with the drive). Click **Windows Explorer** on the taskbar. Click **Show the preview pane** unless the Preview pane is already displayed.

The removable drive shown in Figure 1.8 is titled UDISK 20X (F:), describing the drive manufacturer and the drive letter. Your removable drive will be designated in a different manner, perhaps also identified by manufacturer. The drive letter identifying your flash drive is likely to be different because the configuration of disk drives on your computer is unique.

> **TROUBLESHOOTING:** If you do not have a flash drive, you can use the hard drive. In the next step, simply click drive C in the Navigation Pane instead of the removable drive.

b. Click the removable drive in the Navigation Pane (or click **drive C** if you are using the hard drive). Click **New folder** on the Toolbar, type **Rails and Trails Project**, and then press **Enter**.

You create a folder where you can organize subfolders and files for the Rails and Trails project.

c. Double-click **Rails and Trails Project** in the Content pane (middle pane). The Address bar should show that it is the currently selected folder. Click **New folder**, type **Promotional**, and then press **Enter**.

You decide to create subfolders of the Rails and Trails Project folder to contain promotional material, presentations, and office records. You create three subfolders, appropriately named.

d. Check the Address bar to make sure *Rails and Trails Project* is still the current folder. Click **New folder**, type **Presentations**, and then press **Enter**.

e. Click **New folder**, type **Office Records**, and then press **Enter**.

f. Double-click **Promotional** in the middle pane. Click **New folder**, type **Form Letters**, and then press **Enter**. Click **New folder**, type **Flyers**, and then press **Enter**.

To subdivide the promotional material further, you create two subfolders, one to hold form letters and one to contain flyers. Your screen should appear as in Figure 1.8.

g. Close Windows Explorer.

STEP 2 ▶ CREATE AND SAVE A FILE

As the project gears up, you assign volunteers to take care of certain tasks. After creating an Excel worksheet listing those responsibilities, you will save it in the Office Records folder. Refer to Figure 1.9 as you complete Step 2.

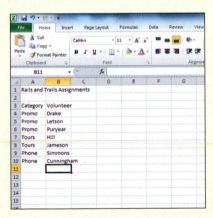

FIGURE 1.9 Volunteers Worksheet ➤

a. Click the **Start button**, and then point to **All Programs**. Scroll down the program list, if necessary, and then click **Microsoft Office**. Click **Microsoft Excel 2010**.

You use Microsoft Excel to create the volunteers worksheet.

b. Type **Rails and Trails Assignments** in **cell A1**. Press **Enter** twice.

Your cursor will be in cell A3.

c. Type **Category**. Press **Tab** to move the cursor one cell to the right, and then type **Volunteer**. Press **Enter**. Complete the remaining cells of the worksheet as shown in Figure 1.9.

d. Click the **File tab** (in the top-left corner of the Excel window). Click **Save**.

The Save As dialog box displays. The Save As dialog box is where you determine the location, file name, and file type of any document. You can also create a new folder in the Save As dialog box.

e. Scroll down if necessary, and then click **Computer** in the left pane. In the Content pane, double-click the drive where you will save the file. Double-click **Rails and Trails Project** in the Content pane. Double-click **Office Records**. Click in the **File name box**. Type **f01h1volunteers_LastnameFirstname** in the **file name box**, replacing *LastnameFirstname* with your own last name and first name. Click **Save**.

The file is now saved as *f01h1volunteers_LastnameFirstname*. You can check the title bar of the workbook to confirm the file has been saved with the correct name.

f. Click the **Close button** in the top-right corner of the Excel window to close Excel.

> **TROUBLESHOOTING:** If you click the lower X instead of the one in the top-right corner, the current Excel worksheet will close, but Excel will remain open. In that case, click the remaining X to close Excel.

The Volunteers workbook is saved in the Office Records subfolder of the Rails and Trails Project folder.

STEP 3 RENAME AND DELETE A FOLDER

As often happens, you find that the folder structure is not exactly what you need. You will remove the Flyers folder and the Form Letters folder and will rename the Promotional folder to better describe the contents. Refer to Figure 1.10 as you complete Step 3.

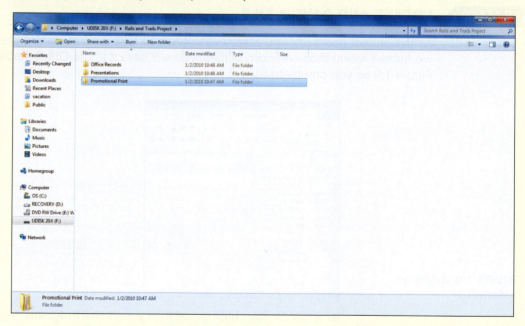

FIGURE 1.10 Rails and Trails Project Folder Structure ➤

a. Right-click the **Start button**. Click **Open Windows Explorer**. Click the disk drive where you save your files (under Computer in the Navigation Pane). Double-click **Rails and Trails Project** in the Content pane.

b. Click the **Promotional folder** to select it.

> **TROUBLESHOOTING:** If you double-click the folder instead of using a single-click, the folder will open and you will see its title in the Address bar. To return to the correct view, click Rails and Trails Project in the Address bar.

c. Click **Organize**, click **Rename**, type **Promotional Print**, and then press **Enter**.

Since the folder will be used to organize all of the printed promotional material, you decide to rename the folder to better reflect the contents.

d. Double-click **Promotional Print**. Click **Flyers**. Hold down **Shift**, and then click **Form Letters**. Both folders should be selected (highlighted). Right-click either folder, and then click **Delete**. If asked to confirm the deletion, click **Yes**. Click **Rails and Trails Project** in the **Address bar**. Your screen should appear as shown in Figure 1.10. Leave Windows Explorer open for the next step.

You decide that dividing the promotional material into flyers and form letters is not necessary, so you delete both folders.

STEP 4 ▶ **OPEN AND COPY A FILE**

You hope to recruit more volunteers to work with the Rails and Trails project. The Volunteers worksheet will be a handy way to keep up with people and assignments, and as the list grows, knowing exactly where the file is saved will be important for easy access. You will modify the Volunteers worksheet and then make a backup copy of the folder hierarchy. Refer to Figure 1.11 as you complete Step 4.

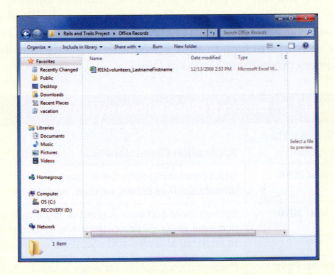

FIGURE 1.11 Rails and Trails Folder Structure ▶

a. Double-click the **Office Records folder**. Double-click *f01h1volunteers_LastnameFirstname*.

Because the file was created with Excel, that program opens, and the volunteers worksheet is displayed.

b. Click **cell A11**, and then type **Office**. Press **Tab**, type **Adams**, and then press **Enter**. Click the **File tab** in the top-left corner of the Excel window, and then click **Save**. The file is automatically saved in the same location with the same file name as before. Close Excel.

A neighbor, Samantha Adams, has volunteered to help in the office. You record that information on the worksheet and save the updated file in the Office Records folder.

c. Click the location where you save files in the Navigation Pane in Windows Explorer. Right-click **Rails and Trails Project** in the right pane. Click **Copy**.

d. Right-click **Desktop** in the Favorites group on the Navigation Pane, and then click **Paste**. Close Windows Explorer. If any other windows are open, close them also.

You make a copy of the Rails and Trails Project folder on the desktop.

e. Double-click **Rails and Trails Project** on the desktop. Double-click **Office Records**. Is the volunteers worksheet in the folder? Your screen should appear as shown in Figure 1.11. Close Windows Explorer.

f. Right-click the **Rails and Trails Project folder** on the desktop, click **Delete**, and then click **Yes** when asked to confirm the deletion.

You delete the Rails and Trails Project folder from the desktop of the computer because you may be working in a computer lab and want to leave the computer as you found it.

Microsoft Office Software

Organizations around the world rely heavily on **Microsoft Office** software to produce documents, spreadsheets, presentations, and databases. Microsoft Office is a productivity software suite including four primary software components, each one specializing in a particular type of output. You can use **Word** to produce all sorts of documents, including memos, newsletters, forms, tables, and brochures. **Excel** makes it easy to organize records, financial transactions, and business information in the form of worksheets. With **PowerPoint**, you can create dynamic presentations to inform groups and persuade audiences. **Access** is relational database software that enables you to record and link data, query databases, and create forms and reports. You will sometimes find that you need to use two or more Office applications to produce your intended output. You might, for example, find that a Word document you are preparing for your investment club should also include a summary of stock performance. You can use Excel to prepare the summary and then incorporate the worksheet in the Word document. Similarly, you can integrate Word tables and Excel charts in a PowerPoint presentation. The choice of which software component to use really depends on what type of output you are producing. Table 1.2 describes the major tasks of the four primary programs in Microsoft Office.

> Microsoft Office is a productivity software suite including four primary software components, each one specializing in a particular type of output.

Microsoft Office is a productivity software suite that includes word processing, spreadsheet, presentation, and database software components.

Word is a word processing program included in Microsoft Office.

Excel is software that specializes in organizing data in worksheet form. It is included in Microsoft Office.

PowerPoint is a Microsoft Office software component that enables you to prepare slideshow presentations for audiences.

Access is a database program included in Microsoft Office.

TABLE 1.2	Microsoft Office Software
Office 2010 Product	**Application Characteristics**
Word 2010	Word processing software is used with text to create, edit, and format documents such as letters, memos, reports, brochures, resumes, and flyers.
Excel 2010	Spreadsheet software is used to store quantitative data and to perform accurate and rapid calculations with results ranging from simple budgets to financial analyses and statistical analyses.
PowerPoint 2010	Presentation graphics software is used to create slide shows for presentation by a speaker, to be published as part of a Web site, or to run as a stand-alone application on a computer kiosk.
Access 2010	Relational database software is used to store data and convert it into information. Database software is used primarily for decision-making by businesses that compile data from multiple records stored in tables to produce informative reports.

As you become familiar with Microsoft Office, you will find that although each software component produces a specific type of output, all components share common features. Such commonality gives a similar feel to each software application so that learning and working with primary Microsoft Office software products is easy. In this section, you will identify features common to Microsoft Office software, including such interface components as the Ribbon, the Backstage view, and the Quick Access Toolbar. You will also learn how to get help with an application.

Identifying Common Interface Components

A **user interface** is a collection of onscreen components that facilitates communication between the software and the user.

As you work with Microsoft Office, you will find that each application shares a similar **user interface**. The user interface is the screen display through which you communicate with the software. Word, Excel, PowerPoint, and Access share common interface elements, as shown in Figure 1.12. As you can imagine, becoming familiar with one application's interface makes it that much easier to work with other Office software.

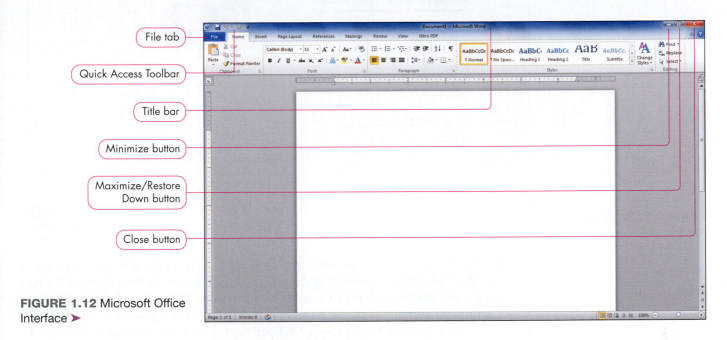

File tab
Quick Access Toolbar
Title bar
Minimize button
Maximize/Restore Down button
Close button

FIGURE 1.12 Microsoft Office Interface ➤

Use the Backstage View and the Quick Access Toolbar

The *Backstage view* is a new component of Office 2010 that provides a concise collection of commands related to an open file. Using the Backstage view, you can print, save, open, close, and share a file. In addition, you can view properties and other information related to the file. A file's properties include the author, file size, permissions, and date modified. You can access the Backstage view by clicking the File tab. The *Quick Access Toolbar*, located at the top-left corner of the Office window, provides handy access to commonly executed tasks such as saving a file and undoing recent actions. The *title bar* identifies the current file name and the application in which you are working. It also includes control buttons that enable you to minimize, maximize, restore down, or close the application window. Refer to Figure 1.12 for the location of those items on the title bar.

> Using the Backstage view, you can print, save, open, close, and share a file.

The **Backstage view** displays when you click the File tab. It includes commands related to common file activities and provides information on an open file.

The **Quick Access Toolbar** provides one-click access to commonly used commands.

The **title bar** contains the current file name, Office application, and control buttons.

When you click the File tab, you will see the Backstage view, as shown in Figure 1.13. Primarily focusing on file activities such as opening, closing, saving, printing, and beginning new files, the Backstage view also includes options for customizing program settings, getting help, and exiting the program. It displays a file's properties, providing important information on file permission and sharing options. When you click the File tab, the Backstage view will occupy the entire application window, hiding the file with which you might be working. For example, suppose that as you are typing a report you need to check the document's properties. Click the File tab to display a Backstage view similar to that shown in Figure 1.13. You can return to the application—in this case, Word—in a couple of ways. Simply click the File tab again (or any other tab on the Ribbon). Alternatively, you can press Esc on the keyboard. The Ribbon is described in the next section.

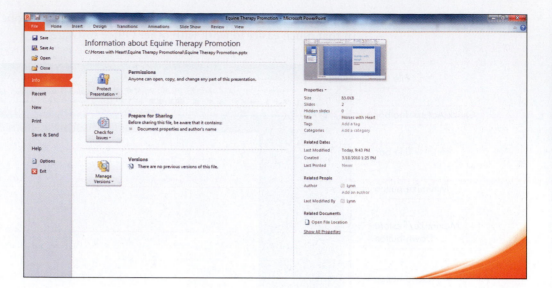

FIGURE 1.13 Backstage View ➤

The Quick Access Toolbar provides one-click access to common activities. Figure 1.14 describes the Quick Access Toolbar. By default, the Quick Access Toolbar includes buttons for saving a file and for undoing or redoing recent actions. You will probably perform an action countless times in an Office application and then realize that you made a mistake. You can recover from the mistake by clicking Undo on the Quick Access Toolbar. If you click the arrow beside Undo, you can select from a list of previous actions in order of occurrence. The Undo list is not maintained when you close a file or exit the application, so you can only erase an action that took place during the current Office session. Similar to Undo, you can also Redo (or Replace) an action that you have just undone. You can customize the Quick Access Toolbar to include buttons for frequently used commands such as printing or opening files. Because the Quick Access Toolbar is onscreen at all times, the most commonly accessed tasks are just a click away.

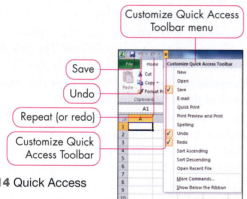

FIGURE 1.14 Quick Access Toolbar ➤

 TIP Customizing the Quick Access Toolbar

To customize the Quick Access Toolbar, click Customize Quick Access Toolbar, as shown in Figure 1.14, and select from a list of commands. If a command that you want to include on the toolbar is not on the list, you can simply right-click the command on the Ribbon, and then click Add to Quick Access Toolbar. Similarly, remove a command from the Quick Access Toolbar by right-clicking the icon on the Quick Access Toolbar, and then clicking Remove from Quick Access Toolbar. If you want to display the Quick Access Toolbar beneath the Ribbon, click Customize Quick Access Toolbar (Figure 1.14), and then click Show Below the Ribbon.

Familiarize Yourself with the Ribbon

The **Ribbon** is the long bar of tabs, groups, and commands located just beneath the Title bar.

Each **tab** on the Ribbon contains groups of related tasks.

A **group** is a subset of a tab that organizes similar tasks together.

A **command** is a button or area within a group that you click to perform tasks.

The **Ribbon** is the command center of Office applications. It is the long bar located just beneath the Title bar, containing tabs, groups, and commands. Each **tab** is designed to appear much like a tab on a file folder, with the active tab highlighted. The File tab is always a darker shade than the other tabs, and a different color depending on the application. Remember that clicking the File tab opens the Backstage view. Other tabs on the Ribbon enable you to create and modify a file. The active tab in Figure 1.15 is the Home tab.

When you click a tab, the Ribbon displays several task-oriented **groups**, with each group containing related **commands**. Microsoft Office is designed to provide the most functionality possible with the fewest clicks. For that reason, the Home tab, displayed when you first open an Office software application, contains groups and commands that are commonly used. For example, because you will often want to change the way text is displayed, the Home tab in each Office application includes a Font group with activities related to modifying text. Similarly, other tabs contain groups of related actions, or commands, many of which are unique to the particular Office application.

FIGURE 1.15 Ribbon ➤

Because Word, PowerPoint, Excel, and Access all share a similar Ribbon structure, you will be able to move at ease among those applications. Although the specific tabs, groups, and commands vary among the Office programs, the way in which you use the Ribbon and the descriptive nature of tab titles is the same regardless of which program you are working with. For example, if you want to insert a chart in Excel, a header in Word, or a shape in PowerPoint, you will click the Insert tab in any of those programs. The first thing that you should do as you begin to work with an Office application is to study the Ribbon. Take a look at all tabs and their contents. That way, you will have a good idea of where to find specific commands and how the Ribbon with which you are currently working differs from one that you might have used previously in another application.

> Because Word, PowerPoint, Excel, and Access all share a similar Ribbon structure, you will be able to move at ease among those applications.

> ### TIP Hiding the Ribbon
>
> The Ribbon occupies a good bit of space at the top of the Office interface. If you are working with a large project, you might want to maximize your workspace by temporarily hiding the Ribbon. You can hide the Ribbon in several ways. Double-click the active tab to hide the Ribbon, and then double-click any tab to redisplay it. Alternatively, you can press Ctrl+F1 to hide the Ribbon, with the same shortcut key combination redisplaying it. Finally, you can click Minimize the Ribbon (see Figure 1.15), located at the right side of the Ribbon, clicking it a second time to redisplay the Ribbon.

A **dialog box** is a window that enables you to make selections or indicate settings beyond those provided on the Ribbon.

A **Dialog Box Launcher** is an icon in Ribbon groups that you can click to open a related dialog box. It is not found in all groups.

The Ribbon provides quick access to common activities such as changing number or text formats or aligning data or text. Some actions, however, are not so common but are related to commands displayed on the Ribbon. For example, you might want to change the background of a PowerPoint slide to include a picture. In that case, you will need to work with a **dialog box** that provides access to more precise, but less frequently used, commands. Figure 1.16 shows a dialog box. Some commands display a dialog box when they are clicked. Other Ribbon groups include a **Dialog Box Launcher** that, when clicked, opens a corresponding dialog box. Figure 1.15 shows a Dialog Box Launcher.

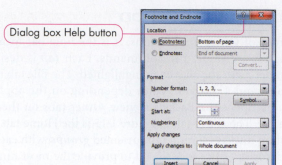

FIGURE 1.16 Dialog Box ➤

A **gallery** is a set of selections that appears when you click a More button, or in some cases when you click a command, in a Ribbon group.

The Ribbon contains many selections and commands, but some selections are too numerous to include in the Ribbon's limited space. For example, Word provides far more text styles than it can easily display at once, so additional styles are available in a *gallery*. A gallery also provides a choice of Excel chart styles and PowerPoint transitions. Figure 1.17 gives an example of a PowerPoint Themes gallery. Most often, you can display a gallery of additional choices by clicking the More button that is found in some Ribbon selections. Figure 1.15 shows a More button.

FIGURE 1.17 PowerPoint Themes Gallery ➤

When editing a document, worksheet, or presentation, it is helpful to see the results of formatting changes before you make final selections. You might be considering changing the font color of a selection in a document or worksheet. As you place the mouse pointer over a color selection in a Ribbon gallery or group, the selected text will temporarily display the color to which you are pointing. Similarly, you can get a preview of how color designs would appear on PowerPoint slides by pointing to specific themes in the PowerPoint Themes group and noting the effect on a displayed slide. When you click the item, such as the font color, the selection is applied. The feature enabling a preview of the results of a selection is called *Live Preview*. It is available in various Ribbon selections among the Office applications.

Live Preview is an Office feature that provides a preview of the results of a selection when you point to an option in a list. Using Live Preview, you can experiment with settings before making a final choice.

A **contextual tab** is a Ribbon tab that displays when an object, such as a picture or clip art, is selected. A contextual tab contains groups and commands specific to the selected object.

Office applications make it easy for you to work with objects such as pictures, clip art, shapes, charts, and tables. When you include such objects in a project, they are considered separate components that you can manage independently. To work with an object, you must click to select it. When you select an object, the Ribbon is modified to include one or more *contextual tabs* containing groups of commands related to the selected object. Figure 1.18 shows a contextual tab related to a selected object in a Word document. When you click outside the selected object, the contextual tab disappears.

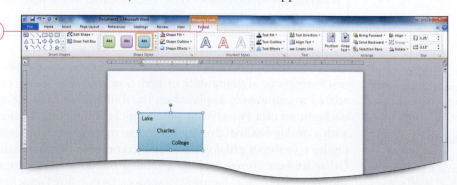

FIGURE 1.18 Contextual Tab ➤

A **Key Tip** is the letter or number that displays over features on the Ribbon and Quick Access Toolbar. Typing the letter or number is the equivalent of clicking the corresponding item.

Use the Status Bar

The *status bar* is found at the bottom of the program window and contains information relative to the open file. It also includes tools for changing the view of the file and for changing the size of onscreen file contents. Contents of the status bar are unique to each specific application. When you work with Word, the status bar informs you of the number of pages and words in an open document. Excel's status bar displays summary information, such as average and sum, of selected cells. The PowerPoint status bar shows the slide number, total slides in the presentation, and the applied theme.

The **status bar** is the horizontal bar located at the bottom of an Office application containing information relative to the open file.

Regardless of the application in which you are working, the status bar includes view buttons and a Zoom slider. You can also use the View tab on the Ribbon to change the current view or zoom level of an open file. The status bar's view buttons, shown in Figure 1.19, enable you to change the *view* of the open file. You might, for example, view a PowerPoint slide presentation with multiple slides displayed (Slide Sorter view) or with only one slide in large size (Normal view). In Word, you could view a document in Print Layout view (showing margins, headers, and footers), Full Screen Reading view, Web Layout view, or Draft view (with the greatest amount of typing space possible). As you learn more about Office applications in the following chapters, you will become aware of the views that are specific to each application.

Changing the **view** of a file changes the way it appears onscreen.

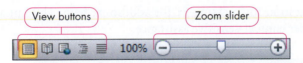

FIGURE 1.19 Word Status Bar ➤

The *Zoom slider* always displays at the far right side of the status bar. You can drag the tab along the slider in either direction to increase or decrease the magnification of the file. Be aware, however, that changing the size of text onscreen does not increase the font size when the file is printed or saved.

The **Zoom slider** enables you to increase or decrease the size of file contents onscreen.

Getting Office Help

One of the most frustrating things about learning new software is determining how to complete a task. Thankfully, Microsoft includes comprehensive help in Office so that you are less likely to feel such frustration. As you work with any Office application, you can access help online as well as within the current software installation. Help is also available through a short description that displays when you rest the mouse pointer on a command. Additionally, you can get help related to a currently open dialog box by clicking a question mark in the top-right corner of the dialog box or when you click the Help button in the Backstage view.

Use Office Help

To access the comprehensive library of Office Help, click the Help button, displayed as a question mark, on the far right side of the Ribbon (see Figure 1.15). You can get the same help by pressing F1 on the keyboard. The Backstage view also includes a Help feature, providing assistance with the current application as well as a direct link to online resources and technical support. Figure 1.20 shows the Help window that will display when you press F1, when you click the Help button, or when you click File, Help, Microsoft Office Help. For general information on broad topics, click a link in the window. However, if you are having difficulty with a specific task, it might be easier to simply type the request in the Search box. Suppose you are seeking help with using the Goal Seek feature in Excel. Simply type *Goal Seek* or a phrase such as *find specific result by changing variables* in the Search box, and press Enter (or click the magnifying glass on the right). Then select from displayed results for more information on the topic.

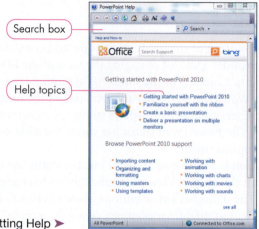

FIGURE 1.20 Getting Help ➤

Use Enhanced ScreenTips

An **Enhanced ScreenTip** provides a brief summary of a command when you place the mouse pointer over the command button.

For quick summary information on the purpose of a command button, place the mouse pointer over the button. An ***Enhanced ScreenTip*** displays, giving the purpose of the command, short descriptive text, and a keyboard shortcut if applicable. Some ScreenTips include a suggestion for pressing F1 for additional help. The Enhanced ScreenTip in Figure 1.21 provides context-sensitive assistance.

FIGURE 1.21 Enhanced ScreenTip ➤

Get Help with Dialog Boxes

Getting help while you are working with a dialog box is easy. Simply click the Help button that appears as a question mark in the top-right corner of the dialog box (see Figure 1.16). The subsequent Help window will offer suggestions relevant to your task.

2 Microsoft Office Software

As the administrative assistant for the Rails and Trails project, you need to get the staff started on a proposed fund-management worksheet. Although you do not have access to information on current donations, you want to provide a suggested format for a worksheet to keep up with donations as they come in. You will use Excel to begin design of the worksheet.

Skills covered: Open an Office Application, Get Enhanced ScreenTip Help, and Use the Zoom Slider • Get Help, Use the Backstage View • Change the View and Use Live Preview • Use the Quick Access Toolbar and Explore PowerPoint Views

---

STEP 1 ▶ **OPEN AN OFFICE APPLICATION, GET ENHANCED SCREENTIP HELP, AND USE THE ZOOM SLIDER**

Because you will use Excel to create the fund-raising worksheet, you will open the application. You will familiarize yourself with items on the Ribbon by getting Enhanced ScreenTip Help. For a better view of worksheet data, you will use the Zoom slider to magnify cell contents. Refer to Figure 1.22 as you complete Step 1.

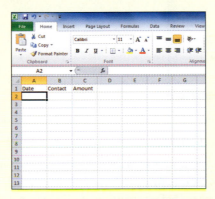

FIGURE 1.22 Fund-Raising Worksheet ➤

a. Click the **Start button** to display the Start Menu. Point to **All Programs**. Scroll down the list, if necessary, and click **Microsoft Office**. Click **Microsoft Excel 2010**.

   You have opened Microsoft Excel because it is the program in which the fund-raising worksheet will be created.

b. Type **Date**. As you type, the text appears in the current worksheet cell, **cell A1**. Press **Tab**, and then type **Contact**. Press **Tab**, and then type **Amount**. Press **Enter**. Your worksheet should look like the one in Figure 1.22.

   The worksheet that you create is only a beginning. Your staff will later suggest additional columns of data that can better summarize the hoped-for donations.

c. Hover the mouse pointer over any command on the Ribbon and note the Enhanced ScreenTip that displays, informing you of the purpose of the command. Explore other commands and identify their purpose.

d. Click the **Page Layout tab**, click **Orientation** in the Page Setup group, and then click **Landscape**.

   The Page Layout tab is also found in Word, enabling you to change margins, orientation, and other page settings. Although you will not see much difference in the Excel screen display after you change the orientation to landscape, the worksheet will be oriented so that it is wider than it is tall when printed.

e. Drag the tab on the **Zoom slider**, located at the far right side of the status bar, to the right to temporarily magnify the text. Click the **View tab**, and then click **100%** in the Zoom group to return the text to its original size. Keep the workbook open for the next step in this exercise.

When you change the zoom, you do not change the text size that will be printed or saved. The change merely magnifies or decreases the view while you work with the file.

STEP 2 ▶ GET HELP, USE THE BACKSTAGE VIEW

Because you are not an Excel expert, you occasionally rely on the Help feature to provide information on tasks. You need assistance with saving a worksheet, previewing it before printing, and printing the worksheet. From what you learn, you will find that the Backstage view enables you to accomplish all of those tasks. Refer to Figure 1.23 as you complete Step 2.

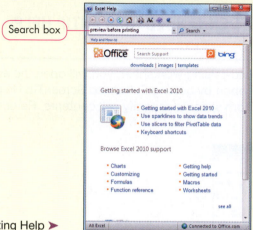

FIGURE 1.23 Getting Help ▶

a. Click the **Help button**, which is the question mark in the top-right corner of the Ribbon.

The Help dialog box displays.

b. Click in the white text box to the left of the word *Search* in the Help dialog box, as shown in Figure 1.23. Type **preview before printing** and click **Search**. In the Help window, click **Preview worksheet pages before printing**. Read about how to preview a worksheet before printing. From what you read, can you identify a keyboard shortcut for previewing worksheets? Click the **Close button**.

Before you print the worksheet, you would like to see how it will look when printed. You can use Help to find information on previewing before printing.

> **TROUBLESHOOTING:** You must be connected to the Internet to get context-sensitive help.

c. Click the **File tab**, and then click **Print**.

Having used Office Help to learn how to preview before printing, you follow the directions to view the document as it will look when printed. The preview of the worksheet displays on the right. To print the worksheet, you would click Print. However, you can first select any print options, such as the number of copies, from the Backstage view.

d. Click the **Help button**. Excel Help presents several links related to the worksheet. Explore any that look interesting. Return to previous Help windows by clicking **Back** at the top-left side of the Help window. Close the Help dialog box.

e. Click the **Home tab**. Point to **Bold** in the Font group.

You will find that, along with Excel, Word and PowerPoint also include formatting features in the Font group, such as Bold and Italic. When the Enhanced ScreenTip appears, identify the shortcut key combination that could be used to bold a selected text item. It is indicated as Ctrl plus a letter. What is the shortcut?

f. Click the **Close button** in the red box in the top-right corner of the Excel window to close both the workbook and the Excel program. When asked whether you want to save changes, click **Don't Save**.

   You decide not to print or save the worksheet right now. Instead, you will get assistance with its design and try it again later.

   > **TROUBLESHOOTING:** If you clicked the Close button on the second row from the top, you closed the workbook but not Excel. Click the remaining Close button to close the program.

STEP 3 **CHANGE THE VIEW AND USE LIVE PREVIEW**

It is important that the documents you prepare or approve are error-free and as attractive as possible. Before printing, you will change the view to get a better idea of how the document will look when printed. In addition, you will use Live Preview to experiment with font settings before actually applying them. Refer to Figure 1.24 as you complete Step 3.

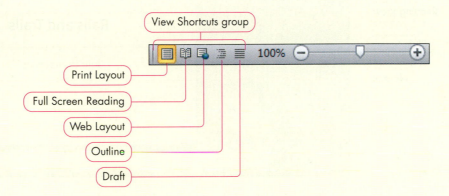

FIGURE 1.24 Word Views ➤

   a. Click the **Start button**, and then point to **All Programs**. Scroll down, if necessary, and click **Microsoft Office**. Click **Microsoft Word 2010**.

   You have opened a blank Word document. You plan to familiarize yourself with the program for later reference.

   b. Type your full name, and then press **Enter**. Drag to select your name (or position the mouse pointer immediately to the left of your name so that the pointer looks like a white arrow, and then click). Your name should be shaded, indicating that it is selected.

   You have selected your name because you want to experiment with using Word to change the way text looks.

   c. Click the **Font Size arrow** in the Font group on the Home tab. If you need help locating Font Size, check for an Enhanced ScreenTip. Place the mouse pointer over any number in the subsequent list, but do not click. As you move to another number, notice the size of your name change. The feature you are using is called Live Preview. Click any number in the list to change the text size of your name.

   d. Click **Draft** in the View Shortcuts group on the status bar to change the view (see Figure 1.24).

   When creating a document, you might find it helpful to change the view. Word's Print Layout view is useful when you want to see both the document text and such features as margins and page breaks. Draft view provides a full screen of typing space without displaying margins or other print features, such as headers or footers. PowerPoint, Excel, and Access also provide view options, although they are unique to the application. The most common view options are accessible from View Shortcuts on the status bar of each application.

   e. Click the **Close button** in the top-right corner of the Word window to close both the current document and the Word program. When asked whether you want to save the file, click **Don't Save**.

During the course of the Rails and Trails project, you will be asked to review documents, presentations, and worksheets. It is important that you explore each application to familiarize yourself with operations and commonalities. Specifically, you know that the Quick Access Toolbar is common to all applications and that you can place commonly used commands there to streamline processes. Also, learning to change views will enable you to see the project in different ways for various purposes. Refer to Figure 1.25 as you complete Step 4.

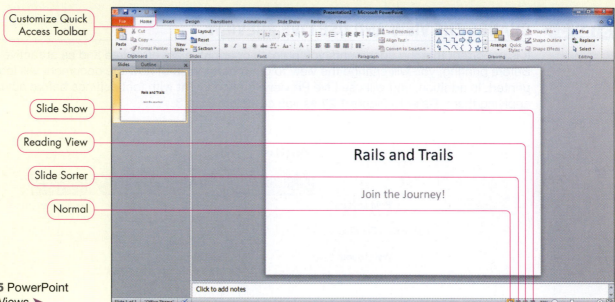

FIGURE 1.25 PowerPoint Presentation Views ▶

a. Click the **Start button**, and then point to **All Programs**. Scroll down, if necessary, and click **Microsoft Office**. Click **Microsoft PowerPoint 2010**.

You have opened PowerPoint. You see a blank presentation.

b. Click **Click to add title**, and then type **Rails and Trails**. Click in the bottom, subtitle box, and then type **Join the Journey!** Click the bottom-right corner of the slide to deselect the subtitle. Your PowerPoint presentation should look like that shown in Figure 1.25.

c. Click **Undo** on the Quick Access Toolbar.

The subtitle on the current slide is removed because it is the most recent action.

d. Click **Slide Sorter** in the View Shortcuts group on the status bar.

The Slide Sorter view shows thumbnails of all slides in a presentation. Because this presentation has only one slide, you see a small version of one slide.

e. Move the mouse pointer to any button on the Quick Access Toolbar and hold it steady. See the tip giving the button name and the shortcut key combination, if any. Move to another button and see the description.

The Quick Access Toolbar has at least three buttons, Save, Undo, and Redo (or Repeat). In addition, a small arrow is included at the far-right side. If you hold the mouse pointer steady on the arrow, you will see the ScreenTip Customize Quick Access Toolbar.

f. Click **Customize Quick Access Toolbar**. From the menu, click **New**. The New button enables you to quickly create a new presentation (also called a document).

g. Click **Customize Quick Access Toolbar**, and then click **New**. The button is removed from the Quick Access Toolbar.

You can customize the Quick Access Toolbar by adding and removing items.

h. Click **Normal** in the View Shortcuts group on the status bar.

The presentation returns to the original view in which the slide displays in full size.

i. Click **Slide Show** in the View Shortcuts group on the status bar.

The presentation is shown in Slide Show view, which is the way it will be presented to audiences.

j. Press **Esc** to end the presentation.

k. Close the presentation without saving it. Exit PowerPoint.

Backstage View Tasks

When you work with Microsoft Office files, you will often want to open previously saved files, create new ones, print items, and save and close files. You will also find it necessary to indicate options, or preferences, of settings. For example, you might want a spelling check to occur automatically, or you might prefer to initiate a spelling check only occasionally. Getting Help is also a common selection that you want to find easily. Because those tasks are applicable to each software application within the Office 2010 suite, they are accomplished through a common area in the Office interface—the Backstage view. Open the Backstage view by clicking the File tab. Figure 1.26 shows the area that displays when you click the File tab. The Backstage view also enables you to exit the application and to identify file information, such as the author or date created. In this section, you will explore the Backstage view, learning to create, open, close, and print files.

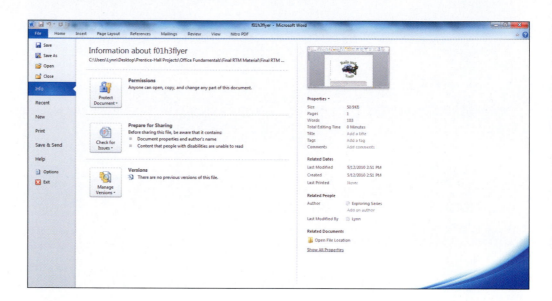

FIGURE 1.26 Backstage View ➤

Opening a File

When working with an Office application, you can begin by opening an existing file that has already been saved to a storage medium, or you can begin work on a new file. Both actions are available when you click the File tab. When you first open Word, Excel, or PowerPoint, you will be presented with a new blank work area that you can begin using immediately. When you first open Access, you will need to save the file before you can begin working with it. You can also open a project that you previously saved to a disk.

Create a New File

After opening an Office application, such as Word, Excel, or PowerPoint, you will be presented with a blank document area. The word *document* is sometimes used generically to refer to any Office file, including a Word document, an Excel worksheet, or a PowerPoint presentation. Perhaps you are already working with a document in an Office application but want to create a new file. Simply click the File tab, and then click New. Double-click Blank document (or Blank presentation or Blank workbook, depending on the specific application). You can also single-click Blank document, and then click Create.

Open a File Using the Open Dialog Box

If you choose to open a previously saved file, as you will need to do when you work with the data files for this book, you will work with the Open dialog box as shown in Figure 1.27. That dialog box appears after you select Open from the File tab. Using the Navigation Pane, you will make your way to the file to be opened. Double-click the file or click the file name once, and then click Open. Most likely, the file will be located within a folder that is appropriately named to make it easy to find related files. Obviously, if you are not well aware of the file's location and file name, the process of opening a file could become quite cumbersome. However, if you have created a well-designed system of folders, as you learned to do in the *Files and Folders* section of this chapter, you will know exactly where to find the file.

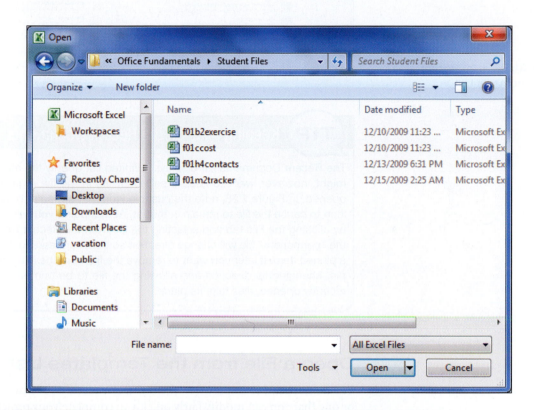

FIGURE 1.27 Open Dialog Box ➤

Open a File Using the Recent Documents List

You will often work with a file, save it, and then continue the project at a later time. Office simplifies the task of reopening the file by providing a Recent Documents list with links to your most recently opened files. See Figure 1.28 for an example of a Recent Documents list. To access the list, click the File tab, and then click Recent. Select from any files listed in the right pane. The list constantly changes to reflect only the most recently opened files, so if it has been quite some time since you worked with a particular file, you might have to work with the Open dialog box instead of the Recent Documents list.

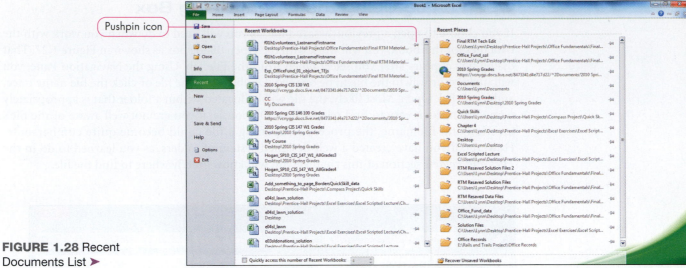

Pushpin icon

FIGURE 1.28 Recent Documents List ➤

> ### TIP ▸ Keeping Files on the Recent Documents List
>
> The Recent Documents list displays a limited list of only the most recently opened files. You might, however, want to keep a particular file in the list regardless of how recently it was opened. In Figure 1.28, note the pushpin icon that appears to the right of each file. Click the icon to cause the file to remain in the list. At that point, you will always have access to the file by clicking the File tab and selecting the file from the Recent Documents list. The pushpin of the "permanent" file will change direction so that it appears to be inserted, indicating that it is a pinned item. If later you want to remove the file from the list, simply click the inserted push-pin, changing its direction and allowing the file to be bumped off the list when other, more recently opened, files take its place.

Open a File from the Templates List

A **template** is a predesigned file that you can modify to suit your needs.

You do not need to create a new file if you can access a predesigned file that meets your needs or one that you can modify fairly quickly to complete your project. Office provides such files, called *templates*, making them available when you click the File tab and then New. Refer to Figure 1.29 for an example of a Templates list. The top area is comprised of template groups available within the current Office installation on your computer. The lower category includes template groups that are available from Office.com. When you click to select a group, you are sometimes presented with additional choices to narrow your selection to a particular file. For example, you might want to prepare a home budget. After opening Excel, click the File tab, and then click New. From the template categories, you could click Budgets from the Office.com Templates area, click Monthly Family Budget, and then click Download to display the associated worksheet (or simply double-click Monthly Family Budget). If a Help window displays along with the worksheet template, click to close it, or explore Help to learn more about the template. If you know only a little bit about Excel, you could then make a few changes so that the worksheet would accurately represent your family's financial situation. The budget would be prepared much more quickly than if you began the project with a blank workbook, designing it yourself.

> You do not need to create a new file if you can access a predesigned file that meets your needs or one that you can modify fairly quickly to complete your project. Office provides such files, called templates.

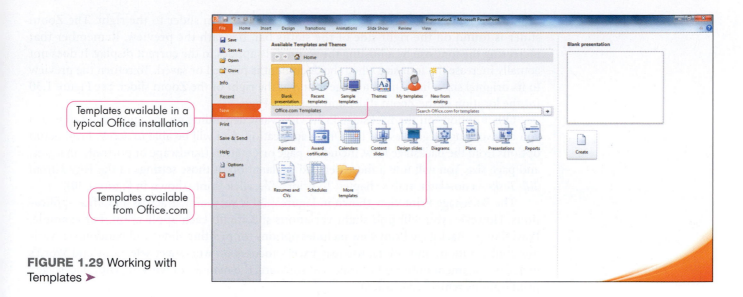

FIGURE 1.29 Working with Templates ➤

Templates available in a typical Office installation

Templates available from Office.com

Printing a File

There will be occasions when you will want to print an Office project. Before printing, you should preview the file to get an idea of how it will look when printed. That way, if there are obvious problems with the page setup, you can correct them before wasting paper on something that is not correct. When you are ready to print, you can select from various print options, including the number of copies and the specific pages to print. If you know that the page setup is correct and that there are no unique print settings to select, you can simply print the project without adjusting any print settings.

It is a good idea to take a look at how your document will appear before you print it. The Print Preview feature of Office enables you to do just that.

It is a good idea to take a look at how your document will appear before you print it. The Print Preview feature of Office enables you to do just that. In Print Preview, you will see all items, including any headers, footers, graphics, and special formatting. To view a project before printing, click the File tab, and then click Print. The subsequent Backstage view shows the file preview on the right, with print settings located in the center of the Backstage screen. Figure 1.30 shows a typical Backstage print view.

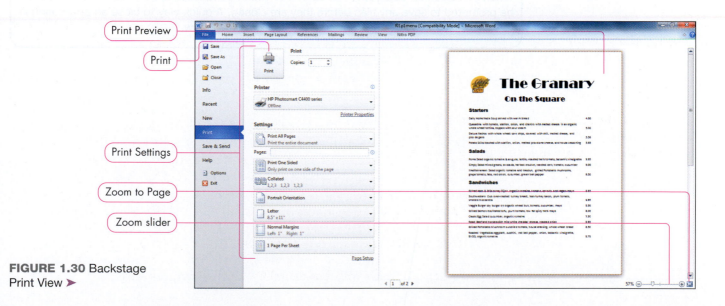

Print Preview

Print

Print Settings

Zoom to Page

Zoom slider

FIGURE 1.30 Backstage Print View ➤

To increase the size of the file preview, drag the Zoom slider to the right. The Zoom slider is found on the right side of the status bar, beneath the preview. Remember that increasing the font size by adjusting the zoom only applies to the current display. It does not actually increase the font size when the document is printed or saved. To return the preview to its original size, click Zoom to Page found at the right of the Zoom slider. See Figure 1.30 for the location of the Zoom slider and Zoom to Page.

Other options on the Backstage Print view vary, depending on the application in which you are working. Regardless of the Office application, you will be able to access Print Setup options from the Backstage view, including page orientation (landscape or portrait), margins, and page size. You will find a more detailed explanation of those settings in the *Page Layout Tab Tasks* section later in this chapter. To print a file, click Print (shown in Figure 1.30).

The Backstage Print view shown in Figure 1.30 is very similar across all Office applications. However, you will find slight variations specific to each application. For example, PowerPoint's Backstage Print view includes options for printing slides and handouts in various configurations and colors, whereas Excel's focuses on worksheet selections and Word's includes document options. Regardless of software, the manner of working with Backstage's print options remains consistent.

Closing a File and Application

Although you can have several documents open at one time, limiting the number of open files is a good idea. Office applications have no problem keeping up with multiple open files, but you can easily become overwhelmed with them. When you are done with an open project, you will need to close it along with the application itself.

You can easily close any files that you no longer need. With the desired file on the screen, click the File tab, and then click the Close button. Respond to any prompt that might appear suggesting that you save the file. The application remains open, but the selected file is closed. To close the application, click the File tab, and then click Exit.

 TIP Closing a File and an Application

When you close an application, all open files within the application are also closed. You will be prompted to save any files before they are closed. A quick way to close an application is to click the X in the top-right corner of the application window.

3 Backstage View Tasks

Projects related to the Rails and Trails project have begun to come in for your review and approval. You have received an informational flyer to be distributed to civic and professional groups around the city. It contains a new logo along with descriptive text. Another task on your agenda is to keep the project moving according to schedule. You will identify a calendar template to print and distribute. You will explore printing options, and you will save the flyer and the calendar to a disk as directed by your instructor.

Skills covered: Open and Save a File • Preview and Print a File • Open a File from the Recent Documents List and Open a Template

---

STEP 1 ▸ OPEN AND SAVE A FILE

You have asked your staff to develop a logo that can be used to promote the Rails and Trails project. You will open a Word document that includes a proposed logo and you will save the document to a disk drive. Refer to Figure 1.31 as you complete Step 1.

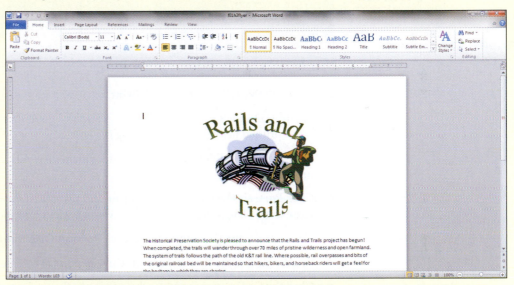

FIGURE 1.31 Promotional Flyer (Word Document) ➤

a. Click the **Start button** to display the Start Menu, and then click **All Programs**. Scroll down the list, if necessary, and then click **Microsoft Office**. Click **Microsoft Word 2010**.

You have opened Microsoft Word because it is the program in which the promotional flyer is saved.

b. Click the **File tab**, and then click **Open**. Navigate to the location of your student files. Because you are working with Microsoft Word, the only files listed are those that were created with Microsoft Word. Double-click *f01h3flyer* to open the file shown in Figure 1.31. Familiarize yourself with the document.

The logo and the flyer are submitted for your approval. A paragraph underneath the logo will serve as the launching point for an information blitz and the beginning of the fund-raising drive.

c. Click the **File tab**, and then click **Save As**.

You choose the Save As command because you know that it enables you to indicate the location to which the file should be saved, as well as the file name.

d. Click the drive where you save your files, and then double-click **Rails and Trails Project**. Double-click **Office Records**, click in the **File name box**, type **f01h3flyer_ LastnameFirstname**, and then click **Save**. Keep the file open for the next step in this exercise.

You approve of the logo, so you will print the document for future reference. You will first preview the document as it will appear when printed. Then you will print the document. Refer to Figure 1.32 as you complete Step 2.

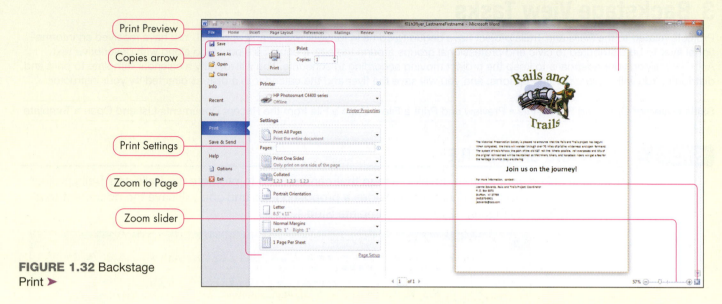

FIGURE 1.32 Backstage Print ➤

a. Click the **File tab**, and then click **Print**.

Figure 1.32 shows the flyer preview. It is always a good idea to check the way a file will look when printed before actually printing it.

b. Drag the **Zoom slider** to increase the document view. Click **Zoom to Page** to return to the original size.

c. Click **Portrait Orientation** in the Print settings area in the center of the screen. Click **Landscape Orientation** to show the flyer in a wider and shorter view.

d. Click **Landscape Orientation**, and click **Portrait Orientation** to return to the original view.

You decide that the flyer is more attractive in portrait orientation, so you return to that setting.

e. Click the **Copies arrow** repeatedly to increase the copies to **5**.

You will need to print five copies of the flyer to distribute to the office assistants for their review.

f. Press **Esc** to leave the Backstage view.

You choose not to print the flyer at this time.

g. Click the **File tab**, and then click the **Close button**. When asked, click **Don't Save** so that changes to the file are not saved. Leave Word open for the next step in this exercise.

A large part of your responsibility is proofreading Rails and Trails material. You will correct a typo in a phone number in the promotional flyer. You must also keep the staff on task, so you will identify a calendar template on which to list tasks and deadlines. Refer to Figure 1.33 as you complete Step 3.

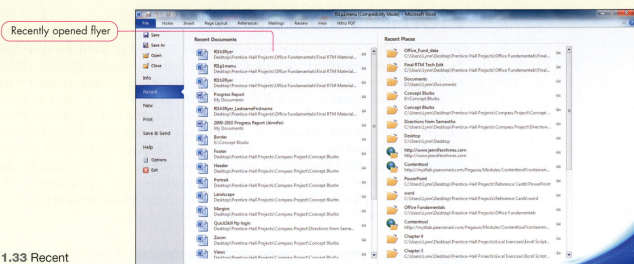

FIGURE 1.33 Recent Documents List ➤

a. Click the **File tab**, click **Recent** if necessary, and then click *f01h3flyer_LastnameFirstname* in the **Recent Documents list**.

Figure 1.33 shows the Recent Documents list. After clicking the document, the promotional flyer opens.

b. Scroll down, and then click after the number 1 in the telephone number in the contact information. Press **Backspace** on the keyboard, and then type **2**.

You find that the phone number is incorrect, so you make a correction.

c. Click **Save** on the Quick Access Toolbar, click the **File tab**, and then click the **Close button**.

When you click Save on the Quick Access Toolbar, the document is saved in the same location with the same file name as was indicated in the previous save.

d. Click the **File tab**, and then click **New**. From the list of template categories available from Office.com, click **Calendars**, and then click the current year's calendar link.

Office.com provides a wide range of calendar choices. You will select one that is appealing and that will help you keep projects on track.

e. Click a calendar of your choice from the gallery, and then click **Download**. Close any Help window that may open.

The calendar that you selected opens in Word.

> **TROUBLESHOOTING:** It is possible to select a template that is not certified by Microsoft. In that case, you might have to confirm your acceptance of settings before you click Download.

f. Click **Save** on the Quick Access Toolbar. If necessary, navigate to **Office Records** (a subfolder of Rails and Trails Project) on the drive where you save your student files. Save the document as **f01h3calendar_LastnameFirstname**. Click **OK**, if necessary. Close the document, and then exit Word.

Because this is the first time to save the calendar file, the Save button on the Quick Access Toolbar opens a dialog box in which you must indicate the location of the file and the file name.

Home Tab Tasks

You will find that you will repeat some tasks often, whether in Word, Excel, or PowerPoint. You will frequently want to change the format of numbers or words, selecting a different font or changing font size or color. You might also need to change the alignment of text or worksheet cells. Undoubtedly, you will find a reason to copy or cut items and paste them elsewhere in the document, presentation, or worksheet. And you might want to modify file contents by finding and replacing text. All of those tasks, and more, are found on the Home tab of the Ribbon in Word, Excel, and PowerPoint. The Access interface is unique, sharing little with other Office applications, so this section will not address Access. In this section, you will explore the Home tab, learning to format text, copy and paste items, and find and replace words or phrases. Figure 1.34 shows Home tab groups and tasks in the various applications. Note the differences and similarities between the groups.

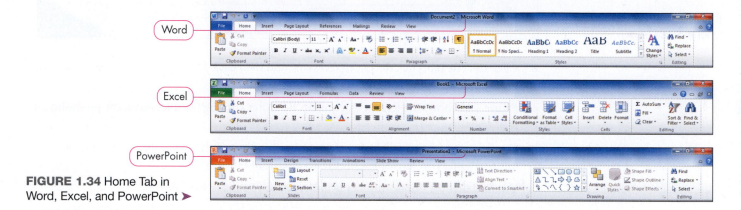

FIGURE 1.34 Home Tab in Word, Excel, and PowerPoint ➤

Selecting and Editing Text

After creating a document, worksheet, or presentation, you will probably want to make some changes. You might prefer to center a title, or maybe you think that certain worksheet totals should be formatted as currency. You can change the font so that typed characters are larger or in a different style. You might even want to underline text to add emphasis. In all Office applications, the Home tab provides tools for selecting and editing text. You can also use the Mini toolbar for quick changes to selected text.

Select Text to Edit

Before making any changes to existing text or numbers, you must first select the characters. A general rule that you should commit to memory is "Select, then do." A foolproof way to select text or numbers is to place the mouse pointer before the first character of the text you want to select, and then drag to highlight the intended selection. Before you drag, be sure that the mouse pointer takes on the shape of the letter *I*, called the I-bar. Although other methods for selecting exist, if you remember only one way, it should be the click-and-drag method. If your attempted selection falls short of highlighting the intended area, or perhaps highlights too much, simply click outside the selection and try again.

> Before making any changes to existing text or numbers, you must first select the characters. A general rule that you should commit to memory is "Select, then do."

Sometimes it can be difficult to precisely select a small amount of text, such as a single character or a single word. Other times, the task can be overwhelming, such as when selecting an entire 550-page document. Shortcut methods for making selections in Word and PowerPoint are shown in Table 1.3. When working with Excel, you will more often need to select multiple cells. Simply drag the intended selection, usually when the mouse pointer appears as a large white plus sign. The shortcuts shown in Table 1.3 are primarily applicable to Word and PowerPoint.

TABLE 1.3 Shortcut Selection in Word and PowerPoint

Item Selected	Action
One Word	Double-click the word.
One Line of Text	Place the mouse pointer at the left of the line, in the margin area. When the mouse changes to a right-pointing arrow, click to select the line.
One Sentence	Press and hold Ctrl while you click in the sentence to select.
One Paragraph	Triple-click in the paragraph.
One Character to the Left of the Insertion Point	Press and hold Shift while you press ←.
One Character to the Right of the Insertion Point	Press and hold Shift while you press →.
Entire Document	Press and hold Ctrl while you press the letter A on the keyboard.

After having selected a string of characters, such as a number, word, sentence, or document, you can do more than simply format the selection. Suppose you have selected a word. If you begin to type another word, the newly typed word will immediately replace the selected word. With an item selected, you can press Delete to remove the selection. You will learn later in this chapter that you can also find, replace, copy, move, and paste selected text.

Use the Mini Toolbar

The **Mini toolbar** is an Office feature that provides access to common formatting commands. It is displayed when text is selected.

You have learned that you can always use commands on the Ribbon to change selected text within a document, cell, or presentation. All it takes is locating the desired command on the Home tab and clicking to select it. Although using Home tab commands is simple enough, an item called the **Mini toolbar** provides an even shorter way to accomplish some of the same formatting changes. When you select any amount of text within a worksheet, document, or presentation, you can move the mouse pointer only slightly within the selection to display the Mini toolbar, as shown in Figure 1.35. The Mini toolbar provides access to the most common formatting selections, such as boldfacing, italicizing, or changing font type or color. Unlike the Quick Access Toolbar, the Mini toolbar is not customizable, which means that you cannot add or remove options from the toolbar. The Mini toolbar will only appear when text is selected. The closer the mouse pointer is to the Mini toolbar, the darker the toolbar. As you move the mouse pointer away from the Mini toolbar, it becomes almost transparent. Make any selections from the Mini toolbar by clicking the corresponding button.

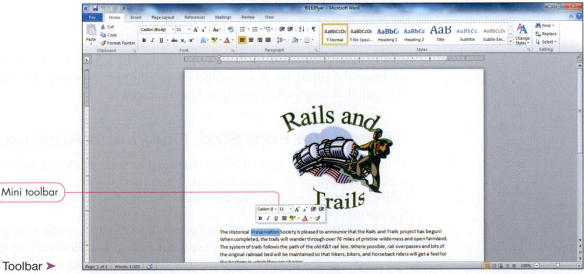

Mini toolbar

FIGURE 1.35 Mini Toolbar ➤

To temporarily remove the Mini toolbar from view, press Esc. If you want to permanently disable the Mini toolbar so that it does not appear in any open file when text is selected, click the File tab and click Options. As shown in Figure 1.36, click General, if necessary. Deselect the Show Mini Toolbar on selection setting by clicking the check box to the left of the setting and clicking OK.

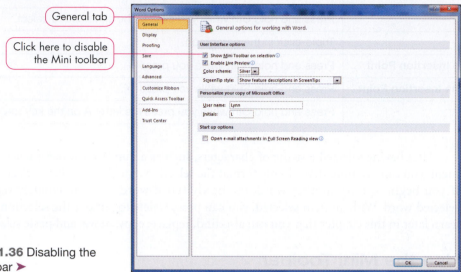

FIGURE 1.36 Disabling the Mini Toolbar ➤

Apply Font Attributes

A **font** is a character design that includes size, spacing, and shape.

A *font* is a character design. More simply stated, it is the way characters appear onscreen, including qualities such as size, spacing, and shape. Each Office application has a default font, which is the font that will be in effect unless you change it. Other font attributes include boldfacing, italicizing, and font color, all of which can be applied to selected text. Some formatting changes, such as Bold and Italic, are called *toggle* commands. They act somewhat like light switches that you can turn on and off. For example, after having selected a word that you want to boldface, click Bold in the Font group of the Home tab to turn the setting "on." If at a later time you want to remove boldface from the word, select it again, and then click Bold. This time, the button turns "off" the bold formatting.

To **toggle** is to switch from one setting to another. Several Home tab tasks, such as Bold and Italic, are actually toggle commands.

Change the Font

All applications within the Office suite provide a set of fonts from which you can choose. If you prefer a font other than the default, or if you want to apply a different font to a section of your project, you can easily make the change by selecting a font from within the Font group on the Home tab. You can also change the font by selecting from the Mini toolbar, although that only works if you have first selected text.

Change the Font Size, Color, and Attributes

At times, you want to make the font size larger or smaller, change the font color, underline selected text, or apply other font attributes. Because such changes are commonplace, Office places those formatting commands in many convenient places within each Office application.

You can find the most common formatting commands in the Font group on the Home tab. As shown in Figure 1.34, Word, Excel, and PowerPoint all share very similar Font groups that provide access to tasks related to changing the character font. Remember that you can place the mouse pointer over any command icon to view a summary of the icon's purpose, so although the icons might at first appear cryptic, you can use the mouse pointer to quickly determine the purpose and applicability to your desired text change. You can also find a subset of those commands plus a few additional choices on the Mini toolbar, which becomes available when you make a text selection.

If the font change that you plan to make is not included as a choice on either the Home tab or the Mini toolbar, you can probably find what you are looking for in the Font dialog box. Click the Dialog Box Launcher in the bottom-right corner of the Font group. Figure 1.37 shows a sample Font dialog box. Since the Font dialog box provides many formatting choices in one window, you can make several changes at once. Depending on the application, the contents of the Font dialog box vary slightly, but the purpose is consistent—providing access to choices related to modifying characters.

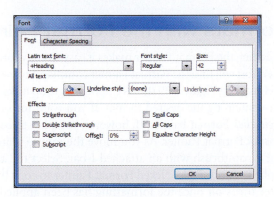

FIGURE 1.37 Font Dialog Box ➤

Using the Clipboard Group Tasks

The **Clipboard** is an Office feature that temporarily holds selections that have been cut or copied. It also enables you to paste those selections in other locations within the current or another Office application.

When you **cut** a selection, you remove it from the original location and place it in the Office Clipboard.

When you **copy** a selection, you duplicate it from the original location and place the copy in the Office Clipboard.

On occasion, you will want to move or copy a selection from one area to another. Suppose that you have included text on a PowerPoint slide that you believe would be more appropriate on a previous slide. Or perhaps an Excel formula should be copied from one cell to another because both cells should be totaled in the same manner. You can easily move the slide text and copy the Excel formula by using options found in the Clipboard group on the Home tab. The *Clipboard* is an area of memory reserved to temporarily hold selections that have been *cut* or *copied*. Although the Clipboard can hold up to 24 items at one time, the usual procedure is to *paste* the cut or copied selection to its final destination fairly quickly. When the computer is shut down or loses power, the contents of the Clipboard are erased, so it is important to finalize the paste procedure during the current session.

The Clipboard group enables you not only to copy and cut items, but also to copy formatting. Perhaps you have applied a font style to a major heading of a report and you realize that the same formatting should be applied to other headings. Especially if the heading includes multiple formatting features, you will save a great deal of time by copying the entire package of formatting to the other headings. In so doing, you will ensure the consistency of formatting for all headings because they will appear exactly alike. Using the Clipboard group's *Format Painter*, you can quickly and easily copy all formatting from one area to another in Word, PowerPoint, and Excel.

> The Clipboard group enables you not only to copy and cut text, but also to copy formatting.

When you **paste** a selection, you place a cut or copied item in another location.

The **Format Painter** is a Clipboard group command that copies the formatting of text from one location to another.

A **shortcut menu** provides choices related to the selection or area at which you right-click.

> ### TIP Using a Shortcut Menu
>
> In Office, you can usually accomplish the same task in several ways. Although the Ribbon provides ample access to formatting and Clipboard commands (such as Format Painter, cut, copy, and paste), you might find it convenient to access the same commands on a **shortcut menu**. Right-click a selected item or text to open a shortcut menu such as the one shown in Figure 1.38. A shortcut menu is also sometimes called a *context menu* because the contents of the menu vary depending on the location at which you right-clicked.

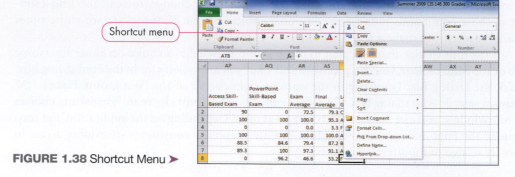

FIGURE 1.38 Shortcut Menu ➤

Copy Formats with the Format Painter

As described earlier, the Format Painter makes it easy to copy formatting features from one selection to another. You will find the Format Painter command conveniently located in the Clipboard group of the Home tab. Figure 1.39 shows Clipboard group tasks. To copy a format, you must first select the text containing the desired format. If you want to copy the format to only one other selection, *single-click* Format Painter. If, however, you plan to copy the same format to multiple areas, *double-click* Format Painter. As you move the mouse pointer, you will find that it has the appearance of a paintbrush with an attached I-bar. Select the area to which the copied format should be applied. If you single-clicked Format Painter to copy the format to one other selection, Format Painter turns off once the formatting has been applied. If you double-clicked Format Painter to copy the format to multiple locations, continue selecting text in various locations to apply the format. Then, to turn off Format Painter, click Format Painter again, or press Esc.

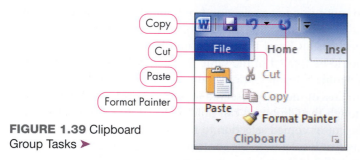

FIGURE 1.39 Clipboard Group Tasks ➤

Move and Copy Text

Undoubtedly, there will be times when you want to revise a project by moving or copying items such as Word text, PowerPoint slides, or Excel cell contents, either within the current application or among others. For example, a section of a Word document might be appropriate as PowerPoint slide content. To keep from retyping the Word text in the PowerPoint slide, you can copy the text and paste it in a blank PowerPoint slide. At other times, it might be necessary to move a paragraph within a Word document or to copy selected cells from one Excel worksheet to another. The Clipboard group contains a Cut command with which you can select text to move. You can also use the Copy command to duplicate items and the Paste command to place moved or copied items in a final location. See those command icons in Figure 1.39.

TIP Using Ribbon Commands with Arrows

Some commands, such as Paste in the Clipboard group, contain two parts: the main command and an arrow. The arrow may be below or to the right of the command, depending on the command, window size, or screen resolution. Instructions in the Exploring series use the command name to instruct you to click the main command to perform the default action (e.g., Click Paste). Instructions include the word *arrow* when you need to select an additional option (e.g., Click the Paste arrow).

The first step in moving or copying text is to select the text. After that, click the appropriate icon in the Clipboard group either to cut or copy the selection. Remember that cut or copied text is actually placed in the Clipboard, remaining there even after you paste it to another location. It is important to note that you can paste the same item multiple times because it will remain in the Clipboard until you power down your computer or until the Clipboard exceeds 24 items. To paste the selection, click the location where you want the text to be placed. The location can be in the current file or in another open file within any Office application. Then click Paste in the Clipboard group. In addition to using the Clipboard group icons, you can also cut, copy, and paste in any of the ways listed in Table 1.4.

TABLE 1.4	Cut, Copy, and Paste Options
Result	**Actions**
Cut	• Click Cut in Clipboard group. • Right-click selection, and then click Cut. • Press Ctrl+X
Copy	• Click Copy in Clipboard group. • Right-click selection, and then click Copy. • Press Ctrl+C.
Paste	• Click in destination location, and then click Paste in Clipboard group. • Right-click in destination location, and then click Paste. • Click in destination location, and then press Ctrl+V. • Click the Clipboard Dialog Box Launcher to open the Clipboard task pane. Click in destination location. With the Clipboard task pane open, click the arrow beside the intended selection, and then click Paste.

Use the Office Clipboard

When you cut or copy selections, they are placed in the Office Clipboard. Especially if you cut or copy multiple items, you might need to view the contents of the Clipboard so that you can select the correct item to paste. Regardless of which Office application you are using, you can view the Clipboard by clicking the Clipboard Dialog Box Launcher as shown in Figure 1.40.

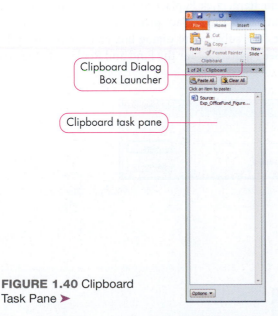

FIGURE 1.40 Clipboard Task Pane ➤

Unless you specify otherwise when beginning a paste operation, the most recently added Clipboard item is pasted. You can, however, select an item from the Clipboard task pane to paste. Similarly, you can delete items from the Clipboard by making a selection in the Clipboard task pane. You can remove all items from the Clipboard by clicking Clear All. The Options button in the Clipboard task pane enables you to control when and where the Clipboard is displayed. Close the Clipboard task pane by clicking the Close button in the top-right corner of the task pane or by clicking the arrow in the title bar of the Clipboard task pane and selecting Close.

Using the Editing Group Tasks

The process of finding and replacing text is easily accomplished through options in the Editing group of the Home tab. You will at times find it necessary to locate each occurrence of a text item so that you can replace it with another or so that you can delete, move, or copy it. If you have consistently misspelled a person's name throughout a document, you can find the misspelling and replace it with the correct spelling in a matter of a few seconds, no matter how many times the misspelling occurs in the document. The Editing group also enables you to select all contents of a project document, all text with similar formatting, or specific objects, such as pictures, clip art, or charts. The Editing group is found at the far-right side of the Home tab in all Office applications except Access.

The Excel Editing group is unique in that it also includes provisions for sorting, filtering, and clearing cell contents; filling cells; and summarizing numeric data. Because those commands are relevant only to Excel, this chapter will not address them specifically. Figure 1.41 shows the Editing group of Excel, Word, and PowerPoint. Note the differences.

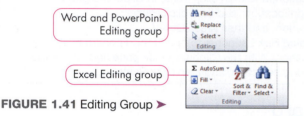

FIGURE 1.41 Editing Group ➤

Find and Replace Text

Find locates a word or phrase that you indicate in a document.

Replace finds text and replaces it with a word or phrase that you indicate.

Especially if you are working with a lengthy project, manually seeking a specific word or phrase can be time-consuming. Office enables you not only to *find* each occurrence of a series of characters, but also to *replace* what it finds with another series.

To begin the process of finding a specific item, click Replace in the Editing group on the Home tab of Word or PowerPoint. To begin a find and replace procedure in Excel, you must click Find & Select, and then click Replace. The subsequent dialog box enables you to indicate a word or phrase to find and replace. See Figure 1.42 for the Find and Replace dialog box in each Office application.

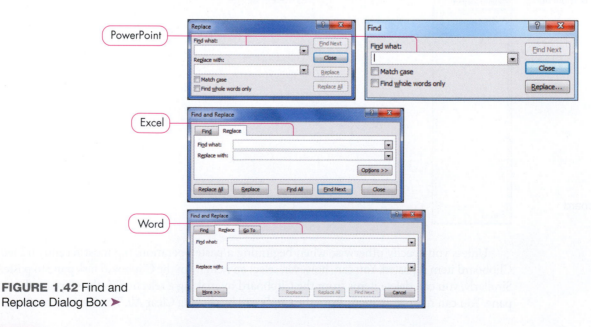

FIGURE 1.42 Find and Replace Dialog Box ➤

TIP Using a Shortcut to Finding Items

Ctrl+F is a shortcut to finding items in a Word, Excel, or PowerPoint file. When you press Ctrl+F, the Find and Replace dialog box shown in Figure 1.42 displays in Excel and PowerPoint. Pressing Ctrl+F in Word displays a feature—the Navigation task pane—at the left side of a Word document. When you type a search term in the Search Document area, Word finds and highlights all occurrences of the search term. The Navigation task pane also makes it easy to move to sections of a document based on levels of headings. The Navigation task pane is only found in Word 2010.

To find and replace selected text, type the text to locate in the *Find what* box and the replacement text in the *Replace with* box. You can narrow the search to require matching case or find whole words only. If you want to replace all occurrences of the text, click Replace All. If you want to replace only some occurrences, click Find Next repeatedly until you reach the occurrence that you want to replace. At that point, click Replace. Click the Close button (or Cancel).

TIP Go to a Location in a File

An Excel worksheet can include more than 1,000,000 rows of data. A Word document's length is unlimited. Moving to a specific point in large files created in either of those applications can be a challenge. That task is simplified by the Go To option, found in the Editing group as an option of the Find command (or under Find & Select in Excel). Click Go To and enter the page number (or other item, such as section, comment, bookmark, or footnote) or the specific Excel cell. Click Go To (in Word) or OK in Excel.

HANDS-ON EXERCISES

4 Home Tab Tasks

You have created a list of potential contributors to the Rails and Trails project. You have used Excel to record that list in worksheet format. Now you will review the worksheet and format its appearance to make it more attractive. You will also modify the promotional flyer that you reviewed in the last Hands-On Exercise. In working with those projects, you will put into practice the formatting, copying, moving, and editing information from the preceding section.

Skills covered: Move, Copy, and Paste Text • Select Text, Apply Font Attributes, and Use the Mini Toolbar • Use Format Painter and Work with a Shortcut Menu • Use the Font Dialog Box and Find and Replace Text

STEP 1 ▶ MOVE, COPY, AND PASTE TEXT

Each contributor to the Rails and Trails project is assigned a contact person from the project. You manage the worksheet that keeps track of those assignments, but the assignments sometimes change. You will copy and paste some worksheet selections to keep from having to retype data. You will also reposition a clip art image to improve the worksheet's appearance. Refer to Figure 1.43 as you complete Step 1.

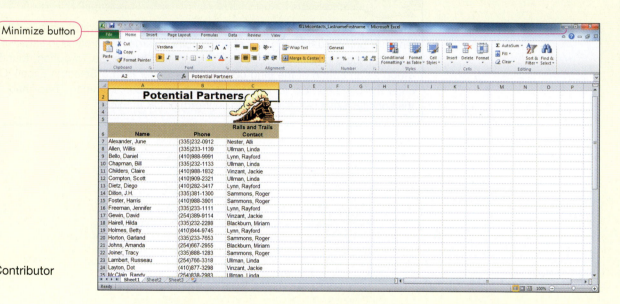

FIGURE 1.43 Contributor List (Excel) ▶

a. Click the **Start button** to display the Start menu, point to **All Programs**, scroll down the list if necessary, and then click **Microsoft Office**. Click **Microsoft Excel 2010**.

The potential contributors list is saved as an Excel worksheet. You will first open Excel.

b. Open the student data file *f01h4contacts*. Save the file as **f01h4contacts_LastnameFirstname** in the Office Records folder on the drive where you save your files.

The potential contributors list shown in Figure 1.43 is displayed.

c. Click **cell C7** to select the cell that contains *Alli Nester*, and then click **Copy** in the Clipboard group on the Home tab. Click **cell C15** to select the cell that contains *Roger Sammons*, click **Paste** in the Clipboard group, and then press **Esc** to remove the selection from *Alli Nester*.

Alli Nester has been assigned as the Rails and Trails contact for Harris Foster, replacing Roger Sammons. You make that replacement on the worksheet by copying and pasting Alli Nester's name in the appropriate worksheet cell.

d. Click the picture of the train. A box displays around the image, indicating that it is selected. Click **Cut** in the Clipboard group, click **cell A2**, click **Paste**, and then click anywhere outside the train picture to deselect it.

> **TROUBLESHOOTING:** A Paste Options icon might appear in the worksheet after you have moved the train picture. It offers additional options related to the paste procedure. You do not need to change any options, so ignore the button.

You decide that the picture of the train will look better if it is placed on the left side of the worksheet instead of the right. You move the picture by cutting and pasting the object.

e. Click **Save** on the Quick Access Toolbar. Click the **Minimize button** to minimize the worksheet without closing it.

STEP 2 ## SELECT TEXT, APPLY FONT ATTRIBUTES, AND USE THE MINI TOOLBAR

As the opening of Rails and Trails draws near, you are active in preparing promotional materials. You are currently working on an informational flyer that is almost set to go. You will make a few improvements before approving the flyer for release. Refer to Figure 1.44 as you complete Step 2.

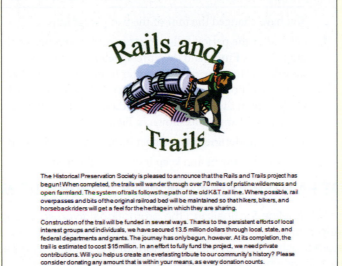

FIGURE 1.44 Promotional Flyer (Word) ➤

a. Click the **Start button** to display the Start menu. Click **All Programs**, scroll down if necessary, and then click **Microsoft Office**. Click **Microsoft Word 2010**. Open *f01h4flyer* and save the document as **f01h4flyer_LastnameFirstname** in the Promotional Print folder (a subfolder of Rails and Trails project) on the drive where you save your files.

You plan to modify the promotional flyer slightly to include additional information about the Rails and Trails project.

> **TROUBLESHOOTING:** If you make any major mistakes in this exercise, you can close the file without saving it, open *f01h4flyer* again, and start this exercise over.

b. Click after the period after the word *sharing* at the end of the first paragraph. Press **Enter**, and then type the text below. As you type, do not press Enter at the end of each line. Word will automatically wrap the lines of text.

Construction of the trail will be funded in several ways. Thanks to the persistent efforts of local interest groups and individuals, we have secured $13.5 million through local, state, and federal departments and grants. The journey has only begun, however. At its completion, the

trail is estimated to cost $15 million. In an effort to fully fund the project, we need private contributions. Will you help us create an everlasting tribute to our community's history? Please consider donating any amount that is within your means, as every donation counts. For further information, please contact Rhea Mancuso at (335)555-9813.

> **TROUBLESHOOTING:** If you make any mistakes while typing, press Backspace and correct them.

c. Scroll down and select all of the text at the end of the document, beginning with **For more information, contact:**. Press **Delete**.

When you press Delete, selected text (or characters to the right of the cursor) are removed. Deleted text is not placed in the Clipboard.

d. Select the words *Join us on the journey!* Click **Italic** in the Font group, and then click anywhere outside the selection to see the result.

e. Select both paragraphs but not the final italicized line. While still within the selection, move the mouse pointer slightly to display the Mini toolbar, click the **font arrow** on the Mini toolbar, and then select **Arial**.

> **TROUBLESHOOTING:** If you do not see the Mini toolbar, you might have moved too far away from the selection. In that case, click outside the selection, and then drag to select it once more. Without leaving the selection, move the mouse pointer slightly to display the Mini toolbar.

You have changed the font of the two paragraphs.

f. Click after the period following the word *counts* before the last sentence in the second paragraph. Press **Enter**, and then press **Delete** to remove the extra space before the first letter, if necessary. Move the mouse pointer to the margin area at the immediate left of the new line. The mouse pointer should appear as a white arrow. Click once to select the line, click **Underline** in the Font group, and then click anywhere outside the selected area. Your document should appear as shown in Figure 1.44.

You have underlined the contact information to draw attention to the text.

g. Save the document and keep it open for the next step in this exercise.

STEP 3 ▶ USE FORMAT PAINTER AND WORK WITH A SHORTCUT MENU

You are on a short timeline for finalizing the promotional flyer, so you will use a few shortcuts to avoid retyping and reformatting more than is necessary. You know that you can easily copy formatting from one area to another using Format Painter. Shortcut menus can also help make changes quickly. Refer to Figure 1.45 as you complete Step 3.

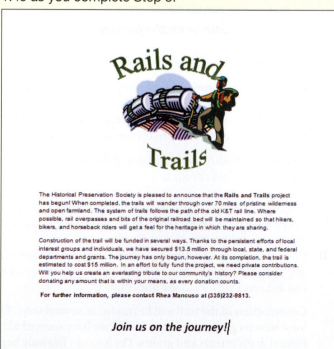

FIGURE 1.45 Promotional Flyer (Word) ➤

a. Select the words **Rails and Trails** in the first paragraph, and then click **Bold** in the Font group.

b. Click **Format Painter** in the Clipboard group, and then select the second to last line of the document, containing the contact information. Click anywhere outside the selection to deselect the line.

The format of the area that you first selected (Rails and Trails) is applied to the line containing the contact information.

c. Select the text *Join us on the journey!* Right-click in the selected area, click **Font** on the shortcut menu, click **22** in the **Size box** to reduce the font size slightly, and then click **OK**. Click outside the selected area.

Figure 1.45 shows the final document as it should now appear.

d. Save the document and close Word.

The flyer will be saved with the same file name and in the same location as it was when you last saved the document in Step 2. As you close Word, the open document will also be closed.

STEP 4 ▶ USE THE FONT DIALOG BOX AND FIND AND REPLACE TEXT

The contributors worksheet is almost complete. However, you first want to make a few more formatting changes to improve the worksheet's appearance. You will also quickly change an incorrect area code by using Excel's Find and Replace feature. Refer to Figures 1.46 and 1.47 as you complete Step 4.

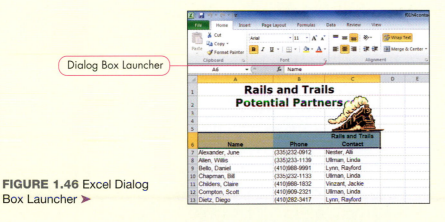

FIGURE 1.46 Excel Dialog Box Launcher ➤

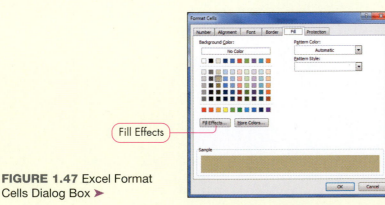

FIGURE 1.47 Excel Format Cells Dialog Box ➤

a. Click the **Excel icon** on the taskbar to redisplay the contributors worksheet that you minimized in Step 1.

The Excel potential contributors list displays.

b. Drag to select **cells A6 through C6**.

> **TROUBLESHOOTING:** Make sure the mouse pointer looks like a large white plus sign before dragging. It is normal for the first cell in the selected area to be a different shade. If you click and drag when the mouse pointer does not resemble a white plus sign, text may have been moved or duplicated. In that case, click Undo on the Quick Access Toolbar.

c. Click the **Dialog Box Launcher** in the Font group as shown in Figure 1.46. Click the **Fill tab**, and then click **Fill Effects** as shown in Figure 1.47. Click any style in the Variants group, click **OK**, and then click **OK** once more to close the Format Cells dialog box. Click outside the selected area to see the final result.

The headings of the worksheet are shaded more attractively.

d. Click **Find & Select** in the Editing group, click **Replace**, and then type **410** in the **Find what box**. Type **411** in the **Replace with box**, click **Replace All**, and then click **OK** when notified that Excel has made 10 replacements. Click **Close**.

You discover that you consistently typed an incorrect area code. You use Find and Replace to make a correction quickly.

e. Save the *f01h4contacts_LastnameFirstname* workbook. Close the workbook and exit Excel.

The workbook will be saved with the same file name and in the same location as it was when you last saved the document in Step 1. As you exit Excel, the open workbook will also be closed.

Insert Tab Tasks

As its title implies, the Insert tab enables you to insert, or add, items into a file. Much of the Insert tab is specific to the particular application, with little commonality to other Office applications. Word's Insert tab includes text-related commands, whereas Excel's is more focused on inserting such items as charts and tables. PowerPoint's Insert tab includes multimedia items and links. Despite their obvious differences in focus, all Office applications share a common group on the Insert tab—the Illustrations group. In addition, all Office applications enable you to insert headers, footers, text boxes, and symbols. Those options are also found on the Insert tab in various groups, depending on the particular application. In this section, you will work with common activities on the Insert tab, including inserting pictures and clip art.

> Despite their obvious differences in focus, all Office applications share a common group on the Insert tab—the Illustrations group.

Inserting Objects

With few exceptions, all Office applications share common options in the Illustrations group of the Insert tab. PowerPoint places some of those common features in the Images group. You can insert pictures, clip art, shapes, screenshots, and SmartArt. Those items are considered objects, retaining their separate nature when they are inserted in files. That means that you can select them and manage them independently of the underlying document, worksheet, or presentation.

After an object has been inserted, you can click the object to select it or click anywhere outside the object to deselect it. When an object is selected, a border of small dots, or "handles," surrounds it, appearing at each corner and in the middle of each side. Figure 1.48 shows a selected object, surrounded by handles. Unless an object is selected, you cannot change or modify it. When an object is selected, the Ribbon expands to include one or more contextual tabs. Items on the contextual tabs relate to the selected object, enabling you to modify and manage it.

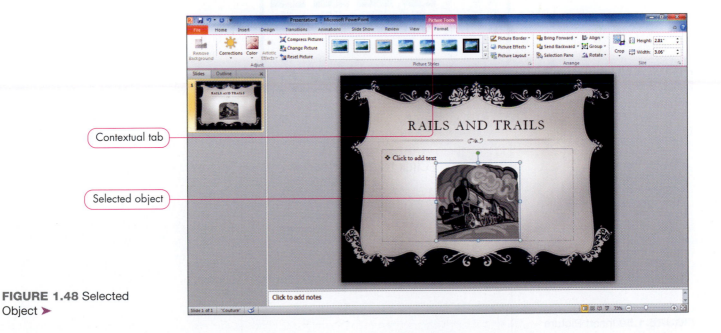

FIGURE 1.48 Selected Object ➤

TIP Resizing and Moving a Selected Object

You can resize and move a selected object. Place the mouse pointer on any handle, and then drag (when the mouse pointer looks like a two-headed arrow) to resize the object. Be careful! If you drag a side handle, the object is likely to be skewed, possibly resulting in a poor image. Instead, drag a corner handle to proportionally resize the image. To move an object, drag the object when the mouse pointer looks like a four-headed arrow.

Insert Pictures

A **picture** is a graphic file that is retrieved from storage media and placed in an Office project.

Documents, worksheets, and presentations can include much more than just words and numbers. You can easily add energy and description to the project by including pictures and other graphic elements. Although a *picture* is usually just that—a digital photo—it is actually defined as a graphic element retrieved from storage media such as a hard drive or a CD. A picture could actually be a clip art item that you saved from the Internet onto your hard drive.

The process of inserting a picture is simple. First, click in the project where you want the picture to be placed. Make sure you know where the picture that you plan to use is stored. Click the Insert tab. Then, in the Illustrations group (or Images group in PowerPoint), click Picture. The Insert Picture dialog box shown in Figure 1.49 displays. Select a picture and click Insert (or simply double-click the picture). In addition, on some slide layouts, PowerPoint displays an Insert Picture from File button (Figure 1.50) that you can click to select and position a picture on the slide.

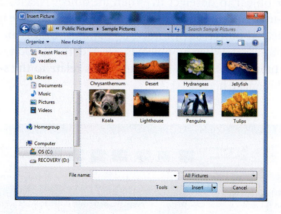

FIGURE 1.49 Insert Picture Dialog Box ➤

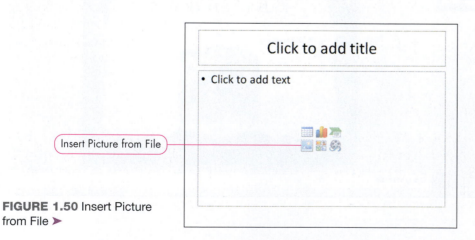

Insert Picture from File

FIGURE 1.50 Insert Picture from File ➤

Insert Clip Art

Clip art is an electronic illustration that can be inserted into an Office project.

A large library of *clip art* is included with each Office installation. Office.com, an online resource providing additional clip art and Office support, is also available from within each Office application. To explore available clip art, click the Insert tab within an Office program, and then click Clip Art in the Illustrations group (or the Images group in PowerPoint). Figure 1.51 shows the Clip Art task pane that displays. Suppose that you are looking for some clip art to support a fund-raising project. Having opened the Clip Art task pane, you could click in the *Search for* box and type a search term, such as *money*. To limit the results to a particular media type, click the arrow beside the *Results should be* box, and make a selection. Click Go to initiate the search.

FIGURE 1.51 Clip Art Task Pane ➤

You can resize and move clip art just as you have learned to similarly manage pictures. All Office applications enable you to insert clip art from the Illustrations group. However, PowerPoint uses a unique approach to working with graphics, including the ability to insert clip art by selecting from a special-purpose area on a slide.

Review Tab Tasks

As a final touch, you should always check a project for spelling, grammatical, and word-usage errors. If the project is a collaborative effort, you and your colleagues might add comments and suggest changes. You can even use a thesaurus to find synonyms for words that are not quite right for your purpose. The Review tab in each Office application provides all these options and more. In this section, you will learn to review a file, checking for spelling and grammatical errors. You will also learn to use a thesaurus to identify synonyms.

Reviewing a File

As you create or edit a file, you will want to make sure no spelling or grammatical errors exist. You will also be concerned with wording, being sure to select words and phrases that best represent the purpose of the document, worksheet, or presentation. On occasion, you might even find yourself at a loss for an appropriate word. Not to worry. Word, Excel, and PowerPoint all provide standard tools for proofreading, including a spelling and grammar checker and a thesaurus.

Check Spelling and Grammar

In general, all Office applications check your spelling and grammar as you type. If a word is unrecognized, it is flagged as misspelled or grammatically incorrect. Misspellings are identified with a red wavy underline, grammatical problems are underlined in green, and word usage errors (such as using *bear* instead of *bare*) have a blue underline. If the word or phrase is truly in error—that is, it is not a person's name or an unusual term that is not in the application's dictionary—you can correct it manually or you can let the software correct it for you. If you right-click a word or phrase that is identified as a mistake, you will see a shortcut menu similar to that shown in Figure 1.52. If the application's dictionary can make a suggestion as to the correct spelling, you can click to accept the suggestion and make the change. If a grammatical rule is violated, you will have an opportunity to select a correction. However, if the text is actually correct, you can click Ignore (to bypass that single occurrence) or Ignore All (to bypass all occurrences of the flagged error in the current document). Click Add to Dictionary if you want the word to be considered correct whenever it appears in all documents. Similar selections on a shortcut menu enable you to ignore grammatical mistakes if they are not errors.

> In general, all Office applications check your spelling and grammar as you type.

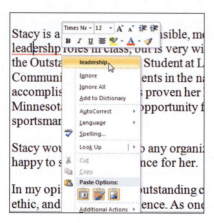

FIGURE 1.52 Correcting Misspelling ➤

You might prefer the convenience of addressing possible misspellings and grammatical errors without having to examine each underlined word or phrase. To do so, click Spelling & Grammar in the Proofing group of the Review tab. Beginning at the top of the document, each identified error is highlighted in a dialog box similar to Figure 1.53. You can then choose how to address the problem by making a selection in the dialog box.

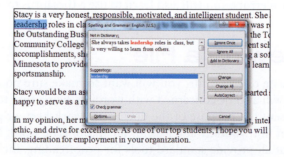

FIGURE 1.53 Checking for Spelling and Grammatical Errors ➤

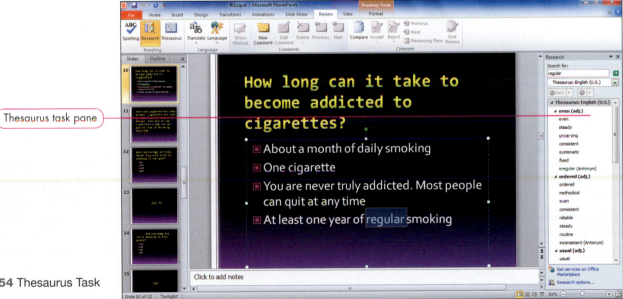

TIP Understanding Software Options

Many Office settings are considered *default* options. Thus, unless you specify otherwise, the default options are in effect. One such default option is the automatic spelling and grammar checker. If you prefer to enable and disable certain options or change default settings in an Office application, you can click the File tab and click Options. From that point, you can work through a series of categories, selecting or deselecting options at will. For example, if you want to change how the application corrects and formats text, you can select or deselect settings in the Proofing group.

A **default** setting is one that is in place unless you specify otherwise.

Use the Thesaurus

As you write, there will be times when you are at a loss for an appropriate word. Perhaps you feel that you are overusing a word and want to find a suitable substitute. The Thesaurus is the Office tool to use in such a situation. Located in the Proofing group of the Review tab, Thesaurus enables you to search for synonyms, or words with similar meanings. Select a word, then click Thesaurus, in the Proofing group on the Review tab. A task pane displays on the right side of the screen, and synonyms are listed similar to those shown in Figure 1.54. You can also use the Thesaurus before typing a word to find substitutes. Simply click Thesaurus and type the word for which you are seeking a synonym in the Search for box. Press Enter or click the green arrow to the right of the Search box for some suggestions. Finally, you can also identify synonyms when you right-click a word and point to Synonyms (if any are available). Click any word to place it in the document.

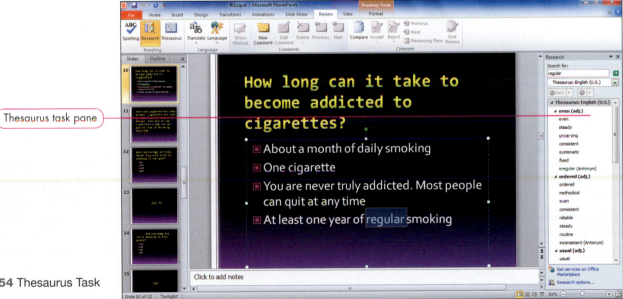

Thesaurus task pane

FIGURE 1.54 Thesaurus Task Pane ➤

Page Layout Tab Tasks

When you prepare a document or worksheet, you are concerned with the way the project appears onscreen and possibly in print. Unlike Word and Excel, a PowerPoint presentation is usually designed as a slide show, so it is not nearly as critical to concern yourself with page layout settings. The Page Layout tab in Word and Excel provides access to a full range of options such as margin settings and page orientation. In this section, you will identify page layout settings that are common to Office applications. These settings include margins and page orientation.

The Page Layout tab in Word and Excel provides access to a full range of options such as margin settings and page orientation.

Changing Page Settings

Because a document is most often designed to be printed, you will want to make sure it looks its best in printed form. That means that you will need to know how to adjust margins and how to change the page orientation. Perhaps the document or spreadsheet should be centered on the page vertically or the text should be aligned in columns. By adjusting page settings, you can do all these things and more. You will find the most common page settings, such as margins and page orientation, in the Page Setup group of the Page Layout tab. For less common settings, such as determining whether headers should print on odd or even pages, you can use the Page Setup dialog box.

Change Margins

A **margin** is the blank space around the sides, top, and bottom of a document or worksheet.

A *margin* is the area of blank space that appears to the left, right, top, and bottom of a document or worksheet. Margins are only evident if you are in Print Layout or Page Layout view or if you are in the Backstage view, previewing a document to print. To change or set margins, click the Page Layout tab. As shown in Figure 1.55, the Page Setup group enables you to change such items as margins and orientation. To change margins, click Margins. If the margins that you intend to use are included in any of the preset margin options, click a selection. Otherwise, click Custom Margins to display the Page Setup dialog box in which you can create custom margin settings. Click OK to accept the settings, and close the dialog box. You can also change margins when you click Print on the File tab.

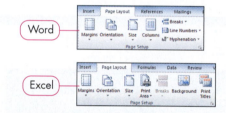

FIGURE 1.55 Page Setup Group ➤

Change Page Orientation

A page or worksheet displayed in **portrait** orientation is taller than it is wide.

A page or worksheet displayed in **landscape** orientation is wider than it is tall.

Documents and worksheets can be displayed in *portrait* orientation or in *landscape*. A page displayed or printed in portrait orientation is taller than it is wide. A page in landscape orientation is wider than it is tall. Word documents are usually more attractive displayed in portrait orientation, whereas Excel worksheets are often more suitable in landscape. To select page orientation, click Orientation in the Page Setup group on the Page Layout tab. See Figure 1.55 for the location of the Orientation command. Orientation is also an option in the Print area of the Backstage view.

Use the Page Setup Dialog Box

The Page Setup group contains the most commonly used page options in the particular Office application. Some are unique to Excel, and others are more applicable to Word. Other less common settings are only available in the Page Setup dialog box, displayed when you click the Page Setup Dialog Box Launcher. The subsequent dialog box includes options for customizing margins, selecting page orientation, centering vertically, printing gridlines, and creating headers and footers, although some of those options are only available when working with Word, and others are unique to Excel. Figure 1.56 gives a glimpse of both the Excel and Word Page Setup dialog boxes.

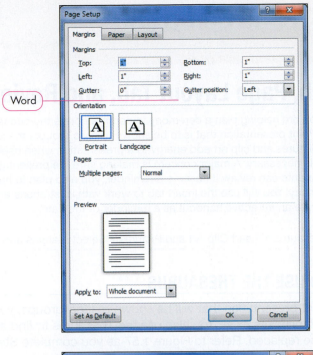

Word

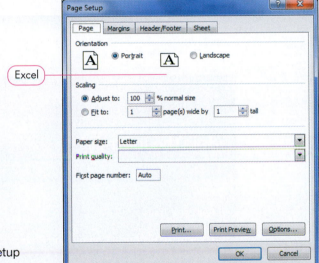

Excel

FIGURE 1.56 Page Setup
Dialog Boxes ➤

HANDS-ON EXERCISES

5 Tasks on the Insert Tab, Page Layout Tab, and Review Tab

The Rails and Trails project is nearing kickoff. You are helping plan a ceremony to commemorate the occasion. To encourage interest and participation, you will edit a PowerPoint presentation that is to be shown to civic groups, the local retiree association, and to city and county leaders. You know that pictures and clip art add energy to a presentation when used appropriately, so you will check for those elements, adding whatever is necessary. A major concern is making sure the presentation is error free and that it is available in print so that meeting participants can review it later. As a reminder, you also plan to have available a handout giving the time and date of the dedication ceremony. You will use the Insert tab to work with illustrations and the Review tab to check for errors, and you will use Word to generate an attractive handout as a reminder of the date.

Skills covered: Check Spelling and Use the Thesaurus • Insert Clip Art and Pictures • Select Margins and Page Orientation

---

STEP 1 ▶ CHECK SPELLING AND USE THE THESAURUS

As you check the PowerPoint presentation that will be shown to local groups, you make sure no misspellings or grammatical mistakes exist. You also use the Thesaurus to find a suitable substitution for a word you feel should be replaced. Refer to Figure 1.57 as you complete Step 1.

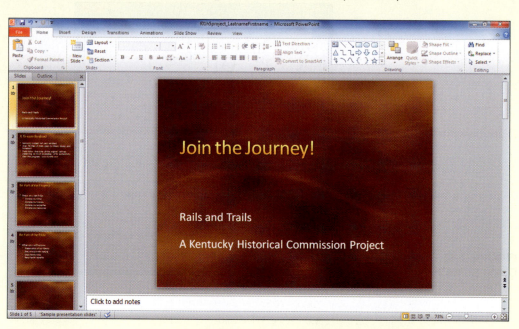

FIGURE 1.57 Project Presentation ▶

a. Click the **Start button** to display the Start menu, and then point to **All Programs**. Click **Microsoft Office**, and then click **Microsoft PowerPoint 2010**. Open *f01h5project* and save it as **f01h5project_LastnameFirstname** in the Presentations folder (a subfolder of Rails and Trails Projects) on the drive where you save your files. The presentation displays as shown in Figure 1.57.

The PowerPoint presentation opens, with Slide 1 shown in Normal view.

b. Click **Slide Show** and the **Slide Show tab**, and then click **From Beginning** in the Start Slide Show group to view the presentation. Click to advance from one slide to another. After the last slide, click to return to Normal view.

c. Click the **Review tab**, and then click **Spelling** in the Proofing group. The first misspelling is not actually misspelled. It is the name of a city. Click **Ignore** to leave it as is. The next flagged misspelling is truly misspelled. With the correct spelling selected, click **Change** to correct the mistake. Correct any other words that are misspelled. Click **OK** when the spell check is complete.

d. Click **Slide 2** in the Slides pane on the left. Double-click the word *route*, click **Thesaurus** in the Proofing group, point to **path** in the Research pane, click the arrow to the right of the word path, and then click **Insert**. Press the **Spacebar**.

The word *route* is replaced with the word *path*.

e. Click the **Close button** in the top-right corner of the Research pane.

f. Save the presentation and keep it open for the next step.

STEP 2 ▷ INSERT CLIP ART AND PICTURES

Although the presentation provides the necessary information and encourages viewers to become active participants in the project, you believe that pictures and clip art might make it a little more exciting. Where appropriate, you will include clip art and a picture. Refer to Figures 1.58 and 1.59 as you complete Step 2.

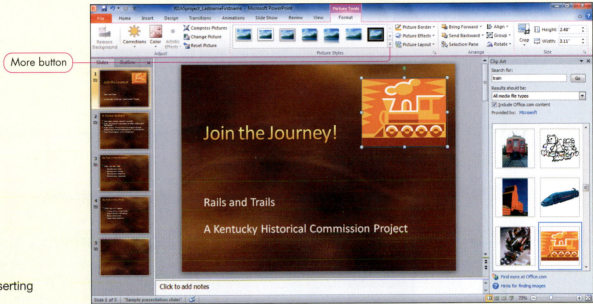

FIGURE 1.58 Inserting Clip Art ➤

a. Display Slide 1, click the **Insert tab**, and then click **Clip Art**.

The Clip Art task pane opens on the right side of the screen.

b. Type **train** in the **Search for box** in the Clip Art task pane. Click the check box beside *Include Office.com content* (unless it is already checked), click the arrow beside *Results should be*, and then click the check box beside *All media types* (unless it is already checked). Narrow results to illustrations by clicking the check box beside *Illustrations*, and then click **Go**.

You will identify clip art to be displayed on Slide 1.

c. Click to select any clip art image of a train.

> **TROUBLESHOOTING:** Be sure to click the clip art image, not the arrow to the right. If you click the arrow, you will then need to click Insert to place the clip art image on the slide.

> **TROUBLESHOOTING:** It is very easy to make the mistake of inserting duplicate clip art images on a slide, perhaps because you clicked the image more than once in the Clip Art task pane. If that should happen, you can remove any unwanted clip art by clicking to select it on the slide and pressing Delete.

The clip art image probably will not be placed as you would like, but you will move and resize it in the next substep. Also, the clip art is selected, as indicated by the box and handles surrounding it.

d. Click a corner handle (small circle) on the border of the clip art. Make sure the mouse pointer appears as a double-headed arrow. Drag to resize the image so that it appears similar to that shown in Figure 1.58. Click in the center of the clip art. The mouse pointer should appear as a four-headed arrow. Drag the clip art to the top-right corner of the slide. Make sure the clip art is still selected (it should be surrounded by a box and handles). If it is not selected, click to select it.

e. Click the **More button** of the Picture Styles group (see Figure 1.58) to reveal a gallery of styles. Position the mouse pointer over any style to see a preview of the style applied to the clip art. Click to apply a style of your choice. Close the Clip Art task pane.

f. On Slide 5, type **The Journey Begins** in the **Title box**. Click **Insert Picture from File** in the Content Placeholder (see Figure 1.50), navigate to the student data files, and then double-click *f01h5rails*.

A picture is placed on the final slide.

g. Click to select the picture, if necessary. Drag a corner handle to resize the picture. Click the center of the picture and drag the picture to reposition it in the center of the slide as shown in Figure 1.59.

> **TROUBLESHOOTING:** You can only move the picture when the mouse pointer looks like a four-headed arrow. If instead, you drag a handle, the picture will be resized instead of moved. Click Undo on the Quick Access Toolbar and try it again.

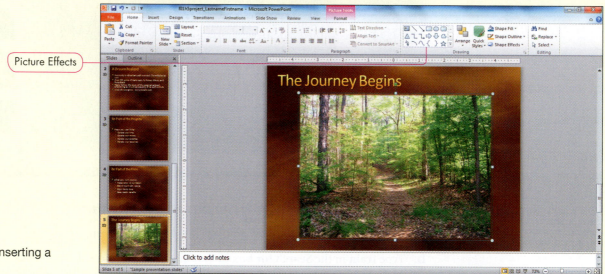

FIGURE 1.59 Inserting a Picture ➤

h. Click **Picture Effects** in the Picture Styles group on the Format tab, point to **Soft Edges**, and then click **5 Point**.

i. Click the **Slide Show tab**, and then click **From Beginning** in the Start Slide Show group. Click to advance from one slide to another. After the last slide, click to return to Normal view.

j. Save the presentation and exit PowerPoint.

You are ready to finalize the flyer, but before printing it you want to see how it will look. You wonder if it would be better in landscape or portrait orientation, so you will try both. After adjusting the margins, you are ready to save the flyer for later printing and distribution. Refer to Figure 1.60 as you complete Step 3.

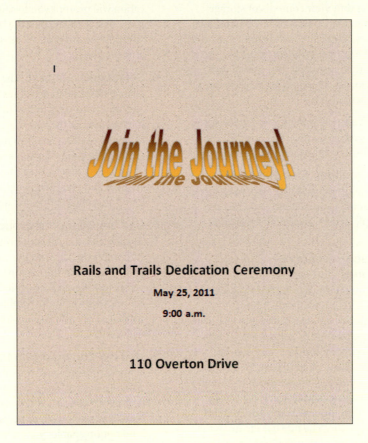

FIGURE 1.60 Word Handout ➤

a. Click the **Start button** to display the Start menu, and then point to **All Programs**. Click **Microsoft Office**, and then click **Microsoft Word 2010**. Open *f01h5handout* and save it as **f01h5handout_LastnameFirstname** in the Promotional Print folder on the drive where you save your files. The handout that you developed to help publicize the dedication ceremony displays as shown in Figure 1.60.

b. Click the **Page Layout tab**, click **Orientation** in the Page Setup group, and then click **Landscape** to view the flyer in landscape orientation.

   You want to see how the handout will look in landscape orientation.

c. Click the **File tab**, click **Print**, and then click **Next Page** (right-directed arrow at the bottom center of the preview page).

   The second page of the handout shows only the address. You can see that the two-page layout is not an attractive option.

d. Click the **Home tab**. Click **Undo** on the Quick Access Toolbar. Click the **File tab**, and then click **Print**.

   The document fits on one page. Portrait orientation is a much better choice for the handout.

e. Click the **Page Layout tab**, click **Margins**, and then select **Custom Margins**. Click the **spin arrow** beside the Left margin box to increase the margin to **1.5**. Similarly, change the right margin to **1.5**. Click **OK**.

f. Save the document and exit Word.

CHAPTER OBJECTIVES REVIEW

After reading this chapter, you have accomplished the following objectives:

1. **Use Windows Explorer.** You can use Windows Explorer to manage files and folders and to view contents of storage media. In addition to viewing the contents of physical folders, you can also manage libraries, which are collections of related data from various physical locations. Windows Explorer provides information on networked resources and shared disk drives, as well. Using the Favorites area of Windows Explorer, you can locate areas of frequent access.

2. **Work with folders and files.** Using Windows Explorer, you can create folders and rename, delete, move, and copy files and folders. You can also open files through Windows Explorer.

3. **Select, copy, and move multiple files and folders.** Backing up, or copying, files and folders is necessary to ensure that you do not lose important data and documents. You can quickly move or copy multiple items by selecting them all at one time.

4. **Identify common interface components.** You can communicate with Office software through the Microsoft Office user interface. Common interface components, found in all Microsoft Office applications, include the Ribbon, Quick Access Toolbar, title bar, status bar, and the Backstage view. The Ribbon is organized by commands within groups within tabs on the Ribbon. The Quick Access Toolbar provides one-click access to such activities as Save, Undo, and Repeat (Redo). The Backstage view is an Office feature that enables such common activities as opening, closing, saving, and printing files. It also provides information on an open file. The status bar contains information relative to the open file. The title bar identifies the open file's name and contains control buttons (minimize, maximize/restore down, and close).

5. **Get Office Help.** You can get help while you are using Microsoft Office by clicking the Help button, which appears as a question mark in the top-right corner of the Ribbon. You can also click the File tab to open the Backstage view, and then click the Help button. Assistance is available from within a dialog box by clicking the Help button in the top-right corner of the dialog box. When you rest the mouse pointer over any command on the Ribbon, you will see an Enhanced ScreenTip that provides a brief summary of the command.

6. **Open a file.** After a file has been saved, you can open it by clicking the File tab and selecting Open. If you recently worked with a file, you can reopen it from the Recent Documents list, which is displayed when you click Recent on the Backstage view. Finally, you can open a file from a template. Templates are predesigned files supplied by Microsoft from within the current Office installation or from Office.com.

7. **Print a file.** Often, you will want to print a file (a document, worksheet, or presentation). The Backstage view makes it easy to preview the file, change print settings, and print the file.

8. **Close a file and application.** When you close a file, it is removed from memory. If you plan to work with the file later, you will need to save the file before closing it. The Office application will prompt you to save the file before closing if you have made any changes since the last time the file was saved. When you close an application, all open files within the application are also closed.

9. **Select and edit text.** The Home tab includes options to change the appearance of text. You can change the size, color, and type of font, as well as other font attributes. The font is the typeface, or the way characters appear and are sized. Before changing existing text, you must select what you want to change. Although shortcuts to text selection exist, you can always select text by dragging to highlight it. Any formatting changes that you identify apply only to selected text or to text typed after the changes are invoked.

10. **Use the Clipboard group tasks.** The Clipboard is a holding area for selections that you have cut or copied. Although you can view the Clipboard by clicking the Dialog Box Launcher in the Clipboard group, doing so is not necessary before pasting a cut or copied item to a receiving location. Another option in the Clipboard group is Format Painter, which enables you to copy formatting from one area to another within a file.

11. **Use the Editing group tasks.** You can easily find selected words or phrases and replace them, if necessary, with substitutions. There may be occasions when you simply want to find an occurrence of selected text without replacing it, whereas at other times you want to make replacements immediately. The Find option enables you to locate text, whereas Replace enables you to find all occurrences of an item quickly and replace it with another.

12. **Insert objects.** Pictures, clip art, shapes, screenshots, headers and footers, and text boxes are objects that you can insert in Office projects. After you have inserted an object, you can click to select it and manage it independently of the underlying worksheet, document, or presentation. When you select an object, a contextual tab appears on the Ribbon to provide formatting options specific to the selected object.

13. **Review a file.** You can check spelling, grammar, and word usage using any Office application. In fact, applications are usually set to check for such errors as you type, underlining possible misspellings in red, grammatical mistakes in green, and incorrect word usage in blue. Errors are not always correctly identified, as the Office application might indicate a misspelling when it is simply a word that is not in its dictionary. You can also check spelling and grammar by selecting Spelling & Grammar in the Proofing group on the Review tab.

14. **Change page settings.** You can change margins and page orientation through commands in the Page Setup group of the Page Layout tab. The Page Setup dialog box, accessible when you click the Dialog Box Launcher in the Page Setup group, provides even more choices of page settings.

KEY TERMS

MULTIPLE CHOICE

1. The Recent Documents list:

   (a) Shows documents that have been previously printed.

   (b) Shows documents that have been previously opened.

   (c) Shows documents that have been previously saved in an earlier software version.

   (d) Shows documents that have been previously deleted.

2. Which of the following Windows Explorer features collects related data from folders and gives them a single name?

   (a) Network

   (b) Favorites

   (c) Libraries

   (d) Computer

3. When you want to copy the format of a selection, but not the content:

   (a) Double-click Copy in the Clipboard group.

   (b) Right-click the selection, and then click Copy.

   (c) Click Copy Format in the Clipboard group.

   (d) Click Format Painter in the Clipboard group.

4. Which of the following is not an object that can be inserted in an Office document?

   (a) Picture

   (b) Clip art

   (c) Paragraph box

   (d) Text box

5. What does a red wavy underline in a document, spreadsheet, or presentation mean?

   (a) A word is misspelled or not recognized by the Office dictionary.

   (b) A grammatical mistake exists.

   (c) An apparent word-usage mistake exists.

   (d) A word has been replaced with a synonym.

6. When you close a file:

   (a) You are prompted to save the file (unless you have made no changes since last saving it).

   (b) The application (Word, Excel, or PowerPoint) is also closed.

   (c) You must first save the file.

   (d) You must change the file name.

7. Live Preview:

   (a) Opens a predesigned document or spreadsheet that is relevant to your task.

   (b) Provides a preview of the results of a choice you are considering before you make a final selection.

   (c) Provides a preview of an upcoming Office version.

   (d) Enlarges the font onscreen.

8. You can get help when working with an Office application in which one of the following areas?

   (a) Help tab

   (b) Status bar

   (c) The Backstage view

   (d) Quick Access Toolbar

9. The Find and Replace feature enables you to do which of the following?

   (a) Find all instances of misspelling and automatically correct (or replace) them.

   (b) Find any grammatical errors and automatically correct (or replace) them.

   (c) Find any specified font settings and replace them with another selection.

   (d) Find any character string and replace it with another.

10. A document or worksheet printed in portrait orientation is:

    (a) Taller than it is wide.

    (b) Wider than it is tall.

    (c) A document with 2″ left and right margins.

    (d) A document with 2″ top and bottom margins.

1 Editing a Menu

You have gone into partnership with a friend to open a health food restaurant in a golf and tennis community. With the renewed emphasis on healthy living and the large number of high-income renters and condominium owners in the community, the specialty restaurant should do well. In preparation for the opening, your partner has begun a menu that you will review and edit. This exercise follows the same set of skills as used in Hands-On Exercises 1, 2, 3, 4, and 5 in the chapter. Refer to Figure 1.61 as you complete this exercise.

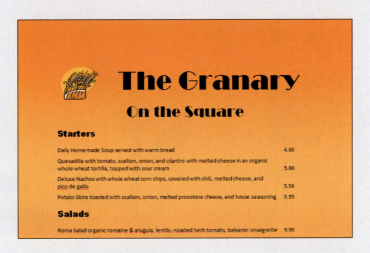

FIGURE 1.61 Restaurant Menu ➤

a. Click **Windows Explorer** on the taskbar, and then select the location where you save your files. Click **New folder**, type **The Granary**, and then press **Enter**. Close Windows Explorer.

b. Start Word. Open *f01p1menu* and save it as **f01p1menu_LastnameFirstname** in the The Granary folder.

c. Click the **Review tab**, and then click **Spelling & Grammar** in the Proofing group. The words *pico*, *gallo*, and *mesclun* are not misspelled, so you should ignore them when they are flagged. Other identified misspellings should be changed.

d. Click after the word *bread* in the first item under *Starters*. Press the **Spacebar**, and then type **or cornbread**.

e. Double-click **Desserts** on page 2 to select the word, and then type **Sweets**.

f. Drag to select the **Sandwiches section**, beginning with the word *Sandwiches* and ending after *8.75*. Click the **Home tab**, click **Cut** in the Clipboard group, click to place the insertion point before the word *Salads*, and then click **Paste** in the Clipboard group. The *Sandwiches* section should be placed before the *Salads* section.

g. Click **Undo** twice on the Quick Access Toolbar to return the *Sandwiches* section to its original location.

h. Change the price of Daily Homemade Soup to **4.95**.

i. Press **Ctrl+End** to place the insertion point at the end of the document, and then type your name.

j. Click the **Page Layout tab**, click **Orientation**, and then click **Landscape**. Click the **File tab**, and then click **Print** to see a preview of the document. Click the **Home tab**. Because the new look does not improve the menu's appearance, click **Undo** to return to the original orientation.

k. Press **Ctrl+Home** to move to the top of the document. Compare your results to Figure 1.61.

l. Drag the **Zoom slider** on the status bar slightly to the right to magnify text. Click the **View tab**, and then click **100%** in the Zoom group to return to the original size.

m. Save and close the file, and submit based on your instructor's directions.

You have always been interested in Web design and have worked in the field for several years. You now have an opportunity to devote yourself full-time to your career as the CEO of a company dedicated to designing and supporting Web sites. One of the first steps in getting the business off the ground is developing a business plan so that you can request financial support. You will use PowerPoint to present your business plan. This exercise follows the same set of skills as used in Hands-On Exercises 2, 3, and 4 in the chapter. Refer to Figure 1.62 as you complete this exercise.

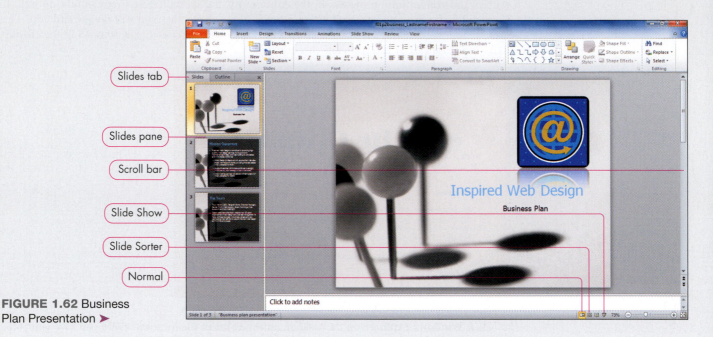

FIGURE 1.62 Business Plan Presentation ➤

a. Start PowerPoint. Open *f01p2business* and save it as **f01p2business_ LastnameFirstname**.

b. Click the **Slides tab** in the Slides pane (on the left), if necessary. Slide 1 should be displayed. If not, click the first slide in the left pane.

c. Position the mouse pointer to the immediate left of the word *Company*. Drag to select the words *Company Name*, and then type **Inspire Web Design**.

d. Click the **Insert tab**, and then click **Clip Art** in the Images group.
   - Click in the **Search for box** in the Clip Art task pane, remove any text that might be in the box, and then type **World Wide Web**. Make sure *Include Office.com content* is checked, and then click **Go**.
   - Select any image (or the one shown in Figure 1.62). Resize and position the clip art as shown. *Hint: To reposition clip art, drag when the mouse pointer is a four-headed arrow.*
   - Click the **Format tab**, click the **More button** in the Picture Styles group, and then click the **Reflected Rounded Rectangle picture style** (fifth from the left on the top row).
   - Click outside the clip art and compare your slide to Figure 1.62. Close the Clip Art task pane.

e. On Slide 2, click after the period on the bulleted point ending with *them*, and then press **Enter**. Type **Support services will include continued oversight, modification, and redesign of client Web sites.**

f. Press **Enter**, and then type **Web hosting services will ensure uninterrupted 24/7 Web presence for clients.**

g. On Slide 3, complete the following steps:
   - Position the mouse pointer over the first bullet so that the pointer appears as a four-headed arrow, and then click the bullet. All of the text in the bullet item is selected. As you type text, it will replace the selected text.
   - Type *your name* **(CEO)** [replacing *your name* with your first and last names]**, Margaret Atkins (Financial Manager), Daniel Finch (Web Design), Susan Cummings (Web Support and Web Hosting).**

h. Click the second bullet, and then type **Team members collectively possess over 28 years' experience in Web design and business management. All have achieved success in business careers and are redirecting their efforts to support Inspire Web Design as full-time employees.**

i. Click to select the third bullet, and then press **Delete**, removing the bullet and text.

j. On Slide 1, click **Slide Show** on the status bar. After viewing a slide, click the mouse button to proceed to the next slide. Continue to click until the slide show ends.

k. Click **Slide Sorter** on the status bar. You and your partners have decided to rename the company. The new name is **Inspired Web Design**.
  • Click the **Home tab**, and then click **Replace** in the Editing group. Be careful to click the button, not the arrow to the right.
  • Type **Inspire** in the **Find what box**. Type **Inspired** in the **Replace with box**.
  • Click **Replace All**. Three replacements should be made. Click **OK**, and then click **Close** in the Replace dialog box.

l. Save and close the file, and submit based on your instructor's directions.

---

3 Planning Ahead

You and a friend are starting a lawn care service and have a few clients already. Billing will be a large part of your record keeping, so you are planning ahead by developing a series of folders to maintain those records. This exercise follows the same set of skills as used in Hands-On Exercises 1 and 4 in the chapter. Refer to Figure 1.63 as you complete this exercise.

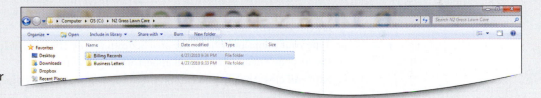

FIGURE 1.63 N2 Grass Folder Structure ➤

a. Click **Windows Explorer** on the taskbar, and then select the location where you save your files. Click **New folder**, type **N2 Grass Lawn Care**, and then press **Enter**.

b. Double-click **N2 Grass Lawn Care** in the Content pane.
  • Click **New folder**, type **Business Letters**, and then press **Enter**.
  • Click **New folder**, type **Billing Records**, and then press **Enter**. Compare your results to Figure 1.63. Close Windows Explorer.

c. Start Word. Open *f01p3lawn*. Use Find and Replace to replace the text *Your Name* with your name.

d. Click the **File tab**, and then click **Save As**.
  • Click **Computer** in the left pane.
  • Click the drive (in the Navigation Pane) where you save your student files. Double-click **N2 Grass Lawn Care**, and then double-click **Business Letters**.
  • Save the file as **f01p3lawn_LastnameFirstname**. Click **OK**, if necessary. Close the document and exit Word.

e. Open Windows Explorer.
  • Click **Computer** in the Navigation Pane.
  • In the Content pane, double-click the drive where you earlier placed the N2 Grass Lawn Care folder. Double-click **N2 Grass Lawn Care**.
  • Right-click **Billing Records**, click **Rename**, type **Accounting Records**, and then press **Enter**.

f. Click the **Start button**, click **All Programs**, click **Accessories**, and then click **Snipping Tool**. You will use the Snipping Tool to capture the screen display for submission to your instructor.
  • Click the **New arrow**, and then click **Full-screen Snip**.
  • Click **File**, and then click **Save As**.

g. Save the file as **f01p3snip_LastnameFirstname**. Close the file and submit based on your instructor's directions.

1 Reference Letter

You are an instructor at a local community college. A student has asked you to provide her with a letter of reference for a job application. You have used Word to prepare the letter, but now you need to make a few changes before it is finalized.

a. Open Windows Explorer. Create a new folder on the drive where you save your student files, naming it **Letters of Reference**. Close Windows Explorer.

b. Start Word. Open *f01m1letter* and save it in the Letters of Reference folder as **f01m1letter_LastnameFirstname**.

c. Type your name, address, and the current date in the address area, replacing the generic text. The letter is to go to **Ms. Samantha Blake, CEO**, **Ridgeline Industries**, **410 Wellington Parkway**, **Huntsville AL 35611**. The salutation should read **Dear Ms. Blake:**.

d. Bold the student's first and last names in the first sentence.

e. Find each occurrence of the word *Stacy* and replace it with **Stacey**.

f. Find and insert a synonym for the word *intelligent* in the second paragraph.

g. Move the last paragraph (beginning with *In my opinion*) to position it before the third paragraph (beginning with *Stacey*).

h. Press **Ctrl+Home** to move the insertion point to the beginning of the document. Check spelling, selecting a correction for each misspelled word and ignoring spelling or grammatical mistakes that are not actually incorrect.

i. Type your name and title in the area beneath the word *Sincerely*.

j. Preview the document as it will appear when printed.

k. Save and close the file, and submit based on your instructor's directions.

2 Medical Monitoring

You are enrolled in a Health Informatics program of study in which you learn to manage databases related to health fields. For a class project, your instructor requires that you monitor your blood pressure, recording your findings in an Excel worksheet. You have recorded the week's data and will now make a few changes before printing the worksheet for submission.

a. Start Excel. Open *f01m2tracker* and save it as **f01m2tracker_LastnameFirstname**.

b. Preview the worksheet as it will appear when printed.

c. Change the orientation of the worksheet to **Landscape**. Preview the worksheet again. Click the **Home tab**.

d. Click in the cell beside *Name*, and then type your first and last names. Press **Enter**.

e. Change the font of the text in **cell C1** to **Verdana** and the font size to **20**.

f. Copy the function in **cell E22** to **cells F22 and G22**. *Hint: After selecting cell E22 and clicking Copy, drag cells F22 and G22. Before you drag, be sure the mouse pointer has the appearance of a large white plus sign. Then click Paste to copy the formula to those two cells. Press **Esc** to remove the selection from around **cell E22**.*

DISCOVER

g. Get Help on showing decimal places. You want to increase the decimal places for the values in **cells E22, F22, and G22**, so that each value shows two places to the right of the decimal. Use Excel Help to learn how to do that. You might use *Increase Decimals* as a Search term. When you find the answer, select the three cells and increase the decimal places to **2**.

h. Click **cell A1**, and insert a clip art image of your choice related to blood pressure. Be sure the images include content from Office.com. If necessary, resize and position the clip art attractively. *Hint: To resize clip art, drag a corner handle (small circle). To reposition, drag the clip art when the mouse pointer is a four-headed arrow.*

i. Open the Backstage view, and adjust print settings to print two copies. You will not actually print two copies unless directed by your instructor.

j. Save and close the file, and submit based on your instructor's directions.

CAPSTONE EXERCISE

You are a member of the Student Government Association (SGA) at your college. As a community project, the SGA is sponsoring a "Stop Smoking" drive designed to provide information on the health risks posed by smoking cigarettes and to offer solutions to those who want to quit. The SGA has partnered with the local branch of the American Cancer Society as well as the outreach program of the local hospital to sponsor free educational awareness seminars. As the SGA Secretary, you will help prepare a PowerPoint presentation that will be displayed on plasma screens around campus and used in student seminars. You will use Microsoft Office to help with those tasks.

Manage Files and Folders

You will open, review, and save an Excel worksheet providing data on the personal monetary cost of smoking cigarettes over a period of years.

a. Create a folder called **SGA Drive** on the drive where you save your files.

b. Start Excel. Open *f01ccost* from the student data files and save it in the SGA Drive folder as **f01ccost_LastnameFirstname**.

c. Click **cell A10**, and then type your first and last names. Press **Enter**.

Modify Font

To highlight some key figures on the worksheet, you will format those cells with additional font attributes.

a. Draw attention to the high cost of smoking for 10, 20, and 30 years by changing the font color in **cells G3 through I4** to **Red**.

b. Italicize the Annual Cost cells (**F3 and F4**).

c. Click **Undo** on the Quick Access Toolbar to remove the italics. Click **Redo** to return the text to italics.

Insert Clip Art

You will add a clip art image to the worksheet and then resize it and position it.

a. Click **cell G7**, and then insert clip art appropriate for the topic of smoking.

b. Resize the clip art and reposition it near cell B7, if necessary.

c. Click outside the clipart to deselect it. Close the Clip Art task pane.

Preview Print, Change Page Layout, and Print

To get an idea of how the worksheet will look when printed, you will preview the worksheet. Then you will change the orientation and margins before printing it.

a. Preview the document as it will appear when printed.

b. Change the page orientation to **Landscape**. Click the **Page Layout tab**, and then change the margins to **Narrow**.

c. Preview the document as it will appear when printed.

d. Adjust the print settings to print two copies. You will not actually print two copies unless directed by your instructor.

e. Save the workbook and exit Excel.

Find and Replace

You have developed a PowerPoint presentation that you will use to present to student groups and for display on plasma screens across campus. The presentation is designed to increase awareness of the health problems associated with smoking. The PowerPoint presentation has come back from the reviewers with only one comment: A reviewer suggested that you spell out Centers for Disease Control and Prevention, instead of abbreviating it. You do not remember exactly which slide or slides the abbreviation might have been on, so you use Find and Replace to make the change quickly.

a. Start PowerPoint. Open *f01c1quit* and save it in the SGA Drive folder as **f01c1quit_LastnameFirstname**.

b. Replace all occurrences of *CDC* with **Centers for Disease Control and Prevention**.

Cut and Paste and Insert a Text Box

The Mark Twain quote on Slide 1 might be more effective on the last slide in the presentation, so you will cut and paste it there in a text box.

a. On Slide 1, select the entire Mark Twain quote, including the author name, and then cut it.

b. On Slide 22, paste the quote, reposition it more attractively, and then format it in a larger font size.

Check Spelling and Change View

Before you call the presentation complete, you will spell check it and view it as a slide show.

a. Check spelling. The word *hairlike* is not misspelled, so it should not be corrected.

b. View the slide show, and then take the smoking quiz. Click after the last slide to return to the presentation.

c. Save and close the presentation. Exit PowerPoint. Submit both files included in this project as directed by your instructor.

Employment Résumé

You have recently graduated from a university and are actively seeking employment. You know how important it is to have a comprehensive résumé to include with job applications, so you will use Word to prepare one. Instead of beginning a new document, you will modify a résumé template that is installed with Word. You can locate an appropriate résumé template by clicking the File tab and then clicking New. Select a résumé template from the Office.com area. Save the résumé as **f01b1resume_LastnameFirstname** in an appropriately named folder where you save your student files. Modify the résumé in any way you like, but make sure to complete the following activities:

- Include your name on the résumé. All other information, including address, education, employment history, and job objective, can be fictional.
- Format some text differently. The choice of text is up to you, but you should change font size and type and apply appropriate character attributes to improve the document's appearance.
- Find and replace all occurrences of the word *education* with **academic preparation**.
- Check the document for spelling errors, correcting or ignoring any that you find.
- Change the margins to **1.5"** right and left. Preview the document as it will appear when printed. Save and close the document. Keep Word open.
- Open a new blank document. Create a cover letter that will accompany the résumé. You can use a template for the cover letter if you find an appropriate one. The letter should serve as your introduction, highlighting anything that you think makes you an ideal employee.
- Save the cover letter as **f01b1cover_LastnameFirstname** and exit Word. Submit the file as directed by your instructor.

Fitness Planner

Microsoft Excel is an excellent organizational tool. You will use it to maintain a fitness planner. Start Excel. Open *f01b2exercise*, and then save it as **f01b2exercise_LastnameFirstname**. The fitness planner is basically a template, which means that all exercise categories are listed, but without actual data. To personalize the planner to improve its appearance, complete the following activities:

- Change the orientation to **Landscape**. Preview the worksheet as it will appear when printed.
- Move the contents of **cell A2** (*Exercise Planner*) to **cell A1**.
- Click **cell A8**, and then use **Format Painter** to copy the format of that selection to **cells A5 and A6**. Increase the font size of **cell A1** to **26**.
- Use Excel Help to learn how to insert a header. Then insert a header on the worksheet with your first and last names.
- Insert a fitness-related clip art item in **cell A21**, positioning and sizing it so that it is attractive. Click outside the clip art to deselect it.
- Begin the fitness planner, entering at least one activity in each category (warm-up, aerobics, strength, and cool-down). Use **Find and Select** to replace all occurrences of *Exercises* with **Activities**. Save and close the file, and submit as directed by your instructor.

Household Records

You recently received a newsletter from the insurance company with which you have homeowners insurance. An article in the newsletter suggested that you maintain detailed records of your household appliances and other items of value that are in your home. In case of burglary or disaster, an insurance claim is expedited if you are able to itemize what was lost along with identifying information such as serial numbers. You will use Excel to prepare such a list. You will then make a copy of the record on another storage device for safekeeping outside your home (in case your home is destroyed by a fire or weather-related catastrophe).

- Connect a flash drive to your computer, and then close any dialog box that may appear (unless it is informing you of a problem with the drive). Use Windows Explorer to create a folder on the hard drive titled **Home Records**.
- Start Excel. Design a worksheet listing at least five fictional appliances and electronic equipment along with the serial number of each. Design the worksheet in any way you like. Save the workbook as **f01b3household_LastnameFirstname** in the Home Records folder of the hard drive. Close the workbook and exit Excel.
- Use Windows Explorer to copy the Home Records folder from the hard drive to your flash drive. Click the **flash drive** in the Navigation Pane of Windows Explorer. Double-click the **Home Records folder** in the Content pane.
- Click the **Start button**, click **All Programs**, click **Accessories**, and then click **Snipping Tool**. Click the **New arrow**, and then click **Full-screen Snip**. Click **File**, and then click **Save As**. Save the screen display as **f01b3disaster_LastnameFirstname**.
- Close all open windows and submit the files as directed by your instructor.

1 INTRODUCTION TO EXCEL

What Is a Spreadsheet?

CASE STUDY | OK Office Systems

You are an assistant manager at OK Office Systems (OKOS) in Oklahoma City. OKOS sells a wide range of computer systems, peripherals, and furniture for small- and medium-sized organizations in the metropolitan area. To compete against large, global big-box office supply stores, OKOS provides competitive pricing by ordering directly from local manufacturers rather than dealing with distributors.

The manager asked you to help prepare a markup, discount, and profit analysis for selected items on sale. The manager has been keeping these data in a ledger, but you will develop a spreadsheet to perform the necessary calculations. Although your experience with Microsoft Office Excel 2010 may be limited, you are excited to apply your knowledge and skills to your newly assigned responsibility.

When you get to the Hands-On Exercises, you will create and format the analytical spreadsheet to practice the skills you learn in this chapter.

OBJECTIVES | AFTER YOU READ THIS CHAPTER, YOU WILL BE ABLE TO:

1. Plan for effective workbook and worksheet design *p.68*
2. Explore the Excel window *p.69*
3. Enter and edit cell data *p.72*
4. Use symbols and the order of precedence *p.77*
5. Use Auto Fill *p.79*
6. Display cell formulas *p.80*
7. Manage worksheets *p.86*
8. Manage columns and rows *p.89*
9. Select, move, copy, and paste *p.93*
10. Apply alignment and font options *p.102*
11. Apply number formats *p.104*
12. Select page setup options *p.110*
13. Print a worksheet *p.113*

Introduction to Spreadsheets

The ability to organize, calculate, and evaluate quantitative data is one of the most important skills needed today for personal, as well as managerial, decision making. In your personal life, you track expenses for your household budget, maintain a savings plan, and determine what amount you can afford for a house or car payment. Retail managers create and analyze their organizations' annual budgets, sales projections, and inventory records. Charitable organizations track the donations they receive, the distribution of those donations, and overhead expenditures. Scientists track the results of their experiments and perform statistical analysis to draw conclusions and recommendations.

> The ability to organize, calculate, and evaluate quantitative data is one of the most important skills needed today.

> A **spreadsheet** is an electronic file that contains a grid of columns and rows containing related data.
>
> A **spreadsheet program** is a computer application used to create and modify spreadsheets.

Regardless of what type of quantitative analysis you need to do, you can use a spreadsheet to help you maintain data and perform calculations. A *spreadsheet* is an electronic file that contains a grid of columns and rows used to organize related data and to display results of calculations, enabling interpretation of quantitative data for decision making. A *spreadsheet program* is a computer application, such as Microsoft Excel, that you use to create and modify electronic spreadsheets.

Performing calculations using a calculator and then entering the results into a ledger can lead to inaccurate values. If an input value is incorrect or needs to be updated, you have to recalculate the results manually, which is time-consuming and can lead to inaccuracies. An electronic spreadsheet makes data-entry changes easy. If the formulas are correctly constructed, the results recalculate automatically and accurately, saving time and reducing room for error. The left side of Figure 1.1 shows the original spreadsheet with the $450 cost, 75% markup rate, and calculated retail price. The right side shows the updated spreadsheet with a $500 cost, 65.5% markup, and automatically updated retail price.

FIGURE 1.1 Original and Modified Values ➤

Original Spreadsheet Values and Results					Modified Spreadsheet Values and Results			
Product	**Cost**	**Markup Rate**	**Retail Price**		**Product**	**Cost**	**Markup Rate**	**Retail Price**
Electronics:					Electronics:			
Computer System	$400.00	50.00%	$ 600.00		Computer System	$400.00	50.00%	$ 600.00
28" Monitor	$195.00	83.50%	$ 357.83		28" Monitor	$195.00	83.50%	$ 357.83
Color Laser Printer	$450.00	75.00%	$ 787.50		Color Laser Printer	$500.00	65.50%	$ 827.50

Callouts: Original calculated retail price; Original values; Changed values; Automatically updated retail price

In this section, you will learn how to design workbooks and worksheets. In addition, you will explore the Excel window and learn the name of each window element. Then, you will enter text, values, dates, and formulas in a worksheet.

Planning for Effective Workbook and Worksheet Design

> A **worksheet** is a spreadsheet that contains formulas, functions, values, text, and visual aids.
>
> A **workbook** is a file containing related worksheets.

Microsoft Excel is the most popular spreadsheet program used today. In Excel, a *worksheet* is a single spreadsheet that typically contains descriptive labels, numeric values, formulas, functions, and graphical representations of data. A *workbook* is a collection of one or more related worksheets contained within a single file. By default, new workbooks contain three worksheets. Storing multiple worksheets within one workbook helps organize related data together in one file and enables you to perform calculations among the worksheets within the workbook. For example, you can create a budget workbook of 13 worksheets, one for each month to store your personal income and expenses and a final worksheet to calculate totals across the entire year.

You should plan the structure before you start entering data into a worksheet. Using the OKOS case study as an example, the steps to design the workbook and a worksheet include the following:

1. **State the purpose of the worksheet.** The purpose of the OKOS worksheet is to provide data, including a profit margin, on selected products on sale.

An **input area** is a range of cells containing values for variables used in formulas.

2. **Decide what input values are needed.** Create an *input area*, a range of cells to enter values for your variables or assumptions. Clearly label an input area so that users know where to change values. For the OKOS worksheet, list the product names, the costs OKOS pays the manufacturers, the markup rates, and the proposed discount rates for the sale. Enter these data in individual cells to enable changes if needed.

An **output area** is a range of cells containing results based on manipulating the variables.

3. **Decide what outputs are needed to achieve the purpose of the worksheet.** Create an *output area*, a range of cells that contains the results of manipulating values in the input area. As the OKOS assistant manager, you need to calculate the retail price (i.e., the selling price to your customers), the sale price, and the profit margin. As you plan your formulas, avoid constants (raw numbers); instead, use references to cells containing numbers.

4. **Assign the worksheet inputs and results into columns and rows, and consider labeling.** Typically, descriptive labels appear in the first column to represent each row of data. For the OKOS worksheet, enter the product names in the first column. Labels at the top of each column represent individual columns of data, such as cost, markup rate, and selling price.

5. **Enter the labels, values, and formulas in Excel.** Change the input values to test that your formulas produce correct results. If necessary, correct any errors in the formulas to produce correct results regardless of the input values. For the OKOS worksheet, change some of the original costs and markup rates to ensure the calculated retail price, selling price, and profit margin percentage results update correctly.

6. **Format the numerical values in the worksheet.** Align decimal points in columns of numbers. In the OKOS worksheet, use Accounting Number Format and the Percent Style to format the numerical data. Adjust the number of decimal places as needed.

7. **Format the descriptive titles and labels attractively but so as not to distract your audience from the purpose of the worksheet.** Include a descriptive title and label for each column. Add bold to headings, increase the font size for readability, and use color to draw attention to important values or trends. In the OKOS worksheet, you will center the main title over all the columns and apply a larger font size to it.

8. **Document the worksheet as thoroughly as possible.** Include the current date, your name as the author of the worksheet, assumptions, and purpose of the worksheet.

9. **Save the completed workbook.** Preview and prepare printouts for distribution in meetings, or send an electronic copy of the workbook to those who need it.

Figure 1.2 shows the completed worksheet in Excel.

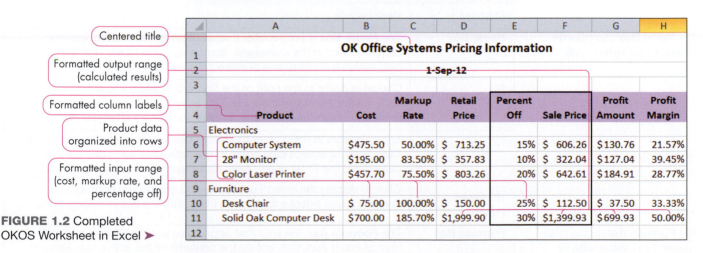

FIGURE 1.2 Completed OKOS Worksheet in Excel ➤

Exploring the Excel Window

By now, you should be familiar with the standard interface of Microsoft Office applications: the Quick Access Toolbar, title bar, control buttons, Ribbon, Home tab, the Backstage view, and scroll bars. The Excel window includes screen elements that are similar to other Office applications and items that are unique to Excel. Figure 1.3 identifies elements specific to the Excel window, and Table 1.1 lists and describes the Excel window elements.

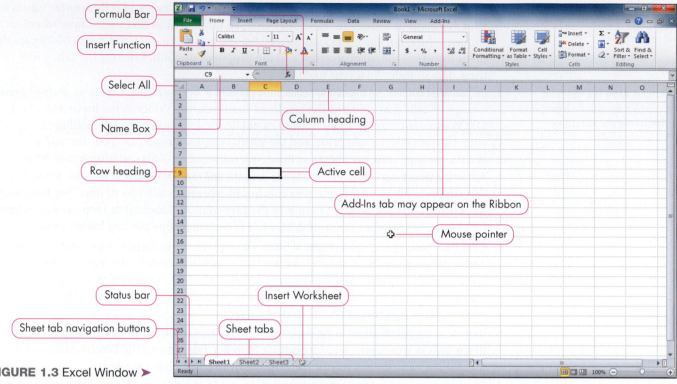

Formula Bar

Insert Function

Select All

Name Box

Row heading

Column heading

Active cell

Add-Ins tab may appear on the Ribbon

Mouse pointer

Status bar

Insert Worksheet

Sheet tab navigation buttons

Sheet tabs

FIGURE 1.3 Excel Window ➤

> **TIP** **Add-Ins Tab**
>
> You may see an Add-Ins tab on the Ribbon. This tab indicates that additional functionality, such as an updated Office feature or an Office-compatible program, has been added to your system. Add-Ins are designed to increase your productivity.

The **Name Box** identifies the address of the current cell.

The **Formula Bar** displays the content (text, value, date, or formula) in the active cell.

TABLE 1.1 Excel Elements

Element	Description
Name Box	The **Name Box** is an identifier that displays the address of the cell currently used in the worksheet. You can use the Name Box to go to a cell, assign a name to one or more cells, or select a function.
☒ **Cancel**	Cancel appears to the right of the Name Box when you enter or edit data. Click Cancel to cancel the data entry or edit and revert back to the previous data in the cell, if any. Cancel disappears after you click it.
✓ **Enter**	Enter appears to the right of the Name Box when you enter or edit data. Click Enter to accept data typed in the active cell and keep the current cell active. The Enter check mark disappears after you enter the data.
fx **Insert Function**	Click to display the Insert Function dialog box, which enables you to search for and select a function to insert into the active cell.
Formula Bar	The **Formula Bar**, the area that appears below the Ribbon and to the right of Insert Function, shows the contents of the active cell. You can enter or edit cell contents here or directly in the active cell. Drag the bottom border of the Formula Bar down to increase the space of the Formula Bar to display large amounts of data or a long formula contained in the active cell.
Select All	The square at the intersection of the row and column headings in the top-left corner of the worksheet. Click it to select everything contained in the active worksheet.

TABLE 1.1 (Continued)

Element	Description
Column headings	The letters above the columns, such as A, B, C, and so on.
Row headings	The numbers to the left of the rows are row headings, such as 1, 2, 3, and so on.
Sheet tabs	*Sheet tabs*, located at the bottom-left corner of the Excel window, show the names of the worksheets contained in the workbook. Three sheet tabs, initially named Sheet1, Sheet2, and Sheet3, are included when you start a new Excel workbook. You can rename sheets with more meaningful names. To display the contents of a particular worksheet, click its sheet tab.
Sheet Tab Navigation buttons	If your workbook contains several worksheets, Excel may not show all the sheet tabs at the same time. Use the buttons to display the first, previous, next, or last worksheet.
Status bar	Located at the bottom of the Excel window, below the sheet tabs and above the Windows taskbar, the status bar displays information about a selected command or operation in progress. For example, it displays *Select destination and press ENTER or choose Paste* after you use the Copy command.

A **sheet tab** displays the name of a worksheet within a workbook.

Identify Columns, Rows, and Cells

A worksheet contains columns and rows, with each column and row assigned a heading. Columns are assigned alphabetic headings from columns A to Z, continuing from AA to AZ, and then from BA to BZ until XFD, which is the last of the possible 16,384 columns. Rows have numeric headings ranging from 1 to 1,048,576 (the maximum number of rows available).

A **cell** is the intersection of a column and row.

A **cell address** identifies a cell by a column letter and a row number.

The intersection of a column and row is a *cell*; a total of over 17 billion cells are available in a worksheet. Each cell has a unique *cell address*, identified by first its column letter and then its row number. For example, the cell at the intersection of column A and row 9 is cell A9. Cell references are useful when referencing data in formulas, or in navigation.

Navigate In and Among Worksheets

The **active cell** is the current cell, indicated by a dark border.

The *active cell* is the current cell. Excel displays a dark border around the active cell in the worksheet window, and the cell address of the active cell appears in the Name Box. The contents of the active cell, or the formula used to calculate the results of the active cell, appear in the Formula Bar. You can change the active cell by using the mouse to click in a different cell. If you work in a large worksheet, you may not be able to see the entire contents in one screen; use the vertical and horizontal scroll bars to display another area of the worksheet, and then click in the desired cell to make it the active cell.

To navigate to a new cell, click it, or use the arrow keys on the keyboard. When you press Enter, the next cell down in the same column becomes the active cell. Table 1.2 lists the keyboard methods for navigating within a worksheet. The Go To command is helpful for navigating to a cell that is not visible onscreen.

TABLE 1.2 Keystrokes and Actions

Keystroke	Used to
↑	Move up one cell in the same column.
↓	Move down one cell in the same column.
←	Move left one cell in the same row.
→	Move right one cell in the same row.
Tab	Move right one cell in the same row.

(Continued)

TABLE 1.2	(Continued)
Keystroke	**Used to**
Page Up	Move the active cell up one screen.
Page Down	Move the active cell down one screen.
Home	Move the active cell to column A of current row.
Ctrl+Home	Make cell A1 the active cell.
Ctrl+End	Make the rightmost, lowermost active corner of the worksheet—the intersection of the last column and row that contains data—the active cell. Does not move to cell XFD1048576 unless that cell contains data.
F5 or Ctrl+G	Display the Go To dialog box to enter any cell address.

To display the contents of another worksheet within the workbook, click the sheet tab at the bottom of the workbook window. The active sheet tab has a white background color. After you click a sheet tab, you can then navigate within that worksheet.

Entering and Editing Cell Data

The four types of data that you can enter in a cell in an Excel worksheet are text; values; dates; and formulas, including functions. Figure 1.4 shows examples of text, values, dates, and formula results.

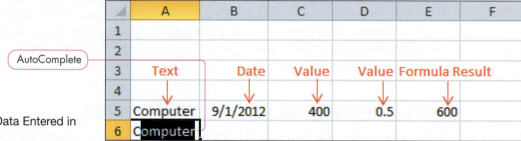

FIGURE 1.4 Data Entered in Cells ➤

Enter Text

Text includes letters, numbers, symbols, and spaces.

Text is any combination of letters, numbers, symbols, and spaces not used in calculations. Excel treats phone numbers, such as 555-1234, and social security numbers, such as 123-45-6789, as text entries. You enter text for a worksheet title to describe the contents of the worksheet, as row and column labels to describe data, and as cell data. Text aligns at the left cell margin by default. To enter text in a cell, do the following:

- Make sure the cell is active where you want to enter text.
- Enter the text.
- Press Enter, press an arrow key on the keyboard, or click Enter—the check mark between the Name Box and the Formula Bar. If you want to enter data without making another cell the active cell, click Enter instead of pressing Enter.

> **TIP** **Line Break in a Cell**
>
> If you have a long text label that does not fit well in a cell, you can insert a line break to display the text label on multiple lines within the cell. To insert a line break while you are typing a label, press Alt+Enter where you want to start the next line of text within the cell.

Enter Values

A **value** is a number that represents a quantity or an amount.

Values are numbers that represent a quantity or a measurable amount. Excel usually distinguishes between text and value data based on what you enter. The primary difference between text and value entries is that value entries can be the basis of calculations, whereas text cannot. Values align at the right cell margin by default. After entering values, you can align decimal places and add identifying characters, such as $ or %.

Enter Dates

You can enter dates and times in a variety of formats in cells, such as 9/15/2012; 9/15/12; September 15, 2012; or 15-Sep-12. You can also enter times, such as 1:30 PM or 13:30. You should enter a static date to document when you create or modify a workbook or to document the specific point in time when the data were accurate, such as on a balance sheet or income statement. Dates are values, so they align at the right cell margin.

Excel displays dates differently from the way it stores dates. For example, the displayed date 9/15/2012 represents the fifteenth day in September in the year 2012. Excel stores dates as serial numbers starting at 1 with January 1, 1900, so 9/15/2012 is stored as 41167 so that you can create formulas to calculate how many days exist between two dates.

Enter Formulas

A **formula** is a combination of cell references, operators, values, and/or functions used to perform a calculation.

Formulas are the combination of cell references, arithmetic operations, values, and/or functions used in a calculation. For Excel to recognize a formula, you must start the formula with an equal sign (=). Because Excel requires that formulas start with =, it treats phone numbers, such as (405) 555-1234, as text, not values. In Figure 1.4, cell E5 contains the formula =C5*D5+C5. The result of the formula (600) displays in the cell.

Edit and Clear Cell Contents

You can edit a cell's contents by doing one of the following:

- Click the cell, click in the Formula Bar, make the changes, and then click Enter on the left side of the Formula Bar.
- Double-click the cell, make changes in the cell, and then press Enter.
- Click the cell, press F2, make changes in the cell, and then press Enter.

You can clear a cell's contents by doing one of the following:

- Click the cell, and then press Delete.
- Click the cell, click Clear in the Editing group on the Home tab, and then select Clear Contents.

1 Introduction to Spreadsheets

As the assistant manager of OKOS, you need to create a worksheet that shows the cost (the amount OKOS pays its suppliers), the markup percentage (the amount by which the cost is increased), and the retail selling price. In addition, you need to list the discount percentage (such as 25% off) for each product, the sale price, and the profit margin percentage. Most of the cells in the worksheet will contain formulas. You have already planned the design as indicated in the steps listed earlier in this chapter.

Skills covered: Enter Text • Enter Unformatted Values • Enter a Date and Clear Cell Contents

---

STEP 1 ▶ ENTER TEXT

Now that you have planned your worksheet, you are ready to enter labels for the title, row labels, and column labels. Refer to Figure 1.5 as you complete Step 1.

	A	B	C	D	E	F	G	H
1	OK Office Systems Pricing Information							
2	1-Sep-12							
3								
4	Product	Cost	Markup Ra	Retail Pric	Percent O	Sale Price	Profit Margin	
5	Computer System							
6	Color Laser Printer							
7	Filing Cabinet							
8	Desk Chair							
9	Solid Oak Computer Desk							
10	28" Monitor							
11								
12								

FIGURE 1.5 Text Entries ➤

FYI

a. Start Excel. Save the new workbook as **e01h1markup_LastnameFirstname**.

When you save files, use your last and first names. For example, as the Excel author, I would save my workbook as e01h1markup_MulberyKeith.

b. Type **OK Office Systems Pricing Information** in **cell A1**, and then press **Enter**.

When you press Enter, the next cell down—cell A2 in this case—becomes the active cell. The text does not completely fit in cell A1, and some of the text appears in cells B1, C1, and D1. If you make cell B1, C1, or D1 the active cell, the Formula Bar is empty, indicating that nothing is stored in those cells. If you were to type data in cell B1, that text would appear in cell B1, and although the contents of cell A1 would appear cut off, cell A1 still would contain the entire text.

c. Click **cell A4**, type **Product**, and then press **Enter**.

d. Continue typing the rest of the text in **cells A5** through **A10** as shown in Figure 1.5. Note that text appears to flow into column B.

When you start typing *Co* in cell A6, AutoComplete displays a ScreenTip suggesting a previous text entry starting with *Co—Computer System*—but keep typing to enter *Color Laser Printer* instead. You just entered the product labels to describe the data on each row.

e. Click **cell B4** to make it the active cell. Type **Cost** and press **Tab**.

Instead of pressing Enter to move down column B, you pressed Tab to make the cell to the right the active cell.

f. Type the following text in the respective cells, pressing **Tab** after typing each column heading:

- **Markup Rate** in **cell C4**
- **Retail Price** in **cell D4**
- **Percent Off** in **cell E4**
- **Sale Price** in **cell F4**
- **Profit Margin** in **cell G4**

Notice that the text looks cut off when you enter data in the cell to the right. Do not worry about this now. You will adjust column widths and formatting later in this chapter.

> **TROUBLESHOOTING:** If you notice a typographical error, click in the cell containing the error, and then retype the label. Or press F2 to edit the cell contents, move the insertion point using the arrow keys, press Backspace or Delete to delete the incorrect characters, type the correct characters, and then press Enter. If you type a label in an incorrect cell, click the cell, and then press Delete.

 FYI

g. Save the changes you made to the workbook.

You should develop a habit of saving periodically. That way if your system unexpectedly shuts down, you won't lose everything you worked on.

STEP 2 ▶ ENTER UNFORMATTED VALUES

Now that you have entered the descriptive labels, you need to enter the cost, markup rate, and percent off for each product. Refer to Figure 1.6 as you complete Step 2.

	A	B	C	D	E	F	G	H
1	OK Office Systems Pricing Information							
2	1-Sep-12							
3								
4	Product	Cost	Markup Ra	Retail Pric	Percent O	Sale Price	Profit Margin	
5	Computer	400	0.5		0.15			
6	Color Lase	457.7	0.75		0.2			
7	Filing Cab	68.75	0.905		0.1			
8	Desk Chai	75	1		0.25			
9	Solid Oak	700	1.857		0.3			
10	28" Monit	195	0.835		0.1			
11								
12								

FIGURE 1.6 Unformatted Values ▶

a. Click **cell B5** to make it the active cell.

You are ready to enter the amount each product cost your company.

b. Type **400** and press **Enter**.

c. Type the remaining costs in **cells B6** through **B10** as shown in Figure 1.6.

> **TIP** Numeric Keypad
>
> To improve your productivity, you should use the numeric keypad on the right side of your keyboard if your keyboard contains a numeric keypad. If you use a laptop, you can purchase a separate numeric keypad device to use. It is much faster to type values and use Enter on the number keypad rather than using the numbers on the keyboard. Make sure Num Lock is active before using the keypad to enter values.

✓ **d.** Click **cell C5**, type **0.5**, and then press **Enter**.

You entered the markup rate as a decimal instead of a percentage. You will apply Percent Style later, but now you can concentrate on data entry. When you enter decimal values less than zero, you can type the period and value without typing the zero first, such as *.5*. Excel will automatically add the zero. You can also enter percentages as 50%, but the approach this textbook takes is to enter raw data without typing formatting such as % and then to use number formatting options through Excel to display formatting symbols.

e. Type the remaining markup rates in **cells C6** through **C10** as shown in Figure 1.6.

f. Click **cell E5**, type **0.15**, and then press **Enter**.

You entered the markdown or percent off sale value as a decimal.

g. Type the remaining markdown rates in **cells E6** through **E10** as shown in Figure 1.6, and then save the changes to the workbook.

STEP 3 ▶ ENTER A DATE AND CLEAR CELL CONTENTS

As you review the worksheet, you realize you need to provide a date to indicate when the sale starts. Refer to Figure 1.7 as you complete Step 3.

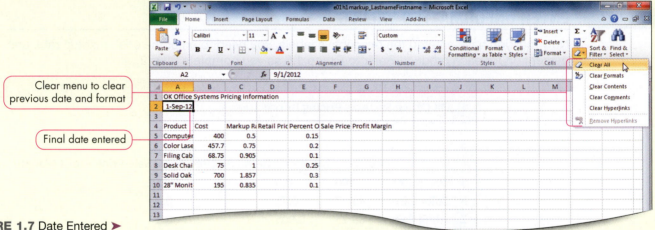

FIGURE 1.7 Date Entered ▶

a. Click **cell A2**, type **9/1/12**, and then press **Enter**.

The date aligns on the right cell margin by default. Note that Excel displays *9/1/2012* instead of *9/1/12* as you entered.

b. Click **cell A2**. Click **Clear** in the Editing group on the Home tab, and then select **Clear All**.

The Clear All command clears both cell contents and formatting in the selected cell(s).

c. Type **September 1, 2012** in **cell A2**, and then press **Enter**.

When you enter a date in the format *September 1, 2012*, Excel displays the date in the customer number format: *1-Sep-12*. However, you can select a date number format in the Format Cells dialog box.

d. Save the workbook. Keep the workbook onscreen if you plan to continue with Hands-On Exercise 2. If not, close the workbook and exit Excel.

Mathematics and Formulas

Formulas transform otherwise static numbers into meaningful results that can update as values change. For example, a payroll manager can build formulas to calculate the gross pay, deductions, and net pay for an organization's employees, or a doctoral student can create formulas to perform various statistical calculations to interpret his or her research data.

> Formulas transform otherwise static numbers into meaningful results.

You can use formulas to help you analyze how results will change as the input data change. You can change the value of your assumptions or inputs and explore the results quickly and accurately. For example, if the interest rate changes from 4% to 5%, how would that affect your monthly payment? Analyzing different input values in Excel is easy after you build formulas. Simply change an input value and observe the change in the formula results.

In this section, you will learn how to use mathematical operations in Excel formulas. You will refresh your memory of mathematical order of precedence and how to construct formulas using cell addresses so that when a value of an input cell changes, the result of the formula changes without you having to modify the formula.

Using Symbols and the Order of Precedence

The four mathematical operations—addition, subtraction, multiplication, and division—are the basis of mathematical calculations. Table 1.3 lists the common arithmetic operators and their symbols.

TABLE 1.3 Arithmetic Operators and Symbols		
Operation	**Common Symbol**	**Symbol in Excel**
Addition	+	+
Subtraction	-	-
Multiplication	X	*
Division	÷	/
Exponentiation	^	^

Enter Cell References in Formulas

Start a formula by typing the equal sign (=), followed by the arithmetic expression. Do not include a space before or after the arithmetic operator. To add the contents of cells A2 and A3, enter =A2+A3 or =A3+A2. Excel uses the value stored in cell A2 (10) and adds it to the value stored in cell A3 (2). The result—12—appears in the cell instead of the formula itself. You can see the formula of the active cell by looking at the Formula Bar. Figure 1.8 shows a worksheet containing data and results of formulas. The figure also displays the actual formulas used to generate the calculated results.

◢	A	B	C	D
1	**Contents**		**Description**	**Results**
2	10		First input value	10
3	2		Second input value	2
4	=A2+A3		Sum of 10 and 2	12
5	=A2-A3		Difference between 10 and 2	8
6	=A2*A3		Product of 10 and 2	20
7	=A2/A3		Results of dividing 10 by 2	5
8	=A2^A3		Results of 10 to the 2nd power	100

Input values

Output (formula results)

FIGURE 1.8 Formula Results ➤

If you type A2+A3 without the equal sign, Excel does not recognize that you entered a formula and stores the data as text.

You should use cell addresses instead of values as references in formulas where possible. You may include values in an input area—such as dates, salary, or costs—that you will need to reference in formulas. Referencing these cells in your formulas, instead of typing the value of the cell to which you are referring, keeps your formulas accurate if the values change. If you change the value of cell A2 to 5, the result of =A2+A3 displays 7 in cell A4. If you had typed actual values in the formula, =10+2, you would have to edit the formula each time a value changes. Always design worksheets in such a way as to be able to change input values without having to modify your formulas if an input value changes later.

> ### TIP Constants in Formulas
>
> Use cell references instead of actual values in formulas, unless the value is a constant. For example, to calculate the reciprocal of a percentage stored in cell B4, type =1-B4. The constant, 1, represents 100%, a value that never changes, although the percentage in cell B4 might change.

Control the Results with the Order of Precedence

Recall the basic rules of performing calculations from a high school or college math class. What is calculated first in the expression =A1+A2*A3? Remember that multiplication is performed before addition, so the value in cell A2 is multiplied by the value in cell A3. Excel then adds the product to the value in cell A1.

The *order of precedence* (also called order of operations) is a rule that controls the sequence in which arithmetic operations are performed, which affects the results of the calculation. Excel performs mathematical calculations left to right in this order: **P**arentheses, **E**xponentiation, **M**ultiplication or **D**ivision, and finally **A**ddition or **S**ubtraction. Some people remember the order of precedence with the phrase **P**lease **E**xcuse **M**y **D**ear **A**unt **S**ally. Therefore, if you want to add the values in A1 and A2 and *then* multiply the sum by the value in cell A3, you need to enclose the addition operation in parentheses =(A1+A2)*A3 since anything in parentheses is calculated first. Without parentheses, multiplication has a higher order of precedence than addition and will be calculated first. Figure 1.9 shows formulas, formula explanations, and formula results based on the order of precedence. The result in cell A12 displays only five digits to the right of the decimal point.

The **order of precedence** controls the sequence in which Excel performs arithmetic operations.

◢	A	B	C	D
1	10			
2	5			
3	2			
4	4			
5				
6	Result		Formula	Explanation
7	20		=A1+A2*A3	5 x 2 = 10. The product 10 is then added to 10 stored in cell A1.
8	30		=(A1+A2)*A3	10 + 5 = 15. The sum of 15 is then multiplied by 2 stored in cell A3.
9	24		=A1+A2*A3+A4	5 x 2 = 10. 10 + 10 + 4 = 24.
10	90		=(A1+A2)*(A3+A4)	10 + 5 = 15; 2+4 = 6. 15 x 6 = 90.
11	10		=A1/A2+A3*A4	10 / 5 = 2; 2 x 4 = 8; 2 + 8 = 10.
12	5.71429		=A1/(A2+A3)*A4	5 + 2 = 7. 10 / 7 = 1.428571429. 1.42857149 * 4 = 5.714285714

FIGURE 1.9 Formula Results Based on Order of Precedence ➤

Using Auto Fill

Auto Fill enables you to copy the contents of a cell or cell range or to continue a sequence by dragging the fill handle over an adjacent cell or range of cells.

The **fill handle** is a small black square at the bottom-right corner of a cell.

Auto Fill enables you to copy the contents of a cell or a range of cells by dragging the *fill handle* (a small black square appearing in the bottom-right corner of a cell) over an adjacent cell or range of cells. To use Auto Fill, do the following:

1. Click the cell with the content you want to copy to make it the active cell.
2. Position the pointer over the bottom-right corner of the cell until it changes to the fill pointer (a thin black plus sign).
3. Drag the fill handle to repeat the content in other cells.

Copying Formulas with Auto Fill. After you enter a formula in a cell, you can duplicate the formula down a column or across a row without retyping it by using Auto Fill. Excel adapts each copied formula based on the type of cell references in the original formula.

Completing Sequences with Auto Fill. You can also use Auto Fill to complete a sequence. For example, if you enter *January* in a cell, you can use Auto Fill to enter the rest of the months in adjacent cells. Other sequences you can complete are quarters (Qtr 1, etc.), weekdays, and weekday abbreviations, by typing the first item and using Auto Fill to complete the other entries. For numeric values, however, you must specify the first two values in sequence. For example, if you want to fill in 5, 10, 15, and so on, you must enter the first two values in two cells, select the two cells, and then use Auto Fill so that Excel knows to increment by 5. Figure 1.10 shows the results of filling in months, abbreviated months, quarters, weekdays, abbreviated weekdays, and increments of 5.

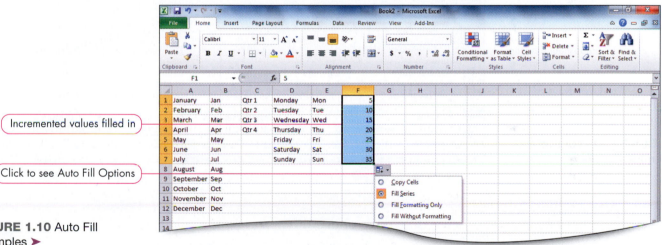

Incremented values filled in

Click to see Auto Fill Options

FIGURE 1.10 Auto Fill Examples ➤

Immediately after you use Auto Fill, Excel displays the Auto Fill Options button in the bottom-right corner of the filled data (see Figure 1.10). Click the button to display four options: Copy Cells, Fill Series, Fill Formatting Only, or Fill Without Formatting.

>  **TIP** **Fill Handle**
>
> To copy a formula down a column, double-click the fill handle. Excel will copy the formula in the active cell for each row of data to calculate in your worksheet. Cell addresses change automatically during the Auto Fill process. For example, if the original formula is =A1+B1 and you copy the formula down one cell, the copied formula is =A2+B2.

Displaying Cell Formulas

When you enter a formula, Excel shows the result of the formula in the cell (see the top half of Figure 1.11); however, you might want to display the formulas instead of the calculated results in the cells (see the bottom half of Figure 1.11). The quickest way to display cell formulas is to press Ctrl and the grave accent (`) key, sometimes referred to as the tilde key, in the top-left corner of the keyboard, below Esc. You can also click Show Formulas in the Formula Auditing group on the Formulas tab to show and hide formulas. This is a toggle feature; do the same step to redisplay formula results.

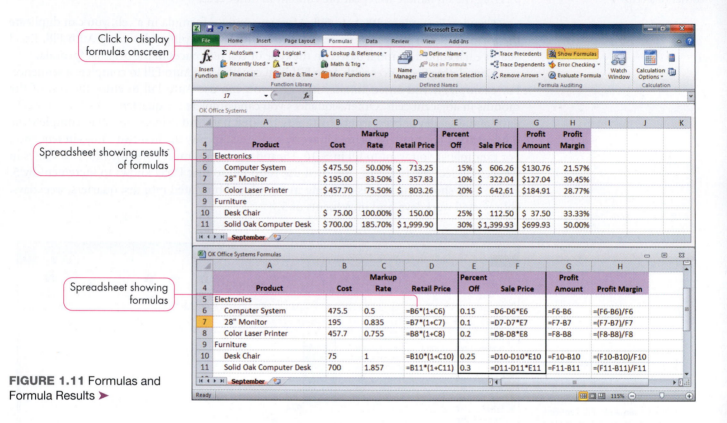

FIGURE 1.11 Formulas and Formula Results ➤

HANDS-ON EXERCISES

2 Mathematics and Formulas

In Hands-On Exercise 1, you created the basic worksheet for OKOS by entering text, values, and a date for items on sale this week. Now you need to insert formulas to calculate the missing results—specifically, the retail (before sale) value, sale price, and profit margin. You will use cell addresses in your formulas, so when you change a referenced value, the formula results will update automatically.

Skills covered: Enter the Retail Price Formula • Enter the Sale Price Formula • Enter the Profit Margin Formula • Copy Formulas with Auto Fill • Change Values and Display Formulas

---

STEP 1 ▶ ENTER THE RETAIL PRICE FORMULA

The first formula you need to create is one to calculate the retail price. The retail price is the price you originally charge. It is based on a percentage of the original cost so that you earn a profit. Refer to Figure 1.12 as you complete Step 1.

Formula displayed in Formula Bar →

Blue border and blue cell reference →

Green border and green cell reference →

SUM — ● X ✓ ƒx =B5*(1+C5)

	A	B	C	D	E	F	G	H
1	OK Office Systems Pricing Information							
2	1-Sep-12							
3								
4	Product	Cost	Markup Ra	Retail Pric	Percent O	Sale Price	Profit Margin	
5	Computer	400	0.5	=B5*(1+C5)				
6	Color Lase	457.7	0.75		0.2			
7	Filing Cab	68.75	0.905		0.1			
8	Desk Chai	75	1		0.25			
9	Solid Oak	700	1.857		0.3			
10	28" Monit	195	0.835		0.1			
11								
12								

FIGURE 1.12 Retail Formula ➤

a. Open the *e01h1markup_LastnameFirstname* workbook if you closed it after the last Hands-On Exercise, and then save it as **e01h2markup_LastnameFirstname**, changing *h1* to *h2*.

> **TROUBLESHOOTING:** If you make any major mistakes in this exercise, you can close the file, open *e01h1markup_LastnameFirstname* again, and then start this exercise over.

b. Click **cell D5**, the cell where you will enter the formula to calculate the retail selling price of the first item.

c. Type **=B5*(1+C5)** and view the formula and the colored cell borders on the screen.

As you type or edit a formula, each cell address in the formula displays in a specific color, and while you type or edit the formula, the cells referenced in the formula have a temporarily colored border. For example, in the formula =B5*(1+C5), B5 appears in blue, and C5 appears in green. Cell B5 has a temporarily blue border and cell C5 has a temporarily green border to help you identify cells as you construct your formulas (see Figure 1.12).

d. Click **Enter** to the left of the Formula Bar and view the formula.

The result of the formula, 600, appears in cell D5, and the formula displays in the Formula Bar. This formula first adds 1 (the decimal equivalent of 100%) to 0.5 (the value stored in cell C5). Excel multiplies that sum of 1.5 by 400 (the value stored in cell B5). The theory behind this formula is that the retail price is 150% of the original cost.

> **TIP** Alternative Formula
>
> An alternative formula also calculates the correct retail price: =B5*C5+B5 or =B5+B5*C5. In this formula, 400 (cell B5) is multiplied by 0.5 (cell C5); that result (200) represents the dollar value of the markup. Excel adds the value 200 to the original cost of 400 to obtain 600, the retail price. You were instructed to enter =B5*(1+C5) to demonstrate the order of precedence.

> **TROUBLESHOOTING:** If the result is not correct, click the cell and look at the formula in the Formula Bar. Click in the Formula Bar, edit the formula to match the formula shown in step 1c, and then click Enter. Make sure you start the formula with an equal sign.

e. Save the workbook with the new formula.

STEP 2 ▶ ENTER THE SALE PRICE FORMULA

Now that you calculated the retail price, you want to calculate a sale price. This week, the computer is on sale for 15% off the retail price. Refer to Figure 1.13 as you complete Step 2.

	F5				f_x	=D5-D5*E5		
	A	B	C	D	E	F	G	H
1	OK Office Systems Pricing Information							
2	1-Sep-12							
3								
4	Product	Cost	Markup Ra	Retail Pric	Percent O	Sale Price	Profit Margin	
5	Computer	400	0.5	600	0.15	510		
6	Color Lase	457.7	0.75		0.2			
7	Filing Cab	68.75	0.905		0.1			
8	Desk Chai	75	1		0.25			
9	Solid Oak	700	1.857		0.3			
10	28" Monit	195	0.835		0.1			
11								
12								

FIGURE 1.13 Sale Price Formula ➤

a. Click **cell F5**, the cell where you will enter the formula to calculate the sale price.

b. Type **=D5-D5*E5** and notice the color-coding in the cell addresses. Press **Ctrl+Enter** to keep the current cell the active cell.

The result is 510. Looking at the formula, you might think D5-D5 equals zero; remember that because of the order of precedence rules, multiplication is calculated before subtraction. The product of 600 (cell D5) and 0.15 (cell E5) equals 90, which is then subtracted from 600 (cell D5), so the sale price is 510. If it helps to understand the formula better, add parentheses: =D5-(D5*E5).

c. View the Formula Bar, and then save the workbook with the new formula.

The Formula Bar displays the formula you entered.

STEP 3 ▶ ENTER THE PROFIT MARGIN FORMULA

After calculating the sale price, you want to know the profit margin you earn. You paid $400 for the computer and will sell it for $510. The profit is $110, which gives you a profit margin of 21.57%. Refer to Figure 1.14 as you complete Step 3.

	G5				f_x	=(F5-B5)/F5		
	A	B	C	D	E	F	G	H
1	OK Office Systems Pricing Information							
2	1-Sep-12							
3								
4	Product	Cost	Markup Ra	Retail Pric	Percent O	Sale Price	Profit Margin	
5	Computer	400	0.5	600	0.15	510	0.215686	
6	Color Lase	457.7	0.75		0.2			
7	Filing Cab	68.75	0.905		0.1			
8	Desk Chai	75	1		0.25			
9	Solid Oak	700	1.857		0.3			
10	28" Monit	195	0.835		0.1			
11								
12								

FIGURE 1.14 Profit Margin Formula ➤

a. Click **cell G5**, the cell where you will enter the formula to calculate the profit margin.

The profit margin is the profit (difference in sales price and cost) percentage of the sale price. This amount represents the amount to cover operating expenses and tax, which are not covered in this analysis.

b. Type **=(F5-B5)/F5** and notice the color-coding in the cell addresses. Press **Ctrl+Enter**.

The formula must first calculate the profit, which is the difference between the sale price (510) and the original cost (400). The difference (110) is then divided by the sale price (510) to determine the profit margin of 0.215686 or 21.6%.

TROUBLESHOOTING: If you type a backslash (\) instead of a forward slash (/), Excel will display an error message box. Make sure you type / as the division operator.

c. Look at the Formula Bar, and then save the workbook with the new formula.

The Formula Bar displays the formula you entered.

After double-checking the accuracy of your calculations for the first product, you are ready to copy the formulas down the columns to calculate the retail price, sale price, and profit margin for the other products. Refer to Figure 1.15 as you complete Step 4.

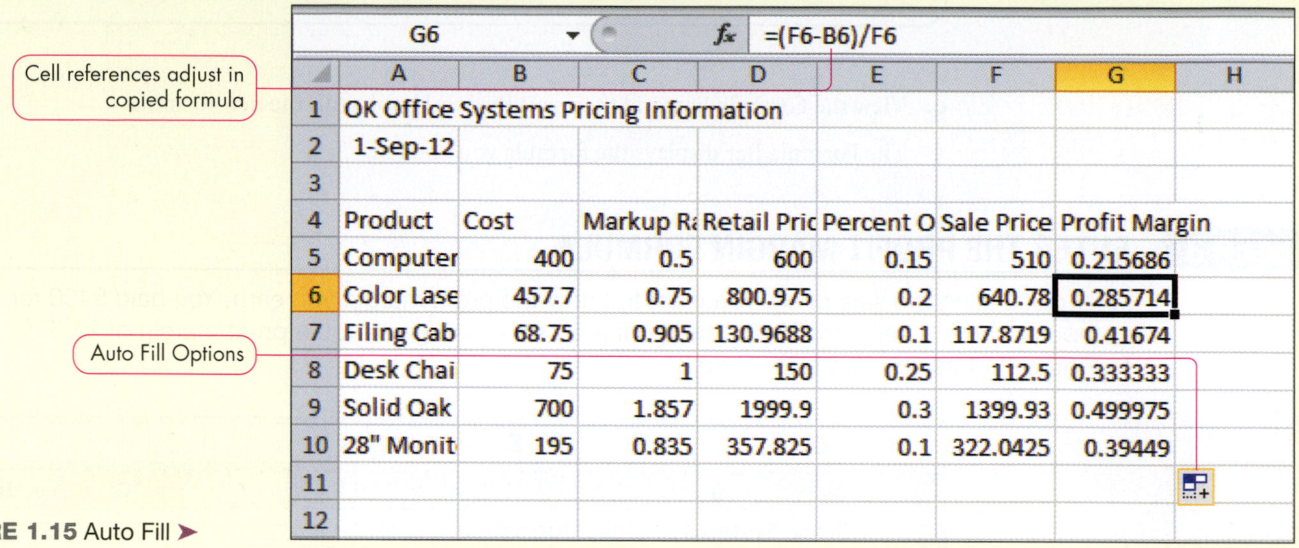

	G6	▾		f_x	=(F6-B6)/F6		
◢	A	B	C	D	E	F	G	H
1	OK Office Systems Pricing Information							
2	1-Sep-12							
3								
4	Product	Cost	Markup Ra	Retail Pric	Percent O	Sale Price	Profit Margin	
5	Computer	400	0.5	600	0.15	510	0.215686	
6	Color Lase	457.7	0.75	800.975	0.2	640.78	0.285714	
7	Filing Cab	68.75	0.905	130.9688	0.1	117.8719	0.41674	
8	Desk Chai	75	1	150	0.25	112.5	0.333333	
9	Solid Oak	700	1.857	1999.9	0.3	1399.93	0.499975	
10	28" Monit	195	0.835	357.825	0.1	322.0425	0.39449	
11								
12								

Cell references adjust in copied formula

Auto Fill Options

FIGURE 1.15 Auto Fill ➤

a. Click **cell D5**, the cell containing the formula to calculate the retail price for the first item.

b. Position the mouse pointer on the fill handle in the bottom-right corner of **cell D5**. When the pointer changes from a white plus sign to a thin black plus sign, double-click the **fill handle**.

Excel's Auto Fill feature copies the retail price formula for the remaining products in your worksheet. Excel detects when to stop copying the formula when it encounters a blank row, such as in row 11.

c. Click **cell D6**, the cell containing the first copied retail price formula, and look at the Formula Bar.

The original formula was =B5*(1+C5). The copied formula in cell D6 is =B6*(1+C6). Excel adjusts the cell addresses in the formula as it copies the formula down a column so that the results are based on each row's data rather than using the original formula's cell addresses for other products.

d. Select the **range F5:G5**. Double-click the **fill handle** in the bottom-right corner of **cell G5**.

Auto Fill copies the selected formulas down their respective columns. Notice Auto Fill Options down and to the right of the cell G10 fill handle, indicating you could select different fill options if you want.

e. Click **cell F6**, the cell containing the first copied sale price formula, and view the Formula Bar.

The original formula was =D5-D5*E5. The copied formula in cell F6 is =D6-D6*E6.

f. Click **cell G6**, the cell containing the first copied profit margin formula, and look at the Formula Bar. Save the changes to your workbook.

The original formula was =(F5-B5)/F5. The copied formula in cell G6 is =(F6-B6)/F6.

CHANGE VALUES AND DISPLAY FORMULAS

You want to see how the prices and profit margins are affected when you change some of the original values. For example, the supplier might notify you that the cost to you will increase. In addition, you want to see the formulas displayed in the cells temporarily. Refer to Figures 1.16 and 1.17 as you complete Step 5.

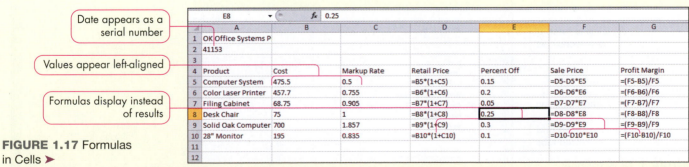

Updated formula results

	E8		*fx*	0.25			
	A	B	C	D	E	F	G	H
1	OK Office Systems Pricing Information						
2	1-Sep-12						
3							
4	Product	Cost	Markup Ra	Retail Pric	Percent O	Sale Price	Profit Margin
5	Computer	475.5	0.5	713.25	0.15	606.2625	0.215686
6	Color Lase	457.7	0.755	803.2635	0.2	642.6108	0.287749
7	Filing Cab	68.75	0.905	130.9688	0.05	124.4203	0.447437
8	Desk Chai	75	1	150	0.25	112.5	0.333333
9	Solid Oak	700	1.857	1999.9	0.3	1399.93	0.499975
10	28" Monit	195	0.835	357.825	0.1	322.0425	0.39449
11							
12							

Changed values

FIGURE 1.16 Results of Changed Values ▶

a. Click **cell B5**, type **475.5**, and then press **Enter**.

The results of the retail price, sale price, and profit margin formulas change based on the new cost.

b. Click **cell C6**, type **0.755**, and then press **Enter**.

The results of the retail price, sale price, and profit margin formulas change based on the new markup rate.

c. Click **cell E7**, type **0.05**, and then press **Enter**.

The results of the sale price and profit margin formulas change based on the new markdown rate. Note that the retail price did not change since that formula is not based on the markdown rate.

d. Press **Ctrl+`** (the grave accent mark).

The workbook now displays the formulas rather than the formula results (see Figure 1.17). This is helpful when you want to review several formulas at one time.

Date appears as a serial number

Values appear left-aligned

Formulas display instead of results

	E8		*fx*	0.25			
	A	B	C	D	E	F	G
1	OK Office Systems P						
2	41153						
3							
4	Product	Cost	Markup Rate	Retail Price	Percent Off	Sale Price	Profit Margin
5	Computer System	475.5	0.5	=B5*(1+C5)	0.15	=D5-D5*E5	=(F5-B5)/F5
6	Color Laser Printer	457.7	0.755	=B6*(1+C6)	0.2	=D6-D6*E6	=(F6-B6)/F6
7	Filing Cabinet	68.75	0.905	=B7*(1+C7)	0.05	=D7-D7*E7	=(F7-B7)/F7
8	Desk Chair	75	1	=B8*(1+C8)	0.25	=D8-D8*E8	=(F8-B8)/F8
9	Solid Oak Computer	700	1.857	=B9*(1+C9)	0.3	=D9-D9*E9	=(F9-B9)/F9
10	28" Monitor	195	0.835	=B10*(1+C10)	0.1	=D10-D10*E10	=(F10-B10)/F10
11							
12							

FIGURE 1.17 Formulas in Cells ▶

e. Press **Ctrl+`** (the grave accent mark).

The workbook now displays the formula results in the cells again.

f. Save the workbook. Keep the workbook onscreen if you plan to continue with Hands-On Exercise 3. If not, close the workbook and exit Excel.

Workbook and Worksheet Management

When you start a new blank workbook in Excel, the workbook contains three worksheets named Sheet1, Sheet2, and Sheet3. The text, values, dates, and formulas you enter into the individual sheets are saved under the one workbook file name. Having multiple worksheets in one workbook is helpful to keep related items together. For example, you might want one worksheet for each month to track your monthly income and expenses for one year. When tax time rolls around, you have all your data stored in one workbook file.

Although you should plan the worksheet and workbook before you start entering data, you might need to add, delete, or rename worksheets. Furthermore, within a worksheet you may want to insert a new row to accommodate new data, delete a column that you no longer need, adjust the size of columns and rows, or move or copy data to other locations.

In this section, you will learn how to manage workbooks by renaming, inserting, and deleting worksheets. You will also learn how to make changes to worksheet columns and rows, such as inserting, deleting, and adjusting sizes. Finally, you will learn how to move and copy data within a worksheet.

Managing Worksheets

Creating a multiple-worksheet workbook takes some planning and maintenance. Worksheet tab names should reflect the contents of the respective worksheets. In addition, you can insert, copy, move, and delete worksheets within the workbook. You can even apply background color to the worksheet tabs so that they stand out onscreen. Figure 1.18 shows a workbook in which the sheet tabs have been renamed, colors have been applied to worksheet tabs, and a worksheet tab has been right-clicked so that the shortcut menu appears.

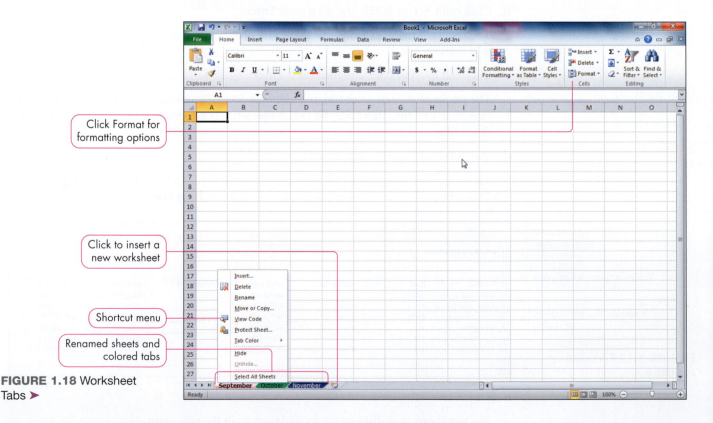

FIGURE 1.18 Worksheet Tabs ➤

Rename Worksheets

The default worksheet names—Sheet1, Sheet2, and Sheet3—are vague; they do not describe the contents of each worksheet. You should rename the worksheet tabs to reflect the sheet contents so that you, and anyone with whom you share your workbook, will be able to find data. For example, if your budget workbook contains monthly worksheets, name the worksheets *September*, *October*, etc. A teacher who uses a workbook to store a grade book for several classes should name each worksheet by class name or number, such as *MIS 1000* and *MIS 3430*. Although you can have spaces in worksheet names, you should keep worksheet names relatively short. The longer the worksheet names, the fewer sheet tabs you will see at the bottom of the workbook window without scrolling.

To rename a worksheet, do one of the following:

- Double-click a sheet tab, type the new name, and then press Enter.
- Click Format in the Cells group on the Home tab (see Figure 1.18), select Rename Sheet (see Figure 1.19), type the new sheet name, and then press Enter.
- Right-click the sheet tab, select Rename from the shortcut menu (see Figure 1.18), type the new sheet name, and then press Enter.

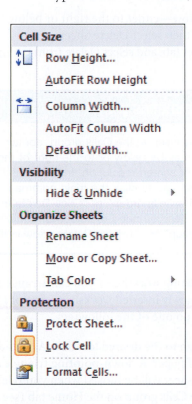

FIGURE 1.19 Format Menu ➤

Change Worksheet Tab Color

The active worksheet tab is white, whereas the default color of the tabs depends on the Windows color scheme. When you use multiple worksheets, you might want to apply a different color to each worksheet tab to make the tab stand out or to emphasize the difference between sheets. For example, you might apply red to the September tab, green to the October tab, and dark blue to the November tab.

To change the color of a worksheet tab, do one of the following:

- Click Format in the Cells group on the Home tab (see Figure 1.18), point to Tab Color (see Figure 1.19), and then click a color on the Tab Color palette.
- Right-click the sheet tab, point to Tab Color on the shortcut menu (see Figure 1.18), and then click a color on the Tab Color palette.

Insert, Delete, Move, and Copy Worksheets

Sometimes you need more worksheets in the workbook than the three default sheets. For example, you might create a workbook that contains 12 worksheets—a worksheet for each month of the year. Each new worksheet you insert starts with a default name, such as Sheet4, numbered consecutively after the last Sheet#. After inserting worksheets, you can rename them to be more descriptive. You can delete extra worksheets from your workbook to keep it streamlined.

To insert a new worksheet, do one of the following:

- Click Insert Worksheet to the right of the last worksheet tab.
- Click the Insert arrow—either to the right or below Insert—in the Cells group on the Home tab, and then select Insert Sheet.
- Right-click any sheet tab, select Insert from the shortcut menu (see Figure 1.18), click Worksheet in the Insert dialog box, and then click OK.
- Press Shift+F11.

To delete a worksheet in a workbook, do one of the following:

- Click the Delete arrow—either to the right or below Delete—in the Cells group on the Home tab, and then select Delete Sheet.
- Right-click any sheet tab, and select Delete from the shortcut menu (see Figure 1.18).

TIP Ribbon Commands with Arrows

Some commands, such as Insert in the Cells group, contain two parts: the main command and an arrow. The arrow may be below or to the right of the command, depending on the command, window size, or screen resolution. Instructions in the Exploring Series use the command name to instruct you to click the main command to perform the default action, such as "Click Insert in the Cells group" or "Click Delete in the Cells group." Instructions include the word *arrow* when you need to select an additional option, such as "Click the Insert arrow in the Cells group" or "Click the Delete arrow in the Cells group."

After inserting and deleting worksheets, you can arrange the worksheet tabs in a different sequence, especially if the newly inserted worksheets do not fall within a logical sequence.

To move a worksheet, do one of the following:

- Drag a worksheet tab to the desired location. As you drag a sheet tab, the pointer resembles a piece of paper. A down-pointing triangle appears between sheet tabs to indicate where the sheet will be moved when you release the mouse button.
- Click Format in the Cells group on the Home tab (see Figure 1.18) or right-click the sheet tab you want to move, and select Move or Copy to see the Move or Copy dialog box (see Figure 1.20). Select the workbook if you want to move the sheet to another workbook. In the *Before sheet* list, select the worksheet on whose left side you want the moved worksheet to be located, and then click OK. For example, assume the October worksheet was selected before displaying the dialog box. You then select November so that the October sheet moves before (or to the left) of November.

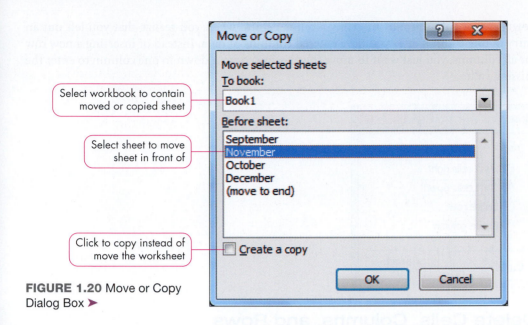

Select workbook to contain moved or copied sheet

Select sheet to move sheet in front of

Click to copy instead of move the worksheet

FIGURE 1.20 Move or Copy Dialog Box ➤

The process for copying a worksheet is similar to moving a sheet. To copy a worksheet, press and hold Ctrl as you drag the worksheet tab. Alternatively, display the Move or Copy dialog box, select the options (see Figure 1.20), click the *Create a copy* check box, and then click OK.

Managing Columns and Rows

As you enter and edit worksheet data, you can adjust the row and column structure. You can add rows and columns to accommodate new data, or you can delete data you no longer need. Adjusting the height and width of columns and rows can present the data better.

Insert Cells, Columns, and Rows

After you construct a worksheet, you might need to insert cells, columns, or rows to accommodate new data. For example, you might need to insert a new column to perform calculations or a new row to list a new product. When you insert cells, rows, and columns, cell addresses in formulas adjust automatically.

To insert a new column or row, do one of the following:

- Click in the column or row for which you want to insert a new column to the left or a new row above, respectively. Click the Insert arrow in the Cells group on the Home tab, and then select Insert Sheet Columns or Insert Sheet Rows.
- Right-click the column letter or row number for which you want to insert a new column to the left or a new row above, respectively, and select Insert from the shortcut menu.

Excel inserts new columns to the *left* of the current column and new rows *above* the current row. If the current column is column C and you insert a new column, the new column becomes column C, and the original column C data are now in column D. Likewise, if the current row is 5 and you insert a new row, the new row is row 5, and the original row 5 data are now in row 6.

You can insert a single cell in a particular row or column. To insert a cell, click in the cell where you want the new cell, click the Insert arrow in the Cells group on the Home tab, and then select Insert Cells. Select an option from the Insert dialog box (see Figure 1.21) to position the new cell, and then click OK. Alternatively, click Insert in the Cells group. The default action of clicking Insert is to insert a cell at the current location, which moves existing data down in that column only. Inserting a cell is helpful when you realize that you left out an entry in one column after you have entered columns of data. Instead of inserting a new row for all columns, you just want to move the existing content down in one column to enter the missing value.

FIGURE 1.21 Insert Dialog Box ➤

Delete Cells, Columns, and Rows

If you no longer need a cell, column, or row, you can delete it. In these situations, you are deleting the entire cell, column, or row, not just the contents of the cell to leave empty cells. As with inserting new cells, any affected formulas adjust the cell references automatically. To delete a column or row, do one of the following:

- Click the column or row heading for the column or row you want to delete. Click Delete in the Cells group on the Home tab.
- Click in any cell within the column or row you want to delete. Click the Delete arrow in the Cells group on the Home tab, and then select Delete Sheet Columns or Delete Sheet Rows, respectively.
- Right-click the column letter or row number for the column or row you want to delete, and then select Delete from the shortcut menu.

To delete a cell or cells, select the cell(s), click the Delete arrow in the Cells group, and then select Delete Cells to display the Delete dialog box (see Figure 1.22). Click the appropriate option to shift cells left or up, and then click OK. Alternatively, click Delete in the Cells group. The default action of clicking Delete is to delete the active cell, which moves existing data up in that column only.

FIGURE 1.22 Delete Dialog Box ➤

Adjust Column Width

Column width is the horizontal measurement of a column.

After you enter data in a column, you often need to adjust the **column width**—the number of characters that can fit horizontally using the default font or the number of horizontal pixels—to show the contents of cells. For example, in the worksheet you created in Hands-On Exercises 1 and 2, the labels in column A displayed into column B when those adjacent cells were empty. However, after you typed values in column B, the labels in column A appeared truncated, or cut off. You will need to widen column A to show the full name of all of your products. Numbers appear as a series of pound signs (######) when the cell is too narrow to display the complete value, and text appears to be truncated.

To widen a column to accommodate the longest label or value in a column, do one of the following:

- Position the pointer on the vertical border between the current column heading and the next column heading. When the pointer displays as a two-headed arrow, double-click the border. For example, if column B is too narrow to display the content in that column, double-click the border between the column B and C headings.
- Click Format in the Cells group on the Home tab (see Figure 1.18), and then select AutoFit Column Width (see Figure 1.19).

You can drag the vertical border to the left to decrease the column width or to the right to increase the column width. As you drag the vertical border, Excel displays a ScreenTip specifying the width (see Figure 1.23). Excel column widths range from 0 to 255 characters. The final way to change column width is to click Format in the Cells group on the Home tab (see Figure 1.18), select Column Width (see Figure 1.19), type a value in the Column width box in the Column Width dialog box, and then click OK.

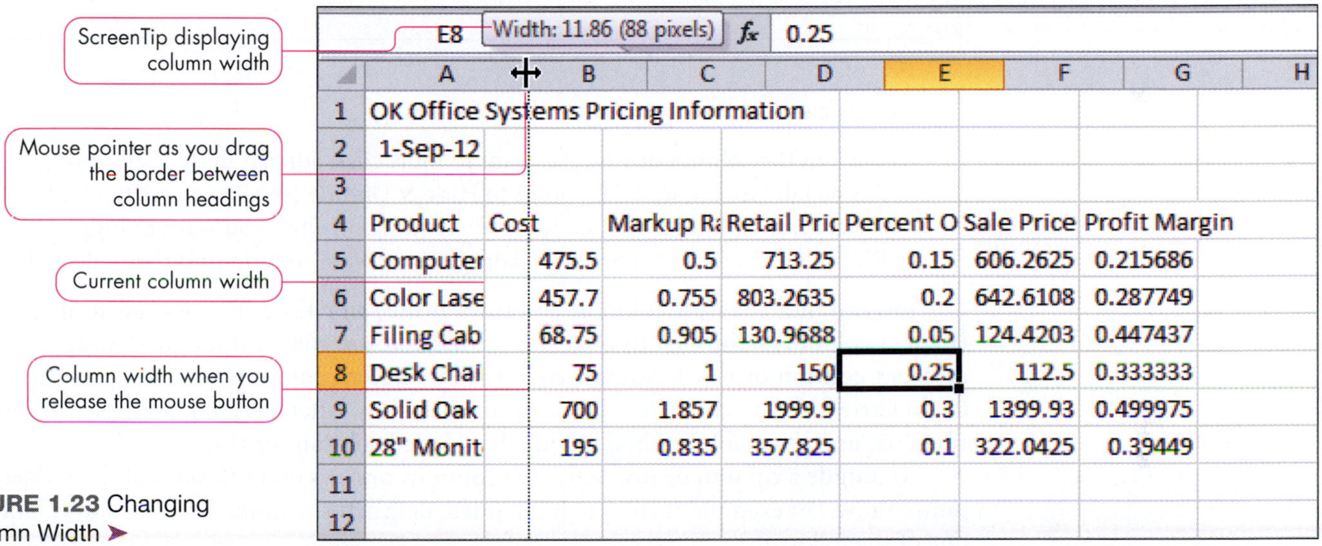

FIGURE 1.23 Changing Column Width ➤

Adjust Row Height

Row height is the vertical measurement of a row.

When you increase the font size of cell contents, Excel automatically increases the *row height*—the vertical measurement of the row. However, if you insert a line break to create multiple lines of text in a cell, Excel might not increase the row height. You can adjust the row height in a way similar to how you change column width by double-clicking the border between row numbers or by selecting Row Height or AutoFit Row Height from the Format menu (see Figure 1.19). In Excel, row height is a value between 0 and 409 based on point size (abbreviated as *pt*). Whether you are measuring font sizes or row heights, one point size is equal to 1/72 of an inch. Your row height should be taller than your font size. For example, with an 11 pt font size, the default row height is 15.

TIP Multiple Column Widths and Row Heights

You can set the size for more than one column or row at a time to make the selected columns or rows the same size. Drag across the column or row headings for the area you want to format, and then set the size using any method.

Hide and Unhide Columns and Rows

If your worksheet contains confidential information, such as social security numbers or salary information, you might need to hide some columns and/or rows before you print a copy for public distribution. When you hide a column or a row, Excel prevents that column or row from displaying or printing. However, the column or row is not deleted. If you hide column B, you will see columns A and C side by side. If you hide row 9, you will see rows 8 and 10 together. Figure 1.24 shows that column B and row 9 are hidden. Excel displays a thicker border between column headings (such as between A and C), indicating one or more columns are hidden, and between row headings (such as between 8 and 10), indicating one or more rows are hidden.

Column B hidden (thicker border)

Row 9 hidden (thicker border)

	A	C	D	E	F	G	H	I	J	K	L
1	OK Office Systems Pricing Information										
2	1-Sep-12										
3											
4	Product	Markup R	Retail Pric	Percent O	Sale Price	Profit Margin					
5	Computer System	0.5	713.25	0.15	606.263	0.21569					
6	Color Laser Printer	0.755	803.264	0.2	642.611	0.28775					
7	Filing Cabinet	0.905	130.969	0.05	124.42	0.44744					
8	Desk Chair	1	150	0.25	112.5	0.33333					
10	28" Monitor	0.835	357.825	0.1	322.043	0.39449					
11											
12											

FIGURE 1.24 Hidden Column and Row ➤

To hide a column or row, do one of the following:

- Click in the column or row you want to hide, click Format in the Cells group on the Home tab (see Figure 1.18), point to Hide & Unhide (see Figure 1.19), and then select Hide Columns or Hide Rows, depending on what you want to hide.
- Right-click the column or row heading(s) you want to hide, and then select Hide.

You can hide multiple columns and rows at the same time. To select adjacent columns (such as columns B through E) or adjacent rows (such as rows 2 through 4), drag across the adjacent column or row headings. To hide nonadjacent columns or rows, press and hold down Ctrl while you click the column or row headings. After selecting multiple columns or rows, use any acceptable method to hide the selected columns or rows.

To unhide a column or row, select the columns or rows on both sides of the hidden column or row. For example, if column B is hidden, drag across column letters A and C. Then do one of the following:

- Click Format in the Cells group on the Home tab (see Figure 1.18), point to Hide & Unhide (see Figure 1.19), and then select Unhide Columns or Unhide Rows, depending on what you want to display again.
- Right-click the column(s) or row(s) you want to hide, and then select Unhide.

TIP Unhiding Column A, Row 1, and All Hidden Rows/Columns

Unhiding column A or row 1 is different because you cannot select the row or column on either side. To unhide column A or row 1, type A1 in the Name Box, and then press Enter. Click Format in the Cells group on the Home tab, point to Hide & Unhide, and then select Unhide Columns or Unhide Rows to display column A or row 1, respectively. If you want to unhide all columns and rows, click Select All, and then use the Hide & Unhide submenu.

Selecting, Moving, Copying, and Pasting

In the Office Fundamentals chapter, you learned the basics of selecting, cutting, copying, and pasting data. These tasks are somewhat different when working in Excel.

Select a Range

A **range** is a rectangular group of cells.

A **range** refers to a group of adjacent or contiguous cells. A range may be as small as a single cell or as large as the entire worksheet. It may consist of a row or part of a row, a column or part of a column, or multiple rows or columns, but will always be a rectangular shape, as you must select the same number of cells in each row or column for the entire range. A range is specified by indicating the top-left and bottom-right cells in the selection. For example, in Figure 1.25, the date is a single-cell range in cell A2, the Color Laser Printer data are stored in the range A6:G6, the cost values are stored in the range B5:B10, and the sales prices and profit margins are stored in range F5:G10. A *nonadjacent range* contains multiple ranges, such as C5:C10 and E5:E10. At times, you need to select nonadjacent ranges so that you can apply the same formatting at the same time, such as formatting the nonadjacent range C5:C10 and E5:E10 with Percent Style.

A **nonadjacent range** contains multiple ranges of cells.

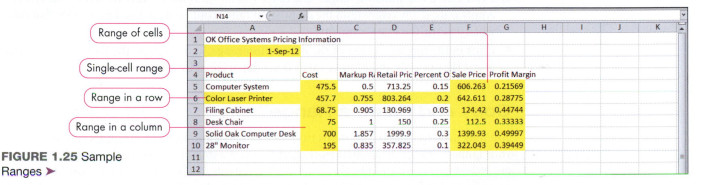

FIGURE 1.25 Sample Ranges ➤

Table 1.4 lists methods you can use to select ranges, including nonadjacent ranges.

TABLE 1.4 Selecting Ranges	
To Select:	**Do This:**
A Range	Click the first cell and drag until you select the entire range. Alternatively, click the first cell in the range, press and hold down Shift, and then click the last cell in the range.
An Entire Column	Click the column heading.
An Entire Row	Click the row heading.
Current Range Containing Data	Click in the range of data and then press Ctrl+A.
All Cells in a Worksheet	Click Select All, or press Ctrl+A twice.
Nonadjacent Range	Select the first range, press and hold down Ctrl, and then select additional range(s).

A border appears around a selected range. Any command you execute will affect the entire range. The range remains selected until you select another range or click in any cell in the worksheet.

Move a Range to Another Location

You can move cell contents from one range to another. For example, you might need to move an input area from the right side of the worksheet to above the output range. When you move a range containing text and values, the text and values do not change. However, any formulas that refer to cells in that range will update to reflect the new cell addresses. To move a range, do the following:

1. Select the range.
2. Use the Cut command to copy the range to the Clipboard. Excel outlines the range you cut with a moving dashed border. Unlike cutting data in other Office applications, the data you cut in Excel remain in their locations until you paste them elsewhere. After you use Cut, the status bar displays *Select destination and press ENTER or choose Paste*.
3. Make sure the destination range—the range where you want to move the data—has enough empty cells. If any cells within the destination range contain data, Excel overwrites that data when you use the Paste command.
4. Click in the top-left corner of the destination range, and then use the Paste command to insert the cut cells and remove them from the original location.

Copy and Paste a Range

You may need to copy cell contents from one range to another. For example, you might copy your January budget to another worksheet to use as a model for creating your February budget. When you copy a range, the original data remain in their original locations. Cell references in copied formulas adjust based on their relative locations to the original data. To copy a range, do the following:

1. Select the range.
2. Use the Copy command to copy the contents of the selected range to the Clipboard. Excel outlines the range you copied with a moving dashed border. After you use Copy, the status bar displays *Select destination and press ENTER or choose Paste*.
3. Make sure the destination range—the range where you want to copy the data—has enough empty cells. If any cells within the destination range contain data, Excel overwrites that data when you use the Paste command.
4. Click in the top-left corner of the destination range where you want the duplicate data, and then use the Paste command. The original selected range remains selected with a moving dashed border around it.
5. Press Esc to deselect the range. Figure 1.26 shows a selected range and a copy of the range.

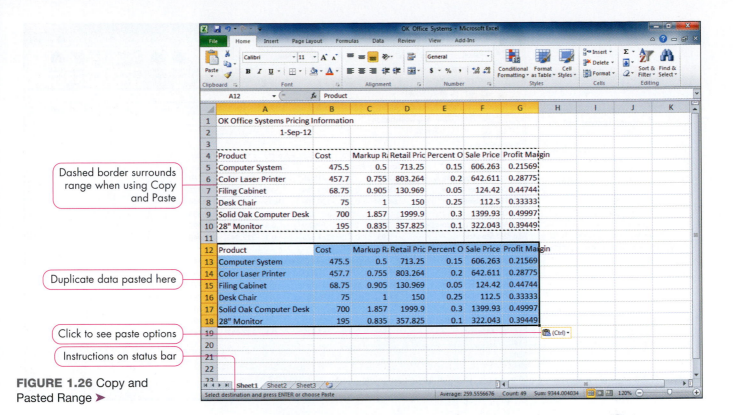

Dashed border surrounds range when using Copy and Paste

Duplicate data pasted here

Click to see paste options

Instructions on status bar

FIGURE 1.26 Copy and Pasted Range ➤

TIP Copy as Picture

Instead of clicking Copy, if you click the Copy arrow in the Clipboard group, you can select Copy (the default option) or Copy as Picture. When you select Copy as Picture, you copy an *image* of the selected data. You can then paste the image elsewhere in the workbook or in a Word document or PowerPoint presentation. However, when you copy the data as an image, you cannot edit individual cell data when you paste the image.

TIP Paste Options Button

When you copy or paste data, Excel displays Paste Options in the bottom-right corner of the pasted data (see Figure 1.26). Click Paste Options to see different results for the pasted data.

Use Paste Special

Sometimes you might want to paste data in a different format than they are in in the Clipboard. For example, you might want to copy a range containing formulas and cell references, and paste the range as values in another workbook that does not have the referenced cells. If you want to copy data from Excel and paste them into a Word document, you can paste the Excel data as a worksheet object, as unformatted text, or in another format. To paste data from the Clipboard into a different format, click the Paste arrow in the Clipboard group, and hover over a command to see a ScreenTip and a preview of how the pasted data will look. In Figure 1.27, the preview shows that a particular paste option will maintain formulas and number formatting; however, it will not maintain the text formatting, such as font color and centered text. After previewing different paste options, click the one you want in order to apply it.

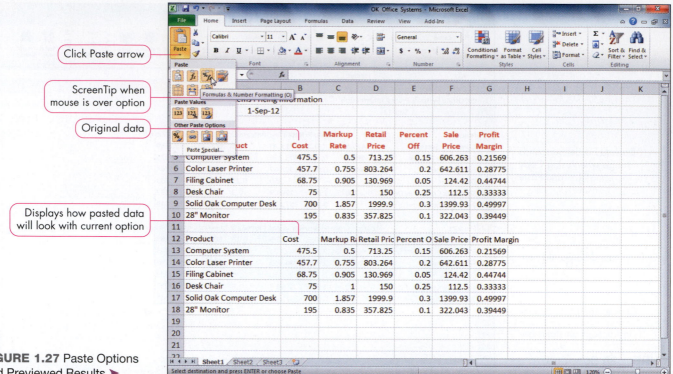

FIGURE 1.27 Paste Options and Previewed Results ➤

The following callouts appear in the figure:
- Click Paste arrow
- ScreenTip when mouse is over option
- Original data
- Displays how pasted data will look with current option

	A	B	C	D	E	F	G
			Markup Rate	Retail Price	Percent Off	Sale Price	Profit Margin
		Cost					
5	Computer System	475.5	0.5	713.25	0.15	606.263	0.21569
6	Color Laser Printer	457.7	0.755	803.264	0.2	642.611	0.28775
7	Filing Cabinet	68.75	0.905	130.969	0.05	124.42	0.44744
8	Desk Chair	75	1	150	0.25	112.5	0.33333
9	Solid Oak Computer Desk	700	1.857	1999.9	0.3	1399.93	0.49997
10	28" Monitor	195	0.835	357.825	0.1	322.043	0.39449
11							
12	Product	Cost	Markup R	Retail Pric	Percent O	Sale Price	Profit Margin
13	Computer System	475.5	0.5	713.25	0.15	606.263	0.21569
14	Color Laser Printer	457.7	0.755	803.264	0.2	642.611	0.28775
15	Filing Cabinet	68.75	0.905	130.969	0.05	124.42	0.44744
16	Desk Chair	75	1	150	0.25	112.5	0.33333
17	Solid Oak Computer Desk	700	1.857	1999.9	0.3	1399.93	0.49997
18	28" Monitor	195	0.835	357.825	0.1	322.043	0.39449

For more specific paste options, click the Paste arrow, and then select Paste Special to display the Paste Special dialog box (see Figure 1.28). This dialog box contains more options than the Paste menu. Click the desired option, and then click OK.

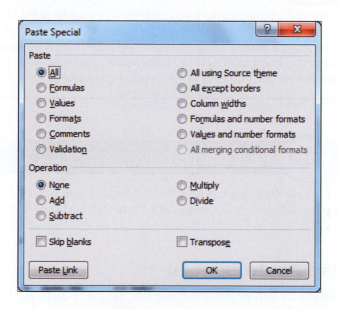

FIGURE 1.28 Paste Special Dialog Box ➤

The Paste Special dialog box contains:

Paste:
- All
- Formulas
- Values
- Formats
- Comments
- Validation
- All using Source theme
- All except borders
- Column widths
- Formulas and number formats
- Values and number formats
- All merging conditional formats

Operation:
- None
- Add
- Subtract
- Multiply
- Divide

Skip blanks
Transpose

Paste Link   OK   Cancel

> **TIP** Transposing Columns and Rows
>
> After entering data into a worksheet, you might want to transpose the columns and rows so that the data in the first column appear as column labels across the first row, or the column labels in the first row appear in the first column. To transpose worksheet data, select and copy the original range, click the top-left corner of the destination range, click the Paste arrow, and then click Transpose.

HANDS-ON EXERCISES

3 Workbook and Worksheet Management

After reviewing the OKOS worksheet, you decide to rename the worksheet that contains the data and delete the other sheets. In addition, you decide to move the 28" Monitor data to display below the Computer System row and insert a column to calculate the amount of markup. You also need to adjust column widths to display data.

Skills covered: Manage Worksheets • Delete a Row • Insert a Column and Three Rows • Move a Row • Adjust Column Width and Row Height • Hide and Unhide Columns

---

STEP 1 ▶ MANAGE WORKSHEETS

You want to rename Sheet1 to describe the worksheet contents and add a color to the sheet tab. In addition, you want to delete the blank worksheets. Refer to Figure 1.29 as you complete Step 1.

FIGURE 1.29 Worksheets Managed ▶

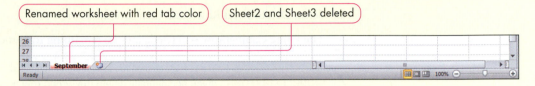

Renamed worksheet with red tab color / Sheet2 and Sheet3 deleted

a. Open the *e01h2markup_LastnameFirstname* workbook if you closed it after the last Hands-On Exercise, and save it as **e01h3markup_LastnameFirstname**, changing *h2* to *h3*.

b. Double-click the **Sheet1 sheet tab**, type **September**, and then press **Enter**.

   You just renamed Sheet1 as September.

c. Right-click the **September sheet tab**, point to **Tab Color**, and then click **Red** in the Standard Colors section.

   The worksheet tab color is red.

d. Click the **Sheet2 sheet tab**, click the **Delete arrow** in the Cells group on the Home tab, and then select **Delete Sheet**.

   You deleted the Sheet2 worksheet from the workbook.

> **TROUBLESHOOTING:** Delete in the Cells group, like some other commands in Excel, contains two parts: the main command icon and an arrow. Click the main command icon when instructed to click Delete to perform the default action. Click the arrow when instructed to click the Delete arrow for additional command options.

> **TROUBLESHOOTING:** Notice that Undo is unavailable on the Quick Access Toolbar. You can't undo deleting a worksheet. It is deleted!

e. Right-click the **Sheet3 sheet tab**, and then select **Delete** to delete the sheet. Save the workbook.

STEP 2 ▶ DELETE A ROW

You just realized that you do not have enough filing cabinets in stock to offer on sale, so you need to delete the Filing Cabinet row. Refer to Figure 1.30 as you complete Step 2.

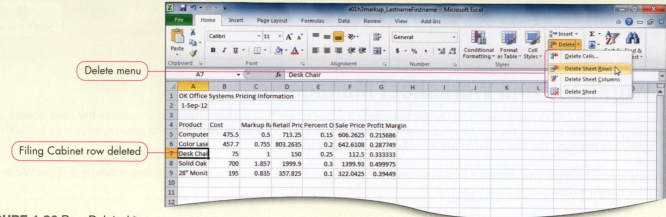

FIGURE 1.30 Row Deleted ▶

Delete menu

Filing Cabinet row deleted

a. Click **cell A7** (or any cell on row 7), the row that contains data for the Filing Cabinet.

b. Click the **Delete arrow** in the Cells group.

c. Select **Delete Sheet Rows**, and then save the workbook.

    The Filing Cabinet row is deleted, and the remaining rows move up one row.

> **TROUBLESHOOTING:** If you accidentally delete the wrong row or accidentally select Delete Sheet Columns instead of Delete Sheet Rows, click Undo on the Quick Access Toolbar to restore the deleted row or column.

STEP 3 INSERT A COLUMN AND THREE ROWS

You decide that you need a column to display the amount of profit. Because profit is a dollar amount, you want to keep the profit column close to another column of dollar amounts. Therefore, you will insert the profit column before the profit margin (percentage) column. You also want to insert new rows for product information and category names. Refer to Figure 1.31 as you complete Step 3.

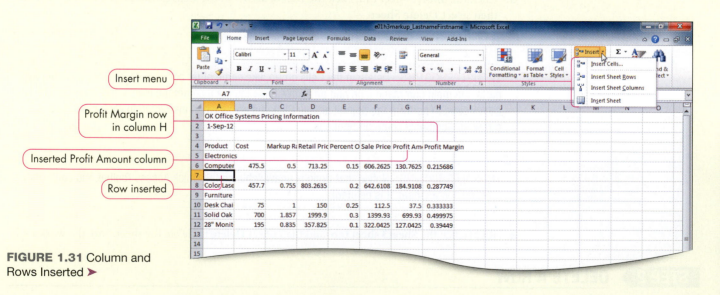

Insert menu

Profit Margin now in column H

Inserted Profit Amount column

Row inserted

FIGURE 1.31 Column and Rows Inserted ▶

a. Click **cell G5** (or any cell in column G), the column containing the Profit Margin.

You want to insert a column between the Sale Price and Profit Margin columns so that you can calculate the profit amount in dollars.

b. Click the **Insert arrow** in the Cells group, and then select **Insert Sheet Columns**.

You inserted a new, blank column G. The data in the original column G are now in column H.

c. Click **cell G4**, type **Profit Amount**, and then press **Enter**.

d. Make sure the active cell is **cell G5**. Type **=F5-B5** and then click **Enter** to the left of the Formula Bar. Double-click the **fill handle** to copy the formula down the column.

You calculated the profit amount by subtracting the original cost from the sale price. Although steps e and f below illustrate one way to insert a row, you can use other methods presented in this chapter.

e. Right-click the **row 5 heading**, the row containing the Computer System data.

Excel displays a shortcut menu consisting of commands you can perform.

f. Select **Insert** from the shortcut menu.

You inserted a new blank row 5, which is selected. The original rows of data move down a row each.

g. Click **cell A5**. Type **Electronics** and then press **Enter**.

You entered the category name Electronics above the list of electronic products.

h. Right-click the **row 8 heading**, the row containing the Desk Chair data, and then select **Insert** from the shortcut menu.

i. Click **cell A8**. Type **Furniture** and then press **Enter**.

You entered the category name Furniture above the list of furniture products. Now you want to insert a blank row after the Computer System row so that you can move the 28" Monitor data to the new row.

j. Insert a row between Computer System and Color Laser Printer. Click **cell A7**, and then save the workbook.

STEP 4 ▶ MOVE A ROW

You want to move the 28" Monitor product to be immediately after the Computer System product. You previously inserted a blank row. Now you need to move the monitor row to this empty row. Refer to Figure 1.32 as you complete Step 4.

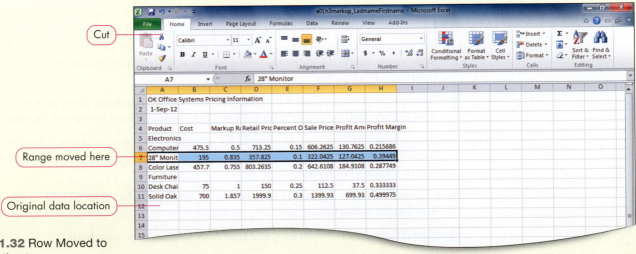

FIGURE 1.32 Row Moved to New Location ➤

a. Click **cell A12**, and then drag to select the **range A12:H12**.

You selected the range of cells containing the 28" Monitor data.

b. Cut the selected range.

A moving dashed border outlines the selected range. The status bar displays the message *Select destination and press ENTER or choose Paste.*

c. Click **cell A7**, the new blank row you inserted in step 3j.

This is the first cell in the destination range.

d. Paste the data that you cut, and then save the workbook.

The 28" Monitor data are now located on row 7.

> **TROUBLESHOOTING:** If you cut and paste a row without inserting a new row first, Excel will overwrite the original row of data, which is why you inserted a new row in step 3.

STEP 5 ▶ ADJUST COLUMN WIDTH AND ROW HEIGHT

As you review your worksheet, you notice that the labels in column A appear cut off. You need to increase the width of that column to display the entire product names. In addition, you want to make row 1 taller. Refer to Figure 1.33 as you complete Step 5.

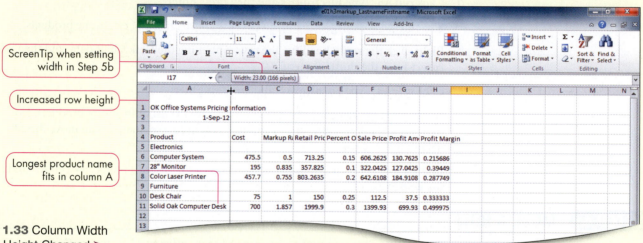

FIGURE 1.33 Column Width and Row Height Changed ▶

a. Position the pointer between the column A and B headings. When the pointer looks like a double-headed arrow, double-click the **border**.

When you double-click the border between two columns, Excel adjusts the width of the column on the left side of the border to fit the contents of that column. In this case, Excel increased the width of column A. However, it is based on the title in cell A1, which will eventually span over all columns. Therefore, you want to decrease the column to avoid so much empty space in column A.

b. Position the pointer between the column A and B headings again. Drag the border to the left until the ScreenTip displays **Width: 23.00 (166 pixels)**. Release the mouse button.

You decreased the column width to 23 for column A. The longest product name is visible. You won't adjust the other column widths until after you apply formats to the column headings in Hands-On Exercise 4.

c. Click **cell A1**. Click **Format** in the Cells group, and then select **Row Height** to display the Row Height dialog box.

d. Type **30** in the **Row height box**, and then click **OK**. Save the workbook.

You doubled the height of the first row.

HIDE AND UNHIDE COLUMNS

To focus on the dollar amounts, you decide to hide the markup rate, discount rate, and profit margin columns. Refer to Figure 1.34 as you complete Step 6.

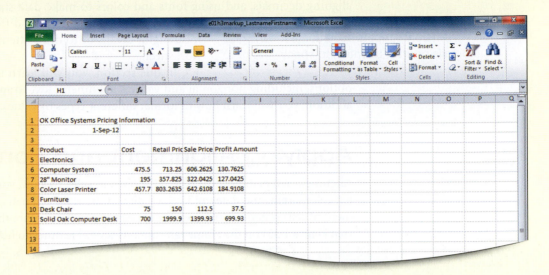

FIGURE 1.34 Hidden Columns ➤

a. Click the **column C heading**, the column containing the Markup Rate values.

b. Press and hold down **Ctrl** as you click the **column E heading** and the **column H heading**.

   Holding down Ctrl enables you to select nonadjacent ranges. You want to hide the rate columns temporarily.

c. Click **Format** in the Cells group, point to **Hide & Unhide**, and then select **Hide Columns**.

   Excel hides the selected columns. You see a gap in column heading letters, indicating columns are hidden (see Figure 1.34).

d. Drag to select the **column G and I headings**.

   You want to unhide column H, so you must select the columns on both sides of the hidden column.

e. Click **Format** in the Cells group, point to **Hide & Unhide**, and then select **Unhide Columns**.

   Column H, which contains the Profit Margin values, is no longer hidden. You will keep the other columns hidden to save the workbook as evidence that you know how to hide columns. You will unhide the remaining columns in the next Hands-On Exercise.

f. Save the workbook. Keep the workbook onscreen if you plan to continue with Hands-On Exercise 4. If not, close the workbook, and exit Excel.

Formatting

After entering data and formulas, you should format the worksheet to achieve a professional appearance. A professionally formatted worksheet—through adding appropriate symbols, aligning decimals, and using fonts and colors to make data stand out—makes finding and analyzing data easy. You apply different formats to accentuate meaningful details or to draw attention to specific ranges in the worksheet.

> Different formats accentuate meaningful details or draw attention to specific ranges.

In this section, you will learn to apply different alignment options, including horizontal and vertical alignment, text wrapping, and indent options. In addition, you will learn how to format different types of values.

Applying Alignment and Font Options

Alignment refers to how data are positioned in cells. By now, you know that text aligns at the left cell margin, and dates and values align at the right cell margin. You can change the alignment of cell contents to improve the appearance of data within the cells. The Alignment group (see Figure 1.35) on the Home tab contains several features to help you align and format data.

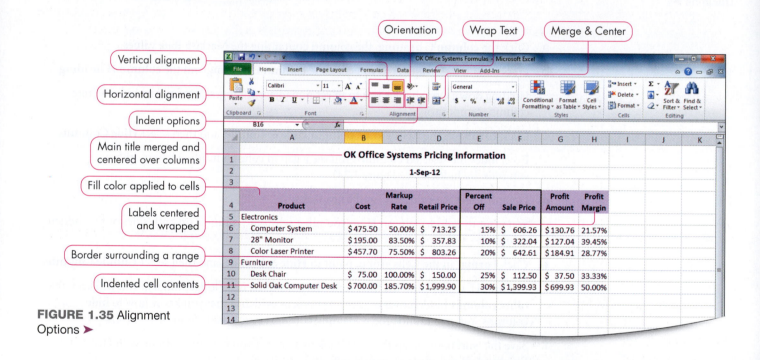

FIGURE 1.35 Alignment Options ➤

Change Horizontal and Vertical Cell Alignment

Horizontal alignment positions data between the left and right cell margins.

Vertical alignment positions data between the top and bottom cell margins.

You can align data horizontally or vertically. *Horizontal alignment* specifies the position of data between the left and right cell margins, and *vertical alignment* specifies the position of data between the top and bottom cell margins. Bottom Align is the default vertical alignment, as indicated by the orange background of Bottom Align on the Ribbon. After adjusting row height, you might need to change the vertical alignment to position data better in conjunction with data in adjacent cells. To change alignments, click the desired horizontal and/or vertical alignment setting in the Alignment group on the Home tab.

Merge and Center Labels

You may want to place a title at the top of a worksheet and center it over the columns of data in the worksheet. You can center main titles over all columns in the worksheet, and you can center category titles over groups of related columns. To create a title, enter the text in the far left cell of the range. Select the range of cells across which you want to center the title, and then click Merge & Center in the Alignment group on the Home tab. Any data in the merge area are lost, except what is in the far left cell in the range. Excel merges the selected cells together into one cell, and the merged cell address is that of the original cell on the left. The data are centered between the left and right sides of the merged cell. In Figure 1.35, the title *OK Office Systems Pricing Information* is merged and centered over the data columns.

If you merge too many cells and want to split the merged cell back into its original multiple cells, click the merged cell, and then click Merge & Center. Unmerging places the data in the top-left cell.

Increase and Decrease Indent

To offset labels, you can indent text within a cell. Accountants often indent the word Totals in financial statements so that it stands out from a list of items above the total row. Indenting helps others see the hierarchical structure of your spreadsheet data. To indent the contents of a cell, click Increase Indent in the Alignment group on the Home tab. The more you click Increase Indent, the more text is indented in the active cell. To decrease the indent, click Decrease Indent in the Alignment group. Figure 1.35 shows an example of an indented label.

Wrap Text

Wrap text enables a label to appear on multiple lines within the current cell.

Sometimes you have to maintain specific column widths, but the data do not fit entirely. You can use **wrap text** to make data appear on multiple lines by adjusting the row height to fit the cell contents within the column width. When you click Wrap Text in the Alignment group, Excel wraps the text on two or more lines within the cell. This alignment option is helpful when the column headings are wider than the values contained in the column. In the next Hands-On Exercise, you will apply the Wrap Text option for the column headings so that you can see the text without widening the columns. Figure 1.35 shows an example of wrapped text.

Apply Borders and Fill Color

A **border** is a line that surrounds a cell or a range.

You can apply a border or fill color to accentuate data in a worksheet. A *border* is a line that surrounds a cell or a range of cells. You can use borders to offset particular data from the rest of the data on the worksheet. To apply a border, select the cell or range that you want to have a border, click the Borders arrow in the Font group, and then select the desired border type. To remove a border, select No Border from the Borders menu.

Fill color is the background color appearing behind data in a cell.

To add some color to your worksheet to add emphasis to data or headers, you can apply a fill color. *Fill color* is a background color that displays behind the data. You should choose a fill color that contrasts with the font color. For example, if the font color is Black, you might want to choose Yellow fill color. If the font color is White, you might want to apply Blue or Dark Blue fill color. To apply a fill color, select the cell or range that you want to have a fill color, click the Fill Color arrow on the Home tab, and then select the color choice from the Fill Color palette. If you want to remove a fill color, select No Fill from the bottom of the palette.

For additional border and fill color options, display the Format Cells dialog box. Click the Border tab to select border options, including the border line style and color. Click the Fill tab to set the background color, fill effects, and patterns. Figure 1.35 shows examples of cells containing a border and fill color.

Applying Number Formats

Values appear in General format (i.e., no special formatting) when you enter data. You should apply number formats based on the type of values in a cell, such as applying either the Accounting or Currency number format to monetary values. Changing the number format changes the way the number displays in a cell, but the format does not change the number's value. If, for example, you entered 123.456 into a cell and format the cell with Currency number type, the value shows as $123.46 onscreen, but the actual value 123.456 is used for calculations. When you apply a number format, you can specify the number of decimal places to display onscreen.

Select an Appropriate Number Format

The default number format is General, which displays values as you originally enter them. General does not align decimal points in a column or include symbols, such as dollar signs, percent signs, or commas. Table 1.5 lists and describes the primary number formats in Excel.

TABLE 1.5 Number Formats	
Format Style	**Display**
General	A number as it was originally entered. Numbers are shown as integers (e.g., 12345), decimal fractions (e.g., 1234.5), or in scientific notation (e.g., 1.23E+10) if the number exceeds 11 digits.
Number	A number with or without the 1000 separator (e.g., a comma) and with any number of decimal places. Negative numbers can be displayed with parentheses and/or red.
Currency	A number with the 1,000 separator and an optional dollar sign (which is placed immediately to the left of the number). Negative values are preceded by a minus sign or are displayed with parentheses or in red. Two decimal places display by default.
Accounting	A number with the 1,000 separator, an optional dollar sign (at the left border of the cell, vertically aligned within a column), negative values in parentheses, and zero values as hyphens. Two decimal places display by default.
Date	The date in different ways, such as March 14, 2012; 3/14/12; or 14-Mar-12.
Time	The time in different formats, such as 10:50 PM or 22:50 (24-hour time).

(Continued)

TABLE 1.5 (Continued)

Format Style	Display
Percentage	The value as it would be multiplied by 100 (for display purpose), with the percent sign. The default number of decimal places is zero if you click Percent Style in the Number group or two decimal places if you use the Format Cells dialog box. However, you should typically increase the number of decimal points to show greater accuracy.
Fraction	A number as a fraction; appropriate when no exact decimal equivalent exists. A fraction is entered into a cell as a formula such as =1/3. If the cell is not formatted as a fraction, you will see the results of the formula.
Scientific	A number as a decimal fraction followed by a whole number exponent of 10; for example, the number 12345 would appear as 1.23E+04. The exponent, +04 in the example, is the number of places the decimal point is moved to the left (or right if the exponent is negative). Very small numbers have negative exponents.
Text	The data left-aligned; is useful for numerical values that have leading zeros and should be treated as text, such as ZIP codes or phone numbers. Apply Text format before typing a leading zero so that the zero displays in the cell.
Special	A number with editing characters, such as hyphens in a Social Security number.
Custom	Predefined customized number formats or special symbols to create your own customized number format.

The Number group on the Home tab contains commands for applying Accounting Number Format, Percent Style, and Comma Style numbering formats. You can click the Accounting Number Format arrow and select other denominations, such as English pounds or euros. For other number formats, click the Number Format arrow and select the numbering format you want to use. For more specific numbering formats than those provided, select More Number Formats from the Number Format menu or click the Number Dialog Box Launcher to open the Format Cells dialog box with the Number tab options readily available. Figure 1.36 shows different number formats applied to values. The first six values are displayed with two decimal places.

	A	B	C
1	General	1234.56	
2	Number	1234.56	
3	Currency	$1,234.56	
4	Accounting	$ 1,234.56	
5	Comma	1,234.56	
6	Percent	12.34%	
7	Short Date	3/1/2012	
8	Long Date	Thursday, March 01, 2012	

FIGURE 1.36 Number Formats ➤

Increase and Decrease Decimal Places

After applying a number format, you may need to adjust the number of decimal places that display. For example, if you have an entire column of monetary values formatted in Accounting Number Format, Excel displays two decimal places by default. If the entire column of values contains whole dollar values and no cents, displaying .00 down the column looks cluttered. You can decrease the number of decimal places to show whole numbers only.

To change the number of decimal places displayed, click Increase Decimal in the Number group on the Home tab to display more decimal places for greater precision or Decrease Decimal to display fewer or no decimal places.

HANDS-ON EXERCISES

4 Formatting

In the first three Hands-On Exercises, you entered data about products on sale, created formulas to calculate markup and profit, and inserted new rows and columns to accommodate additional data. You are ready to format the worksheet. Specifically, you need to center the title, align text, format values, and apply other formatting to enhance the readability of the worksheet.

Skills covered: Merge and Center the Title • Wrap and Align Text • Apply Number Formats and Decimal Places • Apply Borders and Fill Color • Indent Cell Contents

---

STEP 1 ▶ **MERGE AND CENTER THE TITLE**

To make the title stand out, you want to center it over all the data columns. You will use the Merge & Center command to merge cells together and center the title at the same time. Refer to Figure 1.37 as you complete Step 1.

	A	B	C	D	E	F	G	H	I
1				OK Office Systems Pricing Information					
2				1-Sep-12					
3									
4	Product	Cost		Markup Ra	Retail Pric	Percent O	Sale Price	Profit Am	Profit Margin
5	Electronics								
6	Computer System	475.5		0.5	713.25	0.15	606.2625	130.7625	0.215686
7	28" Monitor	195		0.835	357.825	0.1	322.0425	127.0425	0.39449
8	Color Laser Printer	457.7		0.755	803.2635	0.2	642.6108	184.9108	0.287749
9	Furniture								
10	Desk Chair	75		1	150	0.25	112.5	37.5	0.333333
11	Solid Oak Computer Desk	700		1.857	1999.9	0.3	1399.93	699.93	0.499975
12									
13									

FIGURE 1.37 Formatted Title ▶

a. Open the *e01h3markup_LastnameFirstname* workbook if you closed it after the last Hands-On Exercise, and save it as **e01h4markup_LastnameFirstname**, changing *h3* to *h4*.

b. Select the **column B, D, and F headings**. Unhide columns C and E as you learned in Hands-On Exercise 3.

c. Select the **range A1:H1**.

   You want to center the title over all columns of data.

d. Click **Merge & Center** in the Alignment group.

   Excel merges cells in the range A1:H1 into one cell and centers the title horizontally within the merged cell, which is cell A1.

> **TROUBLESHOOTING:** If you merge too many or not enough cells, you can unmerge the cells and start again. To unmerge cells, click in the merged cell. The Merge & Center command has an orange border when the active cell is merged. Click Merge & Center to unmerge the cell. Then select the correct range to merge and use Merge & Center again.

 FYI

e. Bold the title, and then select **14 pt** size.

f. Select the **range A2:H2**. Merge and center the date, and then bold it.

g. Save the workbook.

WRAP AND ALIGN TEXT

You will wrap the text in the column headings to avoid columns that are too wide for the data, but which will display the entire text of the column headings. In addition, you will horizontally center column headings between the left and right cell margins. Refer to Figure 1.38 as you complete Step 2.

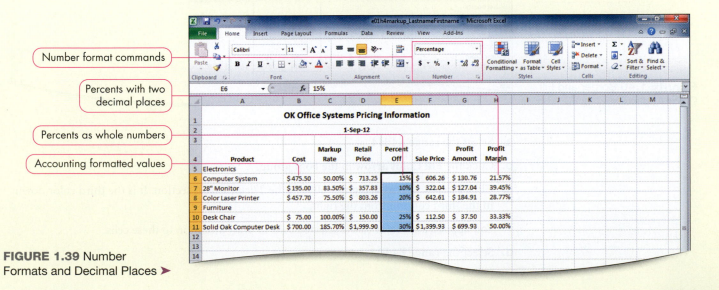

Middle Align applied

Text wrapped, centered, and bold

FIGURE 1.38 Formatted Column Headings ▶

a. Select the **range A4:H4**.

   You selected the multiple-word column headings.

b. Click **Wrap Text** in the Alignment group.

   The column headings are now visible on two lines within each cell.

c. Click **Center** in the Alignment group. Bold the selected column headings.

   The column headings are centered horizontally between the left and right edges of each cell.

d. Click **cell A1**, which contains the title.

e. Click **Middle Align** in the Alignment group. Save the workbook.

   Middle Align vertically centers data between the top and bottom edges of the cell.

APPLY NUMBER FORMATS AND DECIMAL PLACES

You need to format the values to increase readability and look more professional. You will apply number formats and adjust the number of decimal points displayed. Refer to Figure 1.39 as you complete Step 3.

Number format commands

Percents with two decimal places

Percents as whole numbers

Accounting formatted values

FIGURE 1.39 Number Formats and Decimal Places ▶

a. Select the **range B6:B11**, and then click **Accounting Number Format** in the Number group.

You formatted the selected range with Accounting Number Format. The dollar signs align on the left cell margins and the decimals align.

b. Select the **range D6:D11**. Press and hold down **Ctrl** as you select the **range F6:G11**.

Since you want to format nonadjacent ranges with the same formats, you hold down Ctrl.

c. Click **Accounting Number Format** in the Number group.

You formatted the selected nonadjacent ranges with the Accounting Number Format.

d. Select the **range C6:C11**, and then click **Percent Style** in the Number group.

You formatted the values in the selected ranges with Percent Style, showing whole numbers only.

e. Click **Increase Decimal** in the Number group twice.

You increased the decimal places to avoid misleading your readers by displaying the values as whole percentages.

 FYI

f. Use Format Painter to copy the formats of the selected range to values in columns E and H.

g. Select the **range E6:E11**, and then click **Decrease Decimal** twice in the Number group. Save the workbook.

Since this range contained whole percentages, you do not need to show the decimal places.

STEP 4 ▶ APPLY BORDERS AND FILL COLOR

You want to apply a light purple fill color to highlight the column headings. In addition, you want to emphasize the percent off and sale prices. You will do this by applying a border around that range. Refer to Figure 1.40 as you complete Step 4.

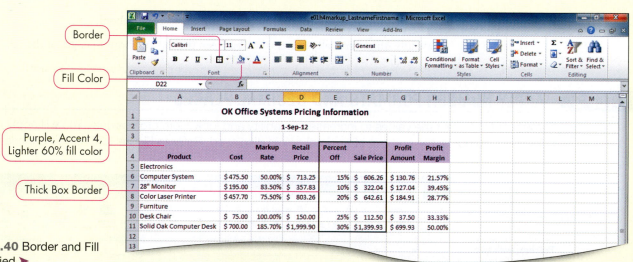

FIGURE 1.40 Border and Fill Color Applied ▶

a. Select the **range A4:H4**.

b. Click the **Fill Color arrow** in the Font group.

c. Click **Purple, Accent 4, Lighter 60%** in the *Theme Colors* section. It is the third color down in the third column from the right.

You applied a fill color to the selected cells to draw attention to these cells.

d. Select the **range E4:F11**.

e. Click the **Border arrow** in the Font group, and then select **Thick Box Border**.

You applied a border around the selected cells.

f. Click in an empty cell below the columns of data to deselect the cells. Save the workbook.

STEP 5 ## INDENT CELL CONTENTS

As you review the first column, you notice that the category names, Electronics and Furniture, don't stand out. You decide to indent the labels within each category to show which products are in each category. Refer to Figure 1.41 as you complete Step 5.

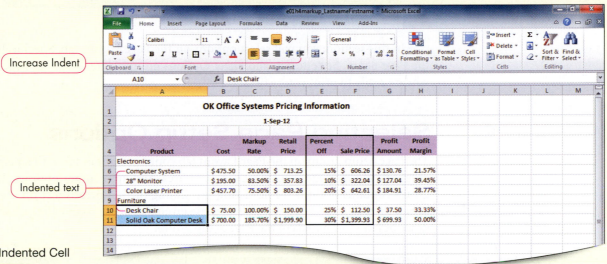

FIGURE 1.41 Indented Cell Contents ➤

a. Select the **range A6:A8**, the cells containing electronic products.

b. Click **Increase Indent** in the Alignment group twice.

The three selected product names are indented below the Electronics heading.

c. Select the **range A10:A11**, the cells containing furniture products, and then click **Increase Indent** twice.

The two selected product names are indented below the Furniture heading. Notice that the product names appear cut off.

d. Increase the **column A** width to **26.00**.

e. Save the workbook. Keep the workbook onscreen if you plan to continue with Hands-On Exercise 5. If not, close the workbook, and exit Excel.

Page Setup and Printing

Although you might distribute workbooks electronically as e-mail attachments or you might upload workbooks to a corporation server, you should prepare the worksheets in the workbook for printing. You should prepare worksheets in case you need to print them or in case others who receive an electronic copy of your workbook need to print the worksheets. The Page Layout tab provides options for controlling the printed worksheet (see Figure 1.42).

Page Setup
Dialog Box Launcher

FIGURE 1.42 Page Layout Tab ➤

In this section, you will select options on the Page Layout tab. Specifically, you will use the Page Setup, Scale to Fit, and Sheet Options groups. After selecting page setup options, you are ready to print your worksheet.

Selecting Page Setup Options

The Page Setup group on the Page Layout tab contains options to set the margins, select orientation, specify page size, select the print area, and apply other options. The Scale to Fit group contains options for adjusting the scaling of the spreadsheet on the printed page. When possible, use the commands in these groups to apply page settings. Table 1.6 lists and describes the commands in the Page Setup group.

TABLE 1.6 Page Setup Commands	
Command	**Description**
Margins	Displays a menu to select predefined margin settings. The default margins are 0.75" top and bottom and 0.7" left and right. You will often change these margin settings to balance the worksheet data better on the printed page. If you need different margins, select Custom Margins.
Orientation	Displays orientation options. The default page orientation is portrait, which is appropriate for worksheets that contain more rows than columns. Select landscape orientation when worksheets contain more columns than can fit in portrait orientation. For example, the OKOS worksheet might appear better balanced in landscape orientation because it has eight columns.
Size	Displays a list of standard paper sizes. The default size is 8.5" by 11". If you have a different paper size, such as legal paper, select it from the list.
Print Area	Displays a list to set or clear the print area. When you have very large worksheets, you might want to print only a portion of that worksheet. To do so, select the range you want to print, click Print Area in the Page Setup group, and select Set Print Area. When you use the Print commands, only the range you specified will be printed. To clear the print area, click Print Area, and select Clear Print Area.
Breaks	Displays a list to insert or remove page breaks.
Background	Enables you to select an image to appear as the background behind the worksheet data when viewed onscreen (backgrounds do not appear when the worksheet is printed).
Print Titles	Enables you to select column headings and row labels to repeat on multiple-page printouts.

Specify Page Options

To apply several page setup options at once or to access options not found on the Ribbon, click the Page Setup Dialog Box Launcher. The Page Setup dialog box organizes options into four tabs: Page, Margins, Header/Footer, and Sheet. All tabs contain Print and Print Preview buttons. Figure 1.43 shows the Page tab.

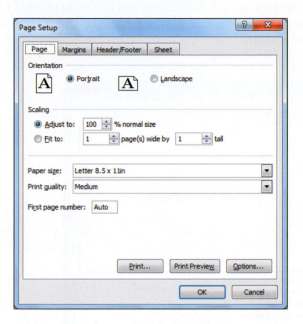

FIGURE 1.43 Page Setup Dialog Box Page Tab ➤

The Page tab contains options to select the orientation and paper size. In addition, it contains scaling options that are similar to the options in the Scale to Fit group on the Page Layout tab. You use scaling options to increase or decrease the size of characters on a printed page, similar to using a zoom setting on a photocopy machine. You can also use the Fit to option to force the data to print on a specified number of pages.

Specify Margins Options

The Margins tab (see Figure 1.44) contains options for setting the specific margins. In addition, it contains options to center the worksheet data horizontally or vertically on the page. To balance worksheet data equally between the left and right margins, Excel users often center the page horizontally.

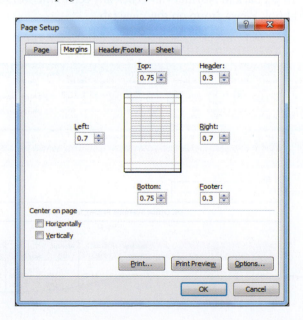

FIGURE 1.44 Page Setup Dialog Box Margins Tab ➤

Create Headers and Footers

The Header/Footer tab (see Figure 1.45) lets you create a header and/or footer that appear at the top and/or bottom of every printed page. Click the arrows to choose from several preformatted entries, or alternatively, you can click Custom Header or Custom Footer, insert text and other objects, and then click the appropriate formatting button to customize your headers and footers. You can use headers and footers to provide additional information about the worksheet. You can include your name, the date the worksheet was prepared, and page numbers, for example.

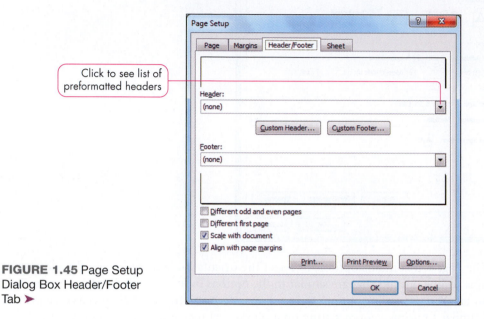

FIGURE 1.45 Page Setup Dialog Box Header/Footer Tab ➤

Instead of creating headers and footers using the Page Setup dialog box, you can click the Insert tab and click Header & Footer in the Text group. Excel displays the worksheet in Page Layout view with the insertion point in the center area of the header. If you click the View tab and then click Page Layout, you see an area that displays *Click to add header* at the top of the worksheet. You can click inside the left, center, or right section of a header or footer. When you do, Excel displays the Header & Footer Tools Design contextual tab (see Figure 1.46). You can enter text or insert data from the Header & Footer Elements group on the tab. To get back to Normal view, click any cell in the worksheet, and then click Normal in the Workbook Views group on the View tab.

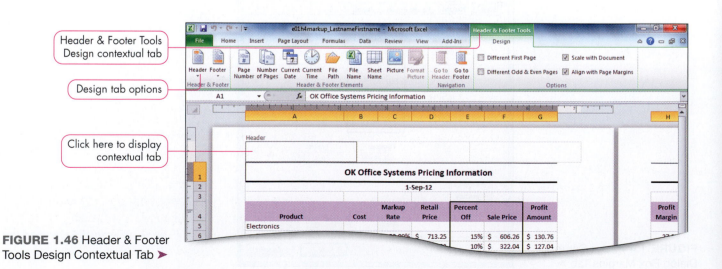

FIGURE 1.46 Header & Footer Tools Design Contextual Tab ➤

Select Sheet Options

The Sheet tab (see Figure 1.47) contains options for setting the print area, print titles, print options, and page order. Some of these options are also located in the Sheet Options group on the Page Layout tab on the Ribbon. By default, Excel displays gridlines onscreen to show you each cell's margins, but the gridlines do not print unless you specifically select the Gridlines check box in the Page Setup dialog box or the Print Gridlines check box in the Sheet Options group on the Page Layout tab. In addition, Excel displays row (1, 2, 3, etc.) and column (A, B, C, etc.) headings onscreen. However, these headings do not print unless you click the Row and column headings check box in the Page Setup dialog box or click the Print Headings check box in the Sheet Options group on the Page Layout tab.

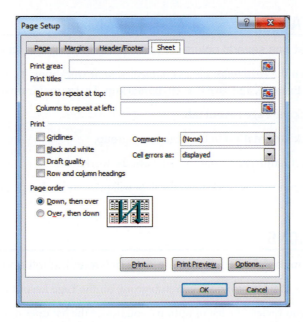

FIGURE 1.47 Page Setup Dialog Box Sheet Tab ➤

TIP Printing Gridlines and Headings

For most worksheets, you do not need to print gridlines and row/column headings. However, when you want to display and print cell formulas instead of formula results, you might want to print the gridlines and row/column headings. Doing so will help you analyze your formulas. The gridlines help you see the cell boundaries, and the headings help you know what data are in each cell. At times, you might want to display gridlines to separate data on a regular print-out to increase readability.

Printing a Worksheet

Before printing a worksheet, you should click the File tab and then select Print. The Backstage view displays print options and displays the worksheet in print preview mode. This mode helps you see in advance if the data are balanced on the page or if data will print on multiple pages. The bottom of the Backstage view indicates how many total pages will print. If the settings are correct, you can specify the print options. If you do not like how the worksheet will print, click the Page Layout tab so that you can adjust margins, scaling, column widths, and so on until the worksheet data appear the way you want them to print.

> The Backstage view helps you see in advance if the data are balanced on the page.

HANDS-ON EXERCISES

5 Page Setup and Printing

You are ready to complete the OKOS worksheet. Before printing the worksheet for your supervisor, you want to make sure the data will appear professional when printed. You will adjust some page setup options to put the finishing touches on the worksheet.

Skills covered: Set Page Orientation • Set Margin Options • Create a Header • Print Preview and Print • Adjust Scaling and Set Sheet Options

---

STEP 1 ▶ SET PAGE ORIENTATION

Because the worksheet has several columns, you decide to print it in landscape orientation.

a. Open the *e01h4markup_LastnameFirstname* workbook if you closed it after the last Hands-On Exercise, and save it as **e01h5markup_LastnameFirstname**, changing *h4* to *h5*.

b. Click the **Page Layout tab**.

c. Click **Orientation** in the Page Setup group.

d. Select **Landscape** from the list. Save the workbook.

If you print the worksheet, the data will print in landscape orientation.

STEP 2 ▶ SET MARGIN OPTIONS

You want to set a 1" top margin and center the data between the left and right margins.

a. Click **Margins** in the Page Setup group on the Page Layout tab.

As you review the list of options, you notice the list does not contain an option to center the worksheet data horizontally.

b. Select **Custom Margins**.

The Page Setup dialog box opens with the Margins tab options displayed.

c. Click the **Top spin box** to display *1*.

You set a 1" top margin. You don't need to change the left and right margins since you will center the worksheet data horizontally between the original margins.

d. Click the **Horizontally check box** in the *Center on page* section, and then click **OK**. Save the workbook.

The worksheet data will be centered between the left and right margins.

STEP 3 ▶ CREATE A HEADER

To document the worksheet, you want to include your name, the current date, and the worksheet tab name in a header. Refer to Figure 1.48 as you complete Step 3.

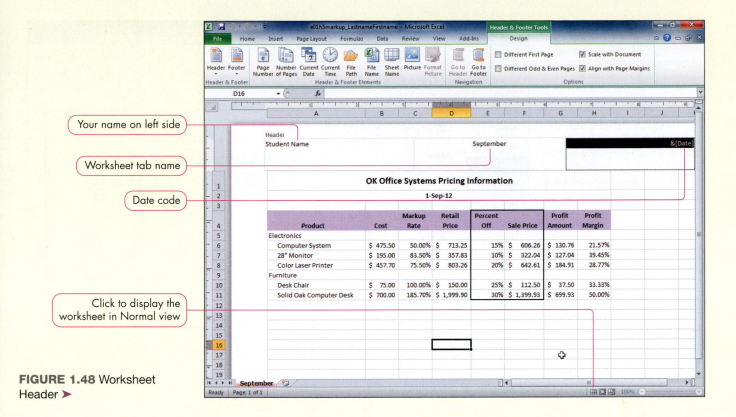

FIGURE 1.48 Worksheet Header ➤

Labels in figure:
- Your name on left side
- Worksheet tab name
- Date code
- Click to display the worksheet in Normal view

a. Click the **Insert tab**, and then click **Header & Footer** in the Text group.

Excel displays the Header & Footer Tools Design tab, and the worksheet displays in Page Layout view. The insertion point blinks inside the center section of the Header.

b. Click in the left section of the header, and then type your name.

c. Click in the center section of the header, and then click **Sheet Name** in the Header & Footer Elements group on the Design tab.

Excel inserts the code &[Tab]. This code displays the name of the worksheet. If you change the worksheet tab name, the header will reflect the new sheet name.

d. Click in the right section of the header, and then click **Current Date** in the Header & Footer Elements group on the Design tab.

Excel inserts the code &[Date]. This code displays the current date based on the computer clock when you print the worksheet. If you want a specific date to appear regardless of the date you open or print the worksheet, you would have to type that date manually. When you click in a different header section, the codes, such as &[Tab], display the actual tab name instead of the code.

e. Click in any cell in the worksheet, click **Normal** on the status bar, and then save the workbook.

STEP 4 ▸ **PRINT PREVIEW AND PRINT**

Before printing the worksheet, you should print preview it. Doing so helps you detect margin problems and other issues, such as a single row or column of data flowing onto a new page. Refer to Figure 1.49 as you complete Step 4.

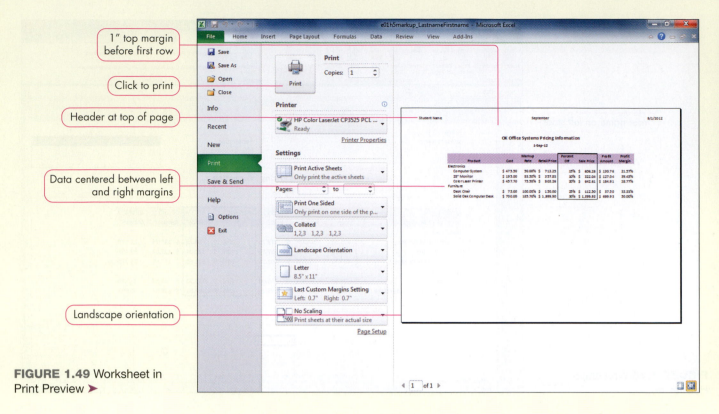

1" top margin before first row

Click to print

Header at top of page

Data centered between left and right margins

Landscape orientation

FIGURE 1.49 Worksheet in Print Preview ➤

a. Click the **File tab**, and then click **Print**.

The Backstage view displays print options and a preview of the worksheet.

b. Verify the Printer name displays the printer that you want to use to print your worksheet.

c. Click **Print** to print the worksheet, and then save the workbook.

Check your printed worksheet to make sure the data are formatted correctly. After you click Print, the Home tab is displayed. If you decide not to print at this time, you need to click the Home tab yourself.

STEP 5 ▸ ADJUST SCALING AND SET SHEET OPTIONS

You want to print a copy of the worksheet formulas to check the logic of the formulas. You need to display the formulas, select options to print gridlines and headings, and then decrease the scaling so that the data print on one page. Refer to Figure 1.50 as you complete Step 5.

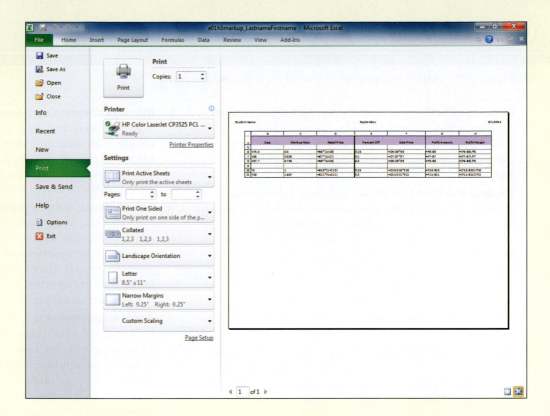

FIGURE 1.50 Worksheet in Print Preview ➤

a. Press **Ctrl+`** to display cell formulas.

b. Click the **Page Layout tab**. Click the **Print Gridlines check box**, and then click the **Print Headings check box** in the Sheet Options group.

   Since you want to print cell formulas, it is helpful to display the gridlines and row and column headings on that printout.

c. Click the **File tab**, and then click **Print**.

   The bottom of the Backstage view displays 1 of 2, indicating the worksheet no longer prints on one page.

d. Click **Next Page** (the right triangle at the bottom of the Backstage view), and then click the **Page Layout tab**.

e. Click **Margins** in the Page Setup group, and then select **Narrow**.

f. Select the **range B4:H11**, click **Print Area** in the Page Setup group, and then select **Set Print Area**.

g. Click the **Scale spin box** in the Scale to Fit group on the Page Layout tab until it displays **90%**.

   The dotted line indicating the page break now appears on the right side of the last column, indicating that the worksheet data will print on one page. If you want to verify that the worksheet will print on one page, display it in print preview.

h. Print the worksheet. Save and close the *e01h5markup_LastnameFirstname* workbook and submit the worksheet based on your instructor's directions.

   Check your printed worksheet to make sure the data are formatted correctly.

CHAPTER OBJECTIVES REVIEW

After reading this chapter, you have accomplished the following objectives:

1. **Plan for effective workbook and worksheet design.** Planning before entering data helps ensure better worksheet design. Planning involves stating the purpose, identifying input values, determining outputs, and deciding what data to add into columns and rows.

2. **Explore the Excel window.** Excel shares many common elements with other Office programs, but also includes unique elements. The Name Box identifies the location of the active cell, indicated first by column letter and then by row number, for example, A10. The Formula Bar displays the contents of the current cell. Select All enables users to select all items in the worksheet. Column and row headings identify column letters and row numbers. Sheet tabs provide different worksheets within the workbook. Navigation buttons enable users to navigate among worksheet tabs.

3. **Enter and edit cell data.** You can enter text, values, dates, and formulas in cells. Text aligns on the left cell margin, and values and dates align on the right cell margin. Values represent quantities that can be used in calculations. Dates may be entered in a variety of formats. You can edit or clear the contents of cells.

4. **Use symbols and order of precedence.** The basic arithmetic symbols are +, −, *, /, and ^ in Excel. The order of operations is the sequence in which mathematical operations is performed: parentheses, exponents, multiplication, division, addition, and subtraction. Formulas start with an equal sign, should include cell references containing values, and should not contain raw values except constants.

5. **Use Auto Fill.** To copy a formula down a column or across a row, double-click or drag the fill handle. You can use Auto Fill to copy formulas, number patterns, names of months, weekdays, etc.

6. **Display cell formulas.** By default, the results of formulas appear in cells instead of the actual formulas. You can display formulas within the cells to help troubleshoot formulas by pressing Ctrl+`.

7. **Manage worksheets.** The default worksheet tab names are Sheet1, Sheet2, and Sheet3. You can rename the worksheet tabs to be more meaningful, delete extra worksheets, insert new worksheets, and apply colors to worksheet tabs. In addition, you can move worksheets or copy worksheets.

8. **Manage columns and rows.** Although you should plan a worksheet before creating it, you can insert new columns and rows or delete columns and rows that you no longer need. You can also increase or decrease the height or width of rows and columns to display data better. Hiding rows and columns protects confidential data from being displayed or printed.

9. **Select, move, copy, and paste.** A range may be a single cell or a rectangular block of cells. After selecting a range, you can cut it to move it to another range or copy it to another location in the worksheet. You should ensure the designation range contains enough empty cells to accommodate the data you cut or copied to avoid overwriting existing data. The Paste Special option enables you to specify how the data are pasted into the worksheet.

10. **Apply alignment and font options.** You can apply horizontal and vertical alignment to format data in cells or use Merge & Center to combine cells and center titles over columns of data. To indicate hierarchy of data or to offset a label you can increase or decrease how much the data are indented in a cell. Use the Wrap Text option to present text on multiple lines in order to avoid having extra-wide columns. You can further improve readability of worksheets by adding appropriate borders around important ranges or applying fill colors to cells.

11. **Apply number formats.** The default number format is General, which does not apply any particular format to values. Apply appropriate formats to values to present the data with the correct symbols and decimal alignment. For example, Accounting is a common number format for monetary values. Other popular number formats include Percentage and Date. After applying a number format, you can increase or decrease the number of decimal points displayed.

12. **Select page setup options.** The Page Layout tab on the Ribbon contains options for setting margins, selecting orientation, specifying page size, selecting the print area, and applying other settings. In addition, you can display the Page Setup dialog box to specify these and other settings to control how data will print. You can insert a header or footer to display documentation, such as your name, date, time, and worksheet tab name.

13. **Print a worksheet.** Before printing a worksheet, you should display a preview in the Backstage view to ensure the data will print correctly. The Backstage view helps you see if margins are correct or if isolated rows or columns will print on separate pages. After making appropriate adjustments, you can print the worksheet.

KEY TERMS

MULTIPLE CHOICE

1. What is the first step in planning an effective worksheet?

   (a) Enter labels, values, and formulas.
   (b) State the purpose of the worksheet.
   (c) Identify the input and output areas.
   (d) Decide how to format the worksheet data.

2. What Excel interface item is not displayed until you start typing or editing data in a cell?

   (a) Insert Function
   (b) Name Box
   (c) Formula Bar
   (d) Enter

3. Given the formula =B1*B2+B3/B4^2 where B1 contains 3, B2 contains 4, B3 contains 32, and B4 contains 4, what is the result?

   (a) 14
   (b) 121
   (c) 76
   (d) 9216

4. Why would you press Ctrl+` in Excel?

   (a) To display the print options
   (b) To undo a mistake you made
   (c) To display cell formulas
   (d) To enable the AutoComplete feature

5. Which of the following is a nonadjacent range?

   (a) C15:D30
   (b) L15:L65
   (c) A1:Z99
   (d) A1:A10, D1:D10

6. If you want to balance a title over several columns, what do you do?

   (a) Enter the data in the cell that is about midway across the spreadsheet.
   (b) Merge and center the data over all columns.
   (c) Use the Increase Indent command until the title looks balanced.
   (d) Click Center to center the title horizontally over several columns.

7. Which of the following characteristics is not applicable to the Accounting Number Format?

   (a) Dollar sign immediately on the left side of the value
   (b) Commas to separate thousands
   (c) Two decimal places
   (d) Zero values displayed as hyphens

8. If you want to see a preview of how a worksheet will appear on a hard copy, what do you do?

   (a) Change the Zoom to 100%.
   (b) Click the Page Layout tab, and then click the Print check box in the Sheet Options group.
   (c) Click the File tab, and then click Print.
   (d) Click the Page Setup Dialog Box Launcher.

9. Assume that the data on a worksheet consume a whole printed page and a couple of columns on a second page. You can do all of the following except what to force the data to print all on one page?

   (a) Decrease the Scale value.
   (b) Increase the left and right margins.
   (c) Decrease column widths if possible.
   (d) Select a smaller range as the print area.

10. What should you do if you see a column of pound signs (###) instead of values or results of formulas?

   (a) Increase the zoom percentage.
   (b) Delete the column.
   (c) Adjust the row height.
   (d) Increase the column width.

1 Mathematics Review

After a nice summer break, you want to brush up on your math skills. Since you are learning Excel, you decide to test your logic by creating formulas in Excel. Your first step is to plan the spreadsheet design. After having read Chapter 1, you realize that you should avoid values in formulas most of the time. Therefore, you will create an input area that contains values you will use in your formulas. To test your knowledge of formulas, you need to create an output area that will contain a variety of formulas using cell references from the input area. You need to include a formatted title, the date prepared, and your name. After creating and verifying formula results, you plan to change the input values and observe changes in the formula results. After verifying the results, you will copy the data to Sheet2, display cell formulas, and apply page layout options. This exercise follows the same set of skills as used in Hands-On Exercises 1, 2, 3, and 5 in the chapter. Refer to Figure 1.51 as you complete this exercise.

	A	B	C	D	E
1			**Excel Formulas and Order of Precedence**		
2	Date Created:	9/1/2012		Student Name	
3					
4	Input Area:			Output Area:	
5	First Value	1		Sum of 1st and 2nd values	3
6	Second Value	2		Difference between 4th and 1st values	3
7	Third Value	3		Product of 2nd and 3rd values	6
8	Fourth Value	4		Quotient of 3rd and 1st values	3
9				2nd value to the power of 3rd value	8
10				1st value added to product of 2nd and 4th values and difference between sum and 3rd value	6
11				Product of sum of 1st and 2nd and difference between 4th and 3rd values	3
12				Product of 1st and 2nd added to product of 3rd and 4th values	14
13					

FIGURE 1.51 Formula Practice ➤

a. Start Excel. If Excel is already open, click the **File tab**, select **New**, and then click **Create** to display a blank workbook. Save the workbook as **e01p1math_LastnameFirstname**.

b. Type **Excel Formulas and Order of Precedence** in **cell A1**, and then press **Enter**.

c. Type the labels in **cells A2** through **A8** as shown in Figure 1.51, type the current date in **cell B2** in the format shown, and then type the values shown in **cells B5:B8**. Column A labels will appear cut off after you enter values in column B, and the column B values will be right-aligned at this point.

d. Type your name in **cell D2**, and then type the labels in **cells D4:D12** as shown in Figure 1.51. Column D labels will overlap into columns E through L at this point.

e. Adjust the column widths by doing the following:
   - Click in any cell in column A, and then click **Format** in the Cells group.
   - Select **Column Width**, type **12.5** in the **Column width box**, and then click **OK**.
   - Use the instructions in the first two bullets above to set a **35.5** width for **column D**.
   - Use the instructions in the first two bullets above to set a **11.43** width for **column B**.

f. Format the title:
   - Select the **range A1:E1**.
   - Click **Merge & Center** in the Alignment group.
   - Bold the title and apply **14 pt** size.

g. Apply the following font and alignment formats:
- Bold **cells A4** and **D4**.
- Select the **range B5:B8**, and then click **Center** in the Alignment group.
- Select the **range D10:D12**, and then click **Wrap Text** in the Alignment group.

h. Enter the following formulas in **column E**:
- Click **cell E5**. Type **=B5+B6** and press **Enter**. Excel adds the value stored in cell B5 (1) to the value stored in cell B6 (2). The result (3) appears in cell E5, as described in cell D5. You can check your results with the results shown in Figure 1.51.
- Enter appropriate formulas in **cells E6:E8**, pressing **Enter** after entering each formula. Subtract to calculate a difference, multiply to calculate a product, and divide to calculate a quotient.
- Type **=B6^B7** in **cell E9**, and then press **Enter**. Estimate the answer: 2*2*2 = 8.
- Enter **=B5+B6*B8-B7** in **cell E10**, and then press **Enter**. Estimate the answer: 2*4=8; 1+8 = 9; 9-3 = 6. Multiplication occurs first, followed by addition, and finally subtraction.
- Enter **=(B5+B6)*(B8-B7)** in **cell E11**, and then press **Enter**. Estimate the answer: 1+2 = 3; 4-3 = 1; 3*1 = 3. Notice that this formula is almost identical to the previous formula; however, the parentheses affect the order of operations. Calculations in parentheses occur before the multiplication.
- Enter **=B5*B6+B7*B8** in **cell E12**, and then press **Enter**. Estimate the answer: 1*2 = 2; 3*4 = 12; 2+12 = 14.

i. Edit a formula and the input values:
- Click **cell E12**, and then click in the **Formula Bar** to edit the formula. Add parentheses as shown: **=(B5*B6)+(B7*B8)**, and then click **Enter** to the left side of the Formula Bar. The answer is still 14. The parentheses do not affect order of precedence since multiplication occurred before the addition. The parentheses help improve the readability of the formula.
- Click **cell B5**, type **2**, and then press **Enter**. Type **4**, press **Enter**, type **6**, press **Enter**, type **8**, and then press **Enter**.
- Double-check the results of the formulas using a calculator or your head. The new results in cells E5:E12 should be 6, 6, 24, 3, 4096, 28, 12, and 56, respectively.

j. Double-click the **Sheet1 tab**, type **Results**, and then press **Enter**. Right-click the **Results tab**, select **Move or Copy**, click (**move to end**) in the *Before sheet* section, click the **Create a copy check box**, and then click **OK**. Double-click the **Results (2) tab**, type **Formulas**, and then press **Enter**. Right-click the **Sheet2 tab**, and then select **Delete**. Delete the Sheet3 tab.

k. Make sure the Formulas worksheet tab is active, click the **Page Layout tab**, and then do the following:
- Click **Orientation** in the Page Setup group, and then select **Landscape**.
- Click the **Print Gridlines check box**, and then click the **Print Headings check box** in the Sheet Options group.

l. Click the **Formulas tab**, and then click **Show Formulas** in the Formula Auditing group. Double-click between the column A and column B headings to adjust the column A width. Double-click between the column B and column C headings to adjust the column B width. Set **24.0** width for **column D**.

m. Click the **File tab**, and then click **Print**. Verify that the worksheet will print on one page. Click the **File tab** again to close the Backstage view.

n. Save and close the workbook, and submit the worksheet based on your instructor's directions.

2 Calendar Formatting

You want to create a calendar for October. The calendar will enable you to practice alignment settings, including center, merge and center, and indents. In addition, you will need to adjust column widths and increase row height to create cells large enough to enter important information, such as birthdays, in your calendar. You will use Auto Fill to complete the days of the week and the days within each week. To improve the appearance of the calendar, you will add fill colors, font colors, borders, and clip art. This exercise follows the same set of skills as used in Hands-On Exercises 1–5 in the chapter. Refer to Figure 1.52 as you complete this exercise.

FIGURE 1.52 October Calendar Page ➤

a. Click the **File tab**, select **New**, and then click **Create** to display a blank workbook. Save the workbook as **e01p2october_LastnameFirstname**.

b. Type **October** in **cell A1**, and then click **Enter** on the left side of the Formula Bar.

c. Format the title:
   - Select the **range A1:G1**, and then click **Merge & Center** in the Alignment group.
   - Apply **48 pt** size.
   - Click the **Fill Color arrow**, and then click **Orange, Accent 6** on the top row of the *Theme Colors* section of the color palette.

d. Complete the days of the week:
   - Type **Sunday** in **cell A2**, and then click **Enter** on the left side of the Formula Bar.
   - Drag the fill handle in **cell A2** across the row through **cell G2** to use Auto Fill to complete the rest of the weekdays.
   - Click the **Fill Color arrow**, and then select **Orange, Accent 6, Lighter 80%**. Click the **Font Color arrow**, and then click **Orange, Accent 6**. Apply bold and **14 pt** size. Click **Middle Align**, and then click **Center** in the Alignment group.

e. Complete the days of the month:
   - Type **1** in **cell B3**, press **Tab**, type **2** in **cell C3**, and then click **Enter** on the left side of the Formula Bar.
   - Select the **range B3:C3**. Drag the fill handle in **cell C3** across the row through **cell G3** to use Auto Fill to complete the rest of the days for the first week.
   - Type **7** in **cell A4**, press **Tab**, type **8** in **cell B4**, and then click **Enter** on the left side of the Formula Bar. Use the fill handle to complete the days for the second week.
   - Type **14** in **cell A5**, press **Tab**, type **15** in **cell B5**, and then click **Enter** on the left side of the Formula Bar. Use the fill handle to complete the days for the third week.
   - Use the fill handle to complete the days of the month (up to 31).

f. Format the columns and rows:
   - Select **columns A:G**. Click **Format** in the Cells group, select **Column Width**, type **16** in the **Column width box**, and then click **OK**.
   - Select **row 2**. Click **Format** in the Cells group, select **Row Height**, type **54**, and then click **OK**.
   - Select **rows 3:7**. Set an **80** row height.
   - Select the **range A2:G7**. Click the **Borders arrow** in the Font group, and then select **All Borders**.
   - Select the **range A3:G7**. Click **Top Align** and **Align Text Left** in the Alignment group. Click **Increase Indent**. Bold the numbers and apply **12 pt** size.

g. Insert and size images:
   - Display the Clip Art task pane. Search for and insert the Halloween image in the **October 31 cell**. Size the image to fit within the cell.
   - Search for and insert an image of Columbus in the **October 15 cell**. Size the image to fit within the cell.

h. Double-click **Sheet1**, type **October**, and then press **Enter**. Right-click **Sheet2**, and then select **Delete**. Delete Sheet3.

i. Click the **Page Layout tab**. Click **Orientation** in the Page Setup group, and then select **Landscape**.

j. Click the **Insert tab**, and then click **Header & Footer** in the Text group. Click in the left side of the header, and then type your name. Click in the center of the header, and then click **Sheet Name** in the Header & Footer Elements group on the Design tab. Click in the right side of the header, and then click **File Name** in the Header & Footer Elements group on the Design tab. Click in any cell in the workbook, and then click **Normal** on the status bar.

k. Save and close the workbook, and submit based on your instructor's directions.

3 Elementary School Attendance

As the principal of Wellsville Elementary School, you have to prepare periodic reports about student attendance. You decided to create a spreadsheet in Excel to store data by each grade level for a particular day. You will complete your spreadsheet by entering formulas to calculate the percentages of students who were present and absent each day. You also want to format the spreadsheet to present the data effectively. This exercise follows the same set of skills as used in Hands-On Exercises 1–5 in the chapter. Refer to Figure 1.53 as you complete this exercise.

	A	B	C	D	E	F
1	**Wellsville Elementary**					
2	**Monday, April 30, 2012**					
3						
4	**Grade Level**	**Total Students**	**Number Present**	**Attendance Rate**	**Absence Rate**	
5	Pre-K	15	10	66.67%	33.33%	
6	Kindergarten	35	30	85.71%	14.29%	
7	First Grade	50	41	82.00%	18.00%	
8	Second Grade	45	44	97.78%	2.22%	
9	Third Grade	47	46	97.87%	2.13%	
10	Fourth Grade	38	38	100.00%	0.00%	
11	Fifth Grade	42	40	95.24%	4.76%	
12						

FIGURE 1.53 Attendance Report ➤

a. Open the *e01p3attend* workbook and save it as **e01p3attend_LastnameFirstname** so that you can return to the original workbook if necessary.

b. Adjust alignments by doing the following from the Alignment group on the Home tab:
   - Select the **range A1:F1**, and then click **Merge & Center** in the Alignment group to center the title over the data columns. Merge and center the date in the second row over the data columns.
   - Select the **range A4:F4**. Click **Wrap Text**, and then click **Center** in the Alignment group to center and word-wrap the column headings.

c. Click **cell D4**. Click the **Delete arrow** in the Cells group, and then select **Delete Sheet Columns** to delete the empty column D.

d. Move the Pre-K row above the Kindergarten row by doing the following:
  - Right-click the **row 5 heading**, and then select **Insert** from the shortcut menu to insert a new row.
  - Select the **range A12:E12**. Cut the selected range, click **cell A5**, and then paste.

e. Select the **range A5:E11**. Click **Format** in the Cells group, and then select **Row Height**. Type **24** and click **OK** to increase the row height.

f. Calculate the percentages of students who were present and absent today by doing the following:
  - Click **cell D5**. Type **=C5/B5** and press **Tab** to enter the formula and make **cell E5** the active cell. This formula divides the number of students present by the total number of students in Pre-K.
  - Type **=(B5-C5)/B5** and click **Enter** on the left side of the Formula Bar to enter the formula and keep **cell E5** as the active cell. This formula must first calculate the number of students who were absent by subtracting the number of students present from the total number of students in Pre-K. The difference is divided by the total number of students to determine the percentage of students absent.
  - Select the **range D5:E5**. Click **Percent Style** in the Number group, and then click **Increase Decimal** twice in the Number group. With both cells still selected, double-click the fill handle in the bottom-right corner of **cell E5** to copy the formulas down the columns.
  - Click the **Formulas tab**, and then click **Show Formulas** in the Formula Auditing group to display cell formulas. Review the formulas, and then click **Show Formulas** to display formula results again.

g. Press **Ctrl+Home** to make **cell A1** the active cell. Spell-check the worksheet and make necessary changes.

h. Click the **Page Layout tab**. Click **Margins** in the Page Setup group, select **Custom Margins**, click the **Horizontally check box**, and then click **OK**.

i. Click the **Insert tab**. Click **Header & Footer** in the Text group. Click in the left side of the header, and then type your name. Press **Tab**, and then click **Current Date** in the Header & Footer Elements group. Press **Tab**, and then click **File Name** in the Header & Footer Elements group. Click **cell A1**, and then click **Normal** on the status bar.

j. Save and close the workbook, and submit based on your instructor's directions.

MID-LEVEL EXERCISES

1 Fuel Efficiency

Your summer vacation involved traveling through several states to visit relatives and to view the scenic attractions. While traveling, you kept a travel log of mileage and gasoline purchases. Now that the vacation is over, you want to determine the fuel efficiency of your automobile. The partially completed worksheet includes the beginning mileage for the vacation trips and the amount of fuel purchased.

a. Open the *e01m1fuel* workbook and save the workbook as **e01m1fuel_LastnameFirstname** so that you can return to the original workbook if necessary.

b. Insert a new column between columns B and C, and then type **Miles Driven** as the column heading.

c. Select the range of beginning miles in **cells A5:A12**. Copy the selected range to duplicate the values in **cells B4:B11** to ensure that the ending mileage for one trip is identical to the beginning mileage for the next trip.

d. Create the formula to calculate the miles driven for the first trip. Copy the formula down the **Miles Driven column**.

e. Create the formula to calculate the miles per gallon for the first trip. Copy the formula down the **Miles Per Gallon column**.

f. Merge and center the title over the data columns. Apply bold, **16 pt** size, and **Blue, Accent 1** font color.

g. Format the column headings: bold, centered, wrap text, and **Blue, Accent 1, Lighter 80% fill color**.

h. Apply **Comma Style** to the values in the Beginning and Ending columns, and then display these values as whole numbers. Display the values in the Miles Per Gallon column with two decimal places.

i. Delete Sheet2 and Sheet3. Rename *Sheet1* as **Mileage**.

j. Set these page settings: **2"** top margin, centered horizontally, **125%** scaling.

k. Insert a header with your name on the left side, the sheet name code in the center, and the file name code on the right side.

l. Save and close the workbook, and submit based on your instructor's directions.

2 Guest House Rental Rates

You manage a beach guest house in Ft. Lauderdale. The guest house contains three types of rental units. You set prices based on peak and off-peak times of the year. You want to calculate the maximum daily revenue for each rental type, assuming all units of each type are rented. In addition, you want to calculate the discount rate for off-peak rental times. After calculating the revenue and discount rate, you want to improve the appearance of the worksheet by applying font, alignment, and number formats. Refer to Figure 1.54 as you complete this exercise.

	A	B	C	D	E	F	G
1	**Beachfront Guest House**						
2	Effective May 1, 2012						
3							
4			Peak Rentals		Off-Peak Rentals		
5	Rental Type	No. Units	Per Day	Maximum Revenue	Per Day	Maximum Revenue	Discount Rate
6	Studio Apartment	6	$ 149.95	$ 899.70	$ 112.50	$ 675.00	25.0%
7	1 Bedroom Suite	4	$ 250.45	$ 1,001.80	$ 174.00	$ 696.00	30.5%
8	2 Bedroom Suite	2	$ 450.00	$ 900.00	$ 247.55	$ 495.10	45.0%

FIGURE 1.54 Beachfront Guest House Rental Summary ➤

a. Open the *e01m2rentals* workbook and save the workbook as **e01m2rentals_LastnameFirstname** so that you can return to the original workbook if necessary.

b. Create and copy the following formulas:
   - Calculate the Peak Rentals Maximum Revenue based on the number of units and the rental price per day.
   - Calculate the Off-Peak Rentals Maximum Revenue based on the number of units and the rental price per day.
   - Calculate the discount rate for the Off-Peak rental price per day. For example, using the peak and off-peak per day values, the studio apartment rents for 75% of its peak rental rate. However, you need to calculate and display the off-peak discount rate, which is 25%.

DISCOVER

c. Format the monetary values with **Accounting Number Format**. Format the discount rate in **Percent Style** with one decimal place.

d. Format the headings on row 4:
   - Merge and center *Peak Rentals* over the two columns of peak rental data. Apply bold, **Dark Red fill color** and **White, Background 1 font color**.
   - Merge and center *Off-Peak Rentals* over the three columns of off-peak rental data. Apply bold, **Blue fill color**, and **White, Background 1 font color**.

e. Center, bold, and wrap the headings on row 5.

f. Apply **Red, Accent 2, Lighter 80% fill color** to the **range C5:D8**. Apply **Blue, Accent 1, Lighter 80% fill color** to the **range E5:G8**.

g. Set **1″** top, bottom, left, and right margins. Center the data horizontally on the page.

h. Insert a header with your name on the left side, the sheet name code in the center, and the file name code on the right side.

i. Insert a new worksheet, and then name it **Formulas**. Copy the data from the Rental Rates worksheet to the Formulas worksheet. On the Formulas worksheet, select **landscape orientation** and the options to print gridlines and headings. Display cell formulas and adjust column widths so that the data will fit on one page. Insert a header with the same specifications that you did for the Rental Rates worksheet.

j. Save and close the workbook, and submit based on your instructor's directions.

3 Real Estate Sales Report

You own a small real estate company in Enid, Oklahoma. You want to analyze sales for selected properties. Your assistant prepared a spreadsheet with some of the data from the files. You need to calculate the number of days that the houses were on the market and their sales percentage of the list price. In one situation, the house was involved in a bidding war between two families that really wanted the house. Therefore, the sale price exceeded the list price.

a. Open the *e01m3sales* workbook and save the workbook as **e01m3sales_LastnameFirstname** so that you can return to the original workbook if necessary.

b. Delete the row that has incomplete sales data. The owners took their house off the market.

c. Calculate the number of days each house was on the market. Copy the formula down that column.

d. Calculate the sale price percentage of the list price. The second house was listed for $500,250, but it sold for only $400,125. Therefore, the sale percentage of the list price is 79.99%. Format the percentages with two decimal places.

e. Format prices with **Accounting Number Format** with zero decimal places.

f. Wrap the headings on row 4.

g. Insert a new column between the Date Sold and List Price columns. Move the Days on Market column to the new location. Then delete the empty column B.

h. Edit the list date of the 41 Chestnut Circle house to be **4/20/2012**. Edit the list price of the house on Amsterdam Drive to be **$355,000**.

i. Select the **property rows**, and then set a **20** row height. Adjust column widths as necessary.

j. Select **landscape orientation**, and then set the scaling to **130%**. Center the data horizontally and vertically on the page.

k. Insert a header with your name, the current date code, and the current time code.

l. Save and close the workbook, and submit based on your instructor's directions.

You manage a publishing company that publishes and sells books to bookstores in Austin. Your assistant prepared a standard six-month royalty statement for one author. You need to insert formulas, format the worksheets, and then prepare royalty statements for other authors.

Enter Data into the Worksheet

You need to enter and format a title, enter the date indicating the end of the statement period, and then delete a blank column. You also need to insert a row for the standard discount rate row, a percentage that you discount the books from the retail price to sell to the bookstores.

a. Open the *e01c1royal* workbook and save it as **e01c1royal_LastnameFirstname**.

b. Type **Royalty Statement** in **cell A1**. Merge and center the title over the four data columns. Select **16 pt** size, and apply **Purple font color**.

c. Type **6/30/2012** in **cell B3**, and then left-align the date.

d. Delete the blank column between the Hardback and Paperback columns.

e. Insert a new row between *Retail Price* and *Price to Bookstore*. Enter **Standard Discount Rate**, **0.55**, and **0.5**. Format the two values as **Percent Style**.

Calculate Values

You need to insert formulas to perform necessary calculations.

a. Enter the **Percent Returned formula** in the Hardback column. The percent returned indicates the percentage of books sold but returned to the publisher.

b. Enter the **Price to Bookstore formula**. This is the price at which you sell the books to the bookstore and is based on the retail price and the standard discount. For example, if a book has a $10 retail price and a 55% discount, you sell the book for $4.50.

c. Enter the **Net Retail Sales formula**. The net retail sales is the revenue from the net units sold at the retail price. Gross units sold minus the returned units equals net units sold.

d. Enter the **Royalty to Author formula**. Royalties are based on net retail sales and the applicable royalty rate.

e. Enter the **Royalty per Book formula**. This amount is the author's earnings on every book sold but not returned.

f. Copy the formulas to the Paperback column.

Format the Values

You are ready to format the values to improve the readability.

a. Apply **Comma Style** with zero decimal places to the quantities in the *Units Sold* section.

b. Apply **Percent Style** with one decimal place to the Units Sold values, **Percent Style** with zero decimal places to the Pricing values, and **Percent Style** with two decimal places to the Royalty Information values.

c. Apply **Accounting Number Format** to all monetary values.

Format the Worksheet

You want to improve the appearance of the rest of the worksheet.

a. Select the **Hardback** and **Paperback labels**. Apply bold, right-alignment, and **Purple font color**.

b. Select the **Units Sold section heading**. Apply bold and **Purple, Accent 4, Lighter 40% fill color**.

c. Use **Format Painter** to apply the formats from the Units Sold label to the Pricing and Royalty Information labels.

d. Select the individual labels within each section (e.g., *Gross Units Sold*) and indent the labels twice. Widen column A as needed.

e. Select the **range A7:C10** (the *Units Sold* section), and then apply the **Outside Borders border style**. Apply the same border style to the *Pricing* and *Royalty Information* sections.

Manage the Workbook

You want to duplicate the royalty statement worksheet to use as a model to prepare a royalty statement for another author. You will apply page setup options and insert a header on both worksheets.

a. Insert a new worksheet on the right side of the Jacobs worksheet. Rename the worksheet as **Lopez**.

b. Change the Jacobs sheet tab to **Red**. Change the Lopez sheet tab to **Dark Blue**.

c. Copy Jacobs' data to the Lopez worksheet.

d. Make these changes on the Lopez worksheet: **Lopez** (author), **5000** (hardback gross units), **15000** (paperback gross units), **400** (hardback returns), **175** (paperback returns), **19.95** (hardback retail price), and **7.95** (paperback retail price).

e. Click the **Jacobs sheet tab**, and then press and hold down **Ctrl** as you click the **Lopez sheet tab** to select both worksheets. Select the margin setting to center the data horizontally on the page. Insert a header with your name on the left side, the sheet name code in the center, and the file name code on the right side.

f. Change back to Normal view. Right-click the **Jacobs sheet name**, and then select **Ungroup Sheets**.

Display Formulas and Print the Workbook

You want to print the formatted Jacobs worksheet to display the calculated results. To provide evidence of the formulas, you want to display and print cell formulas in the Lopez worksheet.

a. Display the cell formulas for the Lopez worksheet.

b. Select options to print the gridlines and headings.

c. Adjust the column widths so that the formula printout will print on one page.

d. Submit either a hard copy of both worksheets or an electronic copy of the workbook to your professor as instructed. Close the workbook.

Server's Tip Distribution

You are a server at a restaurant in Seattle. When you get tips, you calculate the percentage of the subtotal to determine your performance based on the tip. You must tip the bartender 15% of the drink amount and the server assistant 12% of your total tip amount. You started to design a spreadsheet to enter data for one shift. Open *e01b1tips* and save it as **e01b1tips_LastnameFirstname**. Now you need to insert columns for the bartender and assistant tip rates, perform calculations, and format the data. After entering the formulas, use Auto Fill to copy the formulas down the respective columns. Include a notes section that explains the tipping rates for the bartender and server assistant. Decide where to place this information. Add and format a descriptive title, date, and time of shift. To format the data, apply concepts learned in the chapter: font, borders, fill color, alignment, wrap text, and number formats. Select appropriate options on the Page Layout tab. Copy the data to Sheet2, display cell formulas, print gridlines, print headings, set the print area to the column headings and data, and adjust the column widths. Include a footer with appropriate data for the two worksheets. Manage the workbook by deleting extra worksheets, renaming the two worksheets that contain data, and adding worksheet tab colors to both sheets. Save and close the workbook, and submit based on your instructor's directions.

Credit Card Rebate

You recently found out the personal-use Costco TrueEarnings® American Express credit card earns annual rebates on all purchases, whether at Costco or other places. You want to see how much rebate you would have received had you used this credit card for purchases in the past year. Use the Internet to research the percentage rebates for different categories. Plan the design of the spreadsheet. Enter the categories, rebate percentages, amount of money you spent in each category, and a formula to calculate the amount of rebate. Use the Excel Help feature to learn how to add several cells using a function instead of adding cells individually and how to apply a Double Accounting underline. Then insert the appropriate function to total your categorical purchases and rebate amounts. Apply appropriate formatting and page setup options as discussed in this chapter for readability. Underline the last monetary values for the last data row, and apply the Double Accounting underline style to the totals. Insert a header with imperative documentation. Save the workbook as **e01b2rebate_LastnameFirstname**. Save and close the workbook, and submit based on your instructor's directions.

Housing Estimates

One of your friends is starting a house construction business. Your friend developed an Excel workbook to prepare a cost estimate for a potential client. However, the workbook contains several errors. You offer to review the workbook, identify the errors, and correct them. Open *e01b3house* and save it as **e01b3house_LastnameFirstname**. Research how to insert comments in cells. As you identify the errors, insert comments in the respective cells to explain the errors. Correct the errors. Insert your name on the left side of the header. The other header and page setup options are already set. Save and close the workbook, and submit based on your instructor's directions.

EXCEL

2 FORMULAS AND FUNCTIONS

Performing Quantitative Analysis

Watch the
Set-up
Video
for this
Case Study!

CASE STUDY | Denver Mortgage Company

You are an assistant to Erica Matheson, a mortgage broker at the Denver Mortgage Company. Erica spends her days reviewing mortgage rates and trends, meeting with potential clients, and preparing paperwork. She relies on your expertise in using Excel to help you analyze mortgage data.

Today, Erica provided you with a spreadsheet containing data for five mortgages. She asked you to perform some basic calculations so that she can check the output provided by her system. She needs you to calculate the amount financed, the periodic interest rate, the total number of payment periods, monthly payments, and other details for each mortgage. In addition, you will perform some basic statistics, such as totals and averages. After you complete these tasks, Erica wants you to create a separate worksheet with additional input data to automate calculations for future loans.

OBJECTIVES   AFTER YOU READ THIS CHAPTER, YOU WILL BE ABLE TO:

1. Use semi-selection to create a formula *p.130*

2. Use relative, absolute, and mixed cell references in formulas *p.130*

3. Avoid circular references *p.132*

4. Insert a function *p.138*

5. Total values with the SUM function *p.140*

6. Insert basic statistical functions *p.141*

7. Use date functions *p.143*

8. Determine results with the IF function *p.150*

9. Use lookup functions *p.152*

10. Calculate payments with the PMT function *p.154*

11. Create and maintain range names *p.159*

12. Use range names in formulas *p.161*

Formula Basics

By increasing your understanding of formulas, you can build robust spreadsheets that perform a variety of calculations for quantitative analysis. Your ability to build sophisticated spreadsheets and to interpret the results increases your value to any organization. By now, you should be able to build simple formulas using cell references and mathematical operators and using the order of precedence to control the sequence of calculations in formulas.

> Your ability to build sophisticated spreadsheets and to interpret the results increases your value to any organization.

In this section, you will use the semi-selection method to create formulas. In addition, you will create formulas in which cell addresses change or remain fixed when you copy them. Finally, you will learn how to identify and prevent circular references in formulas.

Using Semi-Selection to Create a Formula

You have learned how to create formulas by typing the cell references (for example, =A1+A2) to create a formula. To decrease typing time and ensure accuracy, you can use *semi-selection*, a process of selecting a cell or range of cells for entering cell references as you create formulas. Semi-selection is often called *pointing* because you use the mouse pointer to select cells as you build the formula. To use the semi-selection technique to create a formula, do the following:

Semi-selection (or **pointing**) is the process of using the mouse pointer to select cells while building a formula.

1. Click the cell where you want to create the formula.
2. Type an equal sign (=) to start a formula.
3. Click the cell or drag to select the cell range that contains the value(s) to use in the formula. A moving marquee appears around the cell or range you select, and Excel displays the cell or range reference in the formula.
4. Type a mathematical operator.
5. Continue clicking cells, selecting ranges, and typing operators to finish the formula. Use the scroll bars if the cell is in a remote location in the worksheet, or click a worksheet tab to see a cell in another worksheet.
6. Press Enter to complete the formula.

Using Relative, Absolute, and Mixed Cell References in Formulas

When you copy a formula, Excel either adjusts or preserves the cell references in the copied formulas based on how the cell references appear in the original formula. Excel uses three different ways to reference a cell in a formula: relative, absolute, and mixed. Figure 2.1 shows a worksheet containing various cell references in formulas. When you create an original formula that you will copy to other cells, ask yourself the following: Do the cell references need to adjust for the copied formulas, or should the cell references always refer to the same cell location, regardless where the copied formula is located?

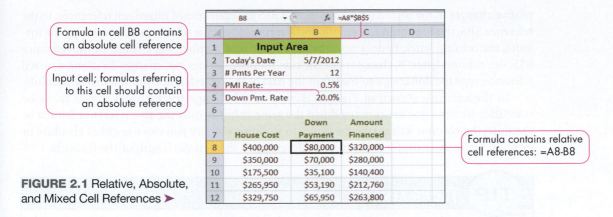

FIGURE 2.1 Relative, Absolute, and Mixed Cell References ➤

Use a Relative Cell Reference

A **relative cell reference** indicates a cell's relative location from the cell containing the formula; the cell reference changes when the formula is copied.

A *relative cell reference* indicates a cell's relative location, such as two rows up and one column to the left, from the cell containing the formula. When you copy a formula containing a relative cell reference, the cell references in the copied formula change relative to the position of the copied formula. Regardless of where you copy the formula, the cell references in the copied formula maintain the same relative distance from the copied formula cell, as the cell references relative location to the original formula cell.

In Figure 2.1, the formulas in column C contain relative cell references. When you copy the original formula =A8-B8 from cell C8 down to cell C9, the copied formula changes to =A9-B9. Because you copy the formula down the column to cell C12, the column letters in the formula stay the same, but the row numbers change, down one row number at a time. Relative references are indicated by using the cell address. Using relative cell addresses to calculate the amount financed ensures that each borrower's down payment is subtracted from his or her respective house cost.

Use an Absolute Cell Reference

An **absolute cell reference** indicates a cell's specific location; the cell reference does not change when you copy the formula.

An *absolute cell reference* provides a permanent reference to a specific cell. When you copy a formula containing an absolute cell reference, the cell reference in the copied formula does not change, regardless of where you copy the formula. An absolute cell reference appears with a dollar sign before both the column letter and row number, such as $B$5.

Figure 2.1 illustrates an effective use of an input area, a range in a worksheet that contains values that you can change. You build formulas using absolute references to the cells in the input area. By using cell references from an input area, you can change the value in the input area and the formulas that refer to those cells update automatically. If an input value changes (e.g., the down payment rate changes from 20% to 25%), enter the new input value in only one cell (e.g., B5), and Excel recalculates the amount of recommended down payment for all the formulas.

In Figure 2.1, the formulas in column B calculate down payments based on the house costs in column A and on the required down payment percentage, which is stored in cell B5. The formula uses an absolute cell reference to cell B5, which currently contains the value 20%. Cell B8 contains the formula to calculate the first borrower's down payment: =A8*$B$5. A8 is a relative address that changes as you copy the formula down the column so that the down payment is based on each borrower's respective house cost (A8 becomes A9 on the 9th row, A10 on the 10th row, etc.). $B$5 is an absolute cell reference to the cell B5, which currently contains 20%. The absolute cell reference $B$5 prevents the cell reference to B5 from changing when you copy the formula to calculate the recommended down payment for the other borrowers.

Use a Mixed Cell Reference

A **mixed cell reference** contains both an absolute and a relative cell reference in a formula; the absolute part does not change but the relative part does when you copy the formula.

A *mixed cell reference* combines an absolute cell reference with a relative cell reference. When you copy a formula containing a mixed cell reference, either the column letter or the row number that has the absolute reference remains fixed while the other part of the cell reference that is relative changes in the copied formula. $B5 and B$5 are examples of mixed cell references. In the reference $B5, the column B is absolute, and the row number is relative; when you copy the formula, the column letter, B, does not change, but the row number will change. In the reference B$5, the column letter, B, changes, but the row number, 5, does not change. To create a mixed reference, type the dollar sign to the left of the part of the cell reference you want to be absolute.

In the example shown in Figure 2.1, you could change the formula in cell B8 to be =A8*B$5. Because you are copying down the same column, only the row reference 5 must be absolute; the column letter stays the same. In situations where you can use either absolute or mixed references, consider using mixed references to shorten the length of the formula.

 TIP The F4 Key

The F4 key toggles through relative, absolute, and mixed references. Click a cell reference within a formula on the Formula Bar, and then press F4 to change it. For example, click in B5 in the formula =A8*B5. Press F4, and the relative cell reference (B5) changes to an absolute cell reference ($B$5). Press F4 again, and $B$5 becomes a mixed reference (B$5); press F4 again, and it becomes another mixed reference ($B5). Press F4 a fourth time, and the cell reference returns to the original relative reference (B5).

Avoiding Circular References

A **circular reference** occurs when a formula directly or indirectly refers to itself.

If a formula contains a direct or an indirect reference to the cell containing the formula, a *circular reference* exists. For example, assume you enter the formula =A8-C8 in cell C8. Because the formula is in cell C8, using the cell address C8 within the formula creates a circular reference. Circular references usually cause inaccurate results, and Excel displays a warning message when you enter a formula containing a circular reference or when you open an Excel workbook that contains an existing circular reference (see Figure 2.2). Click Help to display the *Remove or allow a circular reference* Help topic, or click OK to accept the circular reference. The status bar indicates the location of a circular reference until it has been resolved.

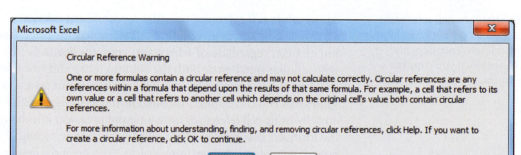

FIGURE 2.2 Circular Reference Warning ➤

If the circular reference warning appears when creating a formula, use Help to activate formula auditing tools to help you identify what is causing the circular reference.

 TIP Green Triangles

Excel displays a green triangle in the top-left corner of a cell if it detects a potential error in a formula. Click the cell to see the Trace Error button (yellow diamond with exclamation mark). When you click Trace Error, Excel displays information about the potential error and how to correct it. In some cases, Excel may anticipate an inconsistent formula or the omission of adjacent cells in a formula. For example, if you add a column of values for the year 2012, the error message indicates that you did not include the year itself. However, the year is merely a label and should not be included; therefore, you would ignore that error message.

HANDS-ON EXERCISES

1 Formula Basics

Erica prepared a workbook containing data for five mortgages financed with the Denver Mortgage Company. The data include house cost, down payment, mortgage rate, number of years to pay off the mortgage, and the financing date for each mortgage.

Skills covered: Use Semi-Selection to Create a Formula • Copy a Formula with a Relative Cell Reference • Enter a Formula with an Absolute Cell Reference • Enter a Formula with a Mixed Cell Reference • Create and Correct a Circular Reference

---

STEP 1 ▶ USE SEMI-SELECTION TO CREATE A FORMULA

Your first step is to calculate the amount financed by each borrower by creating a formula that calculates the difference between the cost of the house and the down payment. You decide to use the semi-selection technique. Refer to Figure 2.3 as you complete Step 1.

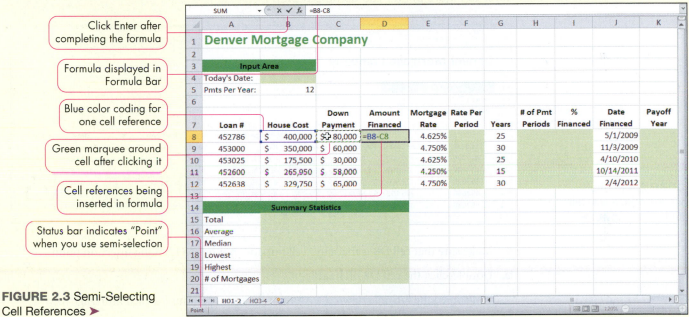

Click Enter after completing the formula

Formula displayed in Formula Bar

Blue color coding for one cell reference

Green marquee around cell after clicking it

Cell references being inserted in formula

Status bar indicates "Point" when you use semi-selection

FIGURE 2.3 Semi-Selecting Cell References ➤

a. Open *e02h1loans* and save it as **e02h1loans_LastnameFirstname**.

> **TROUBLESHOOTING:** If you make any major mistakes in this exercise, you can close the file, open *e02h1loans* again, and then start this exercise over.

The workbook contains two worksheets: HO1-2 (for Hands-On Exercises 1 and 2) and HO3-4 (for Hands-On Exercises 3 and 4). You will enter formulas in the shaded cells.

b. Click the **HO1-2 worksheet tab**, and then click **cell D8**.

This is where you will create a formula to calculate the first borrower's amount financed.

c. Type = and click **cell B8**, the cell containing the first borrower's house cost.

You type an equal sign to start the formula, and then you click the first cell containing a value you want to use in the formula. A blue marquee appears around cell B8, and the B8 cell reference appears to the right of the equal sign in the formula.

d. Type - and click **cell C8**, the cell containing the down payment by the first borrower.

A green marquee appears around cell C8, and the C8 cell reference appears to the right of the subtraction sign in the formula (see Figure 2.3).

> **TROUBLESHOOTING:** If you click the wrong cell, click the correct cell to change the cell reference in the formula. If you realize the mistake after typing an arithmetic operator or after entering the formula, you must edit the formula to change the cell reference.

e. Click **Enter** to the left of the Formula Bar to complete the formula. Save the workbook.

The first borrower financed (i.e., borrowed) $320,000, the difference between the cost ($400,000) and the down payment ($80,000).

STEP 2 ▶ COPY A FORMULA WITH A RELATIVE CELL REFERENCE

After verifying the results of the amount financed by the first borrower, you are ready to copy the formula. Before copying the formula, determine if the cell references should be relative or absolute. For this formula, you want cell references to change for each row. For each borrower, you want to base the amount financed on his or her own data, so you decide to keep the relative cell references in the formula. Refer to Figure 2.4 as you complete Step 2.

Cell references in the first copied formula

Cell containing the first copied formula

Auto Fill Options

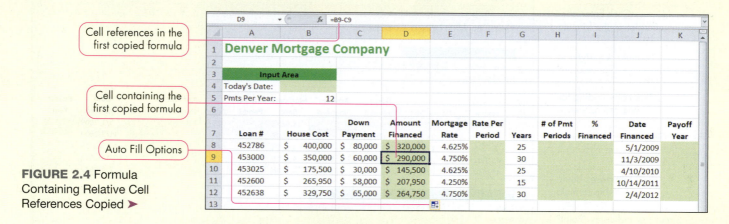

FIGURE 2.4 Formula Containing Relative Cell References Copied ▶

a. Make sure that **cell D8** is the active cell but does not have a blinking insertion point.

b. Double-click the **cell D8 fill handle**.

You copied the formula down the Amount Financed column for each mortgage row.

> **TIP** Auto Fill Options
>
> The Auto Fill Options button appears in the bottom-right corner of the copied formulas. If you click it, you can see that the default is Copy Cells. If you want to copy only formatting, click Fill Formatting Only. If you want to copy data only, click Fill Without Formatting.

c. Click **cell D9**, and then view the formula in the Formula Bar.

The formula in cell D8 is =B8-C8. The formula pasted in cell D9 is =B9-C9. Because the original formula contained relative cell references, when you copy the formula down a column, the row numbers for the cell references change. Each result represents the amount financed for that particular borrower.

d. Press ↓ and look at the cell references in the Formula Bar to see how the references change for each formula you copied. Save the workbook with the new formula you created.

ENTER A FORMULA WITH AN ABSOLUTE CELL REFERENCE

Column E contains the annual percentage rate (APR) for each mortgage. Because the borrowers will make monthly payments, you need to calculate the monthly interest rate by dividing the APR by 12 (the number of payments in one year) for each borrower. Refer to Figure 2.5 as you complete Step 3.

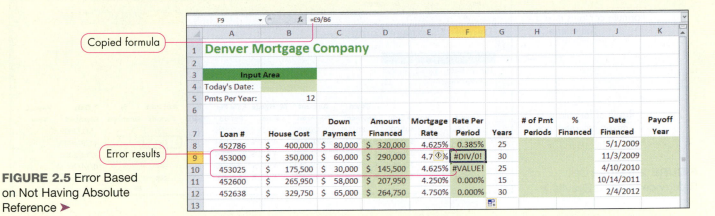

Copied formula

Error results

FIGURE 2.5 Error Based on Not Having Absolute Reference ➤

a. Click **cell F8**.

You need to create a formula to calculate the monthly interest rate for the first borrower.

b. Type = and click **cell E8**, the cell containing the first fixed mortgage rate.

c. Type / and click **cell B5**, the cell containing the value 12.

Typically, you should avoid typing values directly in formulas. Although the number of months in one year will always be 12, you use a cell reference so that the company could change the payment period to bimonthly (24 payments per year) or quarterly (four payments per year) without adjusting the formula.

d. Click **Enter** to the left of the Formula Bar, double-click the **cell F8 fill handle**, click **cell F9**, and then view the results (see Figure 2.5).

An error icon displays to the left of cell F9, cell F9 displays #DIV/0!, and cell F10 displays #VALUE!. The original formula was =E8/B5. Because you copied the formula =E8/B5 down the column, the first copied formula is =E9/B6, and the second copied formula is =E10/B7. Although you want the mortgage rate cell reference (E8) to change (E9, E10, etc.) from row to row, you do not want the divisor to change. You need all formulas to divide by the value stored in cell B5, so you will edit the formula to make B5 an absolute reference.

> **TIP** Error Icons
>
> You can position the mouse pointer over the error icon to see a tip indicating what is wrong, such as *The formula or function used is dividing by zero or empty cells.* You can click the icon to see a menu of options to learn more about the error and how to correct it.

 FYI

e. Undo the Auto Fill process. Click within or to the right of **B5** in the Formula Bar.

f. Press **F4**, and then click **Enter** to the left of the Formula Bar.

Excel changes the cell reference from B5 to $B$5, making it absolute.

g. Copy the formula down the Rate Per Period column. Click **cell F9**, and then view the formula in the Formula Bar. Save the workbook with the new formula you created.

The formula in cell F9 is =E9/$B$5. The reference to E9 is relative and B5 is absolute.

The next formula you need to enter will calculate the total number of payment periods for each loan. Refer to Figure 2.6 as you complete Step 4.

Formula contains mixed cell reference

Result of formula with mixed cell reference

	A	B	C	D	E	F	G	H	I	J	K
	H9		fx	=G9*B$5							
1	Denver Mortgage Company										
2											
3		Input Area									
4	Today's Date:										
5	Pmts Per Year:	12									
6											
7	Loan #	House Cost	Down Payment	Amount Financed	Mortgage Rate	Rate Per Period	Years	# of Pmt Periods	% Financed	Date Financed	Payoff Year
8	452786	$ 400,000	$ 80,000	$ 320,000	4.625%	0.385%	25	300		5/1/2009	
9	453000	$ 350,000	$ 60,000	$ 290,000	4.750%	0.396%	30	360		11/3/2009	
10	453025	$ 175,500	$ 30,000	$ 145,500	4.625%	0.385%	25	300		4/10/2010	
11	452600	$ 265,950	$ 58,000	$ 207,950	4.250%	0.354%	15	180		10/14/2011	
12	452638	$ 329,750	$ 65,000	$ 264,750	4.750%	0.396%	30	360		2/4/2012	
13											

FIGURE 2.6 Mixed Cell Reference Formula Results ▶

a. Click **cell H8**.

b. Type = and click **cell G8**, the cell containing *25*, the number of years to pay off the loan for the first borrower.

You need to multiply the number of years (25) by the number of payment periods in one year (12) using cell references.

c. Type * and click **cell B5**.

You want B5 to be absolute so that the cell reference remains B5 when you copy the formula.

d. Press **F4** to make the cell reference absolute, and then click **Enter** to the left of the Formula Bar.

The product of 25 years and 12 months is 300.

e. Copy the formula down the # of Pmt Periods column.

The first copied formula is =G9*$B$5, and the result is 360. You want to see what happens if you change the absolute reference to a mixed reference and then copy the formula again. Because you are copying down a column, the column letter B can be relative since it will not change either way, but the row number 5 must be absolute.

f. Undo the copied formulas. Click **cell H8**, and then click within the **$B$5 cell reference** in the Formula Bar. Press **F4** to change the cell reference to a mixed cell reference, B$5. Press **Ctrl+Enter**, and then copy the formula down the # of Pmt Periods column. Click **cell H9**. Save the workbook with the new formula you created.

The first copied formula is =G9*B$5, and the result is still 360. In this situation, using either an absolute reference or a mixed reference provides the same results.

Erica wants to know what percentage of the house cost each borrower will finance. As you create the formula, you enter a circular reference. After studying the results, you correct the circular error and plan future formulas that avoid this problem. Refer to Figure 2.7 as you complete Step 5.

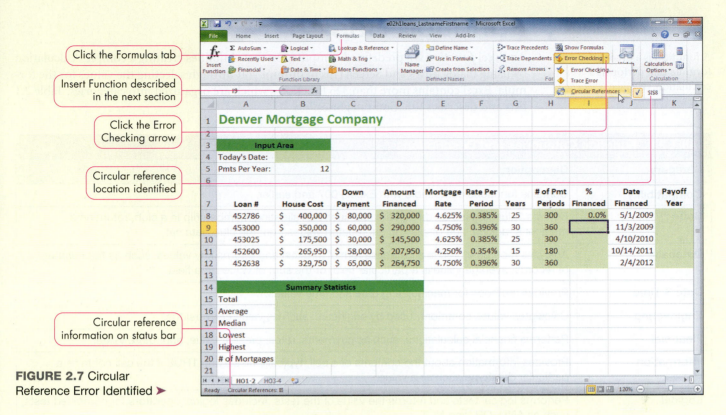

Click the Formulas tab

Insert Function described in the next section

Click the Error Checking arrow

Circular reference location identified

Circular reference information on status bar

FIGURE 2.7 Circular Reference Error Identified ➤

a. Click **cell I8**, type **=I8/B8**, and then press **Enter**.

The Circular Reference Warning message box appears.

b. Read the description of the error, and then click **Help**.

A Help window opens, displaying information about circular references.

c. Read the Help topic information, and then close the Help window.

Notice that the left side of the status bar displays *Circular References: I8*. You will follow the advice given in the Help window to fix it.

d. Click the **Formulas tab**, click the **Error Checking arrow** in the Formula Auditing group, and then point to **Circular References**.

The Circular References menu displays a list of cells containing circular references.

e. Select **$I$8** from the list to make it the active cell.

Because the formula is stored in cell I8, the formula cannot refer to the cell itself. You need to divide the value in the Amount Financed column by the value in the House Cost column.

f. Edit the formula to be **=D8/B8**. Copy the formula down the % Financed column.

The first borrower financed 80% of the cost of the house: $320,000 financed divided by $400,000 cost.

g. Save the workbook. Keep the workbook onscreen if you plan to continue with Hands-On Exercise 2. If not, close the workbook and exit Excel.

Function Basics

A **function** is a predefined formula that performs a calculation.

An Excel *function* is a predefined computation that simplifies creating a complex calculation by using dialog boxes and ScreenTips to prompt you through selecting the values for the formula. Excel contains more than 325 functions, which are organized into categories. Table 2.1 lists and describes function categories.

TABLE 2.1   Function Categories and Descriptions

Category	Description
Compatibility	Contains functions compatible with Excel 2007 and earlier.
Cube	Returns values based on data in a cube, such as validating membership in a club, returning a member's ranking, and displaying aggregated values from the club data set.
Database	Analyzes records stored in a database format in Excel and returns key values, such as the number of records, average value in a particular field, or the sum of values in a field.
Date & Time	Provides methods for manipulating date and time values.
Engineering	Calculates values commonly used by engineers, such as value conversions.
Financial	Performs financial calculations, such as payments, rates, present value, and future value.
Information	Provides information about the contents of a cell, typically displaying TRUE if the cell contains a particular data type such as a value.
Logical	Performs logical tests and returns the value of the tests. Includes logical operators for combined tests, such as AND, OR, and NOT.
Lookup & Reference	Looks up values, creates links to cells, or provides references to cells in a worksheet.
Math & Trig	Performs standard math and trigonometry calculations.
Statistical	Performs common statistical calculations, such as averages and standard deviations.
Text	Manipulates text strings, such as combining text or converting text to lowercase.

Syntax is a set of rules that govern the structure and components for properly entering a function.

An **argument** is an input, such as a cell reference or value, needed to complete a function.

When using functions, you must adhere to correct *syntax*, the rules that dictate the structure and components required to perform the necessary calculations. The basic syntax of a function requires a function to start with an equal sign, to contain the function name, and to specify its arguments. The function name describes the purpose of the function. For example, the function name SUM indicates that the function sums or adds values. A function's *arguments* specify the inputs—such as cells or values—that are required to complete the operation. Arguments are enclosed in parentheses, with the opening parenthesis immediately following the function name. Some functions, such as TODAY, do not require arguments; however, you must include the parentheses with nothing inside them. In some cases, a function requires multiple arguments separated by commas.

In this section, you will learn how to insert common functions using the keyboard and the Insert Function and Function Arguments dialog boxes.

Inserting a Function

Formula AutoComplete displays a list of functions and defined names as you enter a function.

To insert a function by typing, first type an equal sign, and then begin typing the function name. *Formula AutoComplete* displays a list of functions and defined names that match letters as you type a formula. For example, if you type =SU, Formula AutoComplete displays a list of functions and names that start with *SU* (see Figure 2.8). You can double-click the function name from the list or continue typing the function name. You can even scroll through the list to see the ScreenTip describing the function.

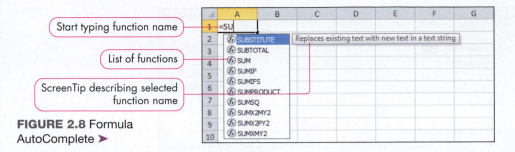

Start typing function name

List of functions

ScreenTip describing selected
function name

FIGURE 2.8 Formula
AutoComplete ➤

A **function ScreenTip** is a small
pop-up description that displays
the arguments for a function as
you enter it.

After you type the function name and opening parenthesis, Excel displays the **function ScreenTip**, a small pop-up description that displays the function's arguments. The argument you are currently entering is bold in the function ScreenTip (see Figure 2.9). Square brackets indicate optional arguments. For example, the SUM function requires the number1 argument, but the number2 argument is optional. Click the argument name in the function ScreenTip to select the actual argument in the cell.

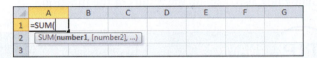

FIGURE 2.9 Function
ScreenTip ➤

You can also use the Insert Function dialog box to search for a function, select a function category, and select a function from the list (see Figure 2.10). The dialog box is helpful if you want to browse a list of functions, especially if you are not sure of the function you need and want to see descriptions. To display the Insert Function dialog box, click Insert Function, which looks like *fx*, between the Name Box and the Formula Bar, or click Insert Function in the Function Library group on the Formulas tab. From within the dialog box, select a function category, such as Most Recently Used, and then select a function to display the syntax and a brief description of that function. Click *Help on this function* to display specific information about the selected function.

Specify type of functions
to display

Selected function

Syntax and description of
selected function

Click to see Help on
selected function

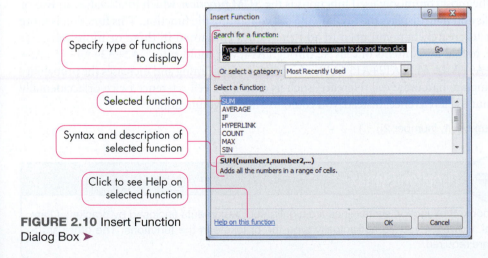

FIGURE 2.10 Insert Function
Dialog Box ➤

When you find the function you want, click OK. The Function Arguments dialog box opens so that you can enter the arguments for that specific function (see Figure 2.11). Bold arguments are required; argument names that are not bold are optional. The function can operate without the optional argument, which is used when you need additional specifications to calculate a result. Type the cell references in the argument boxes, or click a collapse button to the right side of an argument box to select the cell or range of cells in the worksheet to designate as that argument. The value or results of a formula contained in the argument cell displays on the right side of the argument box. If the argument is not valid, Excel displays an error description on the right side of the argument box.

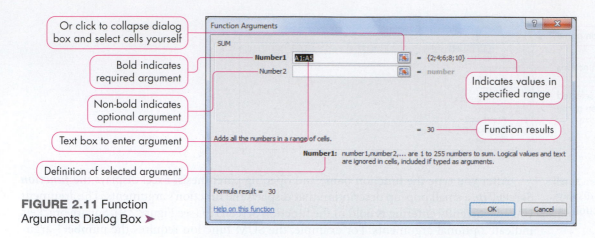

Or click to collapse dialog box and select cells yourself

Bold indicates required argument

Non-bold indicates optional argument

Text box to enter argument

Definition of selected argument

Indicates values in specified range

Function results

FIGURE 2.11 Function Arguments Dialog Box ➤

The bottom of the Function Arguments dialog box displays a description of the function and a description of the argument containing the insertion point. As you enter arguments, the dialog box also displays the results of the function.

> **TIP** #NAME?
>
> If you enter a function, and #NAME? appears in the cell, you might have mistyped the function name. To avoid this problem, select the function name from the Formula AutoComplete list as you type the function name, or use the Insert Function dialog box. You can also type the function name in all lowercase letters. If you enter a function name correctly, Excel converts the name to all capital letters when you press Enter, indicating that you spelled the function name correctly.

Totaling Values with the SUM Function

The **SUM function** calculates the total of values contained in two or more cells.

One of the most commonly used functions is the *SUM function*, which totals values in two or more cells and then displays the result in the cell containing the function. This function is more efficient to create when you need to add the values contained in three or more cells. For example, to add the contents of cells A2 through A14, you could enter =A2+A3+A4+A5+A6+A7+A8+A9+A10+A11+A12+A13+A14, which is time-consuming and increases the probability of entering an inaccurate cell reference, such as entering a cell reference twice or accidentally leaving out a cell reference. Instead, you could use the SUM function:

 =SUM(number 1, [number 2], . . .)

> **TIP** Function Syntax
>
> In this book, the function syntax lines are highlighted. Arguments enclosed by brackets [ ] are optional. However, you do not actually type the brackets in the functions. The other arguments are required.

The SUM function contains one required argument—number1—that represents a range of cells to add. The number2 optional argument is used when you want to sum nonadjacent cells or ranges, such as =SUM(A2:A14,F2:F14).

To insert the SUM function, type =SUM(A2:A14). A2:A14 represents the range containing the values to sum. You can also use semi-selection to select the range of cells. Because the SUM function is the most commonly used function, it is available on the Ribbon: Click Sum in the Editing group on the Home tab, or click AutoSum in the Function Library group on the Formulas tab. Figure 2.12 shows the result of using the SUM function to total scores (898).

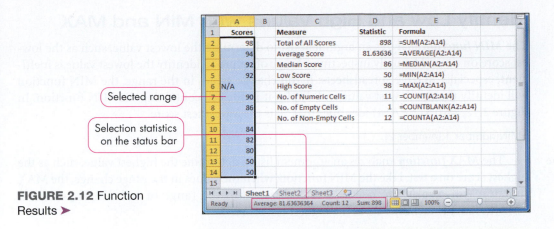

Selected range

Selection statistics on the status bar

	A	B	C	D	E	F
1	Scores		Measure	Statistic	Formula	
2	98		Total of All Scores	898	=SUM(A2:A14)	
3	94		Average Score	81.63636	=AVERAGE(A2:A14)	
4	92		Median Score	86	=MEDIAN(A2:A14)	
5	92		Low Score	50	=MIN(A2:A14)	
6	N/A		High Score	98	=MAX(A2:A14)	
7	90		No. of Numeric Cells	11	=COUNT(A2:A14)	
8	86		No. of Empty Cells	1	=COUNTBLANK(A2:A14)	
9			No. of Non-Empty Cells	12	=COUNTA(A2:A14)	
10	84					
11	82					
12	80					
13	50					
14	50					
15						

Sheet1 Sheet2 Sheet3

Ready   Average: 81.63636364   Count: 12   Sum: 898   100%

FIGURE 2.12 Function Results ➤

> **TIP** Avoiding Functions for Basic Formulas
>
> Do not use a function for a basic mathematical expression. For example, although =SUM(B4/C4) produces the same result as =B4/C4, the SUM function is not needed to perform the basic arithmetic division. Use the most appropriate, clear-cut formula, =B4/C4.

Inserting Basic Statistical Functions

Excel includes commonly used statistical functions that you can use to calculate how much you spend on average per month on DVD rentals, what your highest electric bill is to control spending, and what your lowest test score is so you know what score you need to earn on your final exam to achieve the grade you desire. You can also use statistical functions to create or monitor your budget.

If you click AutoSum, Excel inserts the SUM function. However, if you click the AutoSum arrow in the Editing group on the Home tab, Excel displays a list of basic functions to select: Sum, Average, Count Numbers, Max, and Min. If you want to insert another function, select More Functions from the list.

Find Central Tendency with the AVERAGE and MEDIAN Functions

The AVERAGE function calculates the arithmetic mean, or average, of values in a range.

People often describe data based on central tendency, which means that values tend to cluster around a central value. Excel provides two functions to calculate central tendency: AVERAGE and MEDIAN. The *AVERAGE function* calculates the arithmetic mean, or average, for the values in a range of cells. You can use this function to calculate the class average on a biology test, or the average number of points scored per game by a basketball player. In Figure 2.12, =AVERAGE(A2:A14) returns 81.63636 as the average test score.

=AVERAGE(number 1,[number2], . . .)

The MEDIAN function identifies the midpoint value in a set of values.

The *MEDIAN function* finds the midpoint value, which is the value that one half of the population is above or below. The median is particularly useful because extreme values often influence arithmetic mean calculated by the AVERAGE function. In Figure 2.12, the two extreme test scores of 50 distort the average. The rest of the test scores range from 80 to 98. The median for test scores is 86, which indicates that half the test scores are above 86 and half the test scores are below 86. This statistic is more reflective of the data set than the average is.

=MEDIAN(number 1,[number 2], . . .)

Identify Low and High Values with MIN and MAX

The **MIN function** displays the lowest value in a range.

The **MIN function** analyzes an argument list to determine the lowest value, such as the lowest score on a test. Manually inspecting a range of values to identify the lowest value is inefficient, especially in large spreadsheets. If you change values in the range, the MIN function will identify the new lowest value and display it in the cell containing the MIN function. In Figure 2.12, =MIN(A2:A14) identifies that 50 is the lowest test score.

=MIN(number 1,[number 2], . . .)

The **MAX function** identifies the highest value in a range.

The **MAX function** analyzes an argument list to determine the highest value, such as the highest score on a test. Like the MIN function, when the values in the range change, the MAX function will display the new highest value within the range of cells. In Figure 2.12, =MAX(A2:A14) identifies 98 as the highest test score.

=MAX(number 1,[number 2], . . .)

 TIP Nonadjacent Ranges

You can use multiple ranges as arguments, such as finding the largest number within two nonadjacent (nonconsecutive) ranges. For example, you can find the highest test score where some scores are stored in cells A2:A14, and others are stored in cells K2:K14. Separate each range with a comma in the argument list, so that the formula is =MAX(A2:A14,K2:K14).

Identify the Total Number with COUNT Functions

Excel provides three basic count functions: COUNT, COUNTBLANK and COUNTA to count the cells in a range that meet a particular criterion. The **COUNT function** tallies the number of cells in a range that contain values you can use in calculations, such as numerical and date data, but excludes blank cells or text entries from the tally. In Figure 2.12, the selected range spans 13 cells; however, the COUNT function returns 11, the number of cells that contain numerical data. It does not count the cell containing the text *N/A* or the blank cell.

The **COUNT function** tallies the number of cells in a range that contain values.

The **COUNTBLANK function** tallies the number of blank cells in a range.

The **COUNTA function** tallies the number of cells in a range that are not empty.

The **COUNTBLANK function** tallies the number of cells in a range that are blank. In Figure 2.12, the COUNTBLANK function identifies that one cell in the range A2:A14 is blank. The **COUNTA function** tallies the number of cells in a range that are not blank, that is, cells that contain data whether a value, text, or a formula. In Figure 2.12, =COUNTA(A2:A14) returns 12, indicating the range A2:A14 contains 12 cells that contain some form of data. It does not count the blank cell.

=COUNT(number 1,[number 2], . . .)

=COUNTBLANK(number 1,[number 2], . . .)

=COUNTA(number 1,[number 2], . . .)

 TIP Average, Count, and Sum

When you select a range of cells containing values, by default Excel displays the average, count, and sum of those values on the status bar (see Figure 2.12). You can customize the status bar to show other selection statistics, such as the minimum and maximum values for a selected range. To display or hide particular selection statistics, right-click the status bar, and then select the statistic.

Use Other Math and Statistical Functions

In addition to the functions you have learned in this chapter, Excel provides over 100 other math and statistical functions. Table 2.2 lists and describes some of these functions that you might find helpful in your business, education, and general statistics courses.

TABLE 2.2 Math and Statistical Functions

Function Syntax	Description
=ABS(number)	Displays the absolute (i.e., positive) value of a number.
=FREQUENCY(data_array,bins_array)	Counts how often values appear in a given range.
=INT(number)	Rounds a value number down to the nearest whole number.
=MODE.SNGL(number1,[number2],...)	Displays the most frequently occurring value in a list.
=PI()	Returns the value of *pi* that is accurate up to 15 digits.
=PRODUCT(number1,[number2],...)	Multiplies all values within the argument list.
=RANDBETWEEN(bottom,top)	Generates a random number between two numbers you specify.
=RANK.AVG(number,ref,[order])	Identifies a value's rank within a list of values; returns an average rank for identical values.
=RANK.EQ(number,ref,[order])	Identifies a value's rank within a list of values; the top rank is identified for all identical values.
=ROUND(number,num_digits)	Rounds a value to a specific number of digits. Rounds numbers of 5 and greater up and those less than 5 down.
=SUMPRODUCT(array1,[array2],[array3],...)	Finds the result of multiplying values in one range by the related values in another column and then adding those products.
=TRIMMEAN(array,percent)	Returns the arithmetic average of the internal values in a range by excluding a specified percentage of values at the upper and lower values in the data set. This function helps reduce the effect outliers (i.e., extreme values) have on the arithmetic mean.
=TRUNC(number,[num_digits])	Returns the integer equivalent of a number by truncating or removing the decimal or fractional part of the number. For example, =TRUNC(45.5) returns 45.

> **TIP** ROUND vs. Decrease Decimal Points
>
> When you click Decrease Decimal in the Number group to display fewer or no digits after a decimal point, Excel still stores the original value's decimal places so that those digits can be used in calculations. The ROUND function changes the stored value to its rounded state.

Using Date Functions

Because Excel treats dates as serial numbers, you can perform calculations using dates. For example, assume today is January 1, 2012, and you graduate on May 12, 2012. To determine how many days until graduation, subtract today's date from the graduation date. Excel uses the serial numbers for these dates (40909 and 41041) to calculate the difference of 132 days.

You can use date and time functions to calculate when employees are eligible for certain benefits, how many days it takes to complete a project, or if an account is 30, 60, or more days past due. The Reference table on the next page lists several popular date/time functions.

Insert the TODAY Function

The **TODAY function** displays the current date.

The **TODAY function** displays the current date in a cell. Excel updates the function results when you open or print the workbook. The function is expressed as =TODAY(). The TODAY() function does not require arguments, but you must include the parentheses for the function to work. If you omit the parentheses, Excel displays #NAME? in the cell with a green triangle in the top-left corner of the cell. When you click the cell, an error icon appears that you can click for more information.

Insert the NOW Function

The **NOW function** displays the current date and time.

The *NOW function* uses the computer's clock to display the current date and time you last opened the workbook, so the value will change every time the workbook is opened. Like the TODAY function, the NOW function does not require arguments, but you must include the parentheses. Omitting the parentheses creates a #NAME? error.

 TIP Update the Date and Time

Both the TODAY and NOW functions display the date/time the workbook was last opened or last calculated. These functions do not continuously update the date and time while the workbook is open. To update the date and time, press F9 or click the Formulas tab, and then click Calculate now in the Calculation group.

REFERENCE Date/Time Functions

Function Syntax	Description	Example	Example Results
=TODAY()	Displays today's date: month, day, year.	=TODAY()	5/12/2012
=NOW()	Displays today's date and current military time.	=NOW()	5/12/2012 14:32
=DATE(year,month,day)	Returns the serial number for a date.	=DATE(2012,1,1)	40909 or 1/1/2012
=EDATE(start_date,months)	Displays the serial number of a date a specified number of months in the future or past.	=EDATE(DATE(2012, 1,1),6)	41091
=DAY(serial_number)	Displays the day within a month for a serial number (e.g., 41196 represents 10/14/2012). Entering 41196 as the DAY function argument returns 14 as the 14th day of the month.	=DAY(41196)	14
=EOMONTH(start_date, months)	Identifies the last day of a month a specified number of months from a serial number representing a date (e.g., 40915 represents 1/7/2012, 3 months is 4/7/2012, the last day of April is April 30, which is serial number 41029).	=EOMONTH(40915,3)	41029
=MONTH(serial_number)	Returns the month (1 to 12) for a serial number.	=MONTH(40945)	2
=NETWORKDAYS(start_date,end_date,[holidays])	Calculates the number of work days (excluding weekends and specified holidays) between two dates.	=NETWORKDAYS(40 915,41091,F9:F10)	124
=WEEKDAY(serial_number, [return_type])	Identifies the weekday (1 to 7) for a serial number.	=WEEKDAY(40915,1)	7
=WORKDAY(start_date, days,[holidays])	Calculates a serial number of a date a specified number of days before or after a particular date, excluding specified holidays.	=WORKDAY(41029, 25,E9:E11)	41065
=YEAR(serial_number)	Identifies the year for a serial number.	=YEAR(41029)	2012
=YEARFRAC(start_date, end_date,[basis])	Calculates the fraction of a year between two dates based on the number of whole days.	=YEARFRAC(40915, 41091)	0.483333333

HANDS-ON EXERCISES

2 Function Basics

The Denver Mortgage Company's worksheet contains an area in which you must enter summary statistics. In addition, you need to include today's date and identify what year each mortgage will be paid off.

Skills covered: Use the SUM Function • Use the AVERAGE Function • Use the MEDIAN Function • Use the MIN, MAX, and COUNT Functions • Use the TODAY and YEAR Functions

---

STEP 1 ▶ USE THE SUM FUNCTION

The first summary statistic you need to calculate is the total value of the houses bought by the borrowers. You will use the SUM function. Refer to Figure 2.13 as you complete Step 1.

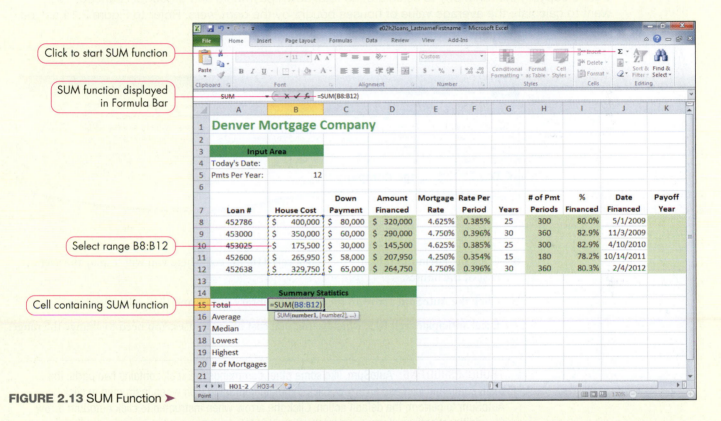

FIGURE 2.13 SUM Function ▶

a. Open *e02h1loans_LastnameFirstname* if you closed it at the end of Hands-On Exercise 1. Save the workbook with the new name **e02h2loans_LastnameFirstname**, changing *h1* to *h2*.

b. Click the **Home tab**, if needed, and then click **cell B15**, the cell where you will enter a formula for the total house cost.

c. Click **AutoSum** in the Editing group.

> **TROUBLESHOOTING:** Click the main part of the AutoSum command. If you click the AutoSum arrow, then select Sum.

Excel anticipates the range of cells containing values you want to sum based on where you enter the formula—in this case, A8:D14. This is not the correct range, so you must enter the correct range.

d. Select the **range B8:B12**, the cells containing house costs.

As you use the semi-selection process, Excel enters the range in the SUM function.

> **TROUBLESHOOTING:** If you accidentally entered the function without changing the arguments, you can repeat steps b–d, or you can edit the arguments in the Formula Bar by deleting the default range, typing B8:B12 between the parentheses, and then pressing Enter.

e. Click **Enter** to the left of the Formula Bar, and then save the workbook.

Cell B15 contains the function = SUM(B8:B12), and the result is $1,521,200.

STEP 2 ▶ USE THE AVERAGE FUNCTION

Before copying the functions to calculate the total down payments and amounts financed, you want to calculate the average value of houses bought by the borrowers. Refer to Figure 2.14 as you complete Step 2.

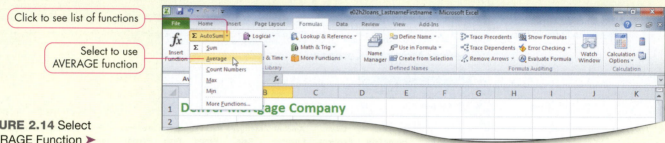

FIGURE 2.14 Select AVERAGE Function ➤

a. Click the **Formulas tab**, and then click **cell B16**, the cell where you will display the average cost of the houses.

b. Click the **AutoSum arrow** in the Function Library group, and then select **Average**.

Excel anticipates cell B15, which is the total cost of the houses. You need to change the range.

> **TROUBLESHOOTING:** AutoSum, like some other commands in Excel, contains two parts: the main command icon and an arrow. Click the main command icon when instructed to click AutoSum to perform the default action. Click the arrow when instructed to click AutoSum arrow for additional options. If you accidentally clicked AutoSum instead of the arrow, press Esc to cancel the SUM function from being completed, and then try step b again.

c. Select the **range B8:B12**, the cells containing the house costs.

The function is =AVERAGE(B8:B12).

d. Press **Enter** to complete the function and make **cell B17** the active cell, and then save the workbook.

The average house cost is $304,240.

You realize that extreme values may distort the average. Therefore, you decide to identify the median value of houses bought to compare it to the average. Refer to Figure 2.15 as you complete Step 3.

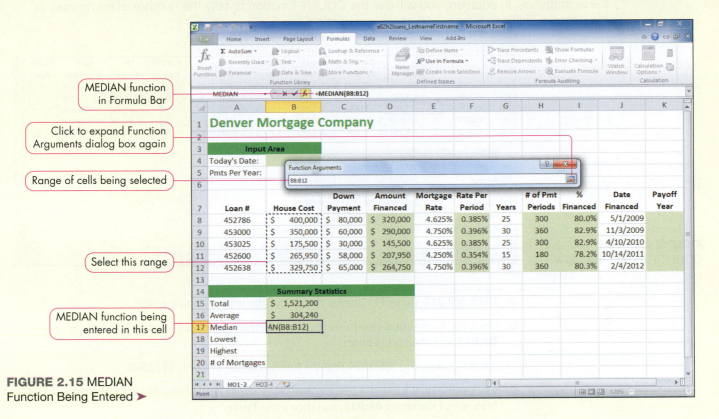

FIGURE 2.15 MEDIAN Function Being Entered ➤

a. Make sure **cell B17** is the active cell. Click **Insert Function** to the left of the Formula Bar or in the Function Library group.

The Insert Function dialog box opens. Use this dialog box to select the MEDIAN function since it is not available on the Ribbon.

b. Type **median** in the **Search for a function box**, and then click **Go**.

Excel displays a list of possible functions in the *Select a function* list. The MEDIAN function is selected at the top of the list; the bottom of the dialog box displays the syntax and the description.

c. Read the MEDIAN function's description, and then click **OK**.

The Function Arguments dialog box opens. It contains one required argument, Number1, representing a range of cells containing values. It has an optional argument, Number2, which you can use if you have nonadjacent ranges that contain values.

d. Click the **collapse button** to the right of the Number1 box.

You collapsed the Function Arguments dialog box so that you can select the range.

e. Select the **range B8:B12**, and then click the **expand button** in the Function Arguments dialog box.

The Function Arguments dialog box expands again.

f. Click **OK** to accept the function arguments and close the dialog box. Save the workbook.

Half of the houses purchased cost over the median, $329,750, and half of the houses cost less than this value. Notice the difference between the median and the average: The average is lower because it is affected by the lowest-costing house, $175,500.

Erica wants to know the least and most expensive houses so that she can analyze typical customers of the Denver Mortgage Company. You will use the MIN and MAX functions to obtain these statistics. In addition, you will use the COUNT function to tally the number of mortgages in the sample. Refer to Figure 2.16 as you complete Step 4.

	Loan #	House Cost	Down Payment	Amount Financed	Mortgage Rate	Rate Per Period	Years	# of Pmt Periods	% Financed	Date Financed	Payoff Year
7											
8	452786	$ 400,000	$ 80,000	$ 320,000	4.625%	0.385%	25	300	80.0%	5/1/2009	
9	453000	$ 425,000	$ 60,000	$ 365,000	4.750%	0.396%	30	360	85.9%	11/3/2009	
10	453025	$ 175,500	$ 30,000	$ 145,500	4.625%	0.385%	25	300	82.9%	4/10/2010	
11	452600	$ 265,950	$ 58,000	$ 207,950	4.250%	0.354%	15	180	78.2%	10/14/2011	
12	452638	$ 329,750	$ 65,000	$ 264,750	4.750%	0.396%	30	360	80.3%	2/4/2012	
13											
14		Summary Statistics									
15	Total	$ 1,596,200	$ 293,000	$1,303,200							
16	Average	$ 319,240	$ 58,600	$ 260,640							
17	Median	$ 329,750	$ 60,000	$ 264,750							
18	Lowest	$ 175,500	$ 30,000	$ 145,500							
19	Highest	$ 425,000	$ 80,000	$ 365,000							
20	# of Mortgages	5	5	5							
21											

FIGURE 2.16 MIN, MAX, and COUNT Function Results ▶

HO1-2 HO3-4

Ready   120%

a. Click **cell B18**, the cell to display the cost of the lowest-costing house.

b. Click the **AutoSum arrow** in the Function Library group, select **Min**, select the **range B8:B12**, and then press **Enter**.

The MIN function identifies that the lowest-costing house is $175,500.

c. Click **cell B19**, if needed. Click the **AutoSum arrow** in the Function Library group, select **Max**, select the **range B8:B12**, and then press **Enter**.

The MAX function identifies that the highest-costing house is $400,000.

d. Click **cell B20**, if needed. Type **=COUNT(B8:B12)** and press **Enter**.

As you type the letter *C*, Formula AutoComplete suggests functions starting with *C*. As you continue typing, the list of functions narrows. After you type the beginning parenthesis, Excel displays the function ScreenTip, indicating the arguments for the function. The range B8:B12 contains five cells.

e. Select the **range B15:B20**.

You want to select the range of original statistics to copy the cells all at one time to the next two columns.

f. Drag the fill handle to the right by two columns to copy the functions. Click **cell D20**.

Because you used relative cell references in the functions, the range changes from =COUNT(B8:B12) to =COUNT(D8:D12).

g. Change the value in **cell B9** to **425000**. Save the workbook.

The results of several formulas and functions change, including the total, average, and max house costs.

STEP 5 › USE THE TODAY AND YEAR FUNCTIONS

You have two date functions to enter to complete the first worksheet. Refer to Figure 2.17 as you complete Step 5.

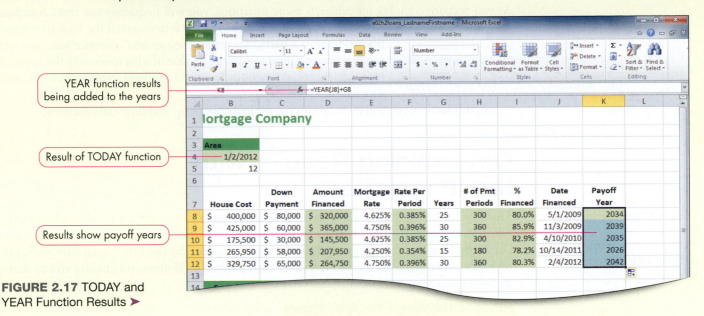

YEAR function results being added to the years

Result of TODAY function

Results show payoff years

FIGURE 2.17 TODAY and YEAR Function Results ➤

a. Click **cell B4**, the cell to contain the current date.

b. Click **Date & Time** in the Function Library group, select **TODAY** to display the Function Arguments dialog box, and then click **OK** to close the dialog box.

   Excel inserts the current date in Short Date format, such as 1/2/2012, based on the computer system's date. The Function Arguments dialog box opens, although no arguments are necessary for this function.

c. Click **cell K8**, click **Date & Time** in the Function Library group, scroll through the list, and then select **YEAR**.

   The Function Arguments dialog box opens so that you can enter the argument, a serial number for a date.

d. Click **cell J8** to enter it in the **Serial_number box**. Click **OK**.

   The function returns 2009, the year the first mortgage was taken out. However, you want the year the mortgage will be paid off. The YEAR function returns the year from a date. You need to add the years to the result of the function to calculate the year that the borrower will pay off the mortgage.

e. Press **F2** to edit the formula stored in cell K8. With the insertion point on the right side of the closing parenthesis, type **+G8**, and then press **Ctrl+Enter**.

   Pressing Ctrl+Enter is the alternative to clicking Enter by the Formula Bar. It keeps the current cell as the active cell. The results show a date: 7/26/1905. You need to apply the Number format to display the year.

f. Click the **Home tab**, click the **Number Format arrow** in the Number group, and then select **Number**. Decrease the number of decimal points to show the value as a whole number.

   You applied the Number format instead of the Comma format because although the Comma format is correct for quantities, such as 2,034 units, it is not appropriate for the year 2034.

g. Copy the formula down the column.

h. Save the workbook. Keep the workbook onscreen if you plan to continue with Hands-On Exercise 3. If not, close the workbook and exit Excel.

Logical, Lookup, and Financial Functions

As you prepare complex spreadsheets using functions, you will frequently use three function categories: logical, lookup and reference, and finance. Logical functions test the logic of a situation and return a particular result. Lookup and reference functions are useful when you need to look up a value in a list to identify the applicable value. Financial functions are useful to anyone who plans to take out a loan or invest money.

> Financial functions are useful to anyone who plans to take out a loan or invest money.

In this section, you will learn how to use the logical, lookup, and financial functions.

Determining Results with the IF Function

The **IF function** evaluates a condition and returns one value if the condition is true and a different value if the condition is false.

The most common logical function is the **IF function**, which returns one value when a condition is met or is true and returns another value when the condition is not met or is false. For example, a company gives a $500 bonus to employees who meet their quarterly goals, but no bonus to employees who did not meet their goals. The IF function enables you to make decisions based on worksheet data.

=IF(logical_test,value_if_true,value_if_false)

The IF function has three arguments: (1) a condition that is tested to determine if it is either true or false, (2) the resulting value if the condition is true, and (3) the resulting value if the condition is false.

Figure 2.18 lists several sample IF functions, how they are evaluated, and their results.

	A	B	C
1	Input Values		
2	$1,000		
3	$2,000		
4	10%		
5	5%		
6	$250		
7			
8			
9	IF Function	Evaluation	Result
10	=IF(A2=A3,A4,A5)	1000 is equal to 2000: FALSE	5%
11	=IF(A2<A3,A4,A5)	1000 is less than 2000: TRUE	10%
12	=IF(A2<A3,A5*A2,MAX(A3*A4,A6))	1000 is less than 2000: TRUE	$50
13	=IF(A2<>A3,"Not Equal","Equal")	1000 and 2000 are not equal: TRUE	Not Equal
14	=IF(A2*A4=A3*A5,A6,0)	100 (A2*A4) is equal to 100 (A3*A5): TRUE	$250

FIGURE 2.18 Sample IF Functions ➤

Design the Logical Test

The **logical test** is an expression that evaluates to true or false.

The first argument for the IF function is the logical test. The **logical test** is a formula that contains either a value or an expression that evaluates to true or false. The logical expression is typically a binary expression, meaning that it requires a comparison between at least two variables, such as the values stored in cells A2 and A3. Table 2.3 lists and describes the logical operators to make the comparison in the logical test.

In Figure 2.18, the first logical test in cell A10 is A2=A3. The logical test compares the values in cells A2 and A3 to see if they are equal. The logical test in cell A14 is A2*A4=A3*A5. The value stored in cell A2 (1,000) is multiplied by the value in cell A4 (10%). The result (100) is then compared to the product of cell A3 (2,000) and cell A5 (5%), which is also 100. Note that the logical test can compare two cell references, or it can perform calculations and then compare the results of those calculations.

TABLE 2.3	Logical Operators
Operator	**Description**
=	Equal to
<>	Not equal to
<	Less than
>	Greater than
<=	Less than or equal to
>=	Greater than or equal to

> **TIP** Using Text in Formulas
>
> You can use text within a formula. For example, to perform a logical test to see if the contents of a cell match text, the logical test would be: B5="Yes". When you compare text, you must surround the text with quotation marks.

Design the Value_If_True and Value_If_False Arguments

The second and third arguments of an IF function are value_if_true and value_if_false. When Excel evaluates the logical test, the result is either true or false. If the logical test evaluates to true, the value_if_true argument executes. If the logical test evaluates to false, the value_if_false argument executes. Only one of the last two arguments is executed; both arguments cannot be executed, since the logical test is either true or false but not both.

The value_if_true and value_if_false arguments can contain text, cell references, formulas, or constants (not recommended). In Figure 2.18, the value_if_true argument in cell A10 is A4, and the value_if_false argument is A5. Since the logical test (A2=A3) is false, the value_if_false argument is executed, and the result displays the same value that is stored in cell A5, which is 5%. In cell A13, the value_if_true argument is "Not Equal", and the value_if_false argument is "Equal". Since the logical test (A2<>A3) is true, the value_if_true argument is executed, and the result displays the text *Not Equal* in the cell containing the function. If you want the result of the function to be blank if a condition is met or not met, type "" (beginning and ending quotation marks).

Nest Basic Functions as Arguments

A **nested function** is a function that contains another function embedded inside one or more of its arguments.

A *nested function* occurs when one function is embedded as an argument within another function. For example, within the function in cell A12 in Figure 2.18, the MAX function is nested in the value_if_false argument of the IF function. Nesting functions enables you to create more complex formulas to handle a variety of situations. In this situation, if the logical test evaluates to false, the value_if_false argument of MAX(A3*A4,A6) would execute. Excel would find the product of A3 and A4 and return the higher of that value (200) or the contents of cell A6 (250). You can even nest functions as part of the logical test or value_if_true argument.

In addition to nesting functions within the IF function, you can nest functions within other functions, such as =SUM(MIN(A1:A5),D10:D15). The nested MIN function identifies the lowest value in the range A1:A5 and adds that value to those stored in the range D10:D15.

Using Lookup Functions

You can use lookup and reference functions to look up values to perform calculations or display results. For example, when you order merchandise on a Web site, the Web server looks up the shipping costs based on weight and distance, or at the end of a semester, your professor uses your numerical average, such as 88%, to look up the letter grade to assign, such as B+.

Create the Lookup Table

A **lookup table** is a range that contains data for the basis of the lookup and data to be retrieved.

Before you insert lookup functions, you need to create a lookup table. A *lookup table* is a range containing a table of values or text that can be retrieved. The table should contain at least two rows and two columns, not including headings. It is important to plan the table so that it conforms to the way in which Excel can utilize the data in it.

Excel cannot interpret the structure of Table 2.4. To look up a value in a range (such as the range 80–89), you must arrange data from the lowest to the highest value and include only the lowest value in the range (such as 80) instead of the complete range. If the values you look up are *exact* values, you can arrange the first column in any logical order. The lowest value for a category or in a series is the *breakpoint*. The first column contains the breakpoints—such as 60, 70, 80, and 90—or the lowest values to achieve a particular grade. The lookup table contains one or more additional columns of related data to retrieve. Table 2.5 shows how to construct the lookup table in Excel.

The **breakpoint** is the lowest value for a specific category or series in a lookup table.

TABLE 2.4	Grading Scale
Range	**Grade**
90–100	A
80–89	B
70–79	C
60–69	D
Below 60	F

TABLE 2.5	Grades Lookup Table
Range	**Grade**
0	F
60	D
70	C
80	B
90	A

Understand the VLOOKUP Function Syntax

The **VLOOKUP function** looks up a value in a vertical lookup table and returns a related result from the lookup table.

The *VLOOKUP function* accepts a value, looks the value up in a vertical lookup table, and returns a result. Use VLOOKUP to search for exact matches or for the nearest value that is less than or equal to the search value, such as assigning a B grade for an 87% class average. The VLOOKUP function has the following three required arguments and one optional argument: (1) lookup_value, (2) table_array, (3) col_index_number, and (4) range_lookup.

=VLOOKUP(lookup_value,table_array,col_index_number,[range_lookup])

Figure 2.19 shows a partial grade book that contains a vertical lookup table, as well as the final scores and letter grades. The function in cell F3 is =VLOOKUP(E3,$A$3:$B$7,2).

F3			f_x =VLOOKUP(E3,$A$3:$B$7,2)			
	A	B	C	D	E	F	G
1	Grading Scale			Partial Gradebook			
2	Breakpoint	Grade		Names	Final Score	Letter Grade	
3	0	F		Abbott	85	B	
4	60	D		Carter	69	D	
5	70	C		Hon	90	A	
6	80	B		Jackson	74	C	
7	90	A		Miller	80	B	
8				Nelsen	78	C	

FIGURE 2.19 VLOOKUP Function for Grade Book ➤

The **lookup value** is a reference to a cell containing a value to look up.

The **table array** is a range containing a lookup table.

The **column index number** is the argument in a VLOOKUP function that identifies which lookup table column from which to return a value.

The *lookup value* is the cell reference of the cell that contains the value to look up. The lookup value for the first student is cell E3, which contains 85. The *table array* is the range that contains the lookup table: $A$3:$B$7. The table array range must be absolute and cannot include column labels for the lookup table. The *column index number* is the column number in the lookup table that contains the return values. In this example, the column index number is 2.

Understand How Excel Processes the Lookup

The VLOOKUP function identifies the value stored in the lookup value argument and then searches the first column of the lookup table until it finds an exact match (if possible). If Excel finds an exact match, it returns the value stored in the column designated by the column index number on that same row. If the table contains breakpoints for ranges rather than exact matches, Excel identifies the correct range based on comparing the lookup value to the breakpoints in the first column. If the lookup value is larger than the breakpoint, it looks to the next breakpoint to see if the lookup value is larger than that breakpoint also. When Excel detects that the lookup value is not greater than the next breakpoint, it stays on that row. It then uses the column index number to identify the column containing the value to return for the lookup value. Because Excel goes sequentially through the breakpoints, it is mandatory that the breakpoints are arranged from the lowest value to the highest value for ranges.

For example, the VLOOKUP function to assign letter grades works like this: Excel identifies the lookup value (85 stored in cell E3) and compares it to the values in the first column of the lookup table (stored in cells A3:B7). It tries to find an exact match for the value 85; however, the table contains breakpoints rather than every conceivable numeric average. Because the lookup table is arranged from the lowest to the highest breakpoints, Excel detects that 85 is greater than the 80 breakpoint but is not greater than the 90 breakpoint. Therefore, it stays on the 80 row. Excel then looks at the column index number of 2 and returns the letter grade of B, which is located in the second column of the lookup table. The returned grade of B is then stored in cell F3, which contains the VLOOKUP function.

Instead of looking up values in a range, you can look up a value for an exact match using the optional range_lookup argument in the VLOOKUP function. By default, the range_lookup is set implicitly to TRUE, which is appropriate to look up values in a range. However, to look up an exact match, you must specify FALSE in the range_lookup argument. For example, if you are looking up product numbers, you must find an exact match to display the price. The function would look like this: =VLOOKUP(D15,$A$1:$B$50,2,FALSE). The VLOOKUP function returns a value for the first lookup value that matches the first column of the lookup table. If no exact match is found, the function returns #N/A.

Use the HLOOKUP Function

The **HLOOKUP function** looks up a value in a horizontal lookup table where the first row contains the values to compare with the lookup value.

You can design your lookup table horizontally, so that the first row contains the values for the basis of the lookup or the breakpoints, and additional rows contain data to be retrieved. With a horizontal lookup table, you must use the *HLOOKUP function*. Table 2.6 shows how the grading scale would look as a horizontal lookup table.

TABLE 2.6	Horizontal Lookup Table			
0	60	70	80	90
F	D	C	B	A

The syntax is almost the same as the syntax for the VLOOKUP function, except the third argument is row_index_number instead of col_index_number.

=HLOOKUP(lookup_value,table_array,row_index_number,[range_lookup])

Calculating Payments with the PMT Function

Excel contains several financial functions to help you perform calculations with monetary values. If you take out a loan to purchase a car, you need to know the monthly payment, which depends on the price of the car, the down payment, and the terms of the loan, in order to determine if you can afford the car. The decision is made easier by developing the worksheet in Figure 2.20 and then by changing the various input values as indicated.

	B9		f_x	=PMT(B6,B8,-B3)	
	A	B	C	D
1	Purchase Price	$25,999.00		
2	Down Payment	$ 5,000.00		
3	Amount to Finance	$20,999.00		
4	Payments per Year	12		
5	Interest Rate (APR)	5.250%		
6	Periodic Rate (Monthly)	0.438%		
7	Term (Years)	5		
8	No. of Payment Periods	60		
9	Monthly Payment	$ 398.69		
10				

FIGURE 2.20 Car Loan Worksheet ➤

Creating a loan model helps you evaluate your options. You realize that the purchase of a $25,999 car is prohibitive because the monthly payment is almost $398.69. Purchasing a less expensive car, coming up with a substantial down payment, taking out a longer term loan, or finding a better interest rate can decrease your monthly payments.

The **PMT function** calculates the periodic payment for a loan with a fixed interest rate and fixed term.

The ***PMT function*** calculates payments for a loan with a fixed amount at a fixed periodic rate for a fixed time period. The PMT function uses up to five arguments, three of which are required and two of which are optional: (1) rate, (2) nper, (3) pv, (4) fv, and (5) type.

=PMT(rate,nper,pv,[fv],[type])

The **rate** is the periodic interest rate, such as a monthly interest rate.

The ***rate*** is the periodic interest rate, the interest rate per payment period. If the annual percentage rate (APR) is 12% and you make monthly payments, the periodic rate is 1% (12%/12 months). With the same APR and quarterly payments, the periodic rate is 3% (12%/4 quarters). Divide the APR by the number of payment periods in one year. However, instead of dividing the APR by 12 within the PMT function, calculate the periodic interest rate in cell B6 in Figure 2.20 and use that calculated rate in the PMT function.

The **nper** is the number of total payment periods.

The ***nper*** is the total number of payment periods. The term of a loan is usually stated in years; however, you make several payments per year. For monthly payments, you make 12 payments per year. To calculate the nper, multiply the number of years by the number of payments in one year. Instead of calculating the number of payment periods in the PMT function, calculate the number of payment periods in cell B8 and use that calculated value in the PMT function.

The **pv** is the present value of the loan.

The ***pv*** is the present value of the loan. The result of the PMT function is a negative value because it represents your debt. However, you can display the result as a positive value by typing a minus sign in front of the present value cell reference in the PMT function.

HANDS-ON EXERCISES

my**it**lab
HOE3 Training

3 Logical, Lookup, and Financial Functions

Erica wants you to complete a similar model that she might use for future mortgage data analysis. As you study the model, you realize you need to incorporate logical, lookup, and financial functions.

Skills covered: Use the VLOOKUP Function • Use the PMT Function • Use the IF Function

---

STEP 1 ▶ USE THE VLOOKUP FUNCTION

Rates vary based on the number of years to pay off the loan. Erica created a lookup table for three common mortgage years, and she entered the current APR. The lookup table will provide efficiency later when the rates change. You will use the VLOOKUP function to display the correct rate for each customer based on the number of years of the respective loans. Refer to Figure 2.21 as you complete Step 1.

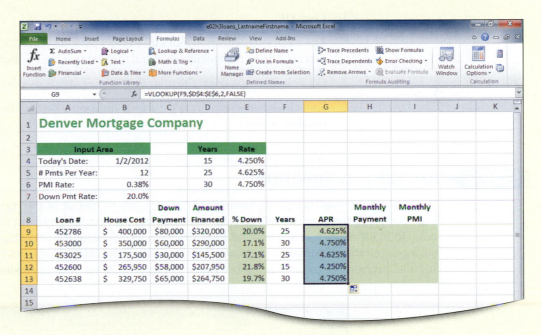

FIGURE 2.21 VLOOKUP Function ➤

a. Open *e02h2loans_LastnameFirstname* if you closed it at the end of Hands-On Exercise 2. Save the workbook with the new name **e02h3loans_LastnameFirstname**, changing *h2* to *h3*.

b. Click the **HO3-4 worksheet tab** to display the worksheet containing the data to complete. Click **cell G9**, the cell that will store the APR for the first customer.

c. Click the **Formulas tab**, click **Lookup & Reference** in the Function Library group, and then select **VLOOKUP**.

   The Function Arguments dialog box opens. You need to enter the three required and one optional argument.

d. Click **F9** to enter F9 in the **Lookup_value box**.

   Cell F9 contains the value you need to look up from the table: 25 years.

> **TROUBLESHOOTING:** If you cannot see the cell you need to use in an argument, click the Function Arguments dialog box title bar, and drag the dialog box on the screen until you can see and click the cell you need for the argument.

e. Press **Tab**, and then select the **range D4:E6** in the **Table_array box**.

This is the range that contains that data for the lookup table. The Years values in the table are arranged in ascending order (from lowest to highest). Do not select the column headings for the range. Anticipate what will happen if you copy the formula down the column. What do you need to do to ensure that the cell references always point to the exact location of the table? If your answer is to make the table array cell references absolute, then you answered correctly.

f. Press **F4** to make the range references absolute.

The Table_array box now contains $D$4:$E$6.

g. Press **Tab**, and then type **2** in the **Col_index_num box**.

The second column of the lookup table contains the APRs that you want to return and display in the cells containing the formulas.

h. Press **Tab**, and then type **False** in the **Range_lookup box**.

You want the formula to display an error if an incorrect number of years has been entered. To ensure an exact match to look up in the table, you enter *False* in the optional argument.

i. Click **OK**.

The VLOOKUP function looks up the first person's years (25), finds an exact match in the first column of the lookup table, and then returns the corresponding APR, which is 4.625%.

j. Copy the formula down the column, and then save the workbook.

Spot check the results to make sure the function returned the correct APR based on the number of years.

STEP 2 ▶ USE THE PMT FUNCTION

The worksheet now has all the necessary data for you to calculate the monthly payment for each loan: the APR, the number of years for the loan, the number of payment periods in one year, and the initial loan amount. You will use the PMT function to calculate the monthly payment, which includes paying back the principal amount with interest. This calculation does not include escrow amounts, such as property taxes or insurance. Refer to Figure 2.22 as you complete Step 2.

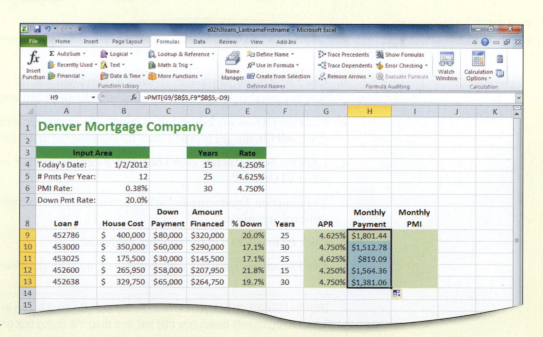

FIGURE 2.22 PMT Function ➤

a. Click **cell H9**, the cell that will store the payment for the first customer.

b. Click **Financial** in the Function Library group, scroll through the list, and then select **PMT**.

> **TROUBLESHOOTING:** Make sure you select PMT, not PPMT. The PPMT function calculates the principal portion of a particular monthly payment, not the total monthly payment itself.

The Function Arguments dialog box opens. You need to enter the three required arguments.

c. Type **G9/B5** in the **Rate box**.

Before going on to the next argument, think about what will happen if you copy the formula. The argument will be G10/B6 for the next customer. Are those cell references correct? G10 does contain the APR for the next customer, but B6 does not contain the correct number of payments in one year. Therefore, you need to make B5 an absolute cell reference because the number of payments per year does not vary.

d. Press **F4** to make the reference absolute.

e. Press **Tab**, and then type **F9*$B$5** in the **Nper box**.

You calculate the nper by multiplying the number of years by the number of payments in one year. Again, you must make B5 an absolute cell reference so that it does not change when you copy the formula down the column.

f. Press **Tab**, and then type **-D9** in the **Pv box**.

The bottom of the dialog box indicates that the monthly payment is 1801.444075 or $1,801.44.

> **TROUBLESHOOTING:** If the payment displays as a negative value, you probably forgot to type the minus sign in front of the D9 reference in the Pv box. Edit the function, and type the minus sign in the correct place.

g. Click **OK**. Copy the formula down the column, and then save the workbook.

STEP 3   USE THE IF FUNCTION

Lenders often want borrowers to have a 20% down payment. If borrowers do not put in 20% of the cost of the house as a down payment, they pay a private mortgage insurance (PMI) fee. PMI serves to protect lenders from absorbing loss if the borrower defaults on the loan, and it enables borrowers with less cash to secure a loan. The PMI fee is about 0.38% of the amount financed. Some borrowers have to pay PMI for a few months or years until the balance owed is less than 80% of the appraised value. The worksheet contains the necessary values input area. You need to use the IF function to determine which borrowers must pay PMI and how much they will pay. Refer to Figure 2.23 as you complete Step 3.

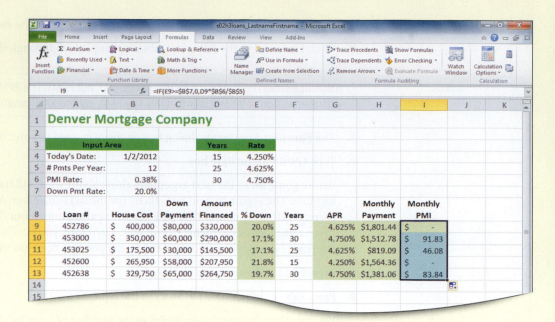

FIGURE 2.23 IF Function ➤

a. Click **cell I9**, the cell that will store the PMI, if any, for the first customer.

b. Click **Logical** in the Function Library group, and then select **IF**.

The Function Arguments dialog box opens. You need to enter the three arguments.

c. Type **E9>=$B$7** in the **Logical_test box**.

The logical test compares the down payment percentage to see if the customer's down payment is at least 20%, the threshold stored in B7, of the amount financed. The customer's percentage cell reference needs to be relative so that it will change when you copy it down the column; however, cell B7 must be absolute because it contains the threshold value.

d. Press **Tab**, and then type **0** in the **Value_if_true box**.

If the customer makes a down payment that is at least 20% of the purchase price, the customer does not pay PMI. The first customer paid 20% of the purchase price, so he or she does not have to pay PMI.

e. Press **Tab**, and then type **D9*$B$6/$B$5** in the **Value_if_false box**.

If the logical test is false, the customer must pay PMI, which is calculated by dividing the yearly PMI (0.38%) by 12 and multiplying the result by the amount financed.

f. Click **OK**, and then copy the formula down the column.

The second, third, and fifth customers must pay PMI because their respective down payments were less than 20% of the purchase price.

> **TROUBLESHOOTING:** If the results are not as you expected, check the logical operators. People often mistype < and > or forget to type = for >= situations. Correct any errors in the original formula, and then copy the formula again.

g. Save the workbook. Keep the workbook onscreen if you plan to continue with Hands-On Exercise 4. If not, close the workbook and exit Excel.

Range Names

A **range name** is a word or string of characters that represents one or more cells.

To simplify entering ranges in formulas, you can use range names. A *range name* is a word or string of characters assigned to one or more cells. Think of range names in this way: Your college identifies you by your student ID; however, your professors call you by an easy-to-remember name, such as Micah or Kristin. Similarly, instead of using cell addresses, you can use descriptive range names in formulas. Going back to the VLOOKUP example shown in Figure 2.19, you can assign the range name *Grades* to cells A3:B7 and then modify the VLOOKUP function to be =VLOOKUP(E3,Grades,2), using the range name *Grades* in the formula. Another benefit of using range names is that they are absolute references, which helps ensure accuracy in your calculations.

In this section, you will work with range names. First, you will learn how to create and maintain range names. Then you will learn how to use a range name in a formula.

Creating and Maintaining Range Names

Before you can use a range name in a formula, you must first create the name. Each range name within a workbook must be unique. For example, you can't assign the name *COST* to ranges on several worksheets or on the same sheet.

After you create a range name, you might need to change its name or change the range of cells. If you no longer need a range name, you can delete it. You can also insert a list of range names and their respective cell ranges for reference.

Create a Range Name

A range name can contain up to 255 characters, but it must begin with a letter or an underscore. You can use a combination of upper- or lowercase letters, numbers, periods, and underscores throughout the range name. A range name cannot include spaces or special characters. You should create range names that describe the range of cells being named, but names cannot be identical to the cell contents. Keep the range names relatively short to make them easier to use in formulas. Table 2.7 lists acceptable and unacceptable range names.

TABLE 2.7	Range Names
Name	**Description**
Grades	Acceptable range name
COL	Acceptable abbreviation for cost-of-living
Tax_Rate	Acceptable name with underscore
Commission Rate	Unacceptable name; can't use spaces in names
Discount Rate %	Unacceptable name; can't use special symbols and spaces
2009_Rate	Unacceptable name; can't start with a number
Rate_2012	Acceptable name with underscore and numbers

To create a range name, select the range of cells you want to name, and do one of the following:

- Click in the Name Box, type the range name, and then press Enter.
- Click the Formulas tab, click Define Name in the Defined Names group to open the New Name dialog box (see Figure 2.24), type the range name in the Name box, and then click OK.
- Click the Formulas tab, click Name Manager in the Defined Names group to open the Name Manager dialog box, click New, type the range name in the Name box, click OK, and then click Close.

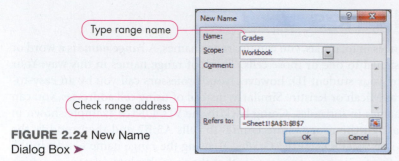

Type range name

Check range address

FIGURE 2.24 New Name
Dialog Box ➤

You can create several range names at the same time if your worksheet already includes ranges with values and descriptive labels. To do this, select the range of cells containing the labels that you want to become names and the cells that contain the values to name, click Create from Selection in the Defined Named group on the Formulas tab, and then select an option in the Create Names from Selection dialog box (see Figure 2.25).

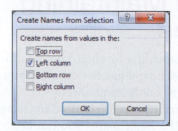

FIGURE 2.25 Create Names
from Selection Dialog Box ➤

Edit or Delete a Range Name

You can use the Name Manager dialog box to edit existing range names, delete range names, and create new range names. To open the Name Manager dialog box shown in Figure 2.26, click Name Manager in the Defined Names group on the Formulas tab. To edit a range or range name, click the range name in the list, and then click Edit. In the Edit Name dialog box, make your edits, and then click OK.

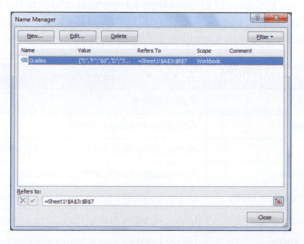

FIGURE 2.26 Name Manager
Dialog Box ➤

To delete a range name, open the Name Manager dialog box, select the name you want to delete, click Delete, and then click OK in the confirmation message box.

If you change a range name, any formulas that use the range name reflect the new name automatically. For example, if a formula contains =cost*rate and you change the name rate to tax_rate, Excel updates the formula to be =cost*tax_rate. If you delete a range name and a formula depends on that range name, Excel displays #NAME?—indicating an Invalid Name Error.

Insert a Table of Range Names

Documentation is an important part of good spreadsheet design. People often document workbooks with date or time stamps that indicate the last date of revision, notes describing how to use a workbook, and so on. One way to document a workbook is to insert a list of range names in a worksheet. To insert a list of range names, click *Use in Formula* in the Defined Names group on the Formulas tab, and then select Paste Names. The Paste Name dialog box opens (see Figure 2.27), listing all range names in the current workbook. Click Paste List to insert a list of range names in alphabetical order. The first column contains a list of range names, and the second column contains the worksheet names and range locations.

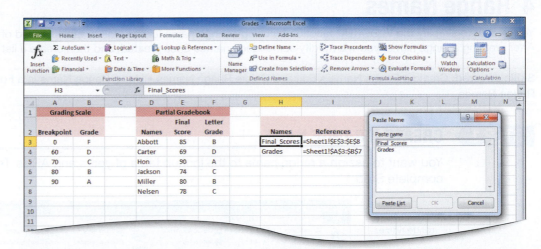

FIGURE 2.27 Paste Name Dialog Box and List of Range Names ➤

TIP List of Range Names

When you paste range names, the list will overwrite any existing data in a worksheet, so consider pasting the list in a separate worksheet. If you add, edit, or delete range names, the list does not update automatically. To keep the list current, you would need to paste the list again.

Using Range Names in Formulas

You can use range names in formulas instead of cell references. For example, if cell C15 contains a purchase amount, and cell C5 contains the sales tax rate, instead of typing =C15*C5, you can type the range names in the formula, such as =purchase*tax_rate. When you type a formula, Formula AutoComplete displays a list of range names, as well as functions, that start with the letters as you type (see Figure 2.28). Double-click the range name to insert it in the formula.

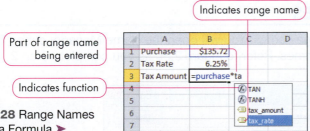

FIGURE 2.28 Range Names Inserted in a Formula ➤

Another benefit of using range names is that if you have to copy the formula, you do not have to make the cell reference absolute in the formula. Furthermore, if you share your workbook with others, range names in formulas help others understand what values are used in the calculations.

TIP Go to a Range Name

Use the Go To dialog box to go to the top-left cell in a range specified by a range name.

HANDS-ON EXERCISES

myitlab
HOE4 Training

4 Range Names

You decide to simplify the VLOOKUP function by using a range name for the lookup table instead of the actual cell references. After creating a range name, you will modify some range names Erica created, and then create a list of range names.

Skills covered: Create a Range Name • Edit and Delete Range Names • Use a Range Name in a Formula • Insert a List of Range Names

---

STEP 1 ▸ CREATE A RANGE NAME

You want to assign a range name to the lookup table of years and APRs. Refer to Figure 2.29 as you complete Step 1.

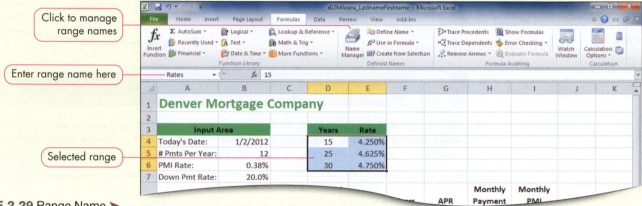

FIGURE 2.29 Range Name ➤

a. Open *e02h3loans_LastnameFirstname* if you closed it at the end of Hands-On Exercise 3. Save the workbook with the new name **e02h4loans_LastnameFirstname**, changing *h3* to *h4*.

b. Make sure the **HO3-4 worksheet tab** is active. Select **range D4:E6** (the lookup table).

c. Type **Rates** in the **Name Box**, and then press **Enter**. Save the workbook.

STEP 2 ▸ EDIT AND DELETE RANGE NAMES

You noticed that Erica added some range names. You will open the Name Manager dialog box to view and make changes to the range names. Refer to Figure 2.30 as you complete Step 2.

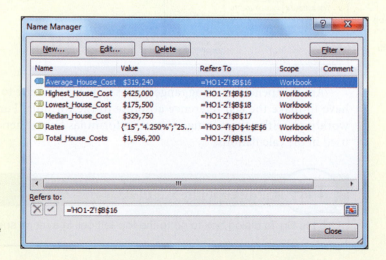

FIGURE 2.30 Updated Range Names ➤

a. Click **Name Manager** in the Defined Names group.

The Name Manager dialog box opens. The first name is *Avg_Cost*. You want to rename it to have a naming structure consistent with the other Cost names, such as Total_House_Costs.

b. Select **Avg_Cost**, and then click **Edit** to open the Edit Name dialog box.

c. Type **Average_House_Cost** in the **Name box**, and then click **OK**.

d. Select **Title** in the Name Manager dialog box.

This range name applies to a cell containing text, which does not need a name as it cannot be used in calculations. You decide to delete the range name.

e. Click **Delete**, read the warning message box, and then click **OK** to confirm the deletion of the Title range name.

f. Click **Close**, and then save the workbook.

STEP 3 ▶ USE A RANGE NAME IN A FORMULA

You will the VLOOKUP function by replacing the existing Table_array argument with the range name. This will help Erica interpret the VLOOKUP function. Refer to Figure 2.31 as you complete Step 3.

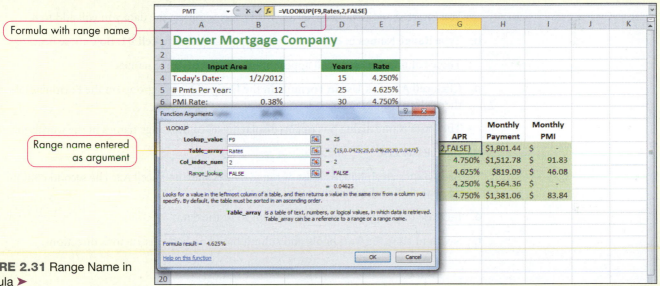

FIGURE 2.31 Range Name in Formula ➤

a. Click **cell G9**, the cell containing the VLOOKUP function.

b. Click **Insert Function** between the Name Box and the Formula Bar to open the Function Arguments dialog box.

The Table_array argument contains $D$4:$E$6, the absolute reference to the lookup table.

c. Select **$D$4:$E$6** in the **Table_array box**, type **Rates**, and then click **OK**.

The new function is =VLOOKUP(F9,Rates,2,FALSE).

d. Copy the updated formula down the column, and then save the workbook.

The results are the same as they were when you used the absolute cell references. However, the formulas are shorter and easier to read with the range names.

Before submitting the completed workbook to Erica, you want to create a documentation worksheet that lists all of the range names in the workbook. Refer to Figure 2.32 as you complete Step 4.

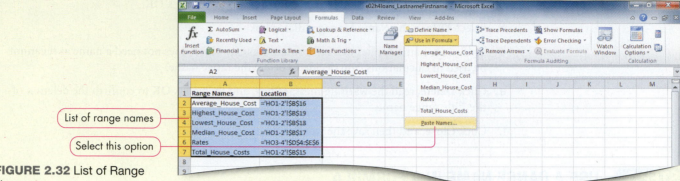

List of range names

Select this option

FIGURE 2.32 List of Range Names ▶

a. Click **Insert Worksheet** to the right of the worksheet tabs, and then double-click the default sheet name, **Sheet1**. Type **Range Names** and press **Enter**.

   You inserted and renamed the new worksheet to reflect the data you will add to it.

b. Type **Range Names** in **cell A1**, and then type **Location** in **cell B1**. Bold these headings.

   These column headings will appear above the list of range names.

c. Click **cell A2**, click **Use in Formula** in the Defined Names group on the Formulas tab, and then select **Paste Names**.

   The Paste Name dialog box opens, displaying all of the range names in the workbook.

d. Click **Paste List**.

   Excel pastes an alphabetical list of range names starting in cell A2. The second column displays the locations of the range names.

e. Increase the widths of columns A and B to fit the data.

f. Save and close the workbook, and submit based on your instructor's directions.

CHAPTER OBJECTIVES REVIEW

After reading this chapter, you have accomplished the following objectives:

1. **Use semi-selection to create a formula.** Semi-selection is a pointing process where you click or drag to select cells to add cell references to a formula.

2. **Use relative, absolute, and mixed cell references in formulas.** Cell references within formulas are relative, absolute, or mixed. A relative reference indicates a cell's location relative to the formula cell. When you copy the formula, the relative cell reference changes. An absolute reference is a permanent pointer to a particular cell, indicated with dollar signs before the column letter and row number, such as $B$5. When you copy the formula, the absolute cell reference does not change. A mixed reference contains part absolute and part relative reference, such as $B5 or B$5. Depending on the type of relative reference, either the column or row reference changes while the other remains constant when you copy the formula.

3. **Avoid circular references.** A circular reference occurs when a formula refers to the cell containing the formula. The status bar indicates the location of a circular reference. You should correct circular references to prevent inaccurate results.

4. **Insert a function.** A function is a predefined formula that performs a calculation. It contains the function name and arguments. Formula AutoComplete, function ScreenTips, and the Insert Function dialog box help you select and create functions. The Function Arguments dialog box guides you through entering requirements for each argument.

5. **Total values with the SUM function.** The SUM function calculates the total of a range of values. The syntax is =SUM(number1,[number2],…) where the arguments are cell references to one or more ranges.

6. **Insert basic statistical functions.** The AVERAGE function calculates the arithmetic mean of values in a range. The MEDIAN function identifies the midpoint value in a set of values. The MIN function identifies the lowest value in a range, whereas the MAX function identifies the highest value in a range. The COUNT function tallies the number of cells in a range, whereas the COUNTBLANK function tallies the number of blank cells in a range. Excel contains other math and statistical functions, such as FREQUENCY and MODE.

7. **Use date functions.** The TODAY function displays the current date, and the NOW function displays the current date and time. Other date functions identify a particular day of the week, identify the number of net working days between two dates, and display a serial number representing a date.

8. **Determine results with the IF function.** The IF function is a logical function that evaluates a logical test using logical operators, such as <, >, and =, and returns one value if the condition is true and another value if the condition is false. The value_if_true and value_if_false arguments can contain cell references, text, or calculations. You can nest or embed other functions inside one or more of the arguments of an IF function to create more complex formulas.

9. **Use lookup functions.** The VLOOKUP function looks up a value for a particular record, compares it to a lookup table, and returns a result in another column of the lookup table. Design the lookup table using exact values or the breakpoints for ranges. If an exact match is required, the optional fourth argument should be FALSE; otherwise, the fourth argument can remain empty. The HLOOKUP function looks up values by row (horizontally) rather than by column (vertically).

10. **Calculate payments with the PMT function.** The PMT function calculates periodic payments for a loan with a fixed interest rate and a fixed term. The PMT function requires the periodic interest rate, the total number of payment periods, and the original value of the loan. You can use the PMT function to calculate monthly car or mortgage payments.

11. **Create and maintain range names.** A range name is a descriptive name that corresponds with one or more cells. A range name may contain letters, numbers, and underscores, but must start with either a letter or an underscore. The quick way to create a range name is to select the range, type the name in the Name Box, and then press Enter. Use the Name Manager dialog box to edit, create, or delete range names. You can insert a list of range names on a worksheet.

12. **Use range names in formulas.** You can use range names in formulas instead of cell references. Range names are absolute and can make your formula easier to interpret by using a descriptive name for the value(s) contained in a cell or range.

KEY TERMS

MULTIPLE CHOICE

1. If cell D15 contains the formula =$C$5*D15, what is the D15 in the formula?

   (a) Mixed reference
   (b) Absolute reference
   (c) Circular reference
   (d) Range name

2. What function would most appropriately accomplish the same thing as =(B5+C5+D5+E5+F5)/5?

   (a) =SUM(B5:F5)/5
   (b) =AVERAGE(B5:F5)
   (c) =MEDIAN(B5:F5)
   (d) =COUNT(B5:F5)

3. When you type a function, what appears after you type the opening parenthesis?

   (a) Function ScreenTip
   (b) Formula AutoComplete
   (c) Insert Function dialog box
   (d) Function Arguments dialog box

4. A formula containing the entry =$B3 is copied to a cell one column to the right and two rows down. How will the entry appear in its new location?

   (a) =$B3
   (b) =B3
   (c) =$C5
   (d) =$B5

5. Cell B10 contains a date, such as 1/1/2012. Which formula will determine how many days are between that date and the current date, given that the cell containing the formula is formatted with Number Format?

   (a) =TODAY()
   (b) =CURRENT()-B10
   (c) =TODAY()-B10
   (d) =TODAY()+NOW()

6. Given that cells A1, A2, and A3 contain values 2, 3, and 10, respectively, and B6, C6, and D6 contain values 10, 20, and 30, respectively, what value will be returned by the function =IF(B6>A3,C6*A1,D6*A2)?

   (a) 10
   (b) 40
   (c) 60
   (d) 90

7. Given the function =VLOOKUP(C6,D12:F18,3), the entries in:

   (a) Range D12:D18 are in ascending order.
   (b) Range D12:D18 are in descending order.
   (c) The third column of the lookup table must be text only.
   (d) Range D12:D18 contain multiple values in each cell.

8. The function =PMT(C5,C7,-C3) is stored in cell C15. What must be stored in cell C7?

   (a) APR
   (b) Periodic interest rate
   (c) Loan amount
   (d) Number of payment periods

9. Which of the following is not an appropriate use of the SUM function?

   (a) =SUM(D15-C15)
   (b) =SUM(F1:G10)
   (c) =SUM(A8:A15,D8:D15)
   (d) =SUM(B3:B45)

10. Which of the following is not an acceptable range name?

    (a) FICA
    (b) Test_Weight
    (c) Goal for 2012
    (d) Target_2012

PRACTICE EXERCISES

1 Blue Skies Airlines

You are an analyst for Blue Skies Airlines, a regional airline headquartered in Kansas City. Blue Skies has up to 10 departures a day from the Kansas City Airport. Your assistant developed a template for you to store daily flight data about the number of passengers per flight. Each regional aircraft can hold up to 70 passengers. You need to calculate the occupancy rate, which is the percent of each flight that is occupied. In addition, you need daily statistics, such as total number of passengers, averages, least full flights, and so forth, so that decisions can be made for future flight departures out of Kansas City. You also want to calculate weekly statistics per flight number. This exercise follows the same set of skills as used in Hands-On Exercises 1 and 2 in the chapter. Refer to Figure 2.33 as you complete this exercise.

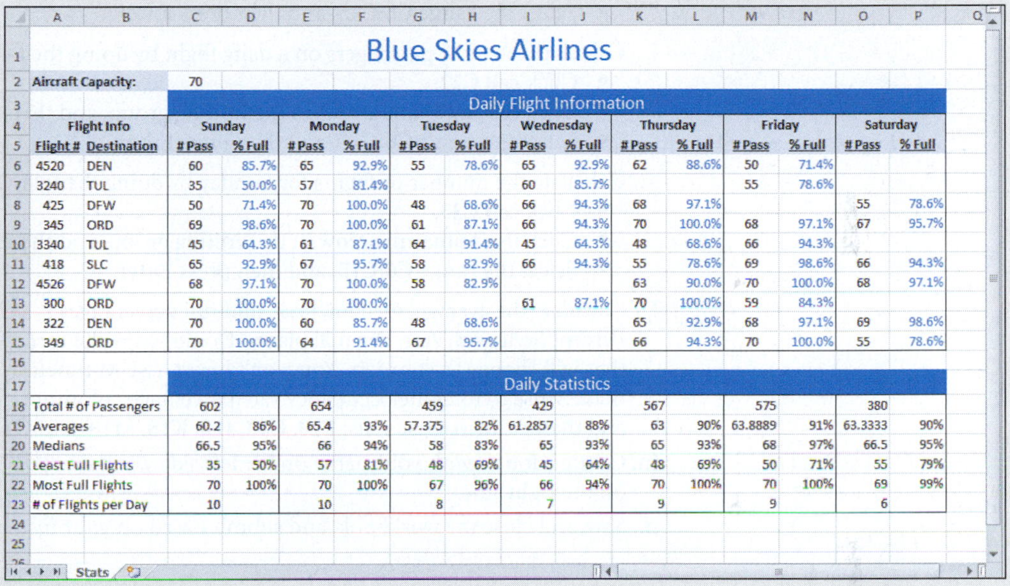

Blue Skies Airlines

Aircraft Capacity:		70													
		Daily Flight Information													
Flight Info		Sunday		Monday		Tuesday		Wednesday		Thursday		Friday		Saturday	
Flight #	Destination	# Pass	% Full	# Pass	% Full	# Pass	% Full	# Pass	% Full	# Pass	% Full	# Pass	% Full	# Pass	% Full
4520	DEN	60	85.7%	65	92.9%	55	78.6%	65	92.9%	62	88.6%	50	71.4%		
3240	TUL	35	50.0%	57	81.4%			60	85.7%			55	78.6%		
425	DFW	50	71.4%	70	100.0%	48	68.6%	66	94.3%	68	97.1%			55	78.6%
345	ORD	69	98.6%	70	100.0%	61	87.1%	66	94.3%	70	100.0%	68	97.1%	67	95.7%
3340	TUL	45	64.3%	61	87.1%	64	91.4%	45	64.3%	48	68.6%	66	94.3%		
418	SLC	65	92.9%	67	95.7%	58	82.9%	66	94.3%	55	78.6%	69	98.6%	66	94.3%
4526	DFW	68	97.1%	70	100.0%	58	82.9%			63	90.0%	70	100.0%	68	97.1%
300	ORD	70	100.0%	70	100.0%			61	87.1%	70	100.0%	59	84.3%		
322	DEN	70	100.0%	60	85.7%	48	68.6%			65	92.9%	68	97.1%	69	98.6%
349	ORD	70	100.0%	64	91.4%	67	95.7%			66	94.3%	70	100.0%	55	78.6%
		Daily Statistics													
Total # of Passengers		602		654		459		429		567		575		380	
Averages		60.2	86%	65.4	93%	57.375	82%	61.2857	88%	63	90%	63.8889	91%	63.3333	90%
Medians		66.5	95%	66	94%	58	83%	65	93%	65	93%	68	97%	66.5	95%
Least Full Flights		35	50%	57	81%	48	69%	45	64%	48	69%	50	71%	55	79%
Most Full Flights		70	100%	70	100%	67	96%	66	94%	70	100%	70	100%	69	99%
# of Flights per Day		10		10		8		7		9		9		6	

Stats

FIGURE 2.33 Blue Skies Airlines ➤

a. Open *e02p1flights* and save it as **e02p1flights_LastnameFirstname**.

b. Click **cell D6**, the cell to display the occupancy percent for Flight 4520 on Sunday, and do the following:
   - Type = and click **cell C6**. Type / and click **cell C2**.
   - Press **F4** to make cell C2 absolute.
   - Click **Enter** to the left of the Formula Bar. The occupancy rate of Flight 4520 is 85.7%.
   - Double-click the **cell D6 fill handle** to copy the formula down the column.

c. Click **cell D7** and notice that the bottom border disappears from cell D15. When you copy a formula, Excel also copies the original cell's format. The cell containing the original formula did not have a bottom border, so when you copied the formula down the column, Excel formatted it to match the original cell with no border. To reapply the border, click **cell D15**, click the **Border arrow** in the Font group on the Home tab, and then select **Bottom Border**.

d. Select the **range D6:D15**, copy it to the Clipboard, and paste it starting in **cell F6**. Notice the formula in cell F6 changes to = E6/$C$2. The first cell reference changes from C6 to E6, maintaining its relative location from the pasted formula. $C$2 remains absolute so that the number of passengers per flight is always divided by the value stored in cell C2. The copied range is still in the Clipboard. Paste the formula into the remaining % Full columns (columns H, J, L, N, and P). Press **Esc** to turn off the marquee around the original copied range.

e. Clean up the data by deleting *0.0%* in cells, such as H7. The 0.0% is misleading as it implies the flight was empty; however, some flights do not operate on all days. Check your worksheet against the *Daily Flight Information* section in Figure 2.33.

f. Calculate the total number of passengers per day by doing the following:
    - Click **cell C18**.
    - Click **AutoSum** in the Editing group.
    - Select the **range C6:C15**, and then press **Enter**.

g. Calculate the average number of passengers per day by doing the following:
    - Click **cell C19**.
    - Click the **AutoSum arrow** in the Editing group, and then select **Average**.
    - Select the **range C6:C15**, and then click **Enter** to the left of the Formula Bar.

h. Calculate the median number of passengers per day by doing the following:
    - Click **cell C20**.
    - Click **Insert Function** to the left of the Formula Bar, type **median** in the **Search for a function box**, and then click **Go**.
    - Click **MEDIAN** in the **Select a function box**, and then click **OK**.
    - Select the **range C6:C15** to enter it in the **Number1 box**, and then click **OK**.

i. Calculate the least number of passengers on a daily flight by doing the following:
    - Click **cell C21**.
    - Click the **AutoSum arrow** in the Editing group, and then select **Min**.
    - Select the **range C6:C15**, and then press **Enter**.

j. Calculate the most passengers on a daily flight by doing the following:
    - Click **cell C22**.
    - Click the **AutoSum arrow** in the Editing group, and then select **Max**.
    - Select the **range C6:C15**, and then press **Enter**.

k. Calculate the number of flights for Sunday by doing the following:
    - Click **cell C23**.
    - Click the **AutoSum arrow** in the Editing group, and then select **Count Numbers**.
    - Select the **range C6:C15**, and then press **Enter**.

l. Calculate the average, median, least, and full percentages in **cells D19:D22**. Format the values with Percent Style with zero decimal places. Do not copy the formulas from column C to column D, as that will change the borders. You won't insert a SUM function in cell D18 because it does not make sense to total the occupancy rate percentage column. Select **cells C18:D23**, copy the range, and then paste in these cells: **E18**, **G18**, **I18**, **K18**, **M18**, and **O18**. Press **Esc** after pasting.

m. Create a footer with your name on the left side, the date code in the center, and the file name code on the right side.

n. Save and close the workbook, and submit based on your instructor's directions.

2 Central Nevada College Salaries

You work in the Human Resources Department at Central Nevada College. You are preparing a spreadsheet model to calculate bonuses based on performance ratings, where ratings between 1 and 1.9 do not receive bonuses, ratings between 2 and 2.9 earn $100 bonuses, ratings between 3 and 3.9 earn $250 bonuses, ratings between 4 and 4.9 earn $500 bonuses, and ratings of 5 or higher earn $1,000 bonuses. In addition, you need to calculate annual raises based on years employed. Employees who have worked five or more years earn a 3.25% raise; employees who have not worked at least five years earn a 2% raise. The partially completed worksheet does not yet contain range names. This exercise follows the same set of skills as used in Hands-On Exercises 1, 2, 3, and 4 in the chapter. Refer to Figure 2.34 as you complete this exercise.

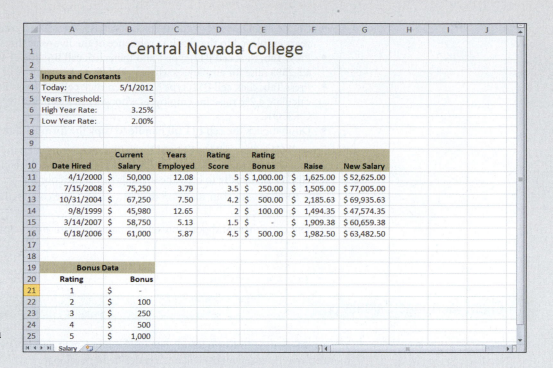

	A	B	C	D	E	F	G	H	I	J
1			Central Nevada College							
2										
3	**Inputs and Constants**									
4	Today:	5/1/2012								
5	Years Threshold:	5								
6	High Year Rate:	3.25%								
7	Low Year Rate:	2.00%								
8										
9										
10	Date Hired	Current Salary	Years Employed	Rating Score	Rating Bonus	Raise	New Salary			
11	4/1/2000	$ 50,000	12.08	5	$ 1,000.00	$ 1,625.00	$ 52,625.00			
12	7/15/2008	$ 75,250	3.79	3.5	$ 250.00	$ 1,505.00	$ 77,005.00			
13	10/31/2004	$ 67,250	7.50	4.2	$ 500.00	$ 2,185.63	$ 69,935.63			
14	9/8/1999	$ 45,980	12.65	2	$ 100.00	$ 1,494.35	$ 47,574.35			
15	3/14/2007	$ 58,750	5.13	1.5	$ -	$ 1,909.38	$ 60,659.38			
16	6/18/2006	$ 61,000	5.87	4.5	$ 500.00	$ 1,982.50	$ 63,482.50			
17										
18										
19		**Bonus Data**								
20	Rating	Bonus								
21	1	$ -								
22	2	$ 100								
23	3	$ 250								
24	4	$ 500								
25	5	$ 1,000								

Salary

FIGURE 2.34 Central Nevada College Salaries ➤

a. Open *e02p2salary* and save it as **e02p2salary_LastnameFirstname**.

b. Click **cell B4**, click the **Formulas tab**, click **Date & Time** in the Function Library, select **TODAY**, and then click **OK** to enter today's date in the cell.

c. Enter a formula to calculate the number of years employed by doing the following:
   • Click **cell C11**.
   • Click **Date & Time** in the Function Library group, scroll through the list, and then select **YEARFRAC**.
   • Click **cell A11** to enter the cell reference in the **Start_date box**.
   • Press **Tab**, and then click **cell B4** to enter the cell reference in the **End_date box**.
   • Ask yourself if the cell references should be relative or absolute. You should answer *relative* for **cell A11** so that it will change as you copy it for the other employees. You should answer *absolute* or *mixed* for **cell B4** so that it always refers to the cell containing the TODAY function as you copy the formula.
   • Press **F4** to make **cell B4** absolute, and then click **OK**. (Although you could have used the formula =($B$4-A11)/365 to calculate the number of years, the YEARFRAC function provides better accuracy since it accounts for leap years and the divisor 365 does not.
   • Double-click the **cell C11 fill handle** to copy the YEARFRAC function down the Years Employed column. Your results will differ based on the date contained in cell B4.

d. Enter the breakpoint and bonus data for the lookup table by doing the following:
   • Click **cell A21**, type **1**, and then press **Ctrl+Enter**.
   • Click the **Home tab**, click **Fill** in the Editing group, and then select **Series**. Click **Columns** in the *Series in* section, leave the Step value at **1**, type **5** in the **Stop value box**, and then click **OK**.
   • Click **cell B21**. Enter **0, 100, 250, 500**, and **1000** down the column. The cells have been previously formatted with Accounting Number Format with zero decimal places.
   • Select **range A21:B25**, click in the **Name Box**, type **Bonus**, and then press **Enter** to name the range.

e. Enter the bonus based on rating by doing the following:
   • Click **cell E11**, and then click the **Formulas tab**.
   • Click **Lookup & Reference** in the Function Library group, and then select **VLOOKUP**.
   • Click **cell D11** to enter the cell reference in the **Lookup_value box**.
   • Press **Tab**, and then type **Bonus** to enter the range name for the lookup table in the **Table_array box**.
   • Press **Tab**, type **2** to represent the second column in the lookup table, and then click **OK**.
   • Double-click the **cell E11 fill handle** to copy the formula down the Rating Bonus column.

f. Enter the raise based on years employed by doing the following:
   • Click **cell F11**.
   • Click **Logical** in the Function Library group, and then select **IF**.

- Click **cell C11**, type >= and then click **cell B5**. Press **F4** to enter C11>=$B$5 to compare the years employed to the absolute reference of the five-year threshold in the **Logical_test box**.
- Press **Tab**, click **cell B11**, type * and then click **cell B6**. Press **F4** to enter B11*$B$6 to calculate a 3.25% raise for employees who worked five years or more in the **Value_if_true box**.
- Press **Tab**, click **cell B11**, type * and then click **cell B7**. Press **F4** to enter B11*$B$7 to calculate a 2% raise for employees who worked less than five years in the **Value_if_false box**. Click **OK**.
- Double-click the **cell F11 fill handle** to copy the formula down the Raise column.

g. Click **cell G11**. Type =B11+E11+F11 to add the current salary, the bonus, and the raise to calculate the new salary. Press **Ctrl+Enter** to keep **cell G11** the active cell, and then double-click the **cell G11 fill handle** to copy the formula down the column.

h. Create a footer with your name on the left side, the date code in the center, and the file name code on the right side.

i. Save and close the workbook, and submit based on your instructor's directions.

3 Client Mortgage Calculator

You are an agent with Koyle Real Estate in Bowling Green, Ohio. Customers often ask you what their monthly mortgage payments will be. You decide to develop an Excel template you can use to enter the house cost, current APR, yearly property tax, and estimated yearly property insurance. Borrowers who want the lowest interest rates make a 20% down payment. You will assign range names and use them in the formulas. This exercise follows the same set of skills as used in Hands-On Exercises 2, 3, and 4 in the chapter. Refer to Figure 2.35 as you complete this exercise.

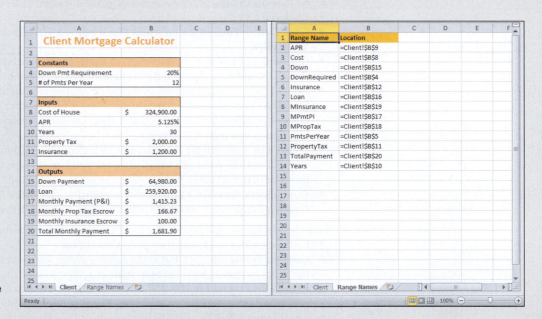

FIGURE 2.35 Client Mortgage Calculator ➤

a. Open *e02p3client* and save it as **e02p3client_LastnameFirstname**.

b. Create a range name for the down payment requirement by doing the following: Click **cell B4**, click in the **Name Box**, type **DownRequired**, and then press **Enter**. The number of payments per year value has already been assigned the range name PmtsPerYear.

c. Name the input values by doing the following:
- Select **range A8:B12**.
- Click the **Formulas tab**, and then click **Create from Selection** in the Defined Names group.
- Make sure *Left column* is selected, and then click **OK**.
- Click each input value cell in **range B8:B12** and look at the newly created names in the Name Box.

d. Edit the range names by doing the following:
- Click **Name Manager** in the Defined Names group.
- Click **Cost_of_House**, click **Edit**, type **Cost**, and then click **OK**.
- Change *Property_Tax* to **PropertyTax**.
- Click **CONSTANTS** in the list, click **Delete**, and then click **OK** to delete it.
- Close the Name Manager.

e. Name the output values using the Create from Selection method you used in step c. Then edit the range names using the same approach you used in step d.
- Change *Down_Payment* to **Down**.
- Change *Monthly_Payment__P_I* to **MPmtPI**.
- Change *Monthly_Property_Tax_Escrow* to **MPropTax**.
- Change *Monthly_Insurance_Escrow* to **MInsurance**.
- Change *Total_Monthly_Payment* to **TotalPayment**.

f. Enter the first two formulas with range names in the Outputs area by doing the following:
- Click **cell B15**. Type **=Cost*down** and double-click **DownRequired** from the **Formula AutoComplete list**. If the list does not appear, type the entire name **DownRequired**. Then press **Enter** to enter the formula =Cost*DownRequired.
- Click **cell B16**. Type **=cost-down** and press **Enter**.

g. Enter the PMT function to calculate the monthly payment of principal and interest by doing the following:
- Click **cell B17**. Click **Financial** in the Function Library group, scroll down, and then select **PMT**.
- Click **cell B9**, type **/** and then click **cell B5** to enter APR/PmtsPerYear in the **Rate box**.
- Press **Tab**, click **cell B10**, type ***** and then click **cell B5** to enter Years*PmtsPerYear in the **Nper box**.
- Press **Tab**, type **-loan** in the **Pv box**, and then click **OK**.

h. Enter the monthly property tax formula by doing the following:
- Click **cell B18**. Type **=** to start the formula.
- Click **Use in Formula** in the Defined Names group, and select **PropertyTax**.
- Type **/** and click **Use in Formula** in the Defined Names group. Select **PmtsPerYear**, and then press **Enter**.

i. Adapt step h to enter the formula =Insurance/PmtsPerYear in **cell B19**.

j. Enter **=SUM(B17:B19)** in **cell B20**.

k. Select **range B15:B20**, and then apply **Accounting Number Format**.

l. Click the **Range Names worksheet tab**, click **cell A2**, click the **Formulas tab**, click **Use in Formula** in the Defined Names group, select **Paste Names**, and then click **Paste List** to paste an alphabetical list of range names in the worksheet. Adjust the column widths.

m. Create a footer with your name on the left side, the date code in the center, and the file name code on the right side for both worksheets.

n. Save and close the workbook, and submit based on your instructor's directions.

1 Sunrise Credit Union Weekly Payroll

As manager of the Sunrise Credit Union, you are responsible for managing the weekly payroll. Your assistant developed a partial worksheet, but you need to enter the formulas to calculate the regular pay, overtime pay, gross pay, taxable pay, withholding tax, FICA, and net pay. In addition, you want to total pay columns and calculate some basic statistics. As you construct formulas, make sure you use absolute and relative cell references correctly in formulas and avoid circular references.

a. Open the *e02m1payroll* workbook and save it as **e02m1payroll_LastnameFirstname**.

b. Study the worksheet structure, and then read the business rules in the Notes section.

c. Use IF functions to calculate the regular pay and overtime pay based on a regular 40-hour workweek. Pay overtime only for overtime hours. Calculate the gross pay based on the regular and overtime pay. Abram's regular pay is $398. With eight overtime hours, Abram's overtime pay is $119.40.

d. Create a formula to calculate the taxable pay. With two dependents, Abram's taxable pay is $417.40.

e. Use the appropriate function to identify and calculate the federal withholding tax. With a taxable pay of $417.40, Abram's tax rate is 25%, and the withholding tax is $104.35.

f. Calculate FICA based on gross pay and the FICA rate, and then calculate the net pay.

g. Calculate the total regular pay, overtime pay, gross pay, taxable pay, withholding tax, FICA, and net pay.

h. Copy all formulas down their respective columns.

i. Apply **Accounting Number Format** to the **range C5:C16**. Apply **Accounting Number Format** to the first row of monetary data and to the total row. Apply **Comma Style** to the monetary values for the other employees. Underline the last employee's monetary values, and then use the Format Cells dialog box to apply **Double Accounting Underline** for the totals.

j. Insert appropriate functions to calculate the average, highest, and lowest values in the Summary Statistics area of the worksheet.

DISCOVER

k. At your instructor's discretion, use Help to learn about the FREQUENCY function. The Help feature contains sample data for you to copy and practice in a new worksheet to learn about this function. You can close the practice worksheet containing the Help data without saving it. You want to determine the number (frequency) of employees who worked less than 20 hours, between 20 and 29 hours, between 30 and 40 hours, and over 40 hours. **Cells J28:J31** list the ranges. You need to translate this range into correct values for the Bin column in **cells I28:I30** and then enter the FREQUENCY function in **cells K28:K31**. The function should identify one employee who worked between 0 and 19 hours and six employees who worked more than 40 hours.

l. Apply other page setup formats as needed.

m. Insert a footer with your name on the left side, the date code in the center, and the file name code on the right side.

n. Save and close the workbook, and submit based on your instructor's directions.

2 First Bank of Missouri

As a loan officer at First Bank of Missouri, you track house loans. You started a spreadsheet that contains client names, the selling price of houses, and the term of the loans. You are ready to calculate the interest rate, which is based on the term. In addition, you need to calculate the required down payment, the amount to be financed, and the monthly payment for each customer. To keep your formulas easy to read, you will create and use range names. Finally, you need to calculate some basic statistics.

a. Open the *e02m2bank* workbook and save it as **e02m2bank_LastnameFirstname**.

b. Enter a function to display the current date in **cell G3**.

c. Assign appropriate range names to the number of payments per year value and to the lookup table.

d. Use range names when possible in formulas, and avoid creating circular references.

e. Use an appropriate function to display the interest rate for the first customer.

f. Use an appropriate lookup function to calculate the amount of the down payment for the first customer. The down payment is based on the term and the selling price. The first customer's amount is $68,975.

g. Calculate the amount to be financed for the first customer.

h. Calculate the monthly payment for the first customer using range names and cell references. The first customer's monthly payment is $1,142.65.

i. Copy the formulas down their respective columns. Format interest rates with **Percent Style** with two decimal places. Format monetary values with **Accounting Number Format** with two decimal places.

j. Calculate the number of loans and other summary statistics. Format the statistics as needed.

k. Create a section, complete with column headings, for the range names. Place this area below the lookup table.

l. Insert a footer with your name on the left side, the sheet name code in the center, and the file name code on the right side.

m. Save and close the workbook, and submit based on your instructor's directions.

3 Professor's Grade Book

You are a teaching assistant for Dr. Denise Gerber, who teaches an introductory C# programming class at your college. One of your routine tasks is to enter assignment and test grades into the grade book. Now that the semester is almost over, you need to create formulas to calculate category averages, the overall weighted average, and the letter grade for each student. In addition, Dr. Gerber wants to see general statistics, such as average, median, low, and high for each graded assignment and test, as well as category averages and total averages. Furthermore, you need to create the grading scale on the documentation worksheet and use it to display the appropriate letter grade for each student.

a. Open the *e02m3grades* workbook and save it as **e02m3grades_LastnameFirstname**.

b. Use breakpoints to enter the grading scale in the correct structure on the Documentation worksheet, and then name the grading scale range **Grades**. The grading scale is as follows:

95+	A
90–94.9	A–
87–89.9	B+
83–86.9	B
80–82.9	B–
77–79.9	C+
73–76.9	C
70–72.9	C–
67–69.9	D+
63–66.9	D
60–62.9	D–
0–59.9	F

c. Calculate the total lab points earned for the first student in **cell T8** in the Grades worksheet. The first student earned 93 lab points.

d. Calculate the average of the two midterm tests for the first student in **cell W8**. The student's midterm test average is 87.

e. Calculate the assignment average for the first student in cell I8. The formula should drop the lowest score before calculating the average. Hint: You need to use a combination of three functions: SUM, MIN, and COUNT. The first student's assignment average is 94.2 after dropping the lowest assignment score.

f. Calculate the weighted total points based on the four category points (assignment average, lab points, midterm average, and final exam) and their respective weights (stored in the range B40:B43) in cell Y8. Use relative and absolute cell references as needed in the formula. The first student's total weighted score is 90.

g. Use the appropriate function to calculate the letter grade equivalent in **cell Z8**. Use the range name in the function. The first student's letter grade is A−.

h. Copy the formulas down their respective columns for the other students.

i. Name the passing score threshold in **cell B5** with the range name **Passing**. Display a message in the last grade book column based on the student's semester performance. If a student earned a final score of 70 or higher, display *Enroll in CS 202*. Otherwise, display *RETAKE CS 101*.

j. Calculate the average, median, low, and high scores for each assignment, lab, test, category average, and total score. Display individual averages with no decimal places; display category and final score averages with one decimal place. Display other statistics with no decimal places.

k. Insert a list of range names in the designated area in the Documentation worksheet. Complete the documentation by inserting your name, today's date, and a purpose statement in the designated areas.

l. At your instructor's discretion, add a column to display each student's rank in the class. Use Help to learn how to insert the RANK function.

m. Select page setup options as needed to print the Grades worksheet on one page.

n. Insert a footer with your name on the left side, the sheet name code in the center, and the file name code on the right side of each worksheet.

o. Save and close the workbook, and submit based on your instructor's directions.

You are a sales representative at the local fitness center, Buff and Tuff Gym. Your manager expects each representative to track weekly new membership data, so you created a spreadsheet to store data. Membership costs are based on membership type. Clients can rent a locker for an additional annual fee. You are required to collect a down payment based on membership type, determine the balance, and then calculate the monthly payment based on a standard interest rate. In addition, you need to calculate general statistics to summarize for your manager. Spot-check results to make sure you created formulas and functions correctly.

Perform Preliminary Work

You need to open the starting workbook you created, acknowledge the existing circular reference error, and assign a range name to the membership lookup table. You will correct the circular reference error later.

a. Open the *e02c1gym* workbook, click **Help**, read about circular references, close the Help window that appears, and save the workbook as **e02c1gym_LastnameFirstname**.

b. Assign the name **Membership** to the **range A18:C20**.

c. Insert a function to display the current date in **cell B2**.

Calculate Cost, Annual Total, and Total Due

You are ready to calculate the basic annual membership cost and the total annual cost. The basic annual membership is determined based on each client's membership type, using the lookup table.

a. Insert a function in **cell C5** to display the basic annual membership cost for the first client.

b. Use a function to calculate the annual total amount, which is the sum of the basic cost and locker fees for those who rent a locker. The Locker column displays *Yes* for clients who rent a locker and *No* for those who don't.

c. Calculate the total amount due for the first client based on the annual total and the number of years in the contract.

d. Copy the three formulas down their respective columns.

Determine the Down Payment and Balance

You need to collect a down payment based on the type of membership for each new client. Then you must determine how much each client owes.

a. Insert the function to display the amount of down payment for the first client.

b. Find and correct the circular reference for the balance. The balance is the difference between the total due and the down payment.

c. Copy the two formulas for the rest of the clients.

Calculate the Monthly Payment

Clients pay the remainder by making monthly payments. Monthly payments are based on the number of years specified in the client's contract and a standard interest rate.

a. Insert the function to calculate the first client's monthly payment, using appropriate relative and absolute cell references.

b. Copy the formula down the column.

c. Edit the formula by changing the appropriate cell reference to a mixed cell reference. Copy the formula down.

Finalize the Workbook

You need to perform some basic statistical calculations and finalize the workbook with formatting and page setup options.

a. Calculate totals on row 14.

b. Insert the appropriate functions in the *Summary Statistics* section of the worksheet: **cells H18:H22**. Format the payments with **Accounting Number Format**, and format the number of new members appropriately.

c. Format the other column headings on rows 4 and 17 to match the fill color in the **range E17:H17**. Wrap text for the column headings.

d. Format the monetary values for Andrews and the total row with **Accounting Number Format**. Use zero decimal places for whole amounts, and display two decimal places for the monthly payment. Apply **Comma Style** to the internal monetary values. Underline the values before the totals, and then apply **Double Accounting Underline** (found in the Format Cells dialog box) for the totals.

e. Set **0.3"** left and right margins, and then ensure the page prints on only one page.

f. Insert a footer with your name on the left side, the date code in the center, and the file name code on the right side.

g. Save and close the workbook, and submit based on your instructor's directions.

Blue Skies Airlines

GENERAL CASE

In Practice Exercise 1, you worked with the Blue Skies Airlines' daily flight statistics. If you did not complete that exercise, review the introductory paragraph, steps, and Figure 2.33. Open *e02b1blue* and save it as **e02b1blue_LastnameFirstName**. It is inefficient to delete 0.0% when a flight does not exist for a particular day, so you will create a formula that enters an empty text string if the number column contains a hyphen (-) using the IF function to evaluate if the # Pass column does not contain a hyphen. The value_if_true argument should calculate the occupancy percentage. The value_if_false argument should enter an empty text string, indicated by "". Copy the function to other days' % Full columns. Calculate the average daily percentage full for Flight 4520 in the Weekly Statistics area of the worksheet. Note that you need to use nonadjacent cell addresses in the function. Include empty % Full cells so that you can copy the formula down for the other flights. The empty cells do not affect the results. The average daily occupancy rate for Flight 4520 is 85.0%. Calculate the low and high daily occupancy rates. For Flight 4520, the lowest occupancy rate is 71.4%, and the highest occupancy rate is 92.9%. Insert a function to count the number of days each flight was made. Reapply the bottom border to the statistics area, if needed. Change the scaling so that the worksheet fits on one page. Include a footer with your name on the left side, the date code in the center, and the file name code on the right side. Save and close the workbook, and submit based on your instructor's directions.

Mall Lease Rates

RESEARCH CASE

As general manager of a shopping mall, you developed a spreadsheet to list current tenant data. Open *e02b2mall*, and save it as **e02b2mall_LastnameFirstname**. You need to calculate the expiration date, price per square foot, annual rent, and monthly rent for each tenant. Use Help to research how you can construct a nested DATE function that will display the expiration date. The function should add the number of years for the lease but should subtract one day. For example, a five-year lease that started on January 1, 2010, expires on December 31, 2014, not on January 1, 2015. Assign three range names: the lookup table and the two constants. The price per square foot is based on two things: length of the lease and the number of square feet. If a tenant's space is less than the threshold, the tenant's price per square footage is based on the regular price. If a tenant's space is at least 3,000 square feet, the tenant's price is based on the adjusted square footage price. Use Help or search the Internet to learn how to nest the VLOOKUP within the IF function. You will need two nested functions. Use range names in the functions. Calculate the annual rent, which is the product of the square footage and price per square footage per tenant. Then calculate the monthly rent. Avoid circular references in your formulas. Format values appropriately. Include a footer with your name on the left side, the date code in the center, and the file name code on the right side. Save and close the workbook, and submit based on your instructor's directions.

Park City Condo Rental

DISASTER RECOVERY

You and some friends are planning a Labor Day vacation to Park City, Utah. You have secured a four-day condominium that costs $1,200. Some people will stay all four days; others will stay part of the weekend. One of your friends constructed a worksheet to help calculate each person's cost of the rental. The people who stay Thursday night will split the nightly cost evenly. To keep the costs down, everyone agreed to pay $30 per night per person for Friday, Saturday, and/or Sunday nights. Depending on the number of people who stay each night, the group may owe more money. Kyle, Ian, Isaac, and Daryl agreed to split the difference in the total rental cost and the amount the group members paid. Open *e02b3parkcity*, address the circular reference error message that appears, and save the workbook as **e02b3parkcity_LastnameFirstname**. Review the worksheet structure, including the assumptions and calculation notes at the bottom of the worksheet. Check the formulas and functions, making necessary corrections. With the existing data, the number of people staying each night is 5, 7, 10, and 10, respectively. The total paid given the above assumptions is $1,110, giving a difference of $90 to be divided evenly among the first four people. Kyle's share should be $172.50. In the cells containing errors, insert comments to describe the error, and then fix the formulas. Verify the accuracy of formulas by entering an IF function in cell I1 to ensure the totals match. Nick, James, and Body inform you they can't stay Sunday night, and Rob wants to stay Friday night. Change the input accordingly. The updated total paid is now $1,200, and the difference is $150. Include a footer with your name on the left side, the date code in the center, and the file name code on the right side. Save and close the workbook, and submit based on your instructor's directions.

EXCEL

3 CHARTS

Depicting Data Visually

Watch the
**Set-up
Video**
for this
Case Study!

CASE STUDY | Hort University Majors

You are an assistant in the Institutional Research Department for Hort University, a prestigious university on the East Coast. You help conduct research using the university's information systems to provide statistics on the student population, alumni, and more. Your department stores an abundance of data to provide needed results upon request.

Dr. Alisha Musto, your boss, asked that you analyze the number of majors by the six colleges: Arts, Business, Education, Humanities & Social Science, Science & Health, and Technology & Computing. In addition, Dr. Musto wants you to include the undeclared majors in your analysis. You created an Excel worksheet with the data, but you want to create a series of charts that will help Dr. Musto analyze the enrollment data.

OBJECTIVES   AFTER YOU READ THIS CHAPTER, YOU WILL BE ABLE TO:

1. Decide which chart type to create *p.178*

2. Create a chart *p.188*

3. Change the chart type *p.197*

4. Change the data source and structure *p.198*

5. Apply a chart layout and a chart style *p.198*

6. Move a chart *p.199*

7. Print charts *p.200*

8. Insert and customize a sparkline *p.200*

9. Select and format chart elements *p.207*

10. Customize chart labels *p.209*

11. Format the axes and gridlines *p.211*

12. Add a trendline *p.212*

Chart Basics

The expression "a picture is worth a thousand words" means that a visual can be a more effective way to communicate or interpret data than words or numbers. Storing, organizing, and performing calculations on quantitative data, such as in the spreadsheets you have created, are important, but you must also be able to analyze the data to determine what they mean. A *chart* is a visual representation of numerical data that compares data and helps reveal trends or patterns to help people make informed decisions. An effective chart depicts data in a clear, easy-to-interpret manner and contains enough data to be useful but not too much that the data overwhelm people.

> An effective chart depicts data in a clear, easy-to-interpret manner....

A **chart** is a visual representation of numerical data.

In this section, you will learn chart terminology and how to choose the best chart type, such as pie or line, to fit your needs. You will select the range of cells containing the numerical values and labels from which to create the chart, choose the chart type, insert the chart, and designate the chart's location.

Deciding Which Chart Type to Create

Before creating a chart, study the data you want to represent visually. Look at the structure of the worksheet—the column labels, the row labels, the quantitative data, and the calculated values. Decide what you want to convey to your audience: Does the worksheet hold a single set of data, such as average snowfall at one ski resort, or multiple sets of data, such as average snowfall at several ski resorts? Do you want to depict data for one specific time period or over several time periods, such as several years or decades? Based on the data on which you want to focus, you decide which type of chart best represents that data. With Excel, you can create a variety of types of charts. The four most common chart types are column, bar, line, and pie.

You should organize the worksheet data before creating a chart by ensuring that the values in columns and rows are on the same value system (such as dollars or units) in order to make comparisons, that labels are descriptive, and that no blank rows or columns exist in the primary dataset. Figure 3.1 shows a worksheet containing the number of students who have declared a major within each college at Hort University. These data will be used to illustrate several chart types. Each cell containing a value is a *data point*. For example, the value 1,330 is a data point for the Arts data in the 2012 column. A group of related data points that appear in row(s) or column(s) in the worksheet create a *data series*. For example, the values 950, 1,000, 1,325, and 1,330 comprise the Arts data series. Textual information, such as column and row labels (college names, months, years, product names, etc.), is used to create *category labels* in charts.

A **data point** is a numeric value that describes a single value on a chart.

A **data series** is a group of related data points.

A **category label** is text that describes a collection of data points in a chart.

	A	B	C	D	E	F
1	**Hort University**					
2	**Number of Majors by College**					
3						
4		**2009**	**2010**	**2011**	**2012**	**Average**
5	Arts	950	1,000	1,325	1,330	1,151
6	Business	3,975	3,650	3,775	4,000	3,850
7	Education	1,500	1,425	1,435	1,400	1,440
8	Humanities & Social Science	2,300	2,250	2,500	3,500	2,638
9	Science & Health	1,895	1,650	1,700	1,800	1,761
10	Technology & Computing	4,500	4,325	4,400	4,800	4,506
11	Undeclared	5,200	5,500	5,000	4,700	5,100
12	**Totals by Year**	**20,320**	**19,800**	**20,135**	**21,530**	**20,446**
13						

FIGURE 3.1 Sample Dataset ➤

Create a Column Chart

A **column chart** displays data comparisons vertically in columns.

The **chart area** contains the entire chart and all of its elements.

The **plot area** contains a graphical representation of values in a data series.

The **X-axis** is a horizontal line that borders the plot area to provide a frame of reference for measurement.

The **Y-axis** is a vertical line that borders the plot area to provide a frame of reference for measurement.

The **category axis** provides descriptive group names for subdividing the data series.

The **value axis** displays incremental values to identify the values of the data series.

A **column chart** displays data vertically in columns. You use column charts to compare values across different categories, such as comparing revenue among different cities or comparing quarterly revenue in one year. Column charts are most effective when they are limited to small numbers of categories—generally seven or fewer. If more categories exist, the columns appear too close together, making it difficult to read the labels.

Before you create a chart, you need to know the names of the different chart elements. The **chart area** contains the entire chart and all of its elements, including the plot area, titles, legend, and labels. The **plot area** is the region containing the graphical representation of the values in the data series. Two axes form a border around the plot area. The **X-axis** is a horizontal border that provides a frame of reference for measuring data horizontally. The **Y-axis** is a vertical border that provides a frame of reference for measuring data vertically. Excel refers to the axes as the category axis and value axis. The **category axis** displays descriptive group names or labels, such as college names or cities, to identify data. The **value axis** displays incremental numbers to identify approximate values, such as dollars or units, of data points in the chart. In a column chart, the category axis is the X-axis, and the value axis is the Y-axis.

The column chart in Figure 3.2 compares the number of majors by college for only one year using the data from the worksheet in Figure 3.1. In Figure 3.2, the college labels stored in the first column—the range A5:A11—form the horizontal category axis, and the data points representing the number of majors in 2012 in the range E5:E11 form the vertical value axis. The height of each column represents the value of the individual data points: The larger the value, the taller the column. For example, Business has a taller column than the Arts and Education columns, indicating that more students major in Business than Arts or Education.

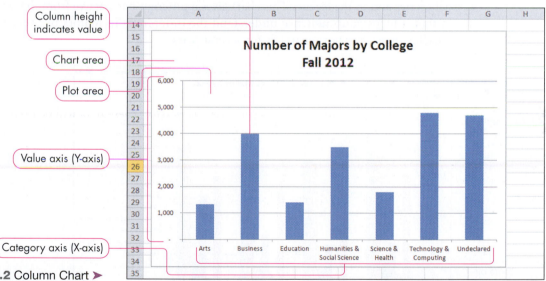

FIGURE 3.2 Column Chart ➤

A **single data series** compares values for one set of data.

A **multiple data series** compares two or more sets of data in one chart.

A **clustered column chart** groups or clusters similar data in columns to compare values across categories.

Figure 3.2 shows a column chart representing a **single data series**—data for only Fall 2012. However, you might want to create a column chart that contains multiple data series. A **multiple data series** chart compares two or more sets of data, such as the number of majors by college for four years. After you select the chart category, such as Column or Line, select a chart subtype. Within each chart category, Excel provides many variations or subtypes, such as clustered, stacked, and 100% stacked.

A **clustered column chart** compares groups or clusters of columns set side-by-side for easy comparison. The clustered column chart facilitates quick comparisons across data series, and it is effective for comparing several data points among categories. Figure 3.3 shows a clustered column chart created from the data in Figure 3.1. By default, the row titles appear on the category axis, and the yearly data series appear as columns with the value axis showing incremental numbers. Excel assigns a different color to each yearly data series and

A **legend** is a key that identifies the color, gradient, picture, texture, or pattern fill assigned to each data series in a chart.

includes a legend. A **_legend_** is a key that identifies the color, gradient, picture, texture, or pattern assigned to each data series in a chart. For example, the 2012 data appear in purple. This chart clusters yearly data series for each college, enabling you to compare yearly trends for each major.

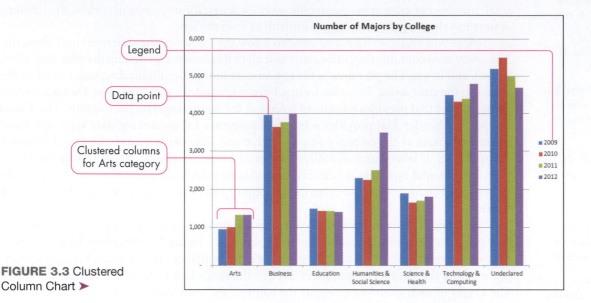

FIGURE 3.3 Clustered Column Chart ➤

Figure 3.4 shows another clustered column chart in which the categories and data series are reversed. The years appear on the category axis, and the colleges appear as color-coded data series and in the legend. This chart gives a different perspective from that in Figure 3.3 in that it helps your audience understand the differences in majors per year rather than focusing on each major separately for several years.

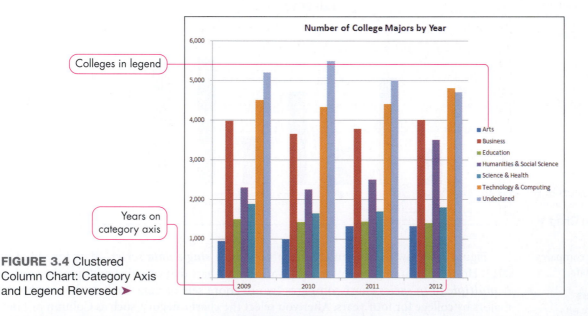

FIGURE 3.4 Clustered Column Chart: Category Axis and Legend Reversed ➤

A **stacked column chart** places stacks of data in segments on top of each other in one column, with each category in the data series represented by a different color.

A **_stacked column chart_** shows the relationship of individual data points to the whole category. Unlike a clustered column chart that displays several columns (one for each data series) for a category (such as Arts), a stacked column chart displays only one column for each category. Each category within the stacked column is color-coded for one data series. Use the stacked column chart when you want to compare total values across categories, as well as to display the individual category values. Figure 3.5 shows a stacked column chart in which a single column represents each categorical year, and each column stacks color-coded data-point segments representing the different colleges. The stacked column chart enables you to determine the total number of majors for each year. The height of each color-coded data point enables you to identify the relative contribution of each college to the total number of yearly majors. A disadvantage of the stacked column chart is that the segments within each column do not start at the same point, making it more difficult to compare individual segment values across categories.

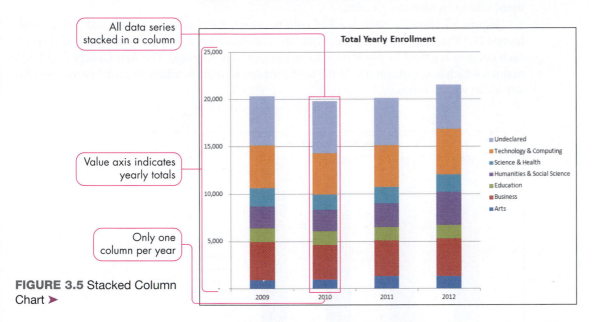

All data series stacked in a column

Value axis indicates yearly totals

Only one column per year

FIGURE 3.5 Stacked Column Chart ➤

When you create a stacked column chart, you must ensure data are *additive*, meaning that each column represents a sum of the data for each segment. Figure 3.5 correctly uses years as the category axis and the colleges as data series. Within each year, Excel adds the number of majors by college, and the columns display the sum of the majors. For example, the total number of majors in 2012 is over 20,000. Figure 3.6 shows an incorrectly constructed stacked column chart because the yearly number of majors by college is *not* additive. It is incorrect to state that the university has 15,000 total business majors for four years. Be careful when constructing stacked column charts to ensure that they lead to logical interpretation of data.

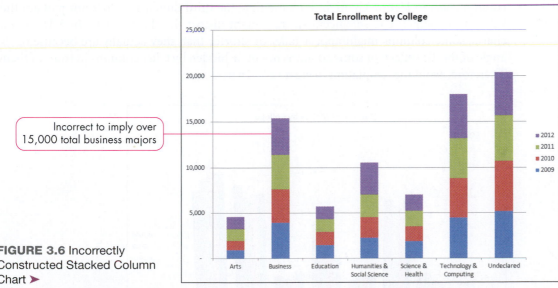

Incorrect to imply over 15,000 total business majors

FIGURE 3.6 Incorrectly Constructed Stacked Column Chart ➤

A **100% stacked column chart** places (stacks) data in one column per category, with each column having the same height of 100%.

A ***100% stacked column chart*** compares the percentage each data point contributes to the total for each category. Similar to the stacked column chart, the 100% stacked column chart displays only one column per category. The value axis displays percentages rather than values, and all columns are the same height: 100%. Excel converts each data point value into a percentage of the total for each category. Use this type of chart when you are more interested in comparing relative percentage contributions across categories rather than actual values across categories. For example, a regional manager for a department store realizes that not every store is the same size and that the different stores have different sales volumes. Instead of comparing sales by department for each store, you might want to display percentage of sales by department to facilitate comparisons of percentage contributions for each department within its own store's sales.

Figure 3.7 shows a 100% stacked column chart. Excel computes the total 2012 enrollment (21,530 in our example), calculates the enrollment percentage by college, and displays each column segment in proportion to its computed percentage. The Arts College had 1,330 majors, which accounts for 6% of the total number of majors, where the total enrollment for any given year is 100%.

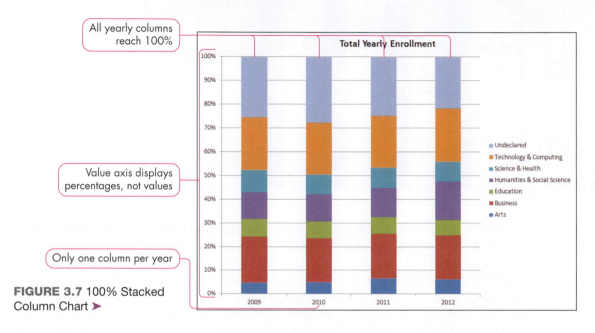

All yearly columns reach 100%

Value axis displays percentages, not values

Only one column per year

FIGURE 3.7 100% Stacked Column Chart ➤

A **3-D chart** adds a third dimension to each data series, creating a distorted perspective of the data.

Excel enables you to create special-effects charts, such as 3-D, cylinder, pyramid, or cone charts. A **3-D chart** adds a third dimension to each data series. Although the 3-D clustered column chart in Figure 3.8 might look exciting, the third dimension does not plot another value. It is a superficial enhancement that might distort the charted data. In 3-D column charts, some columns might appear taller or shorter than they actually are because of the angle of the 3-D effect, or some columns might be hidden by taller columns in front of them. Therefore, avoid the temptation to create 3-D charts.

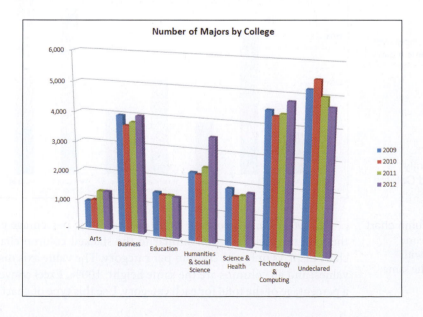

FIGURE 3.8 3-D Clustered Column Chart ➤

Create a Bar Chart

A **bar chart** compares values across categories using horizontal bars.

A **bar chart** compares values across categories using horizontal bars. In a bar chart, the horizontal axis displays values, and the vertical axis displays categories (see Figure 3.9). A bar chart conveys the same type of information as a column chart; however, a bar chart is preferable when category names are long, such as *Humanities & Social Science*. A bar chart enables category names to appear in an easy-to-read format, whereas a column chart might display category names at an awkward angle or smaller font size. Like column charts, bar charts have several subtypes, such as clustered, stacked, 100% stacked, 3-D, cylinder, cone, or pyramid subtypes.

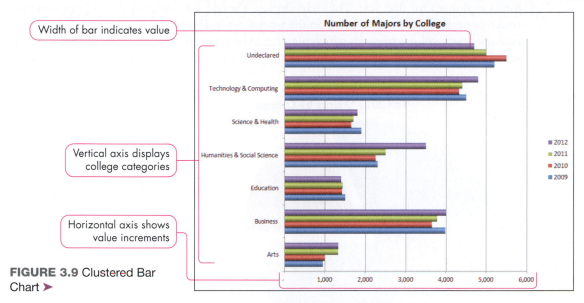

Width of bar indicates value

Vertical axis displays college categories

Horizontal axis shows value increments

FIGURE 3.9 Clustered Bar Chart ➤

Create a Line Chart

A **line chart** uses a line to connect data points in order to show trends over a period of time.

A **line chart** displays lines connecting data points to show trends over equal time periods, such as months, quarters, years, or decades. With multiple data series, Excel displays each data series with a different line color. The category axis (X-axis) represents time, such as ten-year increments, whereas the value axis (Y-axis) represents the value, such as a monetary value or quantity. A line chart enables a user to easily spot trends in the data since the line continues to the next data point. The line, stacked, and 100% stacked line charts do not have specific indicators for each data point. To show each data point, select Line with Markers, Stacked Line with Markers, or 100% Stacked Line with Markers. Figure 3.10 shows a line chart indicating the number of majors by college over time, making it easy to see the enrollment trends. For example, the Arts enrollment spiked in 2010 while enrollments in other colleges decreased that year.

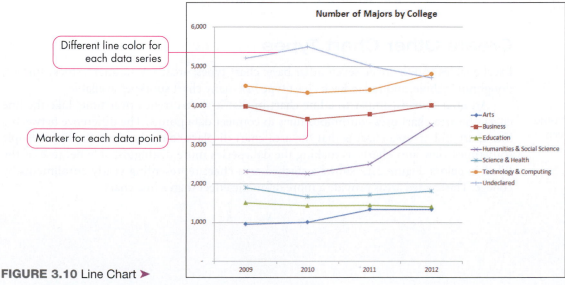

Different line color for each data series

Marker for each data point

FIGURE 3.10 Line Chart ➤

Create a Pie Chart

A **pie chart** shows each data point in proportion to the whole data series as a slice in a circular pie.

A **pie chart** shows each data point as a proportion to the whole data series. The pie chart displays as a circle or "pie," where the entire pie represents the total value of the data series. Each slice represents a single data point. The larger the slice, the larger percentage that data point contributes to the whole. Use a pie chart when you want to convey percentage or market share. Unlike column, bar, and line charts, pie charts represent a single data series only.

The pie chart in Figure 3.11 divides the pie representing total Fall 2012 enrollment into seven slices, one for each college. The size of each slice is proportional to the percentage of total enrollment for that year. The chart depicts a single data series (Fall 2012 enrollment), which appears in the range E5:E11 on the worksheet in Figure 3.1. Excel creates a legend to indicate which color represents which pie slice. When you create a pie chart, limit it to about seven slices. Pie charts with too many slices appear too busy to interpret.

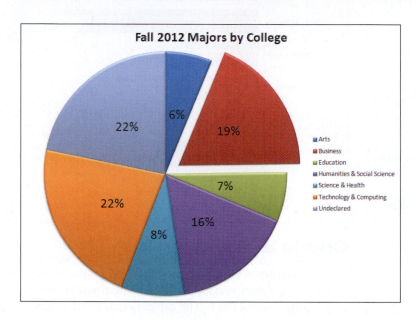

FIGURE 3.11 Pie Chart ➤

Similar to the way it creates a 100% stacked column chart, Excel creates a pie chart by computing the total 2012 enrollment (21,530 in our example), calculating the enrollment percentage by college and drawing each slice of the pie in proportion to its computed percentage. The Business College had 4,000 majors, which accounts for 19% of the total number of majors. You can focus a person's attention on a particular slice by separating one or more slices from the rest of the chart in an **exploded pie chart**, as shown in Figure 3.11. Additional pie subtypes include pie of pie, bar of pie, and 3-D pie charts.

An **exploded pie chart** separates one or more pie slices from the rest of the pie chart.

Create Other Chart Types

Excel enables you to create seven other basic chart types: area, X Y (scatter), stock, surface, doughnut, bubble, and radar. Each chart type has many chart subtypes available.

An **area chart** is similar to a line chart in that it shows trends over time. Like the line chart, the area chart uses continuous lines to connect data points. The difference between a line chart and an area chart is that the area chart displays colors between the lines. People sometimes view area charts as making the data series more distinguishable because of the filled-in colors. Figure 3.12 shows a stacked area chart representing yearly enrollments by college. The shaded areas provide a more dramatic effect than a line chart.

An **area chart** emphasizes magnitude of changes over time by filling in the space between lines with a color.

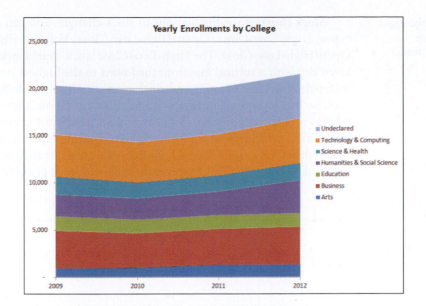

FIGURE 3.12 Stacked Area Chart ➤

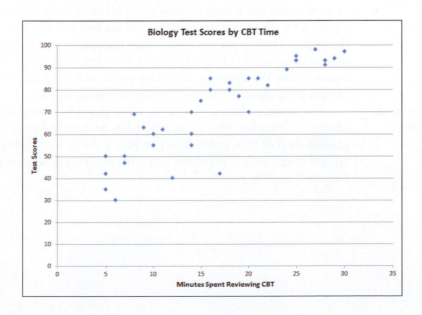

TIP Hidden Data

When creating an area chart, be careful which subtype you select. For some subtypes such as a 3-D area chart, the chart might hide smaller data values behind data series with larger values. If this happens, you can change subtypes or apply a transparency fill to see any hidden data values.

An **X Y (scatter) chart** shows a relationship between two variables.

An **X Y (scatter) chart** shows a relationship between two variables using their X and Y coordinates. Excel plots one variable on the horizontal X-axis and the other variable on the vertical Y-axis. Scatter charts are often used to represent data in educational, scientific, and medical experiments. A scatter chart is essentially the plotted values without any connecting line. A scatter chart helps you determine if a relationship exists between two different sets of numerical data. For example, you can plot the number of minutes students view a computer-based training (CBT) module and their test scores to see if a relationship exists between the two variables (see Figure 3.13).

FIGURE 3.13 Scatter (X Y) Chart ➤

A **stock chart** shows the high, low, and close prices for individual stocks over time.

Stock charts show fluctuations in stock changes. You can select one of four stock sub-types: High-Low-Close, Open-High-Low-Close, Volume-High-Low-Close, and Volume-Open-High-Low-Close. The High-Low-Close stock chart marks a stock's trading range on a given day with a vertical line from the lowest to the highest stock prices. Horizontal bars or rectangles mark the opening and closing prices. Although stock charts may have some other uses, such as showing a range of temperatures over time, they usually show stock prices. To create an Open-High-Low-Close stock chart, you must arrange data with Opening Price, High Price, Low Price, and Closing Price as column labels in that sequence. If you want to create other variations of stock charts, you must arrange data in a structured sequence required by Excel. Figure 3.14 shows three days of stock prices for a particular stock.

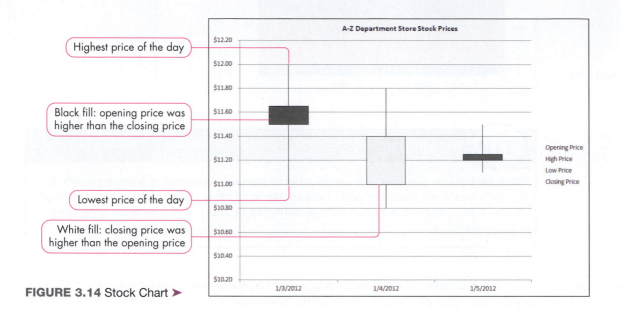

FIGURE 3.14 Stock Chart ➤

The stock chart legend may not explain the chart clearly. However, you can still identify prices. The rectangle represents the difference in the opening and closing prices. If the rectangle has a white fill, the closing price is higher than the opening price. If the rectangle has a black fill, the opening price is higher than the closing price. In Figure 3.14, the opening price was $11.65, and the closing price was $11.50 on January 3. A line below the rectangle indicates that the lowest trading price is lower than the opening and closing prices. In Figure 3.14, the lowest price was $11.00 on January 3. A line above the rectangle indicates the highest trading price is higher than the opening and closing prices. In Figure 3.14, the highest price was $12.00 on January 3. If no line exists below the rectangle, the lowest price equals either the opening or closing price, and if no line exists above the rectangle, the highest price equals either the opening or closing price.

A **surface chart** displays trends using two dimensions on a continuous curve.

The **surface chart** is similar to a line chart; however, it represents numeric data and numeric categories. This chart type takes on some of the same characteristics as a topographic map of hills and valleys (see Figure 3.15). Excel fills in all data points with colors. Surface charts are not as common as other chart types because they require more data points and often confuse people.

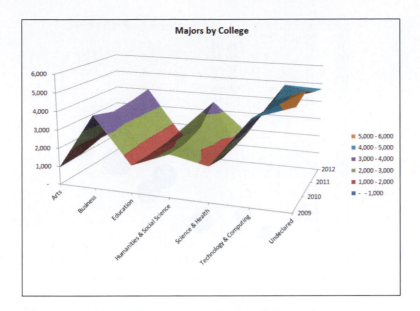

FIGURE 3.15 Surface
Chart ➤

A **doughnut chart** displays
values as percentages of the
whole but may contain more
than one data series.

The **doughnut chart** is similar to a pie chart in that it shows the relationship of parts to
a whole, but the doughnut chart can display more than one series of data, and it has a hole in
the middle. Like a clustered or stacked column chart, a doughnut chart plots multiple data
series. Each ring represents a data series, with the outer ring receiving the most emphasis.
Although the doughnut chart is able to display multiple data series, people often have difficulty interpreting it. Figure 3.16 illustrates the 2011 and 2012 data series, with the 2012 data
series on the outer ring. The chart shows each college as a segment of each ring of the doughnut. The larger the segment, the larger the value.

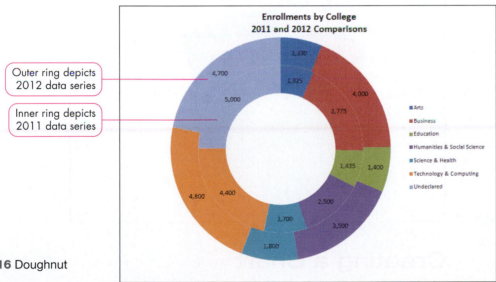

FIGURE 3.16 Doughnut
Chart ➤

A **bubble chart** shows
relationships among three values
by using bubbles.

The **bubble chart** is similar to a scatter chart, but it uses round bubbles instead of data
points to represent a third dimension. Similar to the scatter chart, the bubble chart does not
contain a category axis. The horizontal and vertical axes are both value axes. The third value
determines the size of the bubble where the larger the value, the larger the bubble. People
often use bubble charts to depict financial data. In Figure 3.17, age, years at the company, and
salaries are compared. When creating a bubble chart, do not select the column headings, as
they might distort the data.

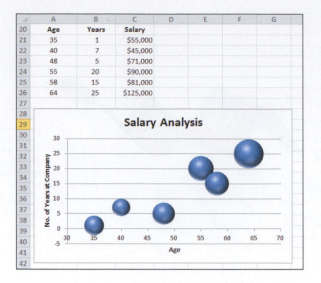

FIGURE 3.17 Bubble Chart ➤

A **radar chart** compares aggregate values of three or more variables represented on axes starting from the same point.

The final chart type is the **_radar chart_**, which uses each category as a spoke radiating from the center point to the outer edges of the chart. Each spoke represents each data series, and lines connect the data points between spokes, similar to a spider web. You can create a radar chart to compare aggregate values for several data series. Figure 3.18 shows a radar chart comparing monthly house sales by house type (rambler, split level, 2 story). The house type categories appear in different colors, while the months appear on the outer edges of the chart.

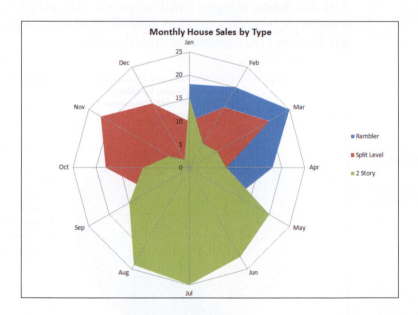

FIGURE 3.18 Radar Chart ➤

Creating a Chart

Creating a chart involves selecting the data source and choosing the chart type. After you insert a chart, you will position and size it.

Select the Data Source

Identify the chart data range by selecting the data series, any descriptive labels you need to construct the category labels, and the series labels you need to create the legend. Edit the row and column labels if they are not clear and concise. Table 3.1 describes what you should select for various charts. If the labels and data series are not stored in adjacent cells, press and hold Ctrl while selecting the nonadjacent ranges. Using Figure 3.1 as a guide, you would select the range A4:E11 to create a clustered column chart with multiple data series. To create the pie chart in Figure 3.11, select the range A5:A11, and then press and hold Ctrl while you select the range E5:E11. If your worksheet has titles and subtitles, you should not select them. Doing so would add unnecessary text to the legend.

TABLE 3.1 Data Selection for Charts		
Chart Type	**What to Select**	**Figure 3.1 Example**
Column, Bar, Line, Area, Doughnut	Row labels (such as colleges), column labels (such as years), and one or more data series	A4:E11
Pie	Row labels (such as colleges) and only one data series (such as 2012), but not column headings	A5:A11,E5:E11
Bubble	Three different data series (such as age, years, and salary)	A21:C26 (in Figure 3.17)
X Y (Scatter)	Two related numeric datasets (such as minutes studying and test scores)	*

*Figure 3.1 does not contain data conducive to an X Y (scatter) chart.

TIP Total Rows and Columns

Make sure that each data series uses the same scale. For example, don't include aggregates, such as totals or averages, along with individual data points. Doing so would distort the plotted data. Compare the clustered column chart in Figure 3.3 to Figure 3.19. In Figure 3.19, the chart's design is incorrect because it mixes individual data points with the totals and yearly averages.

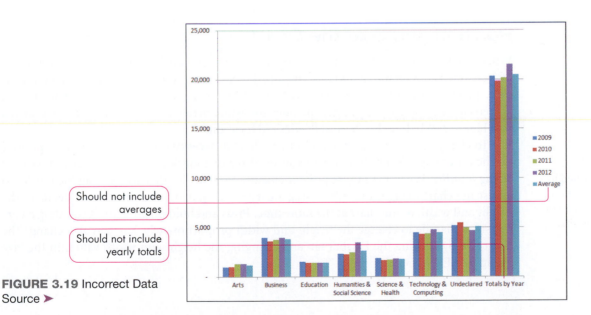

FIGURE 3.19 Incorrect Data Source ➤

Select the Chart Type

After you select the range of cells that you want to be the source for the chart, you need to select the chart type. To insert a chart for the selected range, click the Insert tab, and then do one of the following:

- Click the chart type (such as Column) in the Charts group, and then click a chart subtype (such as Clustered Column) from the chart gallery.

- Click the Charts Dialog Box Launcher to display the Insert Chart dialog box (see Figure 3.20), select a chart type on the left side, select a chart subtype, and then click OK.

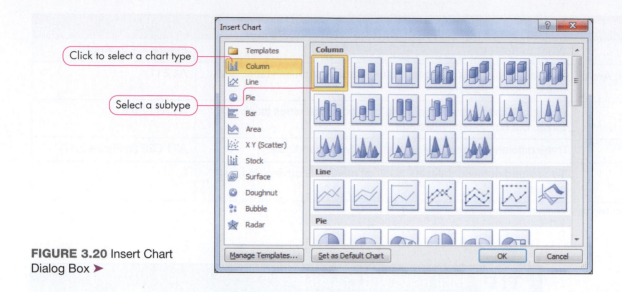

FIGURE 3.20 Insert Chart Dialog Box ➤

A **chart sheet** contains a single chart and no spreadsheet data.

Excel inserts the chart as an embedded object on the current worksheet. You can leave the chart on the same worksheet as the worksheet data used to create the chart, or you can place the chart in a separate worksheet, called a ***chart sheet***. A chart sheet contains a single chart only; you cannot enter data and formulas on a chart sheet. If you leave the chart in the same worksheet (see Figure 3.17), you can print the data and chart on the same page. If you want to print or view a full-sized chart, you can move the chart to its own chart sheet.

Position and Size the Chart

When you first create a chart, Excel inserts the chart in the worksheet, often to the right side of, but sometimes on top of and covering up, the data area. To move the chart to a new location, position the mouse pointer over the chart area. When you see the Chart Area ScreenTip and the mouse pointer includes the white arrowhead and a four-headed arrow (see Figure 3.21), drag the chart to the desired location.

A **sizing handle**, indicated by faint dots on the outside border of a selected chart, enables you to adjust the size of the chart.

To change the size of a chart, select the chart if necessary. Position the mouse pointer on the outer edge of the chart where you see three or four faint dots. These dots are called ***sizing handles***. When the mouse pointer changes to a two-headed arrow, drag the border to adjust the chart's height or width. Drag a corner sizing handle to increase or decrease the height and width of the chart at the same time. Press and hold down Shift as you drag a corner sizing handle to change the height and width proportionately. You can also change the chart size by clicking the Format tab and changing the height and width values in the Size group (see Figure 3.21).

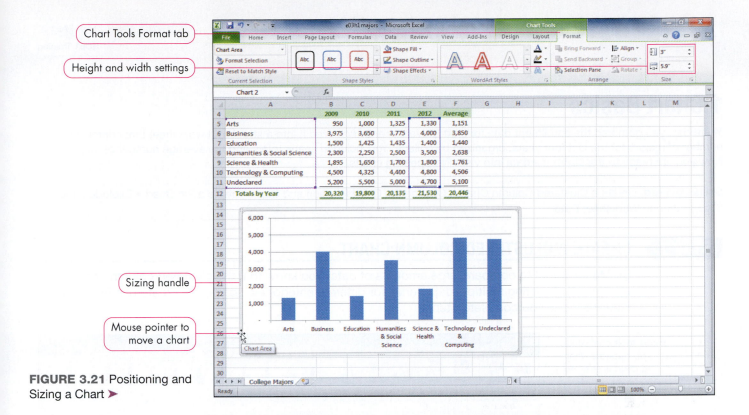

Chart Tools Format tab

Height and width settings

Sizing handle

Mouse pointer to move a chart

FIGURE 3.21 Positioning and Sizing a Chart ➤

TIP Chart Tools Contextual Tab

When you select a chart, Excel displays the Chart Tools contextual tab, containing the Design, Layout, and Format tabs. You can use the commands on these tabs to modify the chart.

1 Chart Basics

Yesterday, you gathered the enrollment data for Hort University and organized it into a structured worksheet that contains the number of majors for the last four years, organized by college. You included yearly totals and the average number of majors. Now you are ready to transform the data into visually appealing charts.

Skills covered: Create a Clustered Column Chart • Change the Chart Position and Size • Create a Pie Chart • Explode a Pie Slice • Change Worksheet Data

STEP 1 ▶ CREATE A CLUSTERED COLUMN CHART

Dr. Musto wants to compare large amounts of data. You know that the clustered column chart is effective at depicting multiple data series for different categories, so you will create one first. Refer to Figure 3.22 as you complete Step 1.

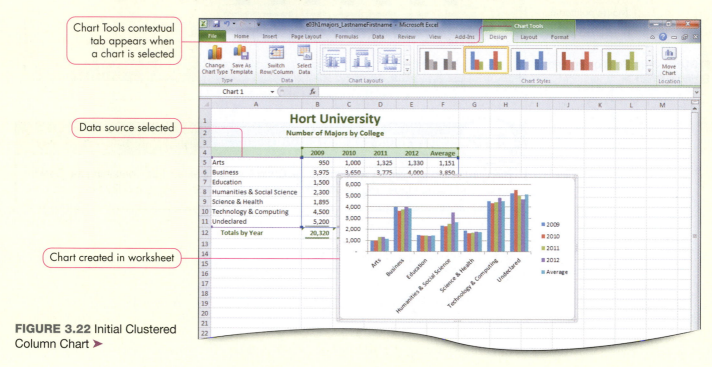

FIGURE 3.22 Initial Clustered Column Chart ➤

a. Open *e03h1majors* and save it as **e03h1majors_LastnameFirstname**.

> **TROUBLESHOOTING:** If you make any major mistakes in this exercise, you can close the file, open *e03h1majors* again, and then start this exercise over.

b. Select the **range A4:F11**.

You included the average column in your selection. Although you should not mix individual values and aggregates such as averages in the same chart, we will do this now and later show you how you can modify the data source after you create the chart.

c. Click the **Insert tab**, and then click **Column** in the Charts group.

The Column gallery opens, displaying the different column subtypes you can create.

d. Click **Clustered Column** in the *2-D Column* section of the gallery. Save the workbook.

Excel inserts the clustered column chart in the worksheet.

Excel inserts the chart next to the worksheet data. You want to reposition the chart and then adjust the size so that the college category labels do not display at an angle to make the chart readable for Dr. Musto. Refer to Figure 3.23 as you complete Step 2.

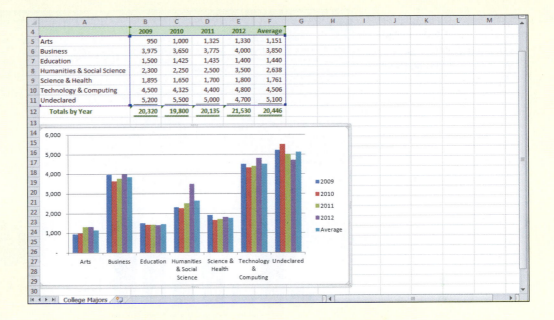

FIGURE 3.23 Repositioned and Resized Chart ➤

a. Position the mouse pointer over the empty area of the chart area.

    The mouse pointer includes a four-headed arrow with the regular white arrowhead, and the Chart Area ScreenTip displays.

> **TROUBLESHOOTING:** Make sure you see the Chart Area ScreenTip as you perform step b. If you move the mouse pointer to another chart element—such as the legend—you will move or size that element instead of moving the entire chart.

b. Drag the chart so that the top-left corner of the chart appears in **cell A14**.

    You positioned the chart below the worksheet data.

c. Drag the bottom-right sizing handle down and to the right to **cell H29**. Save the workbook.

    You increased both the height and the width at the same time. The college labels on the category axis no longer appear at an angle. You will leave the clustered column chart in its current state for the moment while you create another chart.

TIP The F11 Key

Pressing F11 is a fast way to create a column chart in a new chart sheet. Select the worksheet data source, and then press F11 to create the chart.

Dr. Musto has also asked you to create a chart showing the percentage of majors for the current year. You know that pie charts are excellent for illustrating percentages and proportions. Refer to Figure 3.24 as you complete Step 3.

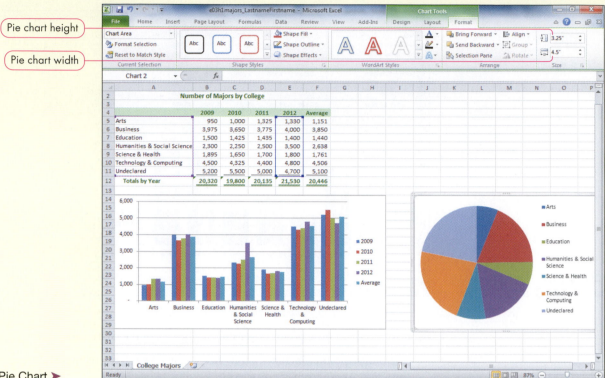

Pie chart height

Pie chart width

FIGURE 3.24 Pie Chart ➤

a. Select the **range A5:A11**, which contains the college category labels.

b. Press and hold **Ctrl** as you select the **range E5:E11**, which contains the 2012 values.

Remember that you have to press and hold Ctrl to select nonadjacent ranges.

> **TIP** Parallel Ranges
>
> Nonadjacent ranges should be parallel so that the legend will correctly reflect the data series. This means that each range should contain the same number of related cells. For example, A5:A11 and E5:E11 are parallel ranges in which E5:E11 contains values that relate to range A5:A11.

c. Click the **Insert tab**, click **Pie** in the Charts group, and then select **Pie** in the 2-D Pie group on the gallery.

Excel inserts a pie chart in the worksheet. The pie chart may overlap part of the worksheet data and the clustered column chart.

d. Drag the chart so that the top-left corner appears in **cell J14**.

> **TROUBLESHOOTING:** Make sure that you see the Chart Area ScreenTip before you start dragging. Otherwise, you might accidentally drag a chart element, such as the legend or plot area. If you accidentally move the legend or plot area, press Ctrl+Z to undo the move.

e. Click the **Format tab**.

f. Type **3.25** in the **Shape Height box** in the Size group, and then press **Enter**.

You increased the chart height to 3.25".

g. Type **4.5** in the **Shape Width box** in the Size group, and then press **Enter**. Save the workbook.

Compare the size of your pie chart to the one shown in Figure 3.24. The zoom in the figure was decreased to display a broader view of the two charts together.

STEP 4 ▸ EXPLODE A PIE SLICE

Dr. Musto is concerned about the number of undeclared majors. You decide to explode the Undeclared pie slice to draw attention to it. Refer to Figure 3.25 as you complete Step 4.

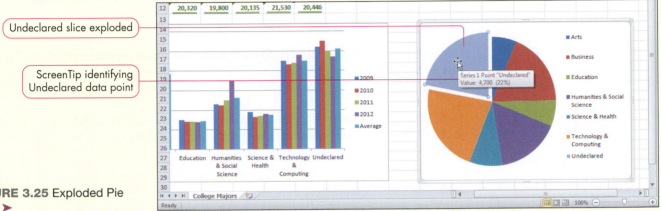

FIGURE 3.25 Exploded Pie Slice ▸

a. Make sure the pie chart is still selected.

b. Click any slice of the chart.

Excel selects all pie slices, as indicated by circular selection handles at the corner of each slice and in the center of the pie.

c. Click the **Undeclared slice**, the light blue slice in the top-left corner of the chart.

The Undeclared slice is the only selected slice.

> **TROUBLESHOOTING:** If you double-click the chart instead of clicking a single data point, the Format Data Point dialog box appears. If this happens, click Close in the dialog box, and then click the individual pie slice to select that slice only.

d. Drag the **Undeclared slice** away from the pie a little bit. Save the workbook.

You exploded the pie slice by separating it from the rest of the pie.

STEP 5 ▸ CHANGE WORKSHEET DATA

While you have been preparing two charts, some updated data came into the Institutional Research Department office. You need to update the worksheet data to update the charts. Refer to Figure 3.26 as you complete Step 5.

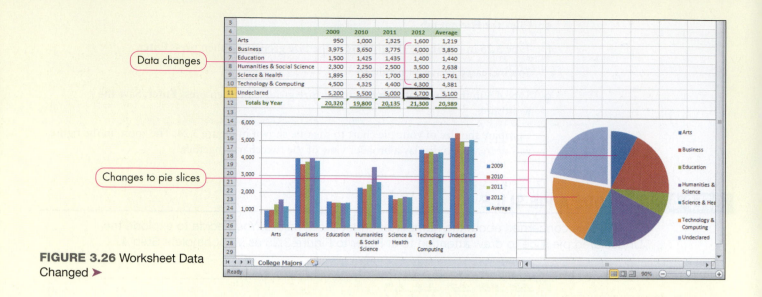

Data changes →

Changes to pie slices →

FIGURE 3.26 Worksheet Data Changed ➤

a. Click **cell E5**, the cell containing *1,330*—the number of students majoring in the College of Arts in 2012.

b. Type **1600** and press **Enter**.

   Notice that the total changes in cell E12, the average yearly number of Arts majors changes in cell F5, the total average students changes in cell F12, and the two charts are adjusted to reflect the new value.

c. Click **cell E10**, the cell containing *4,800*—the number of students majoring in the College of Technology and Computing.

d. Type **4300** and press **Enter**.

   Compare the updated charts to those shown in Figures 3.25 and 3.26. Notice the changes in the worksheet and the chart. With a smaller value, the Technology & Computing slice is smaller, while the other slices represent proportionally higher percentages of the total majors for 2012.

e. Save the workbook. Keep the workbook onscreen if you plan to continue with Hands-On Exercise 2. If not, close the workbook and exit Excel.

Chart Design

When you select a chart, Excel displays the Chart Tools contextual tab. That tab contains three specific tabs: Design, Layout, and Format. You used the Format tab to set the chart height and width in the first Hands-On Exercise. The Chart Tools Design contextual tab contains options to modify the overall chart design. You can change the chart type, modify the data source, select a chart layout, select a chart style, and move the chart. Figure 3.27 shows the Design tab.

FIGURE 3.27 Design Tab ➤

The Design tab provides commands for specifying the structure of a chart. Specifically, you can change the chart type and change the data source to build the chart. In addition, you can specify a chart layout that controls which chart elements display and where, select a chart style, and move the chart to a different location.

In this section, you will learn about the Design tab options and how to make changes to a chart's design. In addition, you will learn how to insert and format sparkline charts.

Changing the Chart Type

After you create a chart, you might want to change how the data are depicted by using other chart types. For example, you might want to change a line chart to a surface chart to see the dramatic effect of the fill colors or change a stacked column chart to a 100% stacked column chart to compare the segment percentages within their respective categories. To change the chart type, do the following:

1. Select the chart.
2. Click the Design tab.
3. Click Change Chart Type in the Type group to open the Change Chart Type dialog box.
4. Select the desired chart type, and then click OK.

> **TIP** Saving a Chart as a Template
>
> Companies often require a similar look for charts used in presentations. After you spend time customizing a chart to your company's specifications, you can save it as a template to create additional charts. To save a chart as a template, select the chart, click the Design tab, and then click Save as Template in the Type group. The Save Chart Template dialog box opens, in which you can select the template location and type a template name. Click Save in the dialog box to save the template. To use a chart template that you have created, click Templates in the Insert Chart dialog box, select the desired chart template, and then click OK.

Changing the Data Source and Structure

By default, Excel displays the row labels in the first column (such as the college names in Figure 3.1) on the category axis and the column labels (such as years) as the data series and in the legend. You can reverse how the chart presents the data—for example, place the column labels (e.g., years) on the category axis and the row labels (e.g., colleges) as data series and in the legend. To reverse the data series, click Switch Row/Column in the Data group. Figure 3.28 shows two chart versions of the same data. The chart on the left shows the row labels (months) on the category axis and the housing types as data series and in the legend. The chart on the right reverses the category axis and data series. The first chart compares house types for each month, and the second chart compares the number of sales of each house type throughout the year.

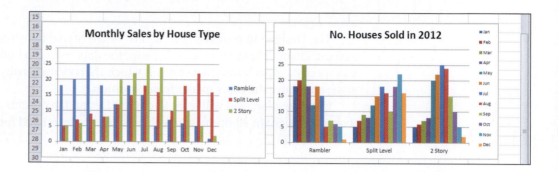

FIGURE 3.28 Original Chart and Reversed Row/Column Chart ➤

After creating a chart, you might notice extraneous data caused by selecting too many cells for the data source, or you might want to add to or delete data from the chart by clicking Select Data in the Data group to open the Select Data Source dialog box (see Figure 3.29). Select the desired range in the worksheet to modify the data source, or adjust the legend and horizontal axis within the dialog box.

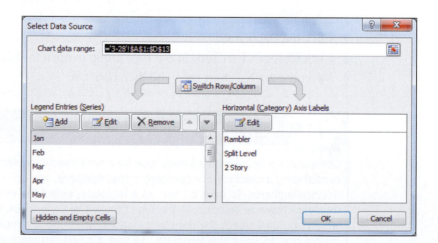

FIGURE 3.29 Select Data Source Dialog Box ➤

Applying a Chart Layout and a Chart Style

The Chart Layouts group enables you to apply predefined layouts to a chart. A chart layout determines which chart elements appear in the chart area and how they are positioned within the chart area. Chart layouts are useful when you are first learning about charts and chart elements or to create consistently laid out charts. As you learn more about charting, you may want to customize your charts by using the commands on the Layout tab.

The Chart Styles group contains predefined styles that control the color of the chart area, plot area, and data series. Styles also affect the look of the data series, such as flat, 3-D, or beveled. Figure 3.30 shows the Chart Styles gallery. When choosing a chart style, make sure the style complements the chart data and is easy to read. Also, consider whether you will display the chart onscreen in a presentation or print the chart. If you will display the chart in a presentation, select a style with a black background. If you plan to print the chart, select a chart style with a white background to avoid wasting toner printing a background. If you print with a black and white printer, use the first column of black and gray styles.

FIGURE 3.30 Chart Styles Gallery ➤

Moving a Chart

By default, Excel creates charts on the same worksheet as the original dataset, but you can move the chart to its own chart sheet in the workbook. To move a chart to another sheet or a new sheet, do the following:

1. Select the chart to display the Chart Tools contextual tab.
2. Click the Design tab.
3. Click Move Chart in the Location group to open the Move Chart dialog box (see Figure 3.31).
4. Click *New sheet* to move the chart to its own sheet, or click *Object in*, click the *Object in* arrow, select the worksheet to which you want to move the chart, and then click OK.

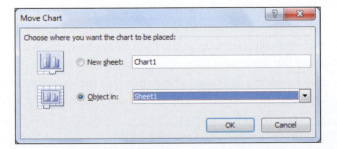

FIGURE 3.31 Move Chart Dialog Box ➤

 Chart Sheet Name

The default chart sheet name is Chart1, Chart2, etc. You can rename the sheet before you click OK in the Move Chart dialog box or by double-clicking the chart sheet tab, typing a new name, and then pressing Enter.

Printing Charts

Just like for printing any worksheet data, preview the chart in the Backstage view before you print to check margins, spacing, and page breaks to ensure a balanced printout.

Print an Embedded Chart

If you embedded a chart on the same sheet as the data source, you need to decide if you want to print the data only, the data *and* the chart, or the chart only. To print the data only, select the data, click the File tab, click Print, click the first arrow in the Settings section and select Print Selection, and then click Print. To print only the chart, select the chart, and then display the Backstage view. The default setting is Print Selected Chart, and clicking Print will print the chart as a full-page chart. If the data and chart are on the same worksheet, print the worksheet contents to print both, but do not select either the chart or the data before displaying the Backstage view. The preview shows you what will print. Make sure it displays what you want to print before clicking Print.

Print a Chart Sheet

If you moved the chart to a chart sheet, the chart is the only item on that worksheet. When you display the print options, the default is Print Active Sheets, and the chart will print as a full-page chart. You can change the setting to Print Entire Workbook.

Inserting and Customizing a Sparkline

A **sparkline** is a miniature chart contained in a single cell.

Excel 2010 enables you to create miniature charts called sparklines. A *sparkline* is a small line, column, or win/loss chart contained in a single cell. The purpose of a sparkline is to present a condensed, simple, succinct visual illustration of data. Unlike a regular chart, a sparkline does not include a chart title or axes labels. Inserting sparklines next to data helps your audience understand data quickly without having to look at a full-scale chart.

> A sparkline presents a condensed, simple, succinct visual illustration of data.

Create a Sparkline

Before creating a sparkline, identify what data you want to depict and where you want to place it. To create a sparkline, do the following:

1. Click the Insert tab.
2. Click Line, Column, or Win/Loss in the Sparklines group. The Create Sparklines dialog box opens (see Figure 3.32).
3. Type the cell references in the Data Range box, or click the collapse button (if necessary), select the range, and then click the expand button.
4. Enter or select the range where you want the sparkline to appear in the Location Range box, and then click OK. The default cell location is the active cell unless you change it.

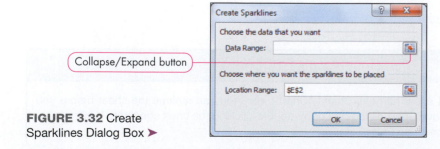

Collapse/Expand button

FIGURE 3.32 Create Sparklines Dialog Box ➤

Apply Design Characteristics to a Sparkline

After you insert a sparkline, the Sparkline Tools Design contextual tab displays, with options to customize the sparkline. Click Edit Data in the Sparkline group to change the data source or sparkline location and indicate how empty cells appear, such as gaps or zeros. You can also change the sparkline type to Line, Column, or Win/Loss in the Type group.

The Show group enables you to display points within the sparkline. For example, click the Markers check box to display markers for all data points on the sparkline, or click High Point to display a marker for the high point, such as for the highest sales or highest price per gallon of gasoline for a time period. The Style group enables you to change the sparkline style, similar to how you can apply different chart styles to charts. Click Sparkline Color to change the color of the sparkline. Click Marker Color, point to a marker type—such as High Point—and then click the color for that marker. Make sure the marker color contrasts with the sparkline color. Figure 3.33 shows a blue sparkline to indicate trends for the yearly students. The High Point marker is red.

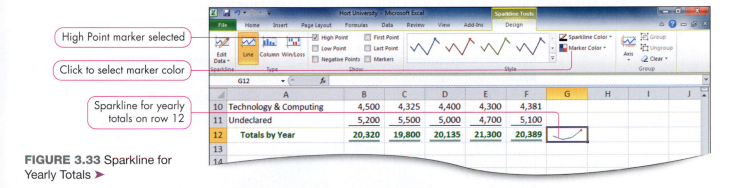

High Point marker selected

Click to select marker color

Sparkline for yearly totals on row 12

FIGURE 3.33 Sparkline for Yearly Totals ➤

TIP Clear Sparklines

To clear the sparklines, select the cells containing sparklines, click the Clear arrow in the Group group on the Sparkline Tools Design tab, and then select either Clear Selected Sparklines or Clear Selected Sparkline Groups.

HANDS-ON EXERCISES

2 Chart Design

You have studied the Design tab and decide to change some design elements on your two charts. You will move the pie chart to a chart sheet so that Dr. Musto can focus on the chart. You will use other options on the Design tab to modify the charts.

Skills covered: Move a Chart • Apply a Chart Style and Chart Layout • Change the Data • Change the Chart Type • Insert a Sparkline • Print a Chart

STEP 1 ▶ MOVE A CHART

Your first task is to move the pie chart to its own sheet so that the worksheet data and the clustered column chart do not distract Dr. Musto. Refer to Figure 3.34 as you complete Step 1.

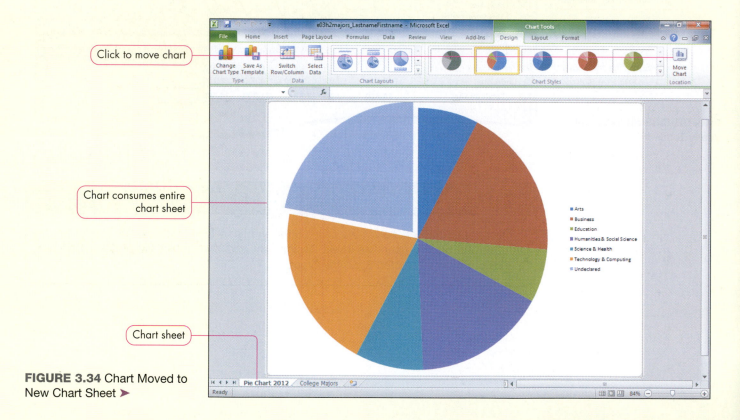

FIGURE 3.34 Chart Moved to New Chart Sheet ▶

a. Open *e03h1majors_LastnameFirstname* if you closed it at the end of Hands-On Exercise 1. Save the workbook with the new name **e03h2majors_LastnameFirstname**, changing *h1* to *h2*.

b. Click the outside border of the pie chart to select it.

c. Click the **Design tab**, and then click **Move Chart** in the Location group.

The Move Chart dialog box opens so that you can specify a new or existing sheet to which to move the chart.

d. Click **New sheet**, type **Pie Chart 2012**, and then click **OK**. Save the workbook.

Excel moves the pie chart out of the original worksheet, creates a new sheet named Pie Chart 2012, and inserts the chart on that sheet.

APPLY A CHART STYLE AND CHART LAYOUT

The pie chart looks a little flat, but you know that changing it to a 3-D pie chart could distort the data. A better solution is to apply an interesting chart style. In addition, you apply a layout to change the location of chart elements. Refer to Figure 3.35 as you complete Step 2.

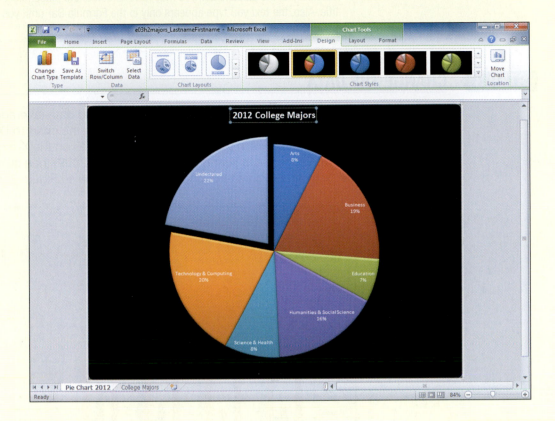

FIGURE 3.35 Chart Style Applied ➤

a. Click the **More button** in the Chart Styles group.

> **TROUBLESHOOTING:** More looks like a horizontal line with a down-pointing triangle.

Excel displays the Chart Styles gallery.

b. Click **Style 42**, the second style from the left on the last row of the gallery.

When you position the mouse pointer over a gallery option, Excel displays a ScreenTip with the style name. When you click Style 42, Excel closes the Chart Styles gallery and applies Style 42 to the chart.

c. Click **Layout 1** in the Chart Layouts group. Save the workbook.

Excel adds a Chart Title placeholder, removes the legend, and inserts the category labels and the respective percentages within the pie slices.

 TIP Pie Chart Labels

The Layout 1 chart layout displays the category names and related percentages on the respective pie slices and removes the legend. This layout is helpful when a pie chart has more than four slices so that you do not have to match pie slice colors with the legend.

d. Click the **Chart Title placeholder**, type **2012 College Majors**, and then press **Enter**. Save the workbook.

> **TROUBLESHOOTING:** If you click inside the Chart Title placeholder instead of just the outer boundary of the placeholder, you may have to delete the placeholder text before typing the new title. Also, the text you type appears only in the Formula Bar until you press Enter. Then it appears in the chart title.

STEP 3 ▶ **CHANGE THE DATA**

You realize that the clustered column chart contains aggregated data (averages) along with the other data series. You need to remove the extra data before showing the chart to Dr. Musto. In addition, you notice that Excel placed the years in the legend and the colleges on the X-axis. Dr. Musto wants to be able to compare all majors for each year (that is, all majors for 2009, then all majors for 2010, and so on) instead of the change in Arts majors throughout the years. Refer to Figure 3.36 as you complete Step 3.

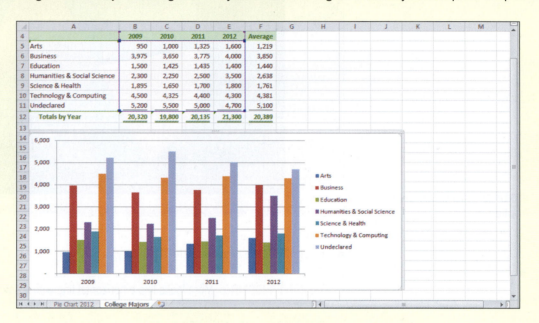

FIGURE 3.36 Adjusted Data for Chart ➤

a. Click the **College Majors worksheet tab** to display the worksheet data and clustered column chart.

b. Click the clustered column chart to select it, and then click the **Design tab**, if necessary.

c. Click **Select Data** in the Data group.

The Select Data Source dialog box opens, and Excel selects the original data source in the worksheet.

d. Click **Average** in the **Legend Entries (Series) list**.

You need to remove the aggregated data.

e. Click **Remove**, and then click **OK**.

f. Click **Switch Row/Column** in the Data group.

Excel reverses the data series and category labels so that the years are category labels and the college data are data series and in the legend.

g. Drag the middle-right sizing handle to the right to the end of column J to widen the chart area. Save the workbook.

After reversing the rows and columns, the columns look tall and thin. You widened the chart area to make the columns appear better proportioned.

CHANGE THE CHART TYPE

Dr. Musto likes what you have done so far, but she would like the column chart to indicate total number of majors per year. You will change the chart to a stacked column chart. Refer to Figure 3.37 as you complete Step 4.

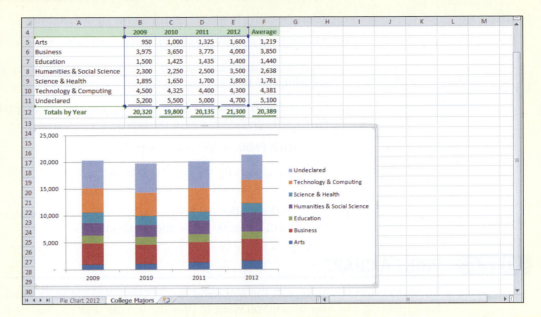

FIGURE 3.37 Stacked Column Chart ➤

a. Click the **Design tab**, if necessary, and then click **Change Chart Type** in the Type group.

The Change Chart Type dialog box opens. The left side displays the main chart types, and the right side contains a gallery of subtypes for each main type.

b. Click **Stacked Column** in the *Column subtype* section, and then click **OK**.

You converted the chart from a clustered column chart to a stacked column chart. The stacked column chart displays the total number of majors per year. Each yearly column contains segments representing each college. Now that you changed the chart to a stacked column chart, the columns look too short and wide.

c. Decrease the chart width so that the right edge ends at the end of column I. Save the workbook.

INSERT A SPARKLINE

You want to insert sparklines to show the enrollment trends for majors in each college at Hort University. After inserting the sparklines, you will display high points to stand out for Dr. Musto and other administrators who want a quick visual of the trends. Refer to Figure 3.38 as you complete Step 5.

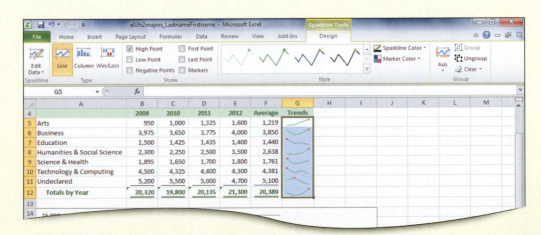

FIGURE 3.38 Sparklines Inserted to Show Trends ➤

FYI

a. Type **Trends** in **cell G4**, use **Format Painter** to apply the styles from **cell F4** to **cell G4**, and then click **cell G5**.

   You entered a heading in the column above where you will insert the sparklines.

b. Click the **Insert tab**, and then click **Line** in the Sparklines group.

c. Select the **range B5:E12** to enter it in the **Data Range box**.

d. Press **Tab**, select the **range G5:G12** to enter it in the **Location Range box**, and then click **OK**.

   Excel inserts sparklines in range G5:G12. Each sparkline depicts data for its row. The sparklines are still selected, and the Sparkline Tools Design contextual tab displays.

e. Click the **More button** in the Style group, and then click **Sparkline Style Colorful #4**, the fourth style on the last row of the gallery.

f. Click **High Point** in the Show group.

   A marker appears for the high point of each data series for each Trendline. You want to change the marker color to stand out.

g. Click **Marker Color** in the Style group, point to **High Point**, and then click **Red** in the *Standard Colors* section. Save the workbook.

STEP 6 ▶ PRINT A CHART

Dr. Musto wants you to print the stacked column chart and the worksheet data for her as a reference for a meeting this afternoon. You want to preview the pie chart to see how it would look when printed as a full page.

a. Click **cell A4** to deselect the sparklines.

   To print both the chart and the worksheet data, you must deselect the chart.

b. Click the **File tab**, and then click **Print**.

   The Backstage view shows a preview that the worksheet data and the chart will print on one page.

c. Click **Print** if you or your instructor wants a printout.

d. Click the **Pie Chart 2012 worksheet tab**, click the **File tab**, click **Print** to preview the printout to ensure it would print on one page, and then click the **Home tab** to go back to the chart window.

e. Save the workbook. Keep the workbook onscreen if you plan to continue with Hands-On Exercise 3. If not, close the workbook and exit Excel.

Chart Layout

The Chart Tools Layout tab (see Figure 3.39) enables you to enhance your charts by selecting specific chart elements, inserting objects, displaying or removing chart elements, customizing the axes, formatting the background, and including analysis. When adding visual elements to a chart, make sure these elements enhance the effectiveness of the chart instead of overpowering it.

> When adding visual elements to a chart, make sure these elements enhance the effectiveness of the chart instead of overpowering it.

FIGURE 3.39 Chart Tools Layout Tab ➤

In this section, you will learn how to modify a chart by adjusting individual chart elements, such as the chart title and data labels. In addition, you will learn how to format chart elements, including applying fill colors to a data series.

Selecting and Formatting Chart Elements

A chart includes several elements—the chart area, the plot area, data series, the horizontal axis, the vertical axis, and the legend—each of which you can customize. When you position the mouse pointer over the chart, Excel displays a ScreenTip with the name of that chart element. To select a chart element, click it when you see the ScreenTip, or click the Chart Elements arrow in the Current Selection group, and then select the element from the list.

After you select a chart element, you can format it and change its settings. You can apply font settings, such as increasing the font size, from the Font group on the Home tab. You can format the values by applying a number style or by changing the number of decimal places on the value axis using the options in the Number group on the Home tab.

You can apply multiple settings at once using a Format dialog box, such as Format Data Series. To format the selected chart element, click Format Selection in the Current Selection group, or right-click the chart element, and then select Format *element* to display the appropriate dialog box (see Figure 3.40).

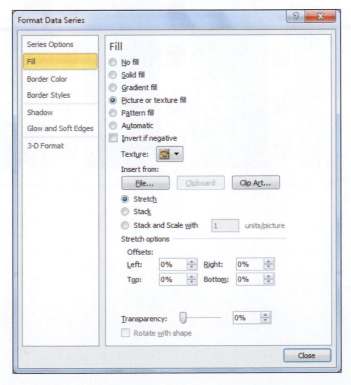

FIGURE 3.40 Format Data Series Dialog Box ➤

The left side of the dialog box lists major categories, such as Fill and Border Color. When you click a category, the right side of the dialog box displays specific options to customize the chart element. For example, when you select the Fill category, the right side displays fill options. When you click a specific option in the right side, such as *Picture or texture fill*, the dialog box displays additional fill options. You can use the Fill options to change the fill color of one or more data series. Avoid making a chart look busy with too many different colors. If you are changing the fill color of a chart area or plot area, make sure the color you select provides enough contrast with the other chart elements.

To format the plot area, click Plot Area in the Background group. Select None to remove any current plot area colors, select Show Plot Area to display the plot area, or select More Plot Area Options to open the Format Plot Area dialog box so that you can apply a fill color to the plot area, similar to selecting fill colors in the Format Data Series dialog box shown in Figure 3.40.

> ### TIP | Use Images or Textures
>
> For less formal presentations, you might want to use images or a texture to fill the data series, chart area, or plot area instead of a solid fill color. To use an image or a texture, click *Picture or texture fill* in the Format Data Series dialog box. Click File or Clip Art in the *Insert from* section, and then insert an image file or search the Microsoft Web site to insert an image. Use the Stack option to avoid distorting the image. To add a texture, click Texture, and then select a textured background. Figure 3.41 shows a stacked image as the first data series fill, a texture fill for the second data series, and a gradient fill for the plot area. Generally, do not mix images and textures; in addition to illustrating different fill options, this figure also shows how adding too many features creates a distracting chart.

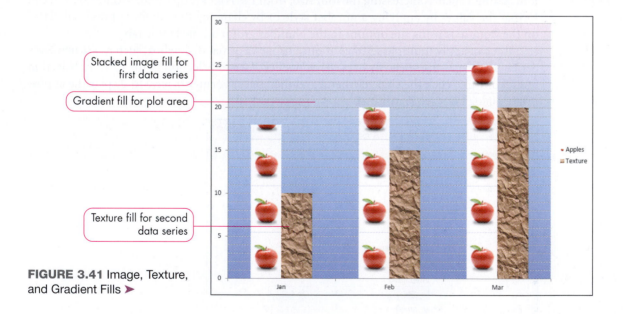

FIGURE 3.41 Image, Texture, and Gradient Fills ➤

Customizing Chart Labels

You should include appropriate labels to describe chart elements. Figure 3.42 identifies basic chart labels.

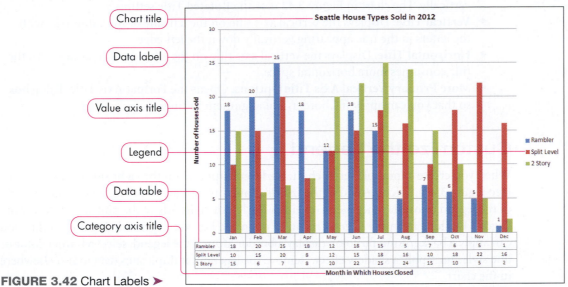

FIGURE 3.42 Chart Labels ➤

Insert and Format the Chart Title

A **chart title** is a label that describes the chart.

A *chart title* is the label that describes the entire chart. Chart titles should reflect the purpose of the chart. For example, *Houses Sold* would be too generic for the chart in Figure 3.42. *Seattle House Types Sold in 2012* indicates the where (Seattle), the what (House Types Sold), and the when (2012).

Excel does not include a chart title by default. Some chart layouts in the Chart Layouts group on the Design tab include a placeholder so that you can enter a title for the current chart. To add, remove, or change the position of a chart title, click Chart Title in the Labels group on the Layout tab, and then select one of the following options:

- **None**. Removes a chart title from the current chart.
- **Centered Overlay Title**. Centers the chart title horizontally without resizing the chart; the title appears over the top of the chart.
- **Above Chart**. Centers the title above the chart (see Figure 3.42), decreasing the chart size to make room for the chart title.
- **More Title Options**. Opens the Format Chart Title dialog box so that you can apply fill, border, and alignment settings.

Position and Format the Axis Titles

An **axis title** is a label that describes either the category axis or the value axis.

Axis titles are labels that describe the category and value axes. If the names on the category axis are not self-explanatory, you can add a label to describe it. The value axis often needs further explanation, such as *In Millions of Dollars* to describe the unit of measurement. To display category axis title options, click Axis Titles in the Labels group, point to Primary Horizontal Axis Title, and then select one of the following:

- **None**. Removes the horizontal axis title from the current chart.
- **Title Below Axis**. Displays the horizontal axis title below the category axis.
- **More Primary Horizontal Axis Title Options**. Opens the Format Axis Title dialog box so that you can apply fill, border, and alignment settings.

To display the value axis title options, click Axis Titles in the Labels group, point to Primary Vertical Axis Title, and then select one of the following:

- **None**. Removes the value axis title from the current chart.
- **Rotated Title**. Displays the value axis title on the left side of the value axis, rotated vertically. The chart in Figure 3.42 uses the Rotated Title setting.
- **Vertical Title**. Displays the vertical axis title on the left side of the value axis, with the letters in the title appearing vertically down the left edge.
- **Horizontal Title**. Displays the vertical axis title on the left side of the value axis; the title consumes more horizontal space.
- **More Primary Vertical Axis Title Options**. Opens the Format Axis Title dialog box so that you can apply fill, border, and alignment settings.

Customize the Legend

When you create a multiple series chart, the legend appears on the right side of the plot area (see Figure 3.42). Click Legend in the Labels group on the Layout tab to change the location of the legend or overlay the legend on either the left or right side of the plot area. Select More Legend Options from the Legend menu to open the Format Legend dialog box so that you can apply a background fill color, display a border around the legend, select a border color or line style, and apply a shadow effect. Remove the legend if it duplicates data found elsewhere in the chart.

Insert and Format Data Labels

A **data label** is the value or name of a data point.

Data labels are descriptive labels that show the exact value of the data points on the value axis. The chart in Figure 3.42 displays data labels for the Rambler data series. Only add data labels when they are necessary for a specific data series; adding data labels for every data point will clutter the chart.

When you select a data label, Excel selects all data labels in that data series. To format the labels, click Format Selection in the Current Selection group, or right-click and select Format Data Labels to open the Format Data Labels dialog box (see Figure 3.43).

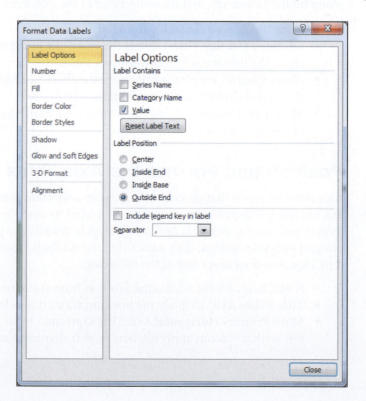

FIGURE 3.43 Format Data Labels Dialog Box ➤

The Format Data Labels dialog box enables you to specify what to display as the label. The default Label Contains setting displays values, but you can display additional data such as the category name. Displaying additional data can clutter the chart. You can also specify the position of the label, such as Center or Outside End. If the numeric data labels are not formatted, click Number on the left side of the dialog box, and then apply number formats.

> **TIP** **Pie Chart Data Labels**
>
> When you first create a pie chart, Excel generates a legend to identify the category labels for the different slice colors, but it does not display data labels. You can display values, percentages, and even category labels on or next to each slice. Pie charts often include percentage data labels. If you also include category labels, hide the legend to avoid duplicating elements.

Include and Format a Data Table

A data table is a grid that contains the data source values and labels. If you embed a chart on the same worksheet as the data source, you do not need to include a data table. Only add a data table with a chart to a chart sheet if you need the audience to know the exact values.

To display a data table, click Data Table in the Labels group, and then select Show Data Table. Figure 3.42 shows a data table at the bottom of the chart area. To see the color-coding along with the category labels, select Show Data Table with Legend Keys, which enables you to omit the legend.

Formatting the Axes and Gridlines

Based on the data source values and structure, Excel determines the starting, incremental, and stopping values that display on the value axis when you create the chart. You might want to adjust the value axis. For example, when working with large values such as 4,567,890, the value axis displays increments, such as 4,000,000 and 5,000,000. You can simplify the value axis by displaying values in millions, so that the values on the axis are 4 and 5 with the word *Millions* placed by the value axis to indicate the units. Figure 3.44 shows two charts—one with original intervals and one in millions.

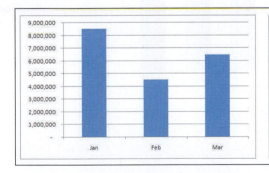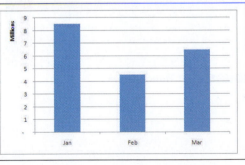

FIGURE 3.44 Value Axis Scaling ➤

To change the number representation, click Axes in the Axes group, and then point to Primary Vertical Axis. Next, select how you want to represent the value axis: Show Default Axis, Show Axis in Thousands, Show Axis in Millions, Show Axis in Billions, or Show Axis in Log Scale. Select More Primary Vertical Axis Options to open the Format Axis dialog box so that you can customize the value axis values.

Although less commonly used, the Primary Horizontal Axis menu enables you to display the axis from left to right (the default), right to left with the value axis on the right side of the chart and the categories in reverse order on the category axis, or without a category axis. Select More Primary Horizontal Axis Options to customize the horizontal axis.

A **gridline** is a horizontal or vertical line that extends from the horizontal or vertical axis through the plot area.

Gridlines are horizontal or vertical lines that span across the chart to help people identify the values plotted by the visual elements, such as a column. Excel displays horizontal gridlines for column, line, scatter, stock, surface, and bubble charts and vertical gridlines for bar charts. If you do not want to display gridlines in a chart, click Gridlines in the Axes group, point to either Primary Horizontal Gridlines or Primary Vertical Gridlines, and then select None. To add more gridlines, select Minor Gridlines or Major & Minor Gridlines.

Adding a Trendline

A **trendline** is a line used to depict trends and forecast future data.

Charts help reveal trends, patterns, and other tendencies that are difficult to identify by looking at values in a worksheet. A *trendline* is a line that depicts trends or helps forecast future data. Trendlines are commonly used in prediction, such as to determine the future trends of sales, or the success rate of a new prescription drug. You can use trendlines in unstacked column, bar, line, stock, scatter, and bubble charts. To add a trendline, click Trendline in the Analysis group, and then select the type you want: Linear Trendline, Exponential Trendline, Linear Forecast Trendline, or Two Period Moving Average. Figure 3.45 shows two linear forecast trendlines, one applied to the Business data series and one applied to the Undeclared data series. Notice that this trendline provides a forecast (prediction) for two additional time periods—2013 and 2014—although the years are not depicted on the X-axis. Excel analyzes the plotted data to forecast values for the next two time periods when you select the Linear Forecast Trendline. If you apply Linear Trendline only, Excel displays the trendline for the data but does not forecast data points for the future.

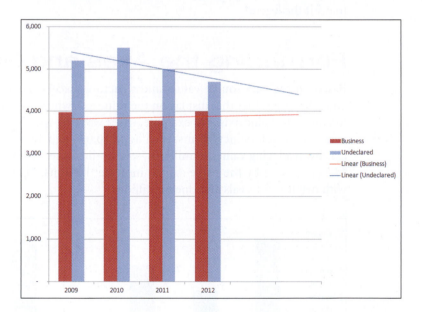

FIGURE 3.45 Trendlines ➤

HANDS-ON EXERCISES

3 Chart Layout

You want to enhance the column chart by using some options on the Layout tab to add the final touches needed before you give the charts to Dr. Musto to review.

Skills covered: Add a Chart Title • Add and Format Axis Titles • Add Data Labels • Apply Fill Colors • Insert a Trendline

---

STEP 1 ▶ ADD A CHART TITLE

When you applied a chart layout to the pie chart, Excel displayed a placeholder for the chart title. However, you need to add a chart title for the column chart. You also want to copy the chart and modify it so that you can provide two different perspectives for Dr. Musto. Refer to Figure 3.46 as you complete Step 1.

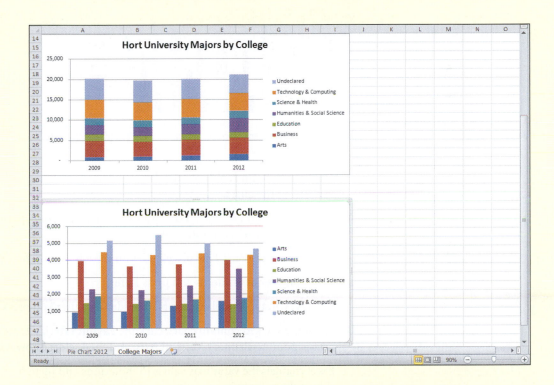

FIGURE 3.46 Charts with Titles ▶

a. Open *e03h2majors_LastnameFirstname* if you closed it at the end of Hands-On Exercise 2. Save the workbook with the new name **e03h3majors_LastnameFirstname**, changing *h2* to *h3*.

b. Click the stacked column chart to select it.

c. Click the **Layout tab**, click **Chart Title** in the Labels group, and then select **Above Chart**.

   Excel displays the Chart Title placeholder, and the plot area decreases to make room for the chart title.

d. Type **Hort University Majors by College** and press **Enter**.

e. Click the **Chart Elements arrow** in the Current Selection group, and then select **Chart Area**.

   You selected the entire chart area so that you can copy it.

f. Press **Ctrl+C**, click **cell A33**, and then press **Ctrl+V** to paste the top-left corner of the chart here. Change the second chart to a **Clustered Column chart**. Save the workbook.

You decide to add an axis title to the value axis to clarify the values in the clustered column chart. For the stacked column chart, you want to change the value axis increments. Refer to Figure 3.47 as you complete Step 2.

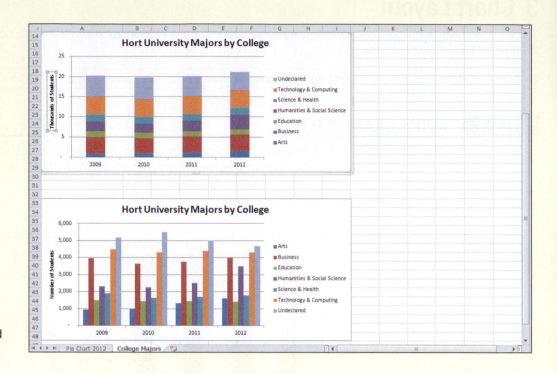

FIGURE 3.47 Axis Titles and Values Changed ➤

a. Make sure the clustered column chart is selected, and then use the scroll bars if necessary to view the entire chart.

b. Click the **Layout tab**, click **Axis Titles** in the Labels group, point to **Primary Vertical Axis Title**, and then select **Rotated Title**.

Excel inserts the Axis Title placeholder on the left side of the value axis.

c. Type **Number of Students** and press **Enter**.

The text you typed replaces the placeholder text after you press Enter.

d. Select the stacked column chart, click the **Layout tab** (if necessary), click **Axes** in the Axes group, point to **Primary Vertical Axis**, and then select **Show Axis in Thousands**.

Excel changes the value axis values to thousands and includes the label *Thousands* to the left side of the value axis.

e. Click **Thousands** to select it, type **Thousands of Students**, and then press **Enter**.

f. Drag the **Thousands of Students label** down to appear vertically centered with the value axis increments. Save the workbook.

Dr. Musto wants you to emphasize the Undeclared majors data series by adding data labels for that data series. You will have to be careful to add data labels for only the Undeclared data series, as adding data labels for all data series would clutter the chart. Refer to Figure 3.48 as you complete Step 3.

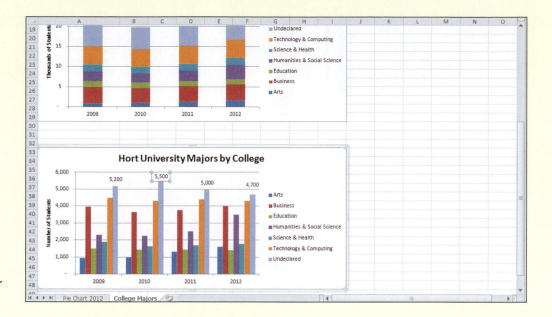

FIGURE 3.48 Data Labels for One Data Series ➤

a. Select the clustered column chart, click the **Chart Elements arrow** in the Current Selection group, and then select **Series "Undeclared"**.

Excel selects all of the Undeclared (light blue) columns in the chart.

b. Click **Data Labels** in the Labels group, and then select **Outside End**.

You added data labels to the selected Undeclared data series.

> **TROUBLESHOOTING:** If data labels appear for all columns, use the Undo feature. Make sure you select only the Undeclared data series columns, and then add data labels again.

c. Look at the data labels to see if they are on gridlines.

The 4,700 and 5,500 data labels are on gridlines.

d. Click the **4,700 data label** twice, pausing between clicks.

Only the 4,700 data label should be selected.

> **TROUBLESHOOTING:** If you double-click a data label instead of pausing between individual clicks, the Format Data Labels dialog box appears. If this happens, click Close in the dialog box, and then repeat step d, pausing longer between clicks.

e. Click the outer edge of the **4,700 data label border**, and then drag the label up a little so that it is off the gridline.

f. Select the **5,500 data label**, and then drag it below the top gridline. Save the workbook.

STEP 4 ▸ APPLY FILL COLORS

Dr. Musto wants the Business data series color to stand out, so you will apply a brighter red fill to that series. In addition, you want to apply a gradient color to the plot area so that the chart stands out from the rest of the page. Refer to Figure 3.49 as you complete Step 4.

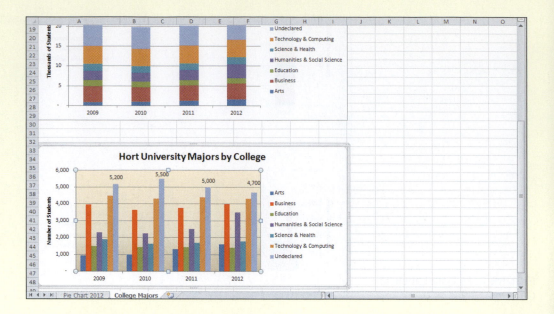

FIGURE 3.49 Chart with Different Fill Colors ➤

a. Make sure the clustered column chart is still selected, click the **Chart Elements arrow** in the Current Selection group, and then select **Series "Business"** or click one of the **Business columns**.

The Business data series columns are selected.

b. Click **Format Selection** in the Current Selection group.

The Format Data Series dialog box opens so that you can format the Business data series.

c. Click **Fill** on the left side of the dialog box, and then click **Solid fill**.

The dialog box displays additional fill options.

d. Click **Color**, click **Red** in the *Standard Colors* section of the gallery, and then click **Close**.

The Business data series appears in red.

e. Click **Plot Area** in the Background group, and then select **More Plot Area Options**.

The Format Plot Area dialog box opens.

f. Click **Gradient fill**, click **Preset colors**, click **Parchment** (using the ScreenTips to help you find the correct preset color), and then click **Close**.

Be careful when selecting plot area colors to ensure that the data series columns, bars, or lines still stand out. Print a sample on a color printer to help make the decision.

STEP 5 ▶ INSERT A TRENDLINE

Identifying trends is important when planning college budgets. Colleges with growing enrollments need additional funding to support more students. It looks like the numbers of humanities and social science majors are increasing, but you want to add a trendline to verify your analysis. Refer to Figure 3.50 as you complete Step 5.

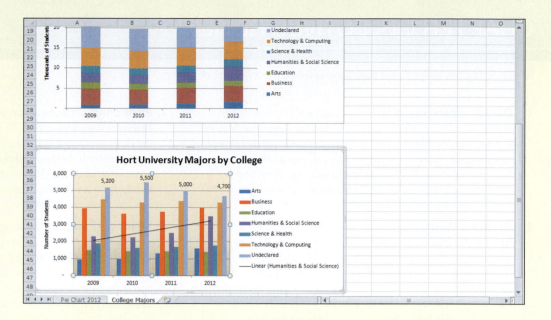

FIGURE 3.50 Trendline ➤

a. Make sure the clustered column chart is still selected.

b. Click **Trendline** in the Analysis group, and then select **Linear Trendline**.

The Add Trendline dialog box opens so that you can select which data series you want to use for the trendline.

c. Click **Humanities & Social Science**, and then click **OK**.

Excel adds a trendline based on the data series you specified. The trend is a steady increase in the number of majors in this discipline.

d. Save and close the workbook, and submit based on your instructor's directions.

After reading this chapter, you have accomplished the following objectives:

1. **Decide which chart type to create.** Choose a chart type that will present the data in a way that communicates the message effectively to your audience. Column charts compare categorical data, bar charts compare categorical data horizontally, line charts illustrate trends over time, and pie charts show proportions to the whole. Variations of each major chart type are called *subtypes*.

2. **Create a chart.** The first step in creating a chart is to identify and select the range of cells that will be used as the data source. Be careful to select similar data series to avoid distorting the chart. After selecting the data source, click the desired chart type on the Insert tab. Excel inserts charts on the same worksheet as the data. You can move the chart and adjust the size of the chart area. When you create a chart or select an existing chart, Excel displays the Chart Tools contextual tab with three tabs: Design, Layout, and Format.

3. **Change the chart type.** You can change a chart to a different chart type if you believe a different chart type will represent the data better.

4. **Change the data source and structure.** You can add or remove data from the data source to change the data in the chart. The Select Data Source dialog box enables you to modify the ranges used for the data series. Excel usually places the first column of data as the category axis and the first row of data as the legend, but you can switch the row and column layout. The Design tab contains options for changing the data source and structure.

5. **Apply a chart layout and a chart style.** You can apply a chart layout to control what chart elements are included and where they are positioned within the chart area. You can apply a chart style, which determines formatting, such as the background color and the data series color. The Design tab contains options for selecting the chart layout and chart style.

6. **Move a chart.** You can position a chart on the same worksheet as the data source, or you can move the chart to its own sheet. The Move Chart dialog box enables you to select a new sheet and name the new chart sheet at the same time. The chart sheet will then contain a full-sized chart and no data. You can also move a chart to an existing worksheet. When you do this, the chart is an embedded object on that sheet, and the sheet may contain other data.

7. **Print charts.** You can print a chart with or without its corresponding data source. To print a chart with its data series, the chart needs to be on the same worksheet as the data source. To ensure both the data and the chart print, make sure the chart is not selected. If the chart is on its own sheet or if you select the chart on a worksheet containing other data, the chart will print as a full-sized chart.

8. **Insert and customize a sparkline.** A sparkline is a miniature chart in one cell representing a single data series. It gives a quick visual of the data to aid in comprehension. You can customize sparklines by changing the data source, location, and style. In addition, you can display markers, such as High Point, and change the line or marker color.

9. **Select and format chart elements.** Because each chart element is an individual object in the chart area, you can select and format each element separately. The Format dialog boxes enable you to apply fill colors, select border colors, and apply other settings. For the value axis, you can format values and specify the number of decimal places to display. For basic formatting, such as font color, use the options in the Font group on the Home tab.

10. **Customize chart labels.** The Labels group on the Layout tab enables you to add or remove chart elements: chart title, axis titles, legend, data labels, and a data table. The chart title should clearly describe the data and purpose of the chart. Include axis titles when you need to clarify the values on the value axis or the categories on the category axis. Customize the legend when you want to change its position within the chart area or hide the legend. Display data labels to provide exact values for data points in one or more data series; however, be careful the data labels do not overlap. If a chart is contained on a chart sheet, you might want to show the data table that contains the values used from the data source.

11. **Format the axes and gridlines.** The Axes group on the Layout tab enables you to control the horizontal and vertical axes. You can select the minimum, maximum, and increments on the value axis, and you can display both major and minor gridlines to help your audience read across the plot area.

12. **Add a trendline.** A trendline is a line that depicts trends. Trendlines are used to help make predictions or forecasts based on the current dataset. Excel enables you to select different types of trendlines based on the type of statistical analysis you want to perform.

KEY TERMS

100% stacked column chart *p.181*
3-D chart *p.182*
Area chart *p.184*
Axis title *p.209*
Bar chart *p.183*
Bubble chart *p.187*
Category axis *p.179*
Category label *p.178*
Chart *p.178*
Chart area *p.179*
Chart sheet *p.190*
Chart title *p.209*
Clustered column chart *p.179*

Column chart *p.179*
Data label *p.210*
Data point *p.178*
Data series *p.178*
Doughnut chart *p.187*
Exploded pie chart *p.184*
Gridline *p.212*
Legend *p.180*
Line chart *p.183*
Multiple data series *p.179*
Pie chart *p.184*
Plot area *p.179*
Radar chart *p.188*

Single data series *p.179*
Sizing handle *p.190*
Sparkline *p.200*
Stacked column chart *p.180*
Stock chart *p.186*
Surface chart *p.186*
Trendline *p.212*
Value axis *p.179*
X Y (scatter) chart *p.185*
X-axis *p.179*
Y-axis *p.179*

MULTIPLE CHOICE

1. Which type of chart is the **least** appropriate for depicting yearly rainfall totals for five cities for four years?

   (a) Pie chart

   (b) Line chart

   (c) Column chart

   (d) Bar chart

2. What is the typical sequence for creating a chart?

   (a) Select the chart type, select the data source, and then size and position the chart.

   (b) Select the data source, size the chart, select the chart type, and then position the chart.

   (c) Select the data source, select the chart type, and then size and position the chart.

   (d) Click the cell to contain the chart, select the chart type, and then select the data source.

3. Which of the following applies to a sparkline?

   (a) Chart title

   (b) Single-cell chart

   (c) Legend

   (d) Multiple data series

4. If you want to show exact values for a data series in a bar chart, what chart element should you display?

   (a) Chart title

   (b) Legend

   (c) Value axis title

   (d) Data labels

5. The value axis currently shows increments such as 50,000 and 100,000. What do you select to display increments of 50 and 100?

   (a) More Primary Vertical Axis Title Options

   (b) Show Axis in Thousands

   (c) Show Axis in Millions

   (d) Show Right to Left Axis

6. You want to create a single chart that shows each of five divisions' proportion of yearly sales for each year for five years. Which type of chart can accommodate your needs?

   (a) Pie chart

   (b) Surface chart

   (c) Clustered bar chart

   (d) 100% stacked column chart

7. Currently, a column chart shows values on the value axis, years on the category axis, and state names in the legend. What should you do if you want to organize data with the states on the category axis and the years shown in the legend?

   (a) Change the chart type to a clustered column chart.

   (b) Click Switch Row/Column in the Data group on the Design tab.

   (c) Click Layout 2 in the Chart Layouts group on the Design tab, and then apply a different chart style.

   (d) Click Legend in the Labels group on the Layout tab, and then select Show Legend at Bottom.

8. Which tab contains commands to apply a predefined chart layout that controls what elements are included, where, and their color scheme?

   (a) Design

   (b) Layout

   (c) Format

   (d) Page Layout

9. A chart and its related data source are located on the same worksheet. What is the default Print option if the chart is selected prior to displaying the Backstage view?

   (a) Print Entire Workbook

   (b) Print Selection

   (c) Print Selected Chart

   (d) Print Active Sheets

10. Which of the following is *not* a way to display the Format Data Series dialog box for the Arts data series in a column chart?

    (a) Press and hold Shift as you click each Arts column.

    (b) Click an Arts column, and then click Format Selection in the Current Selection group on the Layout tab.

    (c) Right-click an Arts column, and then select Format Data Series.

    (d) Click the Chart Elements arrow in the Current Selection group, select the Arts data series, and then click Format Selection in the Current Selection group on the Layout tab.

PRACTICE EXERCISES

1 Family Utility Expenses

Your cousin, Rita Dansie, wants to analyze her family's utility expenses for 2012. She wants to save money during months when utility expenses are lower so that her family will have money budgeted for months when the total utility expenses are higher. She gave you her files for the electric, gas, and water bills for the year 2012. You created a worksheet that lists the individual expenses per month, along with yearly totals per utility type and monthly totals. You will create some charts to depict the data. This exercise follows the same set of skills as used in Hands-On Exercises 1 and 2 in the chapter. Refer to Figure 3.51 as you complete this exercise.

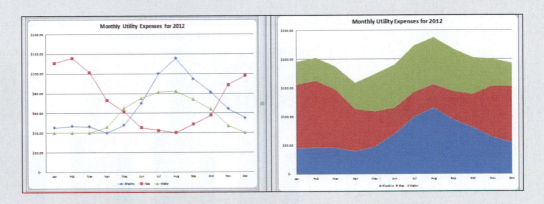

FIGURE 3.51 Dansie Family Utility Expenses ➤

a. Open *e03p1utilities* and save it as **e03p1utilities_LastnameFirstname**.

b. Select the **range A4:E17**, and then click the **Insert tab**.

c. Click **Column** in the Charts group, and then select **Clustered Column**. After creating the chart, you realize you need to adjust the data source because you included the monthly and yearly totals.

d. Click the **Design tab**, if necessary. Click **Select Data** in the Data group to open the Select Data Source dialog box, and then do the following:
  - Click **Monthly Totals** in the **Legend Entries (Series) list,** and then click **Remove**.
  - Click in the **Chart data range box**, and then change *17* to **16** at the end of the range.
  - Click **OK** to finalize removing the monthly and yearly totals from the chart.

e. Position the mouse pointer over the chart area. When you see the Chart Area ScreenTip, drag the chart so that the top-left edge of the chart is in **cell A19**.

f. Click the **Format tab**. Click in the **Shape Width box** in the Size group, type **6**, and then press **Enter**.

g. Click the **Design tab**, and then click **Layout 3** in the Chart Layouts group.

h. Click the **Chart Title placeholder**, type **Monthly Utility Expenses for 2012**, and then press **Enter**.

i. Click the **More button** in the Chart Styles group, and then click **Style 26** (second style, fourth row).

j. Click the clustered column chart, use the **Copy command**, and then paste a copy of the chart in **cell A36**. With the second chart selected, do the following:
  - Click the **Design tab**, click **Change Chart Type** in the Type group, select **Line with Markers** in the *Line* section, and then click **OK**.
  - Click the **More button** in the Chart Styles group, and then click **Style 2** (second style, first row).
  - Copy the selected chart, and then paste it in **cell A52**.

k. Make sure the third chart is selected, and then do the following:
  - Click the **Design tab**, if necessary, click **Change Chart Type** in the Type group, select **Area** on the left side, click **Stacked Area**, and then click **OK**.
  - Click **Move Chart** in the Location group, click **New sheet**, type **Area Chart**, and then click **OK**.

l. Click the **Expenses worksheet tab**, scroll up to see the line chart, and then select the line chart. Click the **Design tab**, if necessary, click **Move Chart** in the Location group, click **New sheet**, type **Line Chart**, and then click **OK**.

m. Create a footer with your name on the left side, the sheet name code in the center, and the file name code on the right side on the worksheet and on the two chart sheets.

n. Click the **File tab**, and then click **Print**. Look at the preview window for each worksheet. Print all three worksheets for your reference, based on your instructor's directions.

o. Save and close the workbook, and submit based on your instructor's directions.

2 U.S. Population Estimates

You work for a major corporation headquartered in Chicago. One of your responsibilities is to analyze population statistics to identify geographic regions in which you can increase your market presence. You often visit the U.S. Census Bureau's Web site to download and analyze the data. You need to create a chart to present at a meeting tomorrow morning. This exercise follows the same set of skills as used in Hands-On Exercises 1, 2, and 3 in the chapter. Refer to Figure 3.52 as you complete this exercise.

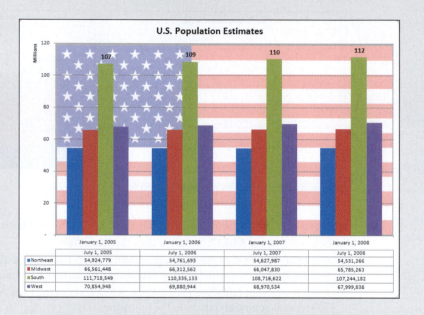

FIGURE 3.52 U.S. Population Estimates ➤

a. Open *e03p2uspop* and save it as **e03p2uspop_LastnameFirstname**.

b. Select the **range A3:E7**, click the **Insert tab**, click **Column** in the Charts group, and then click **Clustered Column** in the *2-D Column* section.

c. Click **Move Chart** in the Location group on the Design tab. Click **New sheet**, type **Column Chart**, and then click **OK**.

d. Click the **Layout tab**, and then add a chart title by doing the following:
   • Click **Chart Title** in the Labels group, and then select **Above Chart**.
   • Type **U.S. Population Estimates** and press **Enter**.

e. Add data labels by doing the following:
   • Click the **Chart Elements arrow** in the Current Selection group, and then select **Series "South"**.
   • Click **Data Labels** in the Labels group, and then select **Outside End**.
   • Click the data labels to select them, apply **bold**, and then apply a **12-pt font** size.

f. Click the **Layout tab**, if necessary, click **Data Table** in the Labels group, and then select **Show Data Table with Legend Keys**.

g. Click **Legend** in the Labels group, and then select **None**.

h. Click **Axes** in the Axes group, point to **Primary Vertical Axis**, and then select **Show Axis in Millions**.

i. Click **Plot Area** in the Background group, and then select **More Plot Area Options**. Do the following in the Format Plot Area dialog box:
   • Click **Picture or texture fill**.
   • Click **Clip Art**, then in the Select Picture dialog box, search for and insert a picture of the **U.S. flag**.

- Select the image, and then click **OK**.
- Drag the **Transparency slider** to **70%**, and then click **Close**.

j. Click the **Population worksheet tab**, click **cell B9**, and create sparklines by doing the following:
- Click the **Insert tab**, and click **Column** in the Sparklines group.
- Select the **range B4:B7** to enter the range in the **Data Range box**.
- Ensure **$B$9** appears in the **Location Range box**, and then click **OK**.
- Increase the row height of row 9 to **42.00**.

k. Adapt step j to create sparklines in the **range C9:E9**.

l. Create a footer with your name on the left side, the sheet name code in the center, and the file name code on the right side of both worksheets.

m. Save and close the workbook, and submit based on your instructor's directions.

3 Gas Prices in Boston

You are interested in moving to Boston, but you want to know about the city's gasoline prices. You downloaded data from a government site, but it is overwhelming to detect trends when you have over 200 weekly data points. You create a chart to help you interpret the data. This exercise follows the same set of skills as used in Hands-On Exercises 1, 2, and 3 in the chapter. Refer to Figure 3.53 as you complete this exercise.

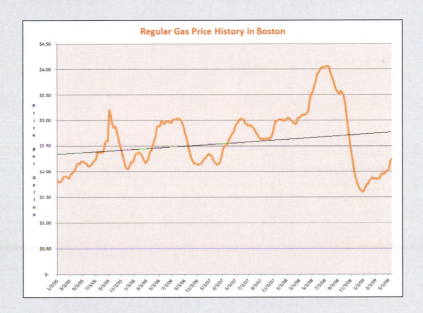

FIGURE 3.53 Boston Gas Prices ➤

a. Open *e03p3boston* and save it as **e03p3boston_LastnameFirstname**.

b. Select **cells A6:B235**, click the **Insert tab**, click **Line** in the Charts group, and then click **Line** in the *2-D Line* section. Excel creates the chart and displays the Chart Tools Design tab.

c. Click **Move Chart** in the Location group, click **New sheet**, type **Line Chart**, and then click **OK**.

d. Click the **Layout tab**, click **Legend** in the Labels group, and then select **None** to remove the legend.

e. Click the chart title to select it, type **Regular Gas Price History in Boston**, and then press **Enter**.

f. Click **Axis Titles** in the Labels group, point to **Primary Vertical Axis Title**, select **Vertical Title**, type **Price per Gallon**, and then press **Enter**.

g. Click **Axes** in the Axes group, point to **Primary Vertical Axis**, and then select **More Primary Vertical Axis Options**. Do the following in the Format Axis dialog box:
- Make sure that **Axis Options** is selected on the left side of the Format Axis dialog box, click the **Display units arrow**, and then select **Hundreds**.
- Click **Number** on the left side of the dialog box, click **Accounting** in the **Category list**, and then click **Close**.

h. Click the **Hundreds label**, and then press **Delete**. You converted the cents per gallon to dollars and cents per gallon.

i. Click **Axes** in the Axes group, point to **Primary Horizontal Axis**, and then select **More Primary Horizontal Axis Options**. Click **Number** on the left side of the Format Axis dialog box, click **Date** in the **Category list** if necessary, select **3/14/01** in the **Type list**, and then click **Close**.

j. Use the Home tab to change the category axis, value axis, and value axis labels to **9-pt** size. Apply the **Orange, Accent 6, Darker 25% font color** to the chart title.

k. Click the **Design tab**, click the **More button** in the Chart styles group, and then click **Style 40** (first style on the right side of the fifth row).

l. Click the **Layout tab**, click **Trendline**, and then select **Exponential Trendline**.

m. Create a footer with your name on the left side, the sheet name code in the center, and the file name code on the right side.

n. Click the **File tab**, click **Print**, and then look at the preview. Print the chart sheet if instructed.

o. Save and close the workbook, and submit based on your instructor's directions.

1 Car Ratings

You work for an independent automobile rating company that provides statistics to consumers. A group of testers recently evaluated four 2012 mid-sized passenger car models and provided the data to you in a worksheet. You need to transform the data into meaningful charts that you will include on your company's Web site. Refer to Figure 3.54 as you complete this exercise.

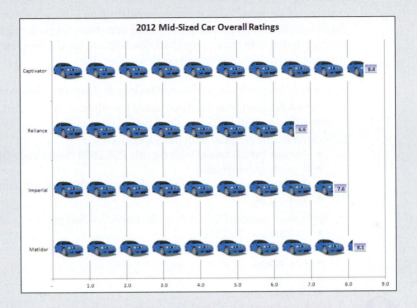

FIGURE 3.54 Automobile Ratings Chart ➤

DISCOVER

a. Open *e03m1autos* and save it as **e03m1autos_LastnameFirstname**.

b. Insert a column sparkline individually for each car model and for the overall category ratings in column H. Include all ratings, including the average. Apply a different style to each sparkline. Change the row height to **20** for rows containing sparklines.

c. Select the **range A3:F8**, and then create a stacked column chart. You realize that the data in this chart is not cumulative and that you included the overall ratings by category. You also notice that the chart is located to the side of the data. Make the following changes:
    - Change the chart to a clustered column chart.
    - Remove the overall category from the data source.
    - Position the chart starting in **cell A11**, and then increase the chart width through **cell G27**.

d. Make the following design changes:
    - Select **Layout 1** as the chart layout style.
    - Edit the chart title to be **2012 Mid-Sized Car Ratings by Category**.
    - Apply the **Red, Accent 2, Darker 25% font color** to the chart title.
    - Apply the **Style 12 chart style**.

e. Create another chart on a new chart sheet:
    - Select the **range A4:A7**, press and hold **Ctrl**, and then select the **range G4:G7**—the models and the overall ratings.
    - Create a clustered bar chart.
    - Move the chart to its own sheet named **Overall Ratings**.

f. Make the following changes to the bar chart (see Figure 3.54):
    - Remove the legend.
    - Add the title **2012 Mid-Sized Car Overall Ratings** above the chart.
    - Apply the **Style 2 chart style**, if necessary.
    - Add data labels in the Outside End position, and then bold the data labels. Apply the **Fog gradient fill color** to the data labels.
    - Select the data series, and then apply a picture fill, searching for clip art of a blue automobile. Select the option to stack the images instead of stretching one image per data marker.

g. Insert a footer with your name on the left side, the sheet name code in the center, and the file name code on the right side on all worksheets.

h. Adjust the page setup option to fit the worksheet to one page with 0.5" left and right margins. Print the worksheet that contains the data and the clustered column chart per your instructor's directions.

i. Save and close the workbook, and submit based on your instructor's directions.

2 Grade Analysis

You are a teaching assistant for Dr. Monica Unice's introductory psychology class. You have maintained her grade book all semester, entering three test scores for each student and calculating the final average. Dr. Unice wants to see a chart that shows the percentage of students who earn each letter grade. You decide to create a pie chart. She wants to see if a correlation exists between attendance and students' final grades, so you will create a scatter chart.

a. Open *e03m2psych* and save it as **e03m2psych_LastnameFirstname**.

b. Create a pie chart from the Final Grade Distribution data located below the student data, and then move the pie chart to its own sheet named **Grades Pie**.

c. Customize the pie chart with these specifications:
   - **Layout 1 chart layout** with the title **PSY 2030 Final Grade Distribution - Fall 2012**
   - F grade slice exploded
   - **20-pt** size for the data labels, with a center label position, and gradient fill
   - Border: no line

d. Apply these standard fill colors to the respective data points:
   - A: Blue
   - B: Green
   - C: Orange
   - D: Purple
   - F: Red

DISCOVER

e. Create a Scatter with only Markers chart using the attendance record and final averages from the Grades worksheet, and then move the scatter chart to its own sheet. Name the sheet **Attend Grades**.

f. Apply these label settings to the scatter chart:
   - Legend: none
   - Chart title above chart: **Attendance - Final Average Relationship**
   - X-axis title: **Percentage of Attendance**
   - Y-axis rotated title: **Student Final Averages**

g. Use Help to learn how to apply the following axis settings:
   - Y-axis: 40 starting point, 100 maximum score, 10 point increments, and a number format with zero decimal places
   - X-axis: 40 starting point, automatic increments, automatic maximum

h. Add the **Parchment gradient fill** to the plot area.

i. Insert a linear trendline.

j. Center the worksheet horizontally between the left and right margins on the Grades worksheet.

k. Insert a footer with your name on the left side, the sheet name code in the center, and the file name code on the right side for all three worksheets.

l. Save and close the workbook, and submit based on your instructor's directions.

CAPSTONE EXERCISE

You are an assistant manager at Premiere Movie Source, an online company that enables customers to download movies for a fee. You are required to track movie download sales by genre. You gathered the data for September 2012 and organized it in an Excel workbook. You are ready to create charts to help represent the data so that you can make a presentation to your manager later this week.

Change Data Source, Position, and Size

You already created a clustered column chart, but you selected too many cells for the data source. You need to open the workbook and adjust the data source for the chart. In addition, you want to position and size the chart.

a. Open the *e03c1movies* workbook and save it as **e03c1movies_LastnameFirstname**.

b. Remove the Category Totals from the legend, and then adjust the data range to exclude the weekly totals.

c. Position and size the chart to fill the **range A18:L37**.

d. Change the row and column orientation so that the weeks appear in the category axis and the genres appear in the legend.

Add Chart Labels

You want to add a chart title and a value axis title and change the legend's position.

a. Add a chart title above the chart.

b. Enter the text **September 2012 Downloads by Genre**.

c. Add a rotated value axis title.

d. Enter the text **Number of Downloads**.

e. Move the legend to the top of the chart, and then drag the bottom of the chart area down to cover row 40.

Format Chart Elements

You are ready to apply the finishing touches to the clustered column chart. You will adjust the font size of the category axis and display additional gridlines to make it easier to identify values for the data series. You will add and adjust data labels to the Drama data series. Finally, you will add a linear trendline to the chart to visualize trends.

a. Format the category axis with **12-pt size**.

b. Display major and minor horizontal gridlines.

c. Select the **Drama data series**, and then add data labels in the Outside End position.

d. Add a **Yellow fill color** to the data labels.

e. Add a linear trendline to the Drama data series.

Insert and Format Sparklines

You want to show weekly trends for each genre by inserting sparklines in the column to the right of Category Totals.

a. Insert a **Line sparkline** for the weekly (but not category totals) data for Action & Adventure in **cell G5**.

b. Copy the sparkline down the column.

c. Format the sparklines by applying **Sparkline Style Dark #6**, display the high point, and format the high point marker in **Red**.

Create Another Chart

You want to create a chart that will show the monthly volume of downloads by genre. You decide to create a bar chart with genre labels along the left side of the chart.

a. Select the genres and weekly totals. Create a clustered bar chart.

b. Move the chart to its own sheet, and then name the sheet **Bar Chart**.

c. Change the chart type to a stacked bar chart.

d. Add a chart title above the chart, and then enter **Sept 2012 Total Monthly Downloads by Genre**.

Format the Bar Chart

You want to enhance the appearance of the chart by applying a chart style and adjusting the axis values.

a. Apply the **Style 31 chart style** to the bar chart.

b. Display the value axis in units of thousands.

c. Display the category axis names in reverse order using the Format Axis dialog box.

d. Apply the **Layout 3 layout style** to the chart.

Printing the Charts

You want to print the bar chart on its own page, but you want to print the clustered column chart with the original data. To ensure the worksheet data and chart print on the same page, you need to adjust the page setup options.

a. Create a footer on each worksheet with your name, the sheet name code, and the file name code.

b. Apply landscape orientation for the original worksheet.

c. Set 0.2" left, right, top, and bottom margins for the original worksheet.

d. Select the option that makes the worksheet print on only one page.

e. Print both worksheets.

f. Save and close the workbook, and submit based on your instructor's directions.

Widget Company Stock Prices

GENERAL CASE

You want to track your investment in Widget Company. Open *e03b1stock* and save it as **e03b1stock_LastnameFirstname**. Create the appropriate stock chart based on the existing sequence of data, keeping in mind that data must be in a specific structure to create the chart. Move the chart to a new chart sheet, and name the sheet **Stock Chart**. Apply the Style 37 chart style, remove the legend, and display the data table. Add a centered overlay title that describes the chart. Select the chart title; apply a solid fill using Olive Green, Accent 3, Darker 50%; and apply White, Background 1 font color. Add a linear trendline for the closing price. Create a footer with your name, the sheet name code, and file name code. Save and close the workbook, and submit based on your instructor's directions.

Box Office Movie Data

RESEARCH CASE

As a contributing writer for an entertainment magazine, you have been asked to gather data on box office opening revenue for movies released in the theaters this month. Conduct some online research to identify six newly released movies, their release dates, and the revenue generated. Start a new workbook. Organize the data from the lowest-grossing movie to the highest-grossing movie. Apply appropriate formatting, and include a main and secondary title for the worksheet. Save the workbook as **e03b2boxoffice_LastnameFirstname**. Use the data to create a bar chart on a separate worksheet, showing the movie names on the vertical axis and revenue on the horizontal axis. Assign names to the worksheet tabs, and delete the extra worksheets. Format the value axis in millions, and apply Accounting or Currency format, if needed. Insert a chart title that describes the data. Apply a different chart style. Use Help to research how to insert text boxes. Insert a text box for the first bar containing the release date. Position the text box on top of the bar, and select a contrasting font color. Copy the text box for the remaining movie bars, and edit each text box to display the respective release dates. Create a footer with your name, the sheet name code, and the file name code. Print a copy of the chart for your records. Save and close the workbook, and submit based on your instructor's directions.

Harper County Houses Sold

DISASTER RECOVERY

You want to analyze the number of houses sold by type (e.g., rambler, two-story, etc.) in each quarter during 2012. Your intern created an initial chart, but it contains a lot of problems. Open *e03b3houses* and save it as **e03b3houses_LastnameFirstname**. Identify the errors and poor design. List the errors and your corrections in a two-column format below the chart. Then correct problems in the chart. Create a footer with your name, the sheet name code, and the file name code. Adjust the margins and scaling to print the worksheet data, including the error list, and chart on one page. Save and close the workbook, and submit based on your instructor's directions.

4 DATASETS AND TABLES

Managing Large Volumes of Data

Watch the
**Set-up
Video**
for this
Case Study!

CASE STUDY | The Spa Experts

Shortly after graduating from college, you and your best friend, Ryan Paap, started a business selling spas and hot tubs. Business has been good, and your expansive showroom and wide selection appeal to a variety of customers. You and Ryan maintain a large inventory to attract the impulse buyer and currently have agreements with three manufacturers: Serenity Spas, The Original Hot Tub, and Port-a-Spa. Each manufacturer offers spas and hot tubs that appeal to different segments of the market, from affordable to exorbitant.

The business has grown rapidly, and you need to analyze the sales data in order to increase future profits. For example, which vendor generates the most sales? Who is the leading salesperson? Do most customers purchase or finance? Are sales promotions necessary to promote business, or will customers pay the full price?

You created a worksheet that has sales data for the current month. Each transaction appears on a separate row and contains the transaction number, date, sales representatives' first and last names, the spa manufacturer, payment type (financed or paid in full), transaction (standard or promotion), and the amount of the sale. You are ready to start analyzing the data in Excel.

Large Datasets

So far you have worked with worksheets that contain small datasets, a collection of structured, related data in columns and rows. In reality, you will probably work with large datasets consisting of hundreds or thousands of rows and columns of data. When you work with small datasets, you can usually view most or all of the data without scrolling. When you work with large datasets, column and row labels scroll offscreen when you scroll through the worksheet. Large, widescreen monitors set at high resolutions display more data onscreen; however, you may not be able to view the entire dataset. You might want to keep some data always in view, even as you scroll throughout the dataset. Figure 4.1 shows the Spa Experts' January sales transactions. Because it contains a lot of transactions, the entire dataset is not visible. You could decrease the zoom level; however, doing so decreases the text size onscreen, making it hard to read the data.

> Working with large datasets is challenging because column and row labels scroll offscreen....

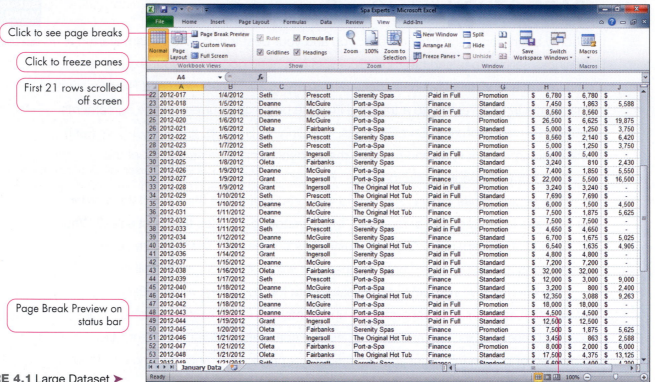

FIGURE 4.1 Large Dataset ➤

In order to view other columns, use the horizontal scroll bar to view one or more columns to the right. When the active cell is in the last visible column (cell J1, for example), pressing → displays one or two more columns on the right. Clicking the down arrow in the vertical scroll bar or pressing ↓ when the active cell is in the bottom visible row moves the screen down one row. As you scroll down and to the right, the rows and columns that were originally visible are no longer visible.

In this section, you will learn how to freeze panes and print large worksheets. In particular, you will learn how to keep labels onscreen as you scroll and how to adjust settings that control how large worksheets print.

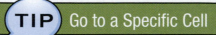

TIP ▶ Go to a Specific Cell

You can navigate through a large worksheet by using the Go To command. Click Find & Select in the Editing group on the Home tab and select Go To (or press F5 or Ctrl+G) to display the Go To dialog box, enter the cell address in the Reference box, and then press Enter to go to the cell. You can also click in the Name Box, type the cell reference, and then press Enter.

Freezing Rows and Columns

Freezing keeps rows and/or columns visible as you scroll through a worksheet.

When you scroll to parts of a dataset not initially visible, some rows and columns disappear from view. When the row and column labels scroll off the screen, you may not remember what each column represents. You can keep labels onscreen by freezing them. ***Freezing*** is the process of keeping rows and/or columns visible onscreen at all times even when you scroll through a large dataset. To freeze labels from scrolling offscreen, click the View tab, click Freeze Panes in the Window group, and then select a freeze option. Table 4.1 describes the three freeze options.

TABLE 4.1 Freeze Options

Option	Description
Freeze Panes	Keeps both rows and columns above and to the left of the active cell visible as you scroll through a worksheet.
Freeze Top Row	Keeps only the top row visible as you scroll through a worksheet.
Freeze First Column	Keeps only the first column visible as you scroll through a worksheet.

To freeze one or more rows and columns, use the Freeze Panes option. Before selecting this option, make the active cell one row below and one column to the right of the rows and columns you want to freeze. For example, to freeze the first five rows and the first two columns, make cell C6 the active cell before clicking a Freeze Panes option. As Figure 4.2 shows, Excel displays a horizontal line below the last frozen row (row 5) and a vertical line to the right of the last frozen column (column B). As you scroll down, the unfrozen rows, such as rows 6–14, disappear. As you scroll to the right, the unfrozen columns, such as columns C and D, disappear.

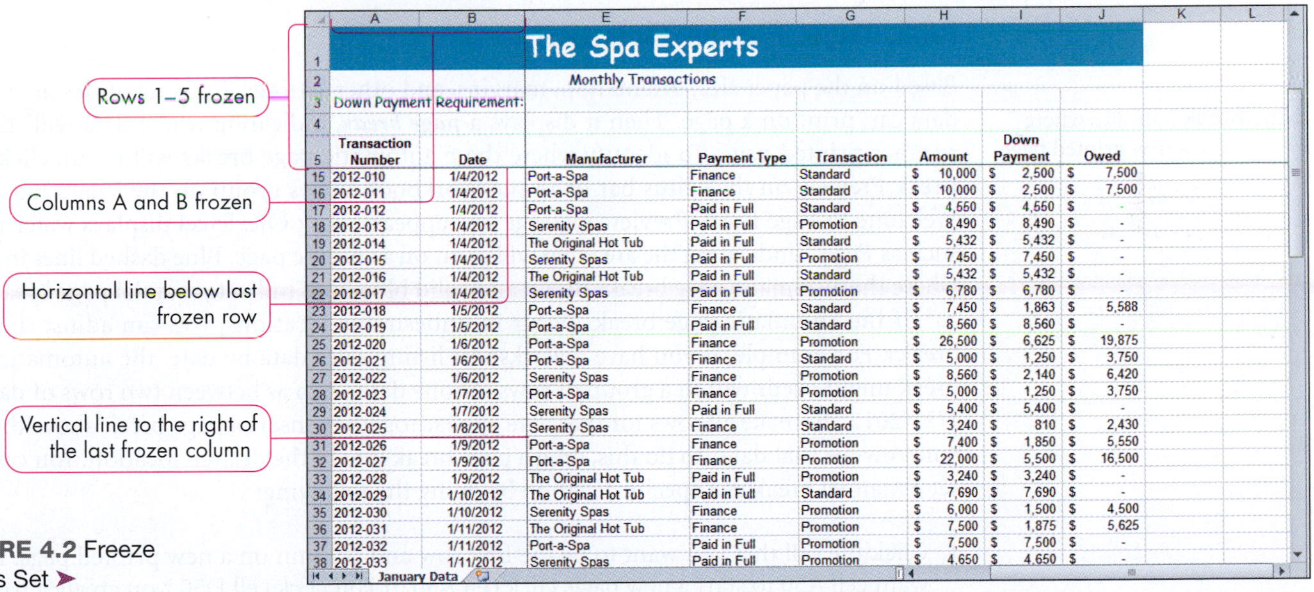

	Transaction Number	Date	Manufacturer	Payment Type	Transaction	Amount	Down Payment	Owed
15	2012-010	1/4/2012	Port-a-Spa	Finance	Standard	$ 10,000	$ 2,500	$ 7,500
16	2012-011	1/4/2012	Port-a-Spa	Finance	Standard	$ 10,000	$ 2,500	$ 7,500
17	2012-012	1/4/2012	Port-a-Spa	Paid in Full	Standard	$ 4,660	$ 4,660	$ -
18	2012-013	1/4/2012	Serenity Spas	Paid in Full	Promotion	$ 8,490	$ 8,490	$ -
19	2012-014	1/4/2012	The Original Hot Tub	Paid in Full	Standard	$ 5,432	$ 5,432	$ -
20	2012-015	1/4/2012	Serenity Spas	Paid in Full	Promotion	$ 7,450	$ 7,450	$ -
21	2012-016	1/4/2012	The Original Hot Tub	Paid in Full	Standard	$ 5,432	$ 5,432	$ -
22	2012-017	1/4/2012	Serenity Spas	Paid in Full	Promotion	$ 6,780	$ 6,780	$ -
23	2012-018	1/5/2012	Port-a-Spa	Finance	Standard	$ 7,450	$ 1,863	$ 5,588
24	2012-019	1/5/2012	Port-a-Spa	Paid in Full	Standard	$ 8,560	$ 8,560	$ -
25	2012-020	1/6/2012	Port-a-Spa	Finance	Promotion	$ 26,500	$ 6,625	$ 19,875
26	2012-021	1/6/2012	Port-a-Spa	Finance	Standard	$ 5,000	$ 1,250	$ 3,750
27	2012-022	1/6/2012	Serenity Spas	Finance	Promotion	$ 8,560	$ 2,140	$ 6,420
28	2012-023	1/7/2012	Port-a-Spa	Finance	Promotion	$ 5,000	$ 1,250	$ 3,750
29	2012-024	1/7/2012	Serenity Spas	Paid in Full	Standard	$ 5,400	$ 5,400	$ -
30	2012-025	1/8/2012	Serenity Spas	Finance	Standard	$ 3,240	$ 810	$ 2,430
31	2012-026	1/9/2012	Port-a-Spa	Finance	Promotion	$ 7,400	$ 1,850	$ 5,550
32	2012-027	1/9/2012	Port-a-Spa	Finance	Promotion	$ 22,000	$ 5,500	$ 16,500
33	2012-028	1/9/2012	The Original Hot Tub	Paid in Full	Promotion	$ 3,240	$ 3,240	$ -
34	2012-029	1/10/2012	The Original Hot Tub	Paid in Full	Standard	$ 7,690	$ 7,690	$ -
35	2012-030	1/10/2012	Serenity Spas	Finance	Promotion	$ 6,000	$ 1,500	$ 4,500
36	2012-031	1/11/2012	The Original Hot Tub	Finance	Promotion	$ 7,500	$ 1,875	$ 5,625
37	2012-032	1/11/2012	Port-a-Spa	Paid in Full	Promotion	$ 7,500	$ 7,500	$ -
38	2012-033	1/11/2012	Serenity Spas	Paid in Full	Promotion	$ 4,650	$ 4,650	$ -

FIGURE 4.2 Freeze Panes Set ➤

To unlock the rows and columns from remaining onscreen as you scroll, click Freeze Panes in the Window group, and then select Unfreeze Panes, which only appears on the menu when you have frozen rows and/or columns. After you unfreeze the panes, the Unfreeze Panes option disappears, and the Freeze Panes option appears on the menu again.

> **TIP** Edit Data in Frozen Range
>
> When you freeze panes and press Ctrl+Home, the first unfrozen cell is the active cell instead of cell A1. For example, with columns A and B and rows 1–5 frozen in Figure 4.2, pressing Ctrl+Home makes cell C6 the active cell. If you need to edit a cell in the frozen area, click the particular cell to make it active, and then edit the data.

Printing Large Datasets

Printing all or parts of a large dataset presents special challenges. For a large dataset, some columns and rows may print on several pages. Analyzing the data for individual printed pages is difficult when each page does not contain column and row labels. To prevent wasting paper, always preview large datasets in the Backstage view before printing data. Doing so enables you to adjust page settings until you are satisfied with how the data will print.

The Page Layout tab (see Figure 4.3) contains many options to help you prepare large datasets to print. Previously, you changed the page orientation, set different margins, and adjusted the scaling. In addition, you can manage page breaks, set the print area, and print titles.

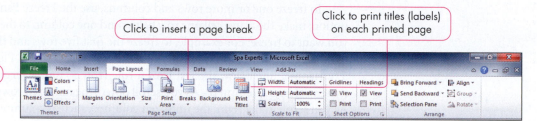

Click to insert a page break

Click to print titles (labels) on each printed page

Click to set the print area

FIGURE 4.3 Page Setup Options ➤

Manage Page Breaks

A **page break** indicates where data starts on a new printed page.

Based on the paper size, orientation, margins, and other settings, Excel identifies how much data can print on a page. Then it displays a *page break*, indicating where data will start on another printed page. To identify where these automatic page breaks will occur, click Page Break Preview on the status bar or in the Workbook Views group on the Views tab. If the Welcome to Page Break Preview message box appears, click OK. Excel displays watermarks, such as *Page 1*, indicating the area that will print on a specific page. Blue dashed lines indicate where the automatic page breaks occur, and solid blue lines indicate manual page breaks.

If the automatic page breaks occur in undesirable locations, you can adjust the page breaks. For example, if you have a worksheet listing sales data by date, the automatic page break might occur within a group of rows for one date, such as between two rows of data for 1/21/2012. To make all rows for that date appear together, insert a page break above the first data row for that date. To do this, drag a page break line to the desired location. You can also set a manual break at a specific location by doing the following:

1. Click the cell that you want to be the first row and column on a new printed page. If you want cell A50 to start a new page, click cell A50. If you click cell D50, you create a page for columns A through C, and then column D starts a new page.
2. Click the Page Layout tab.
3. Click Breaks in the Page Setup group, and then select Insert Page Break. Excel displays a solid blue line in Page Break Preview or a dashed line in Normal view to indicate the manual page breaks you set in the worksheet. Figure 4.4 shows a worksheet with both automatic and manual page breaks.

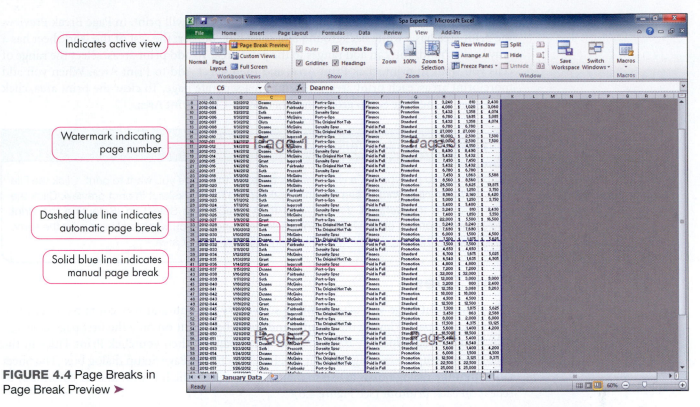

FIGURE 4.4 Page Breaks in Page Break Preview ➤

To remove a manual page break, click the cell below a horizontal page break or the cell to the right of a vertical page break, click Breaks in the Page Setup group, and then select Remove Page Break. To reset all page breaks back to the automatic page breaks, click Breaks in the Page Setup group, and then select Reset All Page Breaks.

Set and Clear a Print Area

The default settings send an entire dataset on the active worksheet to the printer. However, you might want to print only part of the worksheet data. For example, you might want to print an input area only or transactions that occurred on a particular date. You can set the *print area*, which is the range of cells that will print. To print part of a worksheet, do the following:

A **print area** defines the range of data to print.

1. Select the range you want to print.
2. Click the Page Layout tab, and then click Print Area in the Page Setup group.
3. Select Set Print Area. Excel displays solid blue lines in Page Break Preview or thin black dashed lines around the print area in Normal view or Page Layout view (see Figure 4.5).

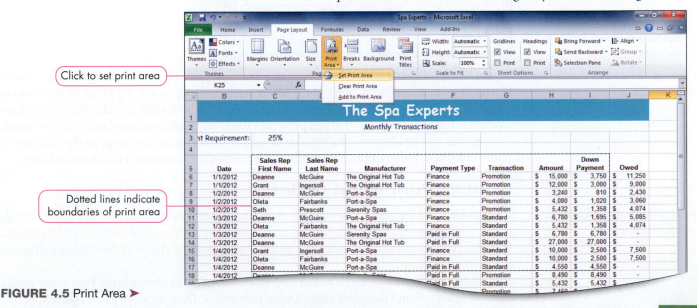

Click to set print area

Dotted lines indicate boundaries of print area

FIGURE 4.5 Print Area ➤

When you use the Print command, only the print area will print. In Page Break Preview, the print area has a white background and solid blue border; the rest of the worksheet has a gray background. You can add ranges to the print area. To add print areas, select the range of cells you want to print, click Print Area, and then select Add to Print Area. When you add more print areas, each print area will print on a separate page. To clear the print area, click Print Area in the Page Setup group, and then select Clear Print Area.

 TIP Print a Selection

Another way to print part of a worksheet is to select the range you want to print. Click the File tab, and then click Print to see the print options and the worksheet in print preview. Click the first arrow in the *Settings* section, and then select Print Selection. Selecting the Print Selection option is a quick way to print a selected range. If you want to always print the same range, select the range in the worksheet, and set it as a print area.

Print Titles

When you print large worksheets, make sure every column and row contains descriptive labels on each page. Having the column and row labels print on only the first page does not help your audience identify data on subsequent pages. When you click Print Titles in the Page Setup group on the Page Layout tab, Excel opens the Page Setup dialog box. The Sheet tab within the dialog box is active so that you can select which row(s) and/or column(s) to repeat on each printout (see Figure 4.6).

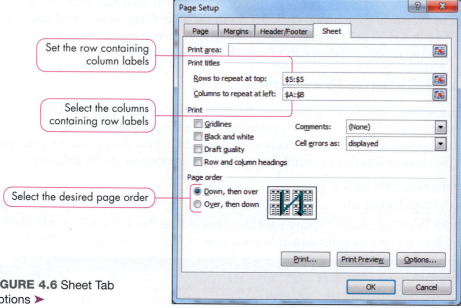

FIGURE 4.6 Sheet Tab Options ➤

In the Spa Experts dataset, not all of the rows will print on the same page as the column labels. To print the column labels at the top of each printout, select the range in the *Rows to repeat at top* box. For example, row 5 contains column labels, such as Manufacturer. If your worksheet has more columns that can print on a page, you might want to display the row labels. To print the row headings on the left side of each printout, select the range in the *Columns to repeat at left* box. For example, columns A and B contain the transaction numbers and dates.

Control Print Page Order

Print order is the sequence in which pages print.

Print order is the sequence in which the pages are printed. By default, the pages print in this order: top-left section, bottom-left section, top-right section, and bottom-right section. However, you might want to print the entire top portion of the worksheet before printing the bottom portion.

To change the print order, click the Page Setup Dialog Box Launcher in the Page Setup group, click the Sheet tab, and then click either *Down, then over* or *Over, then down* (see Figure 4.6).

1 Large Datasets

You want to review the large dataset you created that shows the January transactions for your business, Spa Experts. You want to view the data and adjust some page setup options so that you can print necessary headings on each printed page.

Skills covered: Freeze and Unfreeze Panes • Display and Change Page Breaks • Set and Clear a Print Area • Print Worksheet Titles • Change the Page Order

---

STEP 1 ▶ FREEZE AND UNFREEZE PANES

Before setting up the dataset to print, you want to view the data onscreen. The dataset contains more rows than will display onscreen at the same time. You decide to freeze the headings to stay onscreen as you scroll through the transactions. Refer to Figure 4.7 as you complete Step 1.

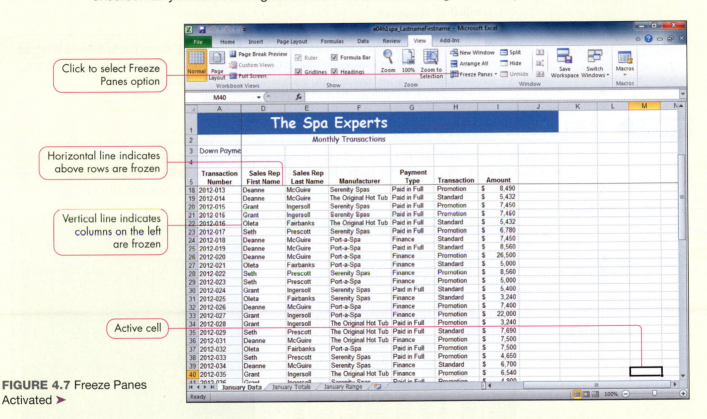

FIGURE 4.7 Freeze Panes Activated ➤

a. Open *e04h1spa* and save it as **e04h1spa_LastnameFirstname**.

> **TROUBLESHOOTING:** If you make any major mistakes in this exercise, you can close the file, open *e04h1spa* again, and then start this exercise over.

The workbook contains three worksheets: January Data (to complete tasks in Hands-On Exercises 1, 2, and 3), January Totals (to complete tasks in Hands-On Exercise 3), and January Range (to complete tasks in Hands-On Exercise 4).

b. Click the **View tab**, click **Freeze Panes** in the Window group, and then select **Freeze Top Row**.

A black horizontal line appears between rows 1 and 2.

c. Press **Page Down** to scroll down through the worksheet.

As rows scroll off the top of the Excel window, the first row remains frozen onscreen. The title by itself is not helpful; you need to freeze the column headings as well.

d. Click **Freeze Panes** in the Window group.

Notice that the first option is now Unfreeze Panes.

e. Select **Unfreeze Panes**.

The top row is no longer frozen.

f. Click **cell B6**, the cell below the row and one column to the right of what you want to freeze. Click **Freeze Panes** in the Window group, and then select **Freeze Panes**.

Excel displays a vertical line between columns A and B, indicating that column A is frozen, and a horizontal line between rows 5 and 6, indicating the first five rows are frozen.

g. Press **Ctrl+G**, type **M40** in the **Reference box** of the Go To dialog box, and then click **OK** to make **cell M40** the active cell. Save the workbook.

Notice that rows 6 through 17 are not visible, and columns B and C are not visible since they scrolled off the screen.

> **TROUBLESHOOTING:** Your screen may differ from what Figure 4.7 shows due to different Windows resolution settings. If necessary, continue scrolling right and down until you see columns and rows scrolling offscreen while column A and the first five rows remain onscreen.

STEP 2 ▷ DISPLAY AND CHANGE PAGE BREAKS

You plan to print the dataset so that you and your business partner Ryan can discuss the transactions in your weekly meeting. You know that large datasets do not fit on one printed page, so you want to see where the automatic page breaks will be. Refer to Figure 4.8 as you complete Step 2.

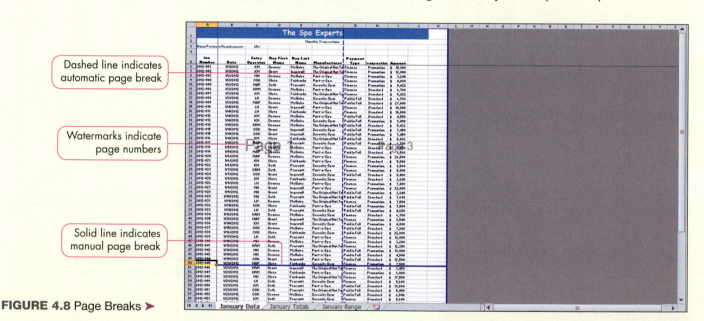

Dashed line indicates automatic page break

Watermarks indicate page numbers

Solid line indicates manual page break

FIGURE 4.8 Page Breaks ➤

a. Press **Ctrl+Home** to jump to **cell B6**, the first cell in the unfrozen area. Click the **View tab** if necessary, and then click **Page Break Preview** in the Workbook Views group or on the status bar.

> **TROUBLESHOOTING:** If the Welcome to Page Break Preview message box opens instructing you how to adjust page breaks, click OK.

b. Drag the **Zoom slider** to the left until the zoom is **50%**.

Excel displays blue dashed lines to indicate the page breaks. The horizontal page break is between rows 51 and 52. You want to make sure all transactions for a particular day do not span between printed pages, so you need to move the page break up to keep all 1/21/2012 transactions together.

c. Click **cell A51**, the cell to start the top of the second page.

d. Click the **Page Layout tab**, click **Breaks** in the Page Setup group, and then select **Insert Page Break**. Save the workbook.

You inserted a page break between rows 50 and 51 so that the 1/21/2012 transactions will be on one page.

> **TROUBLESHOOTING:** If Excel displays a solid line between columns and removes the automatic vertical page break, you selected the wrong cell before inserting a page break. Excel inserts page breaks above and to the left of the active cell. If the page breaks are in the wrong place, click Undo on the Quick Access Toolbar and complete steps c and d again.

> **TIP** Using the Pointer to Move Page Breaks
>
> Instead of clicking Breaks in the Page Setup group, you can use the mouse pointer to adjust a page break. Position the pointer on the page break line to see the two-headed arrow. Drag the page break line to move it where you want the page break to occur.

STEP 3 ▸ SET AND CLEAR A PRINT AREA

You want to focus on the first five days of transactions. To avoid printing more data than you need, you can set the print area to only that data. Refer to Figure 4.9 as you complete Step 3.

White/blue background with yellow border indicates print area

Gray background indicates non-printing area

FIGURE 4.9 Print Area Set ▸

a. Change the zoom back to **100%**. Scroll up to see the first row of January data. Select the **range D5:I25**, the range of data for the first five days of the month.

b. Click the **Page Layout tab**, if necessary, click **Print Area** in the Page Setup group, and then select **Set Print Area**.

Excel displays the print area with a solid yellow border. The rest of the worksheet displays with a gray background, as shown in Figure 4.9.

c. Click the **Page Setup Dialog Box Launcher** in the Page Setup group. Use the dialog box to create a footer with your name on the left side, the sheet name code in the center, and the file name code on the right side.

d. Click the **File tab**, and then click **Print** to verify that only the print area will print. Click the **File tab** to close the Backstage view.

e. Click **Print Area** in the Page Setup group, and then select **Clear Print Area**. Save the workbook.

STEP 4 ▶ PRINT WORKSHEET TITLES

When you looked at the entire dataset in Page Break Preview, you noticed it would print on four pages. Only the first page will print both row and column headings. Page 2 will print the remaining row headings, page 3 will print the remaining column headings, and page 4 will not print either heading. You want to make sure the column and row headings print on all pages. To do this, you will print titles. Refer to Figure 4.10 as you complete Step 4.

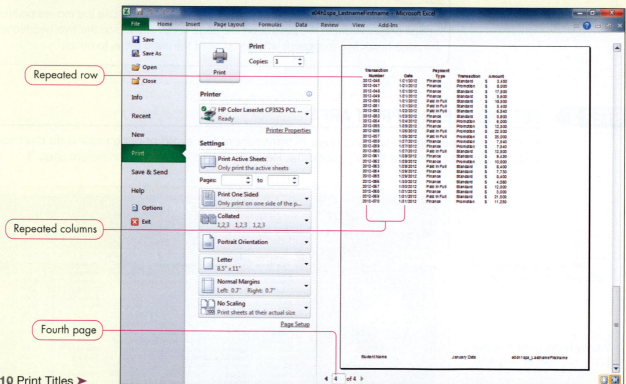

FIGURE 4.10 Print Titles ▶

a. Click **Print Titles** in the Page Setup group.

The Page Setup dialog box opens, displaying the Sheet tab.

b. Click the **Rows to repeat at top collapse button** to collapse the dialog box.

c. Click the **row 5 heading**, and then click the **expand button** to expand the Page Setup dialog box again.

You selected the fifth row, which contains the headings that identify content in the columns.

d. Click in the **Columns to repeat at left box**, type **A:B**, and then click **Print Preview**.

You should verify the page breaks and titles in Print Preview.

e. Click **Next Page** at the bottom of the Backstage view. Look at the second page to see the column headings for the last 11 days of transactions. Click **Next Page** twice to see the third and fourth pages.

Figure 4.10 shows a preview of the fourth page. The fifth row—the descriptive column headings—appears at the top of the page, and the first two columns of row headings (Transaction Number and Date) appear on all pages now.

f. Click the **Page Layout tab** to close the Backstage view. Save the workbook.

STEP 5 ▶ CHANGE THE PAGE ORDER

Although all four pages will print with titles, you want to print all columns for the first half of the monthly transactions rather than printing the first few columns of all transactions and then printing the last columns for all transactions. Refer to Figure 4.11 as you complete Step 5.

FIGURE 4.11 Different Page Order ➤

Page 2 instead of page 3 now

a. Click the **Page Layout tab**, if necessary, and then click the **Page Setup Dialog Box Launcher** in the Page Setup group.

b. Click the **Sheet tab** in the Page Setup dialog box.

c. Click **Over, then down**.

The preview shows that the pages print left to right and then back down left to right, in a Z manner.

d. Click **OK**.

Notice the Page 2 watermark appears on the right side of Page 1 rather than below it.

e. Save the workbook. Keep the workbook onscreen if you plan to continue with Hands-On Exercise 2. If not, close the workbook and exit Excel.

Excel Tables

All organizations maintain lists of data. Businesses maintain inventory lists, educational institutions maintain lists of students and faculty, and governmental entities maintain lists of contracts. Although more complicated related data should be stored in a database management program, such as Access, you can maintain structured lists in Excel tables. A *table* is a structured range that contains related data organized in such a way as to facilitate data management and analysis. Although you can manage and analyze a range of data, a table provides many advantages over a range of data:

> All organizations maintain lists of data.

> A **table** is an area in the worksheet that contains rows and columns of related data formatted to enable data management and analysis.

- Column headings that remain onscreen during scrolling without having to use Freeze Panes
- Filter lists for efficient sorting and filtering
- Predefined table styles to format table rows and columns with complementary fill colors
- Ability to create and edit calculated columns where the formulas copy down the columns automatically
- Calculated total row enabling the user to choose from a variety of functions
- Use of structured references instead of cell references in formulas
- Ability to export the table data to a SharePoint list

In this section, you will learn table terminology and rules for structuring data. You will create a table from existing data, manage records and fields, and remove duplicates. Then, you will apply a table style to format the table.

Understanding Table Design

An Excel table is like a database table: it provides a structured organization of data in columns and rows. Each column represents a *field*, which is an individual piece of data, such as last names or quantities sold. You should create fields with the least amount of data. For example, instead of a Name field, separate data into First Name and Last Name fields. Instead of one large address field, separate addresses into Street Address, City, State, and ZIP Code fields. Storing data into the smallest units possible enables you to manipulate the data in a variety of ways for output.

> A **field** is an individual piece of data, such as a last name.

Each row in an Excel table represents a *record*, which is a collection of data about one entity, such as data for one person. For example, your record in your professor's grade book contains specific data about you, such as your name, ID, test scores, etc. The professor maintains a record of similar data for each student in the class. In an Excel table, each cell represents one piece of data (in the respective field columns) for a particular record.

> A **record** is a complete set of data for an entity.

Often, people create tables from existing worksheet data. For example, a data-entry operator for the Spa Experts might enter data in a worksheet instead of creating a table first. Just as you spend time planning a worksheet, you should plan the structure for a table. Think about who will use the table, what types of reports you need to produce, and what types of searches might be done. The more thorough your planning process, the fewer changes you will have to make to the table after you create it. To help plan your table, follow these guidelines:

- Enter field names on the top row.
- Keep field names relatively short, descriptive, and unique. No two field names should be identical.
- Format the field names so that they stand out from the data.
- Enter data for each record on a row below the field names.
- Do not leave blank rows between records or between the field names and the first record.
- Delete any blank columns between fields in the dataset.

- Make sure each record has something unique about it, such as a transaction number or ID.
- Insert at least one blank row and one blank column between the table and other data, such as the main titles, input area, or other tables. When possible, place separate tables on separate worksheets.

Creating a Table

When your worksheet data are structured correctly, you can easily create a table. To create a table from existing data, do the following:

1. Click within the existing range of data.
2. Click the Insert tab, and then click Table in the Tables group. As Figure 4.12 shows, the Create Table dialog box opens, prompting you to enter the range of data. If Excel does not correctly predict the range, select the range for the *Where is the data for your table?* box. If the existing range contains column headings, select the *My table has headers* check box.
3. Click OK to create the table.

FIGURE 4.12 Create Table Dialog Box ➤

The Table Tools Design tab appears. Excel applies the default Table Style Medium 9 banded rows to your table, and each cell in the header row has filter arrows (see Figure 4.13). Excel assigns a name to each table, such as Table1. You can change the table name by clicking in the Table Name box in the Properties group, typing a new name using the same rules you applied when assigning range names, and then pressing Enter.

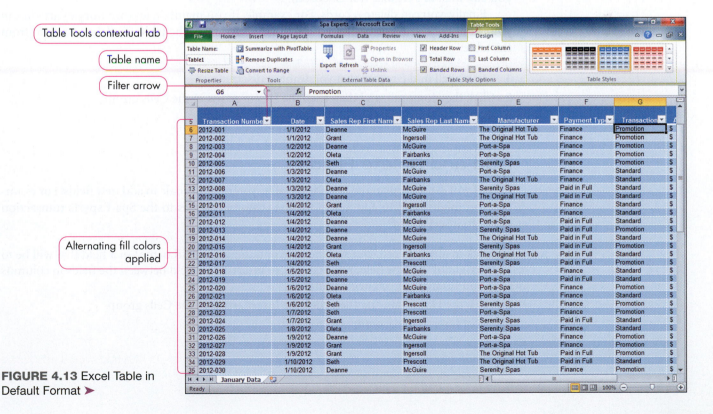

FIGURE 4.13 Excel Table in Default Format ➤

If you do not have existing data, you can create a table structure, and then add data to it later. Select an empty range, and then follow the above steps to create the range for the table. The default table style is Table Style Medium 2, and the default column headings are Column1, Column2, and so on. Click the column heading and type a descriptive label to replace the temporary heading. Excel applies table formatting to the empty rows. You are then ready to add data for each row in the empty table.

> **TIP Converting a Table to a Range**
>
> Tables provide an abundance of advantages to regular ranges. You might want to convert a table back to a range of data to accomplish other tasks. To convert a table back to a range, click within the table range, click the Table Tools Design tab, click Convert to Range in the Tools group, and then click Yes in the message box asking, *Do you want to convert the table to a normal range?*

Add, Edit, and Delete Records

After you create a table, you will need to maintain it, such as by adding new records. For example, you might need to add a new client or employee record, or add a new item to an inventory table or transaction table. To add a record to your table, do the following:

1. Click a cell in the record below where you want the new record inserted. If you want to add a new record below the last record, click the row containing the last record.
2. Click the Home tab, and then click the Insert arrow in the Cells group.
3. Select Insert Table Rows Above to insert a row above the current row, or select Insert Table Row Below if the current row is the last one and you want a row below it.

Sometimes, you need to change data for a record. For example, when a client moves, you need to change the client's address and phone number. You edit data in a table the same way you edit data in a regular worksheet cell.

Finally, you can delete records. For example, if you maintain an inventory of artwork in your house and sell a piece of art, delete that record from the table. To delete a record from the table:

1. Click a cell in the record that you want to delete.
2. Click the Home tab, and then click the Delete arrow in the Cells group.
3. Select Delete Table Rows.

Add and Delete Fields

Even if you carefully plan the fields for a table, you might decide to add new fields. For example, you might want to add a field for the customer names to the Spa Experts transaction table. To insert a field:

1. Click in any data cell (but not the cell containing the field name) in a field that will be to the right of the new field. For example, to insert a new field between the fields in columns A and B, click any cell in column B.
2. Click the Home tab, and then click the Insert arrow in the Cells group.
3. Select Insert Table Columns to the Left.

You can also delete a field if you no longer need any data for that particular field. Although deleting records and fields is easy, you must make sure not to delete data erroneously. If you accidentally delete data, click Undo immediately. To delete a field, do the following:

1. Click a cell in the field that you want to delete.
2. Click the Delete arrow in the Cells group on the Home tab.
3. Select Delete Table Columns.

Remove Duplicate Rows

You might accidentally enter duplicate records in a table, which can give false results when totaling or performing other calculations on the dataset. For a small table, you might be able to detect duplicate records by scanning the data. For large tables, it is more difficult to identify duplicate records by simply scanning the table with the eye. To remove duplicate records, do the following:

1. Click within the table, and then click the Design tab.
2. Click Remove Duplicates in the Tools group to display the Remove Duplicates dialog box (see Figure 4.14).
3. Click Select All to set the criteria to find a duplicate for every field in the record, and then click OK. If you select individual columns, Excel looks for duplicates in that one column only, and deletes all but one record that contains that data. For example, if you delete duplicate records where the manufacturer is Serenity Spas, only one transaction would remain. The other customers' transactions that contain Serenity Spas would be deleted. Excel will display a message box informing you how many duplicate rows it removed.

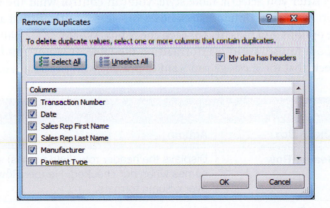

FIGURE 4.14 Remove Duplicates Dialog Box ➤

Applying a Table Style

Formatting tables can make them more attractive and easier to read, and can emphasize data. The Design tab provides a variety of formatting options for tables. Excel applies a table style when you create a table. *Table styles* control the fill color of the header row (the row containing field names) and rows of records. In addition, table styles specify bold and border lines. You can change the table style to a color scheme that complements your organization's color scheme or to emphasize data in the table. Click the More button to see the Table Styles gallery (see Figure 4.15). To see how a table style will format your table using Live Preview, position the pointer over a style in the Table Styles gallery. After you identify a style you want, click it to apply it to the table.

A **table style** controls the fill color of the header row, columns, and records in a table.

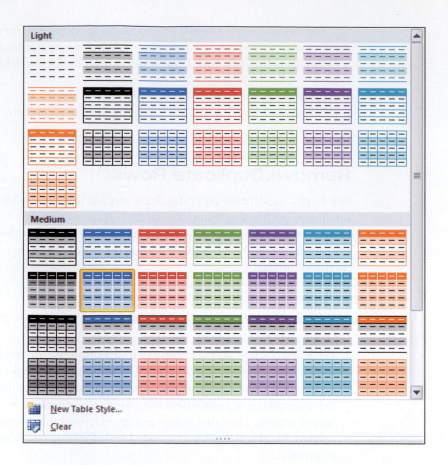

FIGURE 4.15 Table Styles Gallery ➤

After you select a table style, you can control what the style formats. The Table Style Options group contains check boxes to select specific format actions in a table. Table 4.2 lists the options and the effect of each check box. Whatever formatting and formatting effects you choose to use, avoid overformatting the table. It is not good to apply so many formatting effects that the message you want to present with the data is obscured or lost.

TABLE 4.2	Table Style Options
Check Box	**Action**
Header Row	Displays the header row (field names) when checked; removes field names when not checked. Header Row formatting takes priority over column formats.
Total Row	Displays a total row when selected. Total Row formatting takes priority over column formats.
First Column	Applies a different format to the first column so that the row headings stand out. First Column formatting takes priority over Banded Rows formatting.
Last Column	Applies a different format to the last column so that the last column of data stands out; effective for aggregated data, such as grand totals, per row. Last Column formatting takes priority over Banded Rows formatting.
Banded Rows	Displays alternate fill colors for even and odd rows to help distinguish records.
Banded Columns	Displays alternate fill colors for even and odd columns to help distinguish fields.

2 Excel Tables

Now that you understand Excel tables, you need to convert the January transactions data from basic worksheet data to a table. As you review the table, you will adjust its structure by deleting an unnecessary field and adding two missing fields. Then, you will focus on the transaction records by adding a missing record and removing a duplicate record. Finally, you will enhance the table appearance by selecting a table style.

Skills covered: Create a Table • Delete and Add Fields • Add a Record • Remove Duplicate Rows • Apply a Table Style

STEP 1 ▶ CREATE A TABLE

Although the Spa Experts' January transaction data are organized in an Excel worksheet, you know that you will have additional functionality if you convert the range to a table. Refer to Figure 4.16 as you complete Step 1.

Table column headings replace lettered column headings

	Transaction	Date	Data Entry	Sales Rep F	Sales Rep L	Manufacturer	Payment Ty	Transaction	Amount	J
10	2012-005	1/2/2012	MAP	Seth	Prescott	Serenity Spas	Finance	Promotion	$ 5,432	
11	2012-006	1/3/2012	KRM	Deanne	McGuire	Port-a-Spa	Finance	Standard	$ 6,780	
12	2012-007	1/3/2012	KM	Oleta	Fairbanks	The Original Hot Tub	Finance	Standard	$ 5,432	
13	2012-008	1/3/2012	LH	Deanne	McGuire	Serenity Spas	Paid in Full	Standard	$ 6,780	
14	2012-009	1/3/2012	MAP	Deanne	McGuire	The Original Hot Tub	Paid in Full	Standard	$ 27,000	
15	2012-010	1/4/2012	LH	Grant	Ingersoll	Port-a-Spa	Finance	Standard	$ 10,000	
16	2012-011	1/4/2012	LH	Oleta	Fairbanks	Port-a-Spa	Finance	Standard	$ 10,000	
17	2012-012	1/4/2012	KM	Deanne	McGuire	Port-a-Spa	Paid in Full	Standard	$ 4,550	
18	2012-013	1/4/2012	KM	Deanne	McGuire	Serenity Spas	Paid in Full	Promotion	$ 8,490	
19	2012-014	1/4/2012	KRM	Deanne	McGuire	The Original Hot Tub	Paid in Full	Standard	$ 5,432	
20	2012-015	1/4/2012	COK	Grant	Ingersoll	Serenity Spas	Paid in Full	Promotion	$ 7,450	
21	2012-015	1/4/2012	COK	Grant	Ingersoll	Serenity Spas	Paid in Full	Promotion	$ 7,450	
22	2012-016	1/4/2012	KM	Oleta	Fairbanks	The Original Hot Tub	Paid in Full	Standard	$ 5,432	
23	2012-017	1/4/2012	MAP	Seth	Prescott	Serenity Spas	Paid in Full	Promotion	$ 6,780	
24	2012-018	1/5/2012	LH	Deanne	McGuire	Port-a-Spa	Finance	Standard	$ 7,450	
25	2012-019	1/5/2012	MAP	Deanne	McGuire	Port-a-Spa	Paid in Full	Standard	$ 8,560	
26	2012-020	1/6/2012	MAP	Deanne	McGuire	Port-a-Spa	Finance	Promotion	$ 26,500	
27	2012-021	1/6/2012	KM	Oleta	Fairbanks	Port-a-Spa	Finance	Standard	$ 5,000	
28	2012-022					Serenity Spas	Finance	Promotion	$ 8,560	

FIGURE 4.16 Range Converted to a Table ▶

a. Open *e04h1spa_LastnameFirstname* if you closed it at the end of Hands-On Exercise 1, and then save it as **e04h2spa_LastnameFirstname**, changing *h1* to *h2*.

b. Click **Normal** on the status bar, and then click the **Insert tab**.

c. Click in any cell within the transactional data. Click **Table** in the Tables group.

The Create Table dialog box opens. The Where is the data for your table? box displays =$A$5:$I$75. You need to keep the *My table has headers* check box selected so that the headings on the fifth row become the field names for the table.

d. Click **OK**, and then click **cell A5**.

Excel creates a table from the specified range and displays the Table Tools Design tab, filter arrows, and alternating fill colors for every other record. The columns widen to fit the field names, although the wrap text option is still applied to those cells.

e. Set **12.00 column widths** to these fields: Transaction Number, Data Entry Operator, Sales Rep First Name, Sales Rep Last Name, and Payment Type.

f. Unfreeze the panes, and then scroll through the table. Save the workbook.

With a regular range of data, column headings scroll off the top of the screen if you don't freeze panes. When you scroll within a table, the table column headings remain onscreen by moving up to where the Excel column (letter) headings usually display (see Figure 4.16).

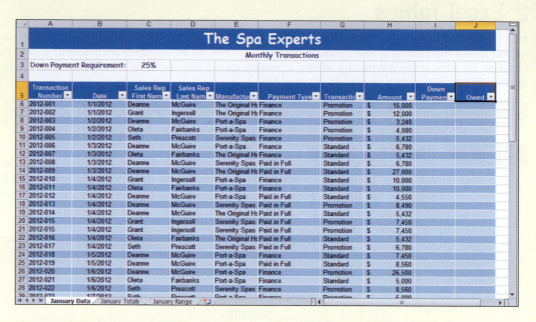

STEP 2 ▶ DELETE AND ADD FIELDS

The original range included the Data Entry Operator's initials. You decide that you no longer need this column, so you will delete it. In addition, you want to add a field to display down payment amounts in the future. Refer to Figure 4.17 as you complete Step 2.

FIGURE 4.17 Field Name Changes ➤

a. Click **cell C6** or any cell containing a value in the Data Entry Operator column.

You need to make a cell active in the field that you want to remove.

b. Click the **Home tab**, click the **Delete arrow** in the Cells group, and then select **Delete Table Columns**.

Excel deletes the Data Entry Operator column. Notice that the 25% remains in cell C3.

> **TROUBLESHOOTING:** If the 25% is deleted in cell C3, you probably selected Delete Sheet Columns instead of Delete Table Columns. Undo the deletion, and then repeat step b.

c. Click **cell I5**, the first blank cell on the right side of the field names.

d. Type **Down Payment** and press **Ctrl+Enter**.

Excel extends the table formatting to column I automatically. A filter arrow appears for the newly created field name, and alternating fill colors appear in the rows below the field name.

e. Click **Wrap Text** in the Alignment group.

f. Click **cell J5**, type **Owed**, and then press **Ctrl+Enter** to keep cell J5 active. Click **Center** in the Alignment group. Save the workbook.

STEP 3 ▶ ADD A RECORD

As you review the January transaction table, you notice that transaction 2012-030 is missing. After finding the paper invoice, you are ready to add a record with the missing transaction data. Refer to Figure 4.18 as you complete Step 3.

	Transaction ▼	Date ▼	Sales Rep f ▼	Sales Rep l ▼	Manufactur ▼	Payment Type ▼	Transaction ▼	Amount ▼	Down Payr ▼	Owed ▼
7	2012-002	1/1/2012	Grant	Ingersoll	The Original Ho	Finance	Promotion	$ 12,000		
8	2012-003	1/2/2012	Deanne	McGuire	Port-a-Spa	Finance	Promotion	$ 3,240		
9	2012-004	1/2/2012	Oleta	Fairbanks	Port-a-Spa	Finance	Promotion	$ 4,080		
10	2012-005	1/2/2012	Seth	Prescott	Serenity Spas	Finance	Promotion	$ 5,432		
11	2012-006	1/3/2012	Deanne	McGuire	Port-a-Spa	Finance	Standard	$ 6,780		
12	2012-007	1/3/2012	Oleta	Fairbanks	The Original Ho	Finance	Standard	$ 5,432		
13	2012-008	1/3/2012	Deanne	McGuire	Serenity Spas	Paid in Full	Standard	$ 6,780		
14	2012-009	1/3/2012	Deanne	McGuire	The Original Ho	Paid in Full	Standard	$ 27,000		
15	2012-010	1/4/2012	Grant	Ingersoll	Port-a-Spa	Finance	Standard	$ 10,000		
16	2012-011	1/4/2012	Oleta	Fairbanks	Port-a-Spa	Finance	Standard	$ 10,000		
17	2012-012	1/4/2012	Deanne	McGuire	Port-a-Spa	Paid in Full	Standard	$ 4,550		
18	2012-013	1/4/2012	Deanne	McGuire	Serenity Spas	Paid in Full	Promotion	$ 8,490		
19	2012-014	1/4/2012	Deanne	McGuire	The Original Ho	Paid in Full	Standard	$ 5,432		
20	2012-015	1/4/2012	Grant	Ingersoll	Serenity Spas	Paid in Full	Promotion	$ 7,450		
21	2012-015	1/4/2012	Grant	Ingersoll	Serenity Spas	Paid in Full	Promotion	$ 7,450		
22	2012-016	1/4/2012	Oleta	Fairbanks	The Original Ho	Paid in Full	Standard	$ 5,432		
23	2012-017	1/4/2012	Seth	Prescott	Serenity Spas	Paid in Full	Promotion	$ 6,780		
24	2012-018	1/5/2012	Deanne	McGuire	Port-a-Spa	Finance	Standard	$ 7,450		
25	2012-019	1/5/2012	Deanne	McGuire	Port-a-Spa	Paid in Full	Standard	$ 8,560		
26	2012-020	1/6/2012	Deanne	McGuire	Port-a-Spa	Finance	Promotion	$ 26,500		
27	2012-021	1/6/2012	Oleta	Fairbanks	Port-a-Spa	Finance	Standard	$ 5,000		
28	2012-022	1/6/2012	Seth	Prescott	Serenity Spas	Finance	Promotion	$ 8,560		
29	2012-023	1/7/2012	Seth	Prescott	Port-a-Spa	Finance	Promotion	$ 5,000		
30	2012-024	1/7/2012	Grant	Ingersoll	Serenity Spas	Paid in Full	Standard	$ 5,400		
31	2012-025	1/8/2012	Oleta	Fairbanks	Serenity Spas	Finance	Standard	$ 3,240		
32	2012-026	1/9/2012	Deanne	McGuire	Port-a-Spa	Finance	Promotion	$ 7,400		
33	2012-027	1/9/2012	Grant	Ingersoll	Port-a-Spa	Finance	Promotion	$ 22,000		
34	2012-028	1/9/2012	Grant	Ingersoll	The Original Ho	Paid in Full	Promotion	$ 3,240		
35	2012-029	1/10/2012	Seth	Prescott	The Original Ho	Paid in Full	Standard	$ 7,690		
36	2012-030	1/10/2012	Deanne	McGuire	Serenity Spas	Finance	Promotion	$ 6,000		
37	2012-031	1/11/2012	Deanne	McGuire	The Original Ho	Finance	Promotion	$ 7,500		
38	2012-032	1/11/2012	Oleta	Fairbanks	Port-a-Spa	Finance	Promotion	$ 7,500		

Duplicate rows

Record added

FIGURE 4.18 Missing Record Added ➤

a. Click **cell A36** or any cell within the table range on row 36.

You need to make a cell active on the row in which you want to insert the new table row.

b. Click the **Home tab**, click the **Insert arrow** in the Cells group, and then select **Insert Table Rows Above**.

Excel inserts a new table row on row 36. The rest of the records move down by one row.

c. Enter the following data in the respective fields on the newly created row. AutoComplete will help you enter the names, manufacturer, payment type, and transaction text. Then save the workbook.

- Transaction Number: **2012-030**
- Date: **1/10/2012**
- Sales Rep First Name: **Deanne**
- Sales Rep Last Name: **McGuire**

- Manufacturer: **Serenity Spas**
- Payment Type: **Finance**
- Transaction: **Promotion**
- Amount: **6000**

STEP 4 ▸ **REMOVE DUPLICATE ROWS**

As you continue checking the transaction records, you think the table contains some duplicate records. To avoid having to look at the entire table row-by-row, you want to have Excel find and remove the duplicate rows for you. Refer to Figure 4.19 as you complete Step 4.

FIGURE 4.19 Duplicate Record Removed ➤

a. Scroll to see rows 20 and 21. Click the **Design tab**.

The records on rows 20 and 21 are identical. You need to remove one row.

b. Click **Remove Duplicates** in the Tools group.

The Remove Duplicates dialog box opens.

c. Click **Select All**, if necessary, to select all table columns.

d. Click the **My data has headers check box**, if necessary, and then click **OK**.

Excel displays a message box indicating the number of duplicate records found and removed. The message box also specifies how many unique records remain.

e. Click **OK** in the message box. Save the workbook.

STEP 5 ▶ APPLY A TABLE STYLE

Now that you have modified fields and records, you want to apply a table style to format the table. Refer to Figure 4.20 as you complete Step 5.

FIGURE 4.20 Table Style Applied ➤

a. Click the **More button** in the Table Styles group to display the Table Styles gallery.

b. Position the mouse pointer over the fourth style on the second row in the *Light* section.

Live Preview shows the table with the Table Style Light 10 style but does not apply it.

c. Click **Table Style Medium 6**, the sixth style on the first row in the *Medium* section.

Excel formats the table with the Table Style Medium 6 format.

d. Click in the **Name Box**, type **A1**, and press **Enter** to go to **cell A1**, the title. Click the **Home tab**, click the **Fill Color arrow** in the Font group, and then click **Aqua, Accent 5**.

You applied a fill color for the title to match the fill color of the field names.

e. Widen column E to **18.14**.

f. Save the workbook. Keep the workbook onscreen if you plan to continue with Hands-On Exercise 3. If not, close the workbook and exit Excel.

Table Manipulation and Aggregation

When you convert data to a table, you have a variety of options to manipulate that data, in addition to managing fields and records and applying predefined table styles. You can arrange data in different sequences, display only particular records instead of the entire dataset, and aggregate data. Although Excel provides many advantages for using tables over a range, you might need to convert a table back to a range to perform a few tasks that are not available for tables.

> You can add more meaning to tables by aggregating data.

In this section, you will learn how to sort records by text, numbers, and dates in a table. In addition, you will learn how to filter data based on conditions you set. You will create structured formulas to perform calculations, and add a total row.

Sorting Data

Table data are easier to understand and work with if you organize the data. In Figure 4.1, the data are arranged by transaction number. You might want to organize the table by showing sales by sales associate, or to display all financed spas together, followed by all paid-in-full spas. *Sorting* arranges records by the value of one or more fields within a table.

> **Sorting** arranges records in a table by the value in field(s) within a table.

Sort One Column

You can sort data by one or more columns. To sort by only one column, you can use any of the following methods for either a range of data or a table:

- Click Sort & Filter in the Editing group on the Home tab.
- Click Sort A to Z, Sort Z to A, or Sort in the Sort & Filter group on the Data tab.
- Right-click the field to sort, point to Sort from the shortcut menu, and select the type of sort you want.

When you format data as a table, the field names appear in a header row, which contains sort and filter arrows. Click the arrow for the column you want to sort and select the type of sort you want. Table 4.3 lists sort options by data type.

TABLE 4.3	Sort Options	
Data Type	**Options**	**Explanation**
Text	Sort A to Z	Arranges data in alphabetical order.
	Sort Z to A	Arranges data in reverse alphabetical order.
Dates	Sort Oldest to Newest	Displays data in chronological order, from oldest to newest.
	Sort Newest to Oldest	Displays data in reverse chronological order, from newest to oldest.
Values	Sort Smallest to Largest	Arranges values from the smallest value to the largest value.
	Sort Largest to Smallest	Arranges values from the largest value to the smallest value.

Use the Sort Dialog Box to Sort Multiple Columns

At times sorting by only one field yields several records that have the same information—for example the same last name or the same manufacturer. Sales representative names and manufacturer names appear several times. A single sort field does not uniquely identify a record. You might need both last name and first name to identify an individual. Using multiple level sorts allows differentiation among records with the same data in the first (primary) sort level.

For example, you might want to sort by sales rep names, manufacturer, and then by price. Excel enables you to sort data on 64 different levels. To perform a multiple level sort:

1. Click in any cell in the table.
2. Click Sort in the Sort & Filter group on the Data tab to display the Sort dialog box.
3. Select the primary sort level by clicking the *Sort by* arrow and selecting the column to sort by, and then clicking the Order arrow and selecting the sort order from the list.
4. Click Add Level, select the second sort level by clicking the *Then by* arrow and selecting the column to sort by, clicking the Order arrow, and then selecting the sort order from the list.
5. Continue to click Add Level and add sort levels until you have entered all sort levels. See Figure 4.21. Click OK.

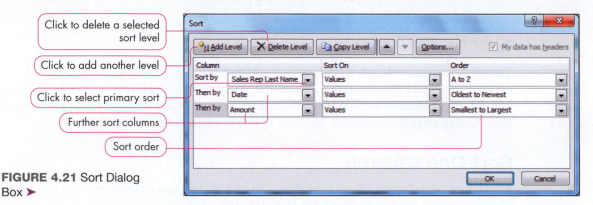

FIGURE 4.21 Sort Dialog Box ➤

Create a Custom Sort

Excel arranges data in defined sequences, such as alphabetical order. For example, weekdays are sorted alphabetically: Friday, Monday, Saturday, Sunday, Thursday, Tuesday, and Wednesday. However, you might want to create a custom sort sequence. For example, you can create a custom sort to arrange weekdays in order from Sunday to Saturday.

To create a custom sort sequence, click Sort in the Sort & Filter group on the Data tab. Click the Order arrow, and then select Custom List to display the Custom Lists dialog box (see Figure 4.22). Select an existing sort sequence in the *Custom lists* box, or select NEW LIST, click Add, and then type the entries in the desired sort sequence in the *List entries* box, pressing Enter between entries. Click Add, and then click OK.

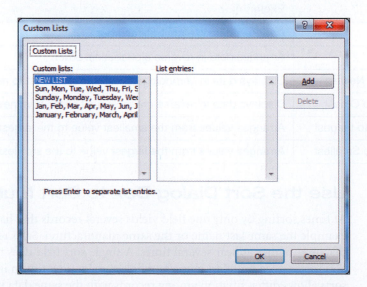

FIGURE 4.22 Custom Lists Dialog Box ➤

Filtering Data

Filtering is the process of displaying only records that meet specific conditions.

You might want to show only particular records. **Filtering** is the process of specifying conditions to display only those records that meet certain conditions. For example, you might want to filter the data to show transactions for only Oleta Fairbanks. To filter records by a particular field, click the column's filter arrow. The list displays each unique label, value, or date contained in the column. Deselect the (Select All) check box, and then click the check box for each value you want to include in the filtered results.

Often you will need to apply more than one filter to display the needed records. You can filter more than one column. Each additional filter is based on the current filtered data and further reduces a data subset. To apply multiple filters, click each column's filter arrow, and select the values to include in the filtered data results.

> **TIP** Copying Before Filtering Data
>
> Often, you need to show different filters applied to the same dataset. You can copy the data to another worksheet, and then filter the copied data to preserve the original dataset.

Apply Text Filters

When you apply a filter to a text column, the filter menu displays each unique text item. You can select one or more text items from the list. For example, select Fairbanks to show only records for this salesperson. To display records for both Fairbanks and Prescott, deselect the (Select All) check mark, and then click the Fairbanks and Prescott check boxes. You can also select Text Filters to see a submenu of additional options, such as *Begins With*, to select all records where the name begins with the letter G, for example.

Figure 4.23 shows the Last Name filter menu with two names selected. Excel displays records for these two reps only. The records for the other sales reps are hidden but not deleted. The filter arrow displays a filter icon, indicating which column is filtered. Excel displays the row numbers in blue, indicating that you applied a filter. The missing row numbers indicate hidden rows of data. When you remove the filter, all the records display again.

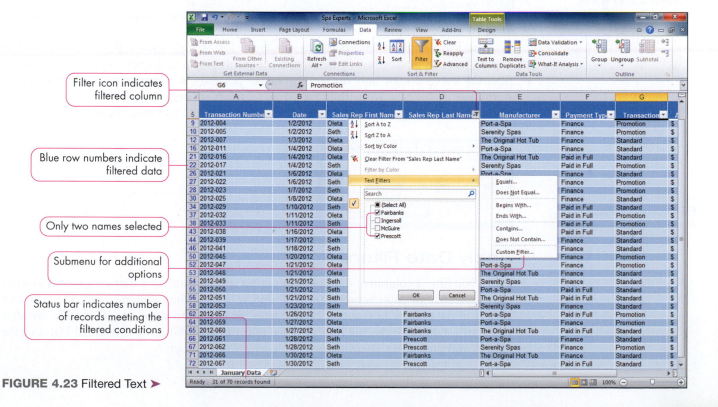

Filter icon indicates filtered column

Blue row numbers indicate filtered data

Only two names selected

Submenu for additional options

Status bar indicates number of records meeting the filtered conditions

FIGURE 4.23 Filtered Text ➤

Apply Number Filters

When you filter a column of numbers, you can select specific numbers. You might want to filter numbers by a range, such as numbers greater than $5,000 or numbers between $4,000 and $5,000. The submenu enables you to set a variety of number filters. In Figure 4.24, the amounts are filtered to show only those that are above the average amount. In this situation, Excel calculates the average amount as $9,577. Only records above that amount display.

If the field contains a large number of unique entries, you can click in the Search box, and then type a value, text label, or date. Doing so narrows the visible list so that you do not have to scroll through the entire list. For example, if you enter $7, the list will display only values that start with $7.

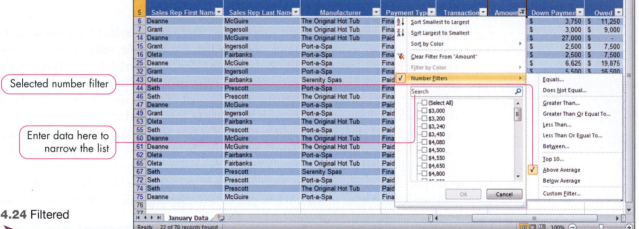

Selected number filter

Enter data here to narrow the list

FIGURE 4.24 Filtered Numbers ➤

The Top 10 option enables you to specify the top records. Although the option name is Top 10, you can specify the number or percentage of records to display. For example, you can filter the list to display only the top five or the bottom 7%. Figure 4.25 shows the Top 10 AutoFilter dialog box. Click the first arrow to select either Top or Bottom, click the spin arrows to indicate a value, and then click the last arrow to select either Items or Percent.

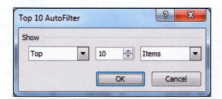

FIGURE 4.25 Top 10 AutoFilter Dialog Box ➤

Apply Date Filters

When you filter a column of dates, you can select specific dates or a date range, such as dates after 1/15/2012 or dates between 1/1/2012 and 1/7/2012. The submenu enables you to set a variety of date filters. In Figure 4.26, the dates are filtered to show only those that are after 1/15/2012. For more specific date options, point to Date Filters, point to All Dates in the Period, and then select a period, such as Quarter 2 or October.

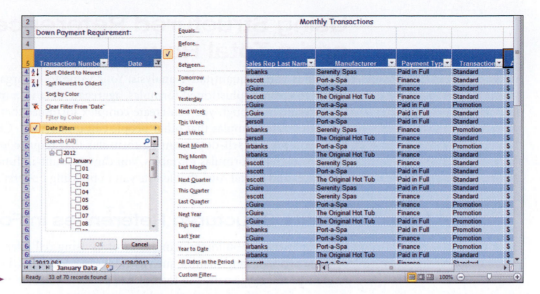

FIGURE 4.26 Filtered Dates ➤

Apply a Custom Filter

If you select options such as *Greater Than* or *Before*, Excel displays the Custom AutoFilter dialog box (see Figure 4.27). You can also select Custom Filter from the menu to display this dialog box, which is designed for more complex filtering requirements.

Date is the column being filtered

FIGURE 4.27 Custom AutoFilter Dialog Box ➤

The dialog box indicates the column being filtered, such as Date. To set the filters, click the arrows to select the comparison type, such as equals or contains. Click the arrow on the right to select a specific text, value, or date entry, or type the data yourself. For ranges of dates or values, click And, and then specify the comparison operator and value or date for the next condition row. For text, click Or. For example, if you want both Kansas and Kentucky, you must select Or because one data entry contains either Kansas or Kentucky but not both at the same time.

You can use wildcards to represent characters. For example, to select all states starting with New, type New * in the second box. The asterisk (*) represents any number of characters. If you want a wildcard for only a single character, type the question mark (?).

Clear Filters

After reviewing the filtered data, you can remove the filters to see the entire dataset again. To remove only one filter and keep the other filters, click the filter arrow for the column from which you wish to clear the filter, and then select Clear Filter From. Excel then removes that column's filter and displays records previously hidden by that filter. To remove all filters, click Filter in the Sort & Filter group on the Data tab, or click Sort & Filter in the Editing group on the Home tab and select Filter. Excel clears all filters and displays all records in the dataset.

Using Structured References and a Total Row

Excel aids you in quantitative analysis. Your value to an organization increases with your ability to create sophisticated formulas, aggregate data in a meaningful way, and interpret those results. Although you can create complex formulas that you understand, you should strive to create formulas that other people can understand. Creating easy-to-read formulas helps you present self-documenting formulas that require less explanation on your part. When you create formulas for tables, you can use built-in functionality (such as structured references and a total row) that assists you in building understandable formulas.

Create Structured References in Formulas

A **structured reference** is a tag or use of a table element as a reference in a formula.

Your experience in building formulas involves using cell references, such as =SUM(B1:B15) or =H6*$B$3, or range names, such as grades in =VLOOKUP(E5,grades,2). You can use cell references and range names in formulas to perform calculations in a table, as well as another type of reference for formulas in tables: structured references. A ***structured reference*** is a tag or use of a table element, such as a column heading, as a reference in a formula. Structured references in formulas clearly indicate what type of data is used in the calculations.

A structured reference requires brackets around column headings or field names, such as =[Amount]-[Down Payment]. The use of column headings without row references in a structured formula is called an *unqualified reference.* While creating a formula by typing, Formula AutoComplete displays a list of column headings after you type the equal sign and the opening bracket (see Figure 4.28). Type or double-click the name from the list, and then type the closing bracket. Excel displays a colored border around the column being referenced. When you enter a formula using structured references, Excel copies the formula down the rest of the column in the table automatically, compared to typing references in formulas and copying the formula down a column.

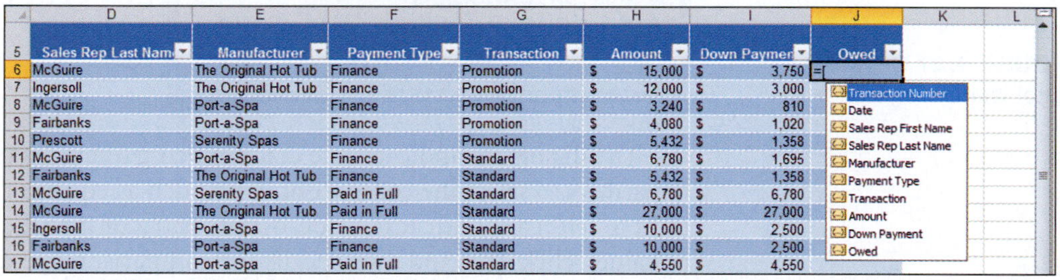

	D	E	F	G	H		I		J
5	Sales Rep Last Nam	Manufacturer	Payment Type	Transaction	Amount		Down Paymen		Owed
6	McGuire	The Original Hot Tub	Finance	Promotion	$	15,000	$	3,750	=[
7	Ingersoll	The Original Hot Tub	Finance	Promotion	$	12,000	$	3,000	
8	McGuire	Port-a-Spa	Finance	Promotion	$	3,240	$	810	
9	Fairbanks	Port-a-Spa	Finance	Promotion	$	4,080	$	1,020	
10	Prescott	Serenity Spas	Finance	Promotion	$	5,432	$	1,358	
11	McGuire	Port-a-Spa	Finance	Standard	$	6,780	$	1,695	
12	Fairbanks	The Original Hot Tub	Finance	Standard	$	5,432	$	1,358	
13	McGuire	Serenity Spas	Paid in Full	Standard	$	6,780	$	6,780	
14	McGuire	The Original Hot Tub	Paid in Full	Standard	$	27,000	$	27,000	
15	Ingersoll	Port-a-Spa	Finance	Standard	$	10,000	$	2,500	
16	Fairbanks	Port-a-Spa	Finance	Standard	$	10,000	$	2,500	
17	McGuire	Port-a-Spa	Paid in Full	Standard	$	4,550	$	4,550	

FIGURE 4.28 Structured Reference Creation ➤

You can still use the semi-selection process to create a formula. If you use the pointing process to enter a formula in a table, Excel builds a formula like this: =[@Amount]-[@Down Payment], where the @ indicates the current row. If you use the semi-selection process to create a formula outside the table, the formula includes the table name and row as well, such as =Table1[@Amount]-Table1[@Down Payment]. Table1 is the name of the table, and Amount and Down Payment are column headings. This structured formula that includes references, such as table numbers, is called a *fully qualified reference.* When you build formulas *within* a table, you can use either unqualified or fully qualified structured references. If you need to use table data in a formula *outside* the table boundaries, you must use fully qualified structured references.

> **TIP** Complex Structured References
>
> You can create structured reference tags to other elements, such as headers and totals. The more you know how to incorporate structured references, the more powerful your tables are to you. Look up *structured references* in Help for detailed explanations and examples of more complex use of structured references.

Create a Total Row

Aggregating data provides more meaningful quantitative interpretation than individual values at times. For regular ranges of data, you use basic statistical functions, such as SUM, AVERAGE, MIN, and MAX, to provide meaning for a dataset. An Excel table provides the advantage of being able to display a total row automatically without creating the aggregate function yourself. A **total row** appears below the last row of records in an Excel table and enables you to display summary statistics, such as a sum of values displayed in a column. To display and use the total row:

A **total row** appears as the last row of a table to display summary statistics, such as a sum.

1. Click the Design tab.
2. Click Total Row in the Table Style Options group. Excel displays the total row below the last record in the table. Excel displays *Total* in the first column of the total row. Excel either sums or counts data for the last column, depending on the type of data stored in that column. If the last column consists of values, Excel sums the values. If the last column is text, Excel counts the number of records.
3. Click a cell in the total row, and then click that cell's total row arrow and select the function results, such as Average, that you desire. To add a total to another column, click in the empty cell for that column in the total row, and then click the arrow to select the desired function. Select None to remove the function.

Figure 4.29 shows the active total row with totals applied to the Amount and Down Payment columns. A list of functions displays to change the function for the last column.

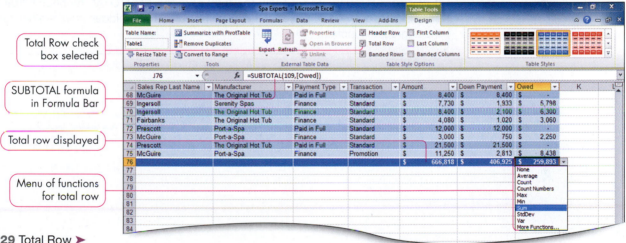

FIGURE 4.29 Total Row ➤

=SUBTOTAL(function_num,ref1,...

The **SUBTOTAL function** calculates an aggregate for values in a range or database.

The SUBTOTAL function calculates results on the total row. The **SUBTOTAL function** calculates an aggregate value, such as totals, for values in a range or database. The function for the total row looks like this: =SUBTOTAL(109,[Owed]). The function_num argument is a number that represents a function (see Table 4.4). The number 109 represents the SUM function. The ref1 argument indicates the range of values to calculate. In this case, [Owed] represents the Owed field. A benefit of the SUBTOTAL function is that it subtotals data for filtered records, so you have an accurate total for the visible records.

TABLE 4.4	SUBTOTAL Function Numbers	
Function	**Database Number**	**Table Number**
AVERAGE	1	101
COUNT	2	102
COUNTA	3	103
MAX	4	104
MIN	5	105
PRODUCT	6	106
STDEV	7	107
STDEVP	8	108
SUM	9	109
VAR	10	110
VARP	11	111

 TIP Filtering Data and Subtotals

If you filter the data and display the total row, the SUBTOTAL function's 109 argument ensures that only the displayed data are summed; data for hidden rows are not calculated in the aggregate function.

HANDS-ON EXERCISES

3 Table Manipulation and Aggregation

You want to start analyzing the January transactions for Spa Experts by sorting and filtering data in a variety of ways to help you understand the transactions better. In addition, you need to calculate the required down payment amount and how much customers owe for their spas. Finally, you will convert the table back to a range.

Skills covered: Sort Individual Columns • Use the Sort Dialog Box • Apply Text Filters • Apply a Number Filter • Apply a Date Filter • Create Structured References • Add a Total Row • Convert a Table to a Range

---

STEP 1 ▷ SORT INDIVIDUAL COLUMNS

First, you want to compare the number of transactions by sales rep, so you will sort the data by the Last Name field. After reviewing the transactions by sales reps, you want to see what manufacturer's spas are sold most often. Refer to Figure 4.30 as you complete Step 1.

FIGURE 4.30 Sorted Data ▶

a. Open *e04h2spa_LastnameFirstname* if you closed it at the end of Hands-On Exercise 2. Save the workbook with the new name **e04h3spa_LastnameFirstname**, changing *h2* to *h3*.

b. Click the **Sales Rep Last Name filter arrow**, and then select **Sort A to Z**.

Excel arranges the records in alphabetical order by last name. All transactions completed by Fairbanks display first. Within each sales rep, records appear in their original sequence by transaction number. Without actually counting the records, which sales rep appears to have the most sales? According to the sorted list, McGuire sold the most spas in January. The up arrow icon on the Last Name filter arrow indicates records are sorted in alphabetical order by that column.

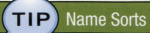

TIP Name Sorts

Always check the table to determine how many levels of sorting you need to apply. If your table contains several people with the same last name but different first names, you would first sort by the Last Name field, and then sort by First Name field individually. All the people with the last name Fairbanks would be grouped together and then further sorted by first name, such as Amanda and then Bradley. To ensure that Excel sorts in the sequence you desire, use the Sort dialog box instead of sorting columns individually.

c. Click the **Manufacturer filter arrow**, and then select **Sort A to Z**.

Excel arranges the records in alphabetical order by manufacturer. Port-a-Spa displays first. Within the Port-a-Spa group, the records are further sorted by the previous sort: last name. Fairbanks appears before Ingersoll. The up arrow icon within the Manufacturer filter arrow indicates that records are sorted in alphabetical order by this column (see Figure 4.30).

d. Click the **Transaction Number filter arrow**, and then select **Sort A to Z**. Save the workbook.

Excel arranges the records back in their original sequence—by transaction number.

STEP 2 ▶ USE THE SORT DIALOG BOX

You want to review the transactions by payment type (financed or paid in full). Within each payment type, you want to further compare the transaction type (promotion or standard). Finally, you want to compare costs within the sorted records by displaying the highest costs first. You will use the Sort dialog box to perform a three-level sort. Refer to Figure 4.31 as you complete Step 2.

FIGURE 4.31 Three-Level Sort ▶

a. Click inside the table. Click the **Data tab**.

Both the Data and Home tabs contain commands to open the Sort dialog box.

b. Click **Sort** in the Sort & Filter group.

The Sort dialog box opens. You start by specifying the column for the primary sort. In this case, you want to sort the records first by the Payment Type column.

c. Click the **Sort by arrow**, and then select **Payment Type**.

The default Sort On is Values, and the default Order is A to Z.

d. Click **Add Level**.

The Sort dialog box adds the *Then by* row, which adds a secondary sort.

e. Click the **Then by arrow**, and then select **Transaction**.

Excel will first sort the records by the Payment Type. Within each Payment Type, Excel will further sort records by Transaction.

f. Click **Add Level** to add another *Then by* row. Click the second **Then by arrow**, and then select **Amount**.

g. Click the **Order arrow** for the Amount sort, and then select **Largest to Smallest**.

Within the Payment Type and Transaction sorts, this will arrange the records with the largest amount first in descending order to the smallest amount.

h. Click **OK** and scroll through the records. Save the workbook.

Figure 4.31 shows the sorted records. Most customers finance their spas instead of paying for their spas in full. For the financed spas, about half were promotional sales and half were standard sales. For those spas paid in full, a majority of the transactions were standard sales, indicating that people with money don't necessarily wait for a promotional sale to buy their spas.

STEP 3 ▶ APPLY TEXT FILTERS

Now that you know McGuire had the most transactions, you want to focus on her sales for January. In particular, you want to filter the table to show only her records. You notice that she sells more Port-a-Spas and The Original Hot Tub than the Serenity Spas, so you will filter out the Serenity Spa sales. Refer to Figure 4.32 as you complete Step 3.

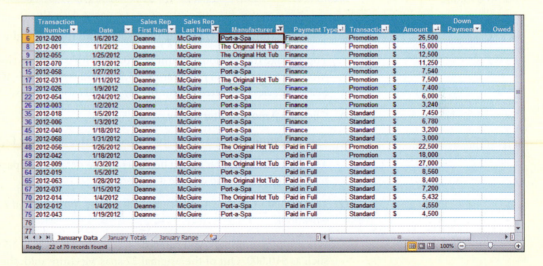

FIGURE 4.32 McGuire Sales for Two Manufacturers ➤

a. Click the **Sales Rep Last Name filter arrow**.

The (Select All) check box is selected.

b. Click the **(Select All) check box** to deselect all last names.

c. Click the **McGuire check box**, and then click **OK**.

The status bar indicates that 27 out of 70 records meet the filtering condition. The Last Name filter arrow includes a funnel icon, indicating that this column is filtered.

d. Click the **Manufacturer filter arrow**.

e. Click the **Serenity Spas check box** to deselect this manufacturer, and then click **OK**. Save the workbook.

You filtered out the Serenity Spas brand that McGuire sold. The remaining 22 records show McGuire's sales for the Port-a-Spas and The Original Hot Tub brands sold. The Manufacturer filter arrow includes a funnel icon, indicating that this column is also filtered.

STEP 4 ▶ APPLY A NUMBER FILTER

You now want to focus on the amount of sales for McGuire. In particular, you are interested in how much gross revenue she generated for spas that cost at least $10,000 or more. Refer to Figure 4.33 as you complete Step 4.

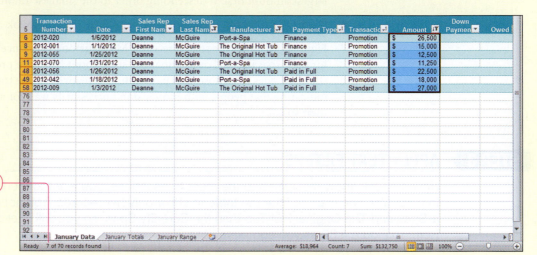

Number of filtered records

FIGURE 4.33 Filtered to Amounts Greater Than or Equal To $10,000 ➤

a. Select the **range H6:H75** of the filtered list, and then view the status bar.

The average transaction amount is $10,159 with 22 transactions (i.e., 22 filtered records). McGuire's total January sales are $223,502. You will use this total to see how much of the $223,502 sales generated are for higher-priced models she sold.

b. Click the **Amount filter arrow**.

c. Point to **Number Filters**, and then select **Greater Than Or Equal To**.

The Custom AutoFilter dialog box opens. The default comparison is *is greater than or equal to*, although you could change it if needed.

d. Type **10000** in the box to the right of *is greater than or equal to*, and then click **OK**. Save the workbook.

When typing numbers, you can type raw numbers such as 10000 or formatted numbers such as $10,000. Out of the original 27 spas McGuire sold, she sold only 7 of the Port-a-Spas and The Original Hot Tub brands that cost $10,000 or more. Out of the $223,502 total sales for those two brands, McGuire sold $132,750 in the higher-priced models costing $10,000 or more.

> **TROUBLESHOOTING:** If no records display or if too many records display, you might have entered 100000 or 1000. Repeat steps b–d.

STEP 5 › APPLY A DATE FILTER

Finally, you want to study McGuire's sales records for the week of January 22. You will add a date filter to identify those sales records. Refer to Figure 4.34 as you complete Step 5.

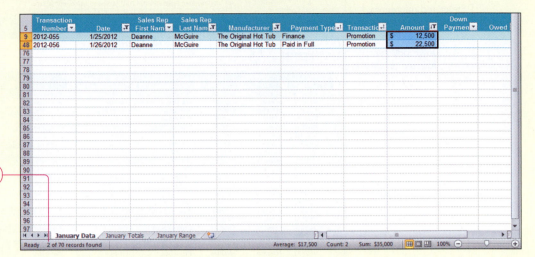

FIGURE 4.34 Filtered by Dates Between 1/22/2012 and 1/28/2012 ➤

a. Click the **Date filter arrow**.

b. Point to **Date Filters**, and then select **Between**.

> The Custom AutoFilter dialog box opens. The default comparisons are *is after or equal to* and *is before or equal to*, ready for you to enter the date specifications.

c. Type **1/22/2012** in the box on the right side of *is after or equal to*.

> You specified the starting date of the range of dates to include. You will keep the *And* option selected.

d. Type **1/28/2012** in the box on the right side of *is before or equal to*. Click **OK**. Save the workbook.

> McGuire had only two sales during that week, totaling $35,000.

STEP 6 › CREATE STRUCTURED REFERENCES

To continue reviewing the January transactions, you need to calculate the required down payment for customers who financed their spas. The required down payment is located above the table data so that you can change that value if needed later. In addition, you need to calculate how much customers owe on their spas if they did not pay in full. You will use structured formulas to perform these calculations. Refer to Figure 4.35 as you complete Step 6.

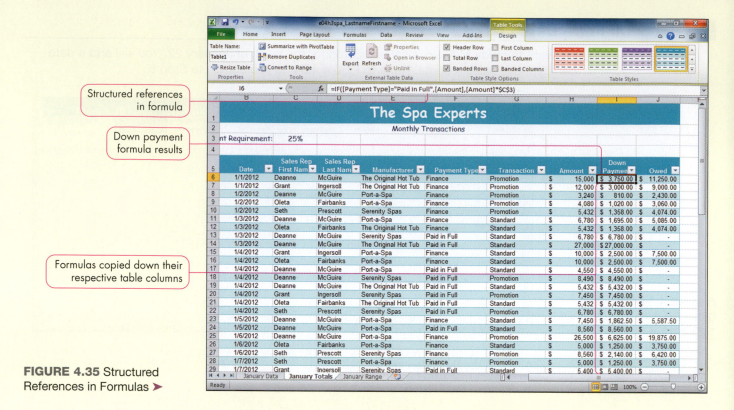

FIGURE 4.35 Structured References in Formulas ➤

a. Click the **January Totals worksheet tab**.

To preserve the integrity of the sorting and filtering in case your instructor wants to verify your work, you will continue with an identical table on another worksheet.

b. Click in the **Name Box**, type **I6**, and then press **Enter** to go to **cell I6**. Click **Insert Function** on the Formula Bar to open the Insert Function dialog box, select **IF** in the **Select a function list**, and then click **OK**.

c. Type **[Payment Type]="Paid in Full"** in the **Logical_test box**.

The logical test evaluates whether a customer paid in full, indicated in the Payment Type column. Remember to type the brackets around the column heading.

d. Type [**Amount**] in the **Value_if_true box**.

If a customer pays in full, their down payment is the full amount.

e. Type [**Amount**]*$C$3 in the **Value_if_false box**.

If a customer does not pay in full, they must pay a required down payment. You use [Amount] to refer to the Amount column in the table. You must enclose the column heading in brackets. The amount of the spa is multiplied by the absolute reference to C3, the cell containing the required down payment percentage. You make this cell reference absolute so that it does not change when Excel copies the formula down the Down Payment column. Figure 4.35 shows the formula in the formula bar.

f. Click **OK** to enter the formula (see Figure 4.35).

Because you are entering formulas in a table, Excel copies the formula down the column automatically. The first customer must finance $3,750 (25% of $15,000). The columns in the current worksheet have been formatted as Accounting Number Format for you.

> **TROUBLESHOOTING:** If the results seem incorrect, check your function. Errors will result if you do not enclose the field names in brackets, if you have misspelled a field name, if you omit the quotation marks around *Paid in Full*, and so on. Correct any errors.

g. Click **cell J6**. Type the formula =[**Amount**]-[**Down Payment**] and press **Enter**. Save the workbook.

The formula calculates how much customers owe if they finance their hot tubs. Excel copies the formula down the column.

STEP 7 **ADD A TOTAL ROW**

The table is almost complete, but you want to see the monthly totals for the Amount, Down Payment, and Owed columns. Instead of entering SUM functions yourself, you will add a total row. Refer to Figure 4.36 as you complete Step 7.

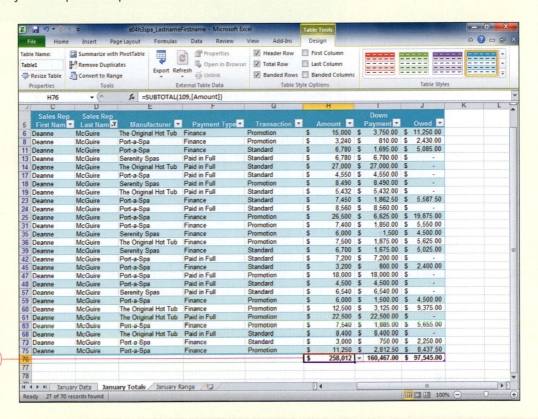

FIGURE 4.36 Totals for Filtered Table ➤

a. Click the **Design tab**, and then click **Total Row** in the Table Style Options group.

Excel displays the total row after the last record. It sums the last column of values automatically. The total amount customers owe is $259,893.00.

b. Click the **Down Payment cell** in row 76, click the **total arrow**, and then select **Sum**. Increase the Down Payment column width as needed.

You added a total to the Down Payment column. The total amount of down payment collected is $406,925.00. The formula appears as =SUBTOTAL(109,[Down Payment]) in the Formula Bar.

c. Click the **Amount cell** in row 76, click the **total arrow**, and then select **Sum**.

You added a total to the Amount column. The total amount of spa sales is $666,818. The formula appears as =SUBTOTAL(109,[Amount]) in the Formula Bar.

d. Filter by McGuire again. Save the workbook.

Notice that the total row values change to display the totals for only the filtered records.

Your last task for now is to convert a copy of the table to a range again so that you can apply other formats. Refer to Figure 4.37 as you complete Step 8.

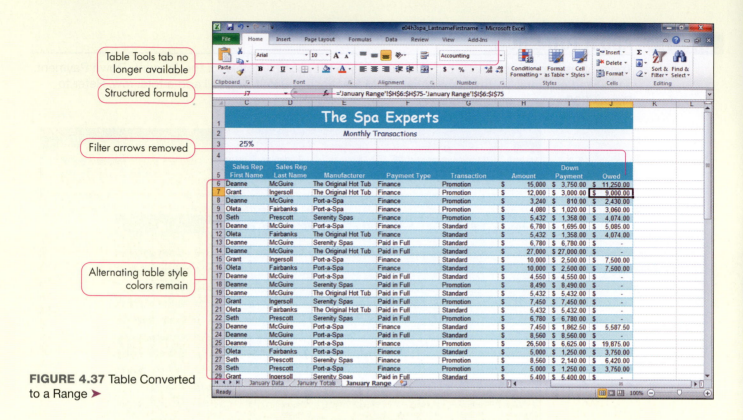

FIGURE 4.37 Table Converted to a Range ➤

a. Click the **January Range worksheet tab**.

To preserve the integrity of the sorting and filtering in case your instructor wants to verify your work, you will continue with an identical table on another worksheet.

b. Click within the table, and then click the **Design tab**, if necessary.

c. Click **Convert to Range** in the Tools group.

Excel displays a message box asking if you want to convert the table to a range.

d. Click **Yes**.

Excel converts the table to a range. The filter arrows disappear, and the Table Tools no longer display. The range is still formatted using the table style you applied. The structured formula =[Amount]-[Down Payment] changes (see Figure 4.37).

e. Double-click the border between the column I and J headers to increase the width of column I so that the down payment total displays on the last row.

f. Save the workbook. Keep the workbook onscreen if you plan to continue with Hands-On Exercise 4. If not, close the workbook and exit Excel.

Conditional Formatting

You use table styles, or a variety of font, alignment, and number formats on the Home tab, to format a worksheet. You can also apply special formatting to cells that contain particular values or text using conditional formatting. *Conditional formatting* applies special formatting to highlight or emphasize cells that meet specific conditions. For example, a sales manager might want to highlight cells containing the top 10 sales amounts, or a professor might want to highlight test scores that fall below the average. You can also apply conditional formatting to point out data for a specific date or duplicate values in a range.

In this section, you will learn about the five conditional formatting categories and how to apply conditional formatting to a range of values based on a condition you set.

Conditional formatting highlights or emphasizes cells that meet certain conditions.

Applying Conditional Formatting

Conditional formatting helps you and your audience understand a dataset better because it adds a visual element to the cells. The term is called *conditional* because the formatting occurs when a condition is met. This is similar logic to the IF function you have used. Remember with an IF function, you create a logical test that is evaluated. If the logical or conditional test is true, the function produces one result. If the logical or conditional test is false, the function produces another result. With conditional formatting, if the condition is true, Excel formats the cell automatically based on that condition. If the condition is false, Excel does not format the cell. If you change a value in a conditionally formatted cell, Excel examines the new value to see if it should apply the conditional format. Table 4.5 lists and describes a number of different conditional formats that you can apply.

> Conditional formatting helps you and your audience understand a dataset better because it adds a visual element to the cells.

TABLE 4.5	Conditional Formatting Options
Conditional Formatting	**Description**
Highlight Cells Rules	Highlights cells with a fill color, font color, or border (such as Light Red Fill with Dark Red Text) if values are greater than, less than, between two values, equal to a value, or duplicate values; text that contains particular characters; or dates when a date meets a particular condition, such as *In the last 7 days*.
Top/Bottom Rules	Formats cells with values in the top 10 items, top 10%, bottom 10 items, bottom 10%, values, above average, or below average. You can change the exact values to format the top or bottom items or percentages, such as top 5 or bottom 15%.
Data Bars	Applies a gradient or solid fill bar in which the width of the bar represents the current cell's value compared to other cells' values.
Color Scales	Formats different cells with different colors, assigning one color to the lowest group of values and another color to the highest group of values, with gradient colors to other values.
Icon Sets	Inserts an icon from an icon palette in each cell to indicate values compared to each other.

To apply a conditional format, select the cells for which you want to apply a conditional format, click the Home tab, click Conditional Formatting in the Styles group, and select the conditional formatting category you want to apply.

Apply the Highlight Cells Rules

The Highlight Cells Rules category enables you to apply a highlight to cells that meet a condition, such as a value greater than a particular value. This option contains predefined combinations of fill colors, font colors, and/or borders. This category is useful because it helps you identify and format automatically values of interest. For example, a weather tracker who developed a worksheet containing the temperatures for each day of a month might want to apply a conditional format to cells that contain temperatures between 70 and 75 degrees. To apply this conditional formatting, she would select Highlight Cells Rules, and then select Between. In the Between dialog box (see Figure 4.38), the weather tracker would type 70 in the *Format cells that are BETWEEN* box and 75 in the *and* box, select the type of conditional formatting, such as *Light Red Fill with Dark Red Text*, and then click OK to apply the formats.

FIGURE 4.38 Between Dialog Box ➤

Figure 4.39 shows two columns of data that contain conditional formats. The Manufacturer column contains a conditional format to highlight text with a Light Red Fill with Dark Red Text for cells that contain *Serenity Spas*, and the Amount column contains a conditional format to highlight with Red Border values between $10,000 and $20,000.

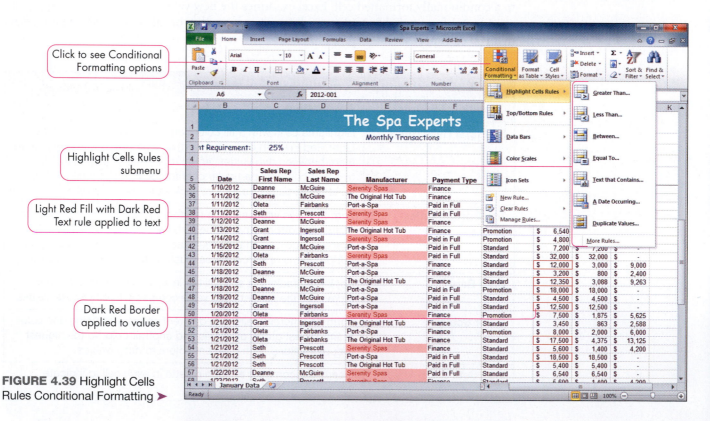

FIGURE 4.39 Highlight Cells Rules Conditional Formatting ➤

Specify Top/Bottom Rules

You may not know the exact values to format conditionally. You might be interested in identifying the top five sales to reward the sales associates, or want to identify the bottom 15% of automobile dealers so that you can close underperforming locations. The Top/Bottom Rules category enables you to specify the top or bottom number or percentage in a selected range. In addition, the Top/Bottom Rules category enables you to identify values that are above or below the average value in that range. In Figure 4.40, the selected range is conditionally formatted to highlight the top three amounts. Although the menu option is Top 10 Items, you can specify the exact number of items to highlight.

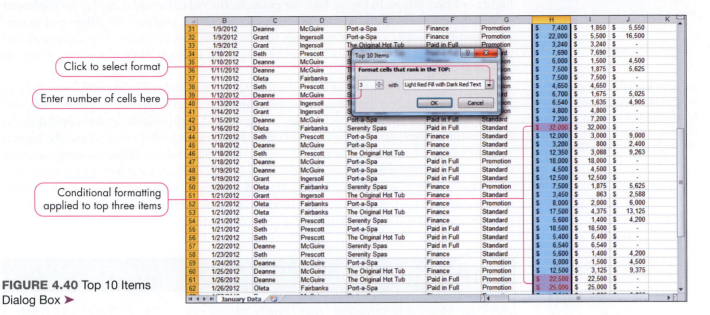

Click to select format

Enter number of cells here

Conditional formatting applied to top three items

FIGURE 4.40 Top 10 Items Dialog Box ➤

Display Data Bars, Color Scales, and Icon Sets

A **data bar** is a horizontal gradient or solid fill indicating the cell's relative value compared to other selected cells.

Data bars help you visualize the value of a cell relative to other cells, as shown in Figure 4.41. The width of the gradient or solid data bar represents the value in a cell, with a wider bar representing a higher value and a shorter bar a lower value. Use data bar conditional formatting when identifying high and low values. Excel locates the largest value and displays the widest data bar in that cell. Excel then finds the smallest value and displays the smallest data bar in that cell. Excel sizes the data bars for the remaining cells based on their relative values. If you change the values in your worksheet, Excel automatically updates the widths of the data bars. Data bars are more effective with wider columns than narrow columns. Figure 4.41 shows data bar conditional formatting applied to the Amount column. The widest data bar displays in the cell containing the largest amount of $27,000, and the smallest data bar appears in the cells containing the smallest value of $3,240. The data bar widths of other cells help you see the value differences. Excel uses the same color for each data bar, but each bar differs in size based on the value in the respective cells.

Data bars applied to Amount column

Icon set applied to Owed column

Color scales applied to Down Payment column

FIGURE 4.41 Data Bars, Color Scales, and Icon Sets ➤

A **color scale** is a conditional format that displays a particular color based on the relative value of the cell contents to other selected cells.

Color scales format cells with different colors based on the relative value of a cell compared to other selected cells. You can apply a two- or three-color scale. This scale assists in comparing a range of cells using gradations of those colors. The shade of the color represents higher or lower values. In Figure 4.41, for example, the red color scales display for the lowest values, the green color displays for the highest values, and gradients of yellow and orange represent the middle range of values in the Down Payment column. Use color scales to understand variation in the data to identify trends, for example to view good stock returns and weak stock returns.

An **icon set** is a conditional format that displays an icon representing a value in the top third, quarter, or fifth based on values in the selected range.

Icon sets are little symbols or signs that display in cells to classify data into three, four, or five categories, based on the values in the selected range. Excel determines categories of value ranges and assigns an icon to each range. In Figure 4.41, a three-icon set was applied to the Owed column. Excel divided the range of values between the lowest value $0 and the highest value of $19,875 into thirds. The red diamond icon displays for the cells containing values in the lowest third ($0 to $6,625), the yellow triangle icon displays for cells containing the values in the middle third ($6,626 to $12,150), and the green circle icon displays for cells containing values in the top third ($13,251 to $19,875). This helps you identify the spas with the most financing. Most spa purchases fall into the lowest third.

 TIP Don't Overdo It!

Although conditional formatting helps identify trends, you should use this feature wisely. Apply conditional formatting when you want to emphasize important data. When you decide to apply conditional formatting, think about which category is best to highlight the data. Sometimes simple highlighting will suffice when you want to point out data meeting a particular condition; other times, you might want to apply data bars to point out relative differences among values. Finally, don't apply conditional formatting to too many columns.

Clear Rules

To clear conditional formatting from the entire worksheet, click Conditional Formatting in the Styles group on the Home tab, point to Clear Rules, and select Clear Rules from Entire Sheet. To remove conditional formatting from a range of cells, select cells. Then click Conditional Formatting, point to Clear Rules, and then select Clear Rules from Selected Cells.

Creating a New Rule

The default conditional formatting categories provide a variety of options. Excel also enables you to create your own rules to specify different fill colors, borders, or other formatting if you don't want the default settings. Excel provides three ways to create a new rule:

- Click Conditional Formatting in the Cell Styles group, and then select New Rule.
- Click Conditional Formatting in the Cell Styles group, select Manage Rules to open the Conditional Formatting Rules Manager dialog box, and then click New Rule.
- Click Conditional Formatting in the Cell Styles group, select a rule category such as Highlight Cells Rules, and then select More Rules.

The New Formatting Rule dialog box opens (see Figure 4.42) so that you can define your new conditional formatting rule. First, select a rule type, such as *Format all cells based on their values*. The *Edit the Rule Description* section changes, based on the rule type you select. With the default rule type selected, you can specify the format style (2-Color Scale, 3-Color Scale, Data Bar, or Icon Sets). You can then specify the minimum and maximum values, the fill colors for color sets or data bars or the icons for icon sets. After you edit the rule description, click OK to save your new conditional format.

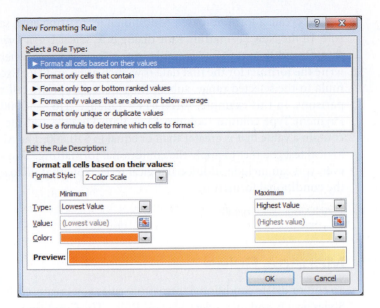

FIGURE 4.42 New Formatting Rule Dialog Box ➤

If you select any rule type except the *Format all cells based on their values* rule, the dialog box contains a Format button. When you click Format, the Format Cells dialog box opens so that you can specify number, font, border, and fill formats to apply to your rule.

TIP Format Only Cells That Contain

This option provides a wide array of things you can format: values, text, dates, blanks, no blanks, errors, or no errors. Formatting blanks is helpful to see where you are missing data, and formatting cells containing errors helps you find those errors quickly.

Use Formulas in Conditional Formatting

Excel provides a vast number of conditional formatting options. If you need to create a complex conditional formatting rule, you can select a rule that uses a formula to format cells. For example, you might want to format amounts of financed spas *and* amounts that are $10,000 or more. Figure 4.43 shows the Edit Formatting Rule dialog box and the corresponding conditional formatting applied to cells.

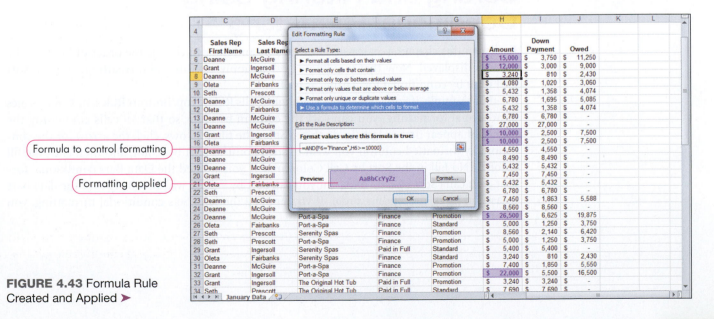

Formula to control formatting

Formatting applied

FIGURE 4.43 Formula Rule Created and Applied ➤

To create a formula-based conditional formatting rule, select the data and create a new rule. In the New Formatting Rule dialog box, select *Use a formula to determine which cells to format*, and then type the formula in the *Format values where this formula is true* box. You write the formula for the first data row, such as F6 and H6. Excel then applies the general formula to the selected range, substituting the appropriate cell reference as it makes the comparisons. In this example, =AND(F6="Finance",H6>=10000) requires that the text in the Payment Type column (column F) contain Finance and the Amount column (column H) contain a value that is greater than or equal to $10,000. The AND function requires that both logical tests be met to apply the conditional formatting. Two logical tests are required; however, you can include additional logical tests. Note that *all* logical tests must be true to apply the conditional formatting.

= AND(logical1,logical2,...)

Manage Rules

To edit or delete conditional formatting rules you create, click Conditional Formatting in the Styles group, and then select Manage Rules. The Conditional Formatting Rules Manager dialog box opens (see Figure 4.44). Click the *Show formatting rules for* arrow and select from current selection, the entire worksheet, or a specific table. Then select the rule, and then click Edit Rule or Delete Rule.

FIGURE 4.44 Conditional Formatting Rules Manager Dialog Box ➤

Sorting and Filtering Using Conditional Formatting

Earlier in this chapter, you learned how to sort and filter to change the order of fields or the records displayed. Now that you know how to apply conditional formatting, you can sort and filter by conditional formatting as well.

For example, if you applied the Highlight Cells Rules, Top/Bottom Rules, or Color Scales conditional formatting, you can sort the column by color so that all cells containing the highlight appear first or last. To do this, display the filter arrows, click the arrow for the conditionally formatted column you wish to sort, point to Sort by Color, and then click the fill color or No Fill in the Sort by Cell Color area. If you applied the Data Bars conditional format, you can't sort by data bars, but you can sort by values, which will arrange the data bars in ascending or descending order. If you applied the Icon Sets conditional formatting, you can filter by icon.

4 Conditional Formatting

Your business partner, Ryan, wants to review the transactions with you. He is interested in Fairbanks' sales record and the five highest spa amounts. In addition, he wants to compare the down payment amounts visually. Finally, he wants to analyze the amounts owed for sales completed by Prescott.

Skills covered: Highlight Cells Rules • Specify Top/Bottom Rules • Display Data Bars • Create a New Rule • Filter by Rule

---

STEP 1 ▶ HIGHLIGHT CELLS RULES

You want to identify Fairbanks' spa sales for January without filtering the data. You will apply a conditional format to apply a fill and font color so that cells containing her last name stand out. Refer to Figure 4.45 as you complete Step 1.

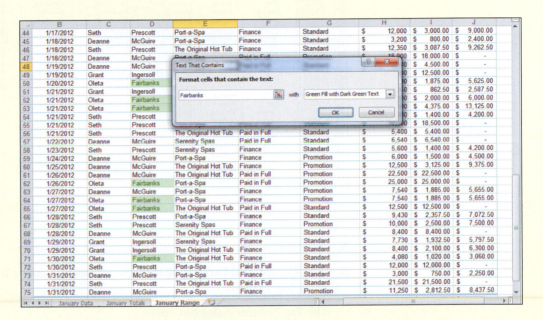

FIGURE 4.45 Text Formatted with Highlight Text Rules ▶

a. Open *e04h3spa_LastnameFirstname* if you closed it at the end of Hands-On Exercise 3. Save the workbook with the new name **e04h4spa_LastnameFirstname**, changing *h3* to *h4*.

b. Select **row headings 6 through 75** in the January Range worksheet. Click the **Home tab**, if necessary, click the **Fill Color arrow**, and then select **No Fill**.

You removed the previous table style with banded rows. This will avoid having too many fill colors when you apply conditional formatting rules.

c. Select the **range D6:D75**, which is the column containing the sales representatives' last names.

d. Click **Conditional Formatting** in the Styles group, point to **Highlight Cells Rules**, and then select **Text that Contains**.

The Text That Contains dialog box opens.

e. Type **Fairbanks** in the box, click the **with arrow**, and then select **Green Fill with Dark Green Text**. Click **OK**. Deselect the range, and then save the workbook.

Excel formats only cells that contain Fairbanks with the fill and font color.

TIP Apply Multiple Formats to One Column

While the range is selected, you can apply another conditional format, such as Light Yellow with Dark Yellow text for another last name.

STEP 2 ▶ SPECIFY TOP/BOTTOM RULES

Ryan is now interested in identifying the highest five spa sales in January. Instead of sorting the records, you will use the Top/Bottom Rules conditional formatting. Refer to Figure 4.46 as you complete Step 2.

	B	C	D	E	F	G	H	I	J
14	1/3/2012	Deanne	McGuire	The Original Hot Tub	Paid in Full	Standard	$ 27,000	$ 27,000.00	$ -
15	1/4/2012	Grant	Ingersoll	Port-a-Spa	Finance	Standard	$ 10,000	$ 2,500.00	$ 7,500.00
16	1/4/2012	Oleta	Fairbanks	Port-a-Spa	Finance	Standard	$ 10,000	$ 2,500.00	$ 7,500.00
17	1/4/2012	Deanne	McGuire	Port-a-Spa	Paid in Full	Standard	$ 4,550	$ 4,550.00	$ -
18	1/4/2012	Deanne	McGuire	Serenity Spas	Paid in Full	Promotion	$ 8,490	$ 8,490.00	$ -
19	1/4/2012	Deanne	McGuire	The Original Hot Tub	Paid in Full	Standard	$ 5,432	$ 5,432.00	$ -
20	1/4/2012	Grant	Ingersoll	Serenity Spas	Paid in Full	Promotion	$ 7,450	$ 7,450.00	$ -
21	1/4/2012	Oleta	Fairbanks	The Original Hot Tub	Paid in Full	Standard	$ 5,432	$ 5,432.00	$ -
22	1/4/2012	Seth	Prescott	Serenity Spas	Paid in Full	Promotion	$ 6,780	$ 6,780.00	$ -
23	1/5/2012	Deanne	McGuire	Port-a-Spa	Finance	Standard	$ 7,450	$ 1,862.50	$ 5,587.50
24	1/5/2012	Deanne	McGuire	Port-a-Spa	Paid in Full	Standard	$ 8,560	$ 8,560.00	$ -
25	1/6/2012	Deanne	McGuire	Port-a-Spa	Finance	Promotion	$ 26,500	$ 6,625.00	$ 19,875.00
26	1/6/2012	Oleta	Fairbanks	Port-a-Spa	Finance	Standard	$ 5,000	$ 1,250.00	$ 3,750.00
27	1/6/2012	Seth	Prescott	Serenity Spas	Finance	Promotion	$ 8,560	$ 2,140.00	$ 6,420.00
28	1/7/2012	Seth	Prescott	Port-a-Spa	Finance	Promotion	$ 5,000	$ 1,250.00	$ 3,750.00
29	1/7/2012	Grant	Ingersoll	Serenity Spas	Paid in Full	Standard	$ 5,400	$ 5,400.00	$ -
30	1/8/2012	Oleta	Fairbanks	Serenity Spas	Finance	Standard	$ 3,240	$ 810.00	$ 2,430.00
31	1/9/2012	Deanne	McGuire	Port-a-Spa	Finance	Promotion	$ 7,400	$ 1,850.00	$ 5,550.00
32	1/9/2012	Grant	Ingersoll	Port-a-Spa	Finance	Promotion	$ 22,000	$ 5,500.00	$ 16,500.00
33	1/9/2012	Grant	Ingersoll	The Original Hot Tub	Paid in Full	Promotion	$ 3,240	$ 3,240.00	$ -
34	1/10/2012	Seth	Prescott	The Original Hot Tub	Paid in Full	Standard	$ 7,690	$ 7,690.00	$ -
35	1/10/2012	Deanne	McGuire	Serenity Spas	Finance	Promotion	$ 6,000	$ 1,500.00	$ 4,500.00
36	1/11/2012	Deanne	McGuire	The Original Hot Tub	Finance	Promotion	$ 7,500	$ 1,875.00	$ 5,625.00
37	1/11/2012	Oleta	Fairbanks	Port-a-Spa	Paid in Full	Promotion	$ 7,500	$ 7,500.00	$ -
38	1/11/2012	Seth	Prescott	Serenity Spas	Paid in Full	Promotion	$ 4,650	$ 4,650.00	$ -
39	1/12/2012	Deanne	McGuire	Serenity Spas	Finance	Standard	$ 6,700	$ 1,675.00	$ 5,025.00
40	1/13/2012	Grant	Ingersoll	The Original Hot Tub	Finance	Promotion	$ 6,540	$ 1,635.00	$ 4,905.00
41	1/14/2012	Grant	Ingersoll	Serenity Spas	Paid in Full	Promotion	$ 4,800	$ 4,800.00	$ -
42	1/15/2012	Deanne	McGuire	Port-a-Spa	Paid in Full	Standard	$ 7,200	$ 7,200.00	$ -
43	1/16/2012	Oleta	Fairbanks	Serenity Spas	Paid in Full	Standard	$ 32,000	$ 32,000.00	$ -
44	1/17/2012	Seth	Prescott	Port-a-Spa	Finance	Standard	$ 12,000	$ 3,000.00	$ 9,000.00
45	1/18/2012	Deanne	McGuire	Port-a-Spa	Finance	Standard	$ 3,200	$ 800.00	$ 2,400.00

January Data / January Totals / **January Range**

FIGURE 4.46 Top 5 Amounts Conditionally Formatted ▶

a. Select the **range H6:H75**, the range containing the amounts.

b. Click **Conditional Formatting** in the Styles group, point to **Top/Bottom Rules**, and then select **Top 10 Items**.

    The Top 10 Items dialog box opens.

c. Click the **spin arrow** to display 5, click the **with arrow**, and then select **Light Red Fill**. Click **OK**.

d. Scroll through the worksheet to see the top five amounts (three of which are shown in Figure 4.46). Save the workbook.

STEP 3 ▶ DISPLAY DATA BARS

Now Ryan wants to compare all of the down payments. Data bars would add a nice visual element as Ryan compares down payment amounts. Refer to Figure 4.47 as you complete Step 3.

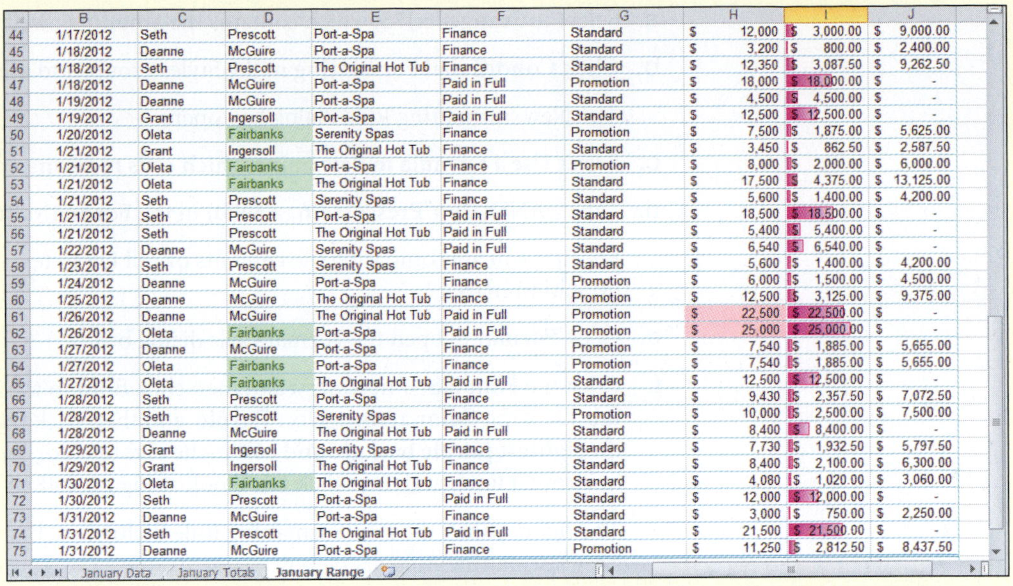

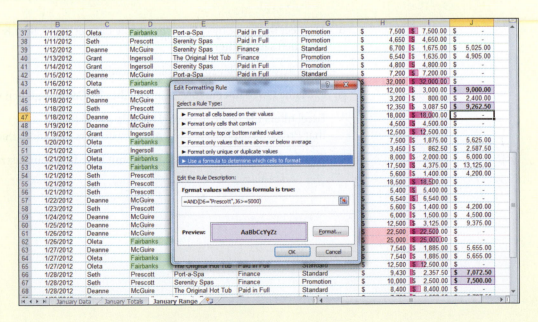

FIGURE 4.47 Data Bars
Conditional Formatting ➤

a. Select the **range I6:I75**, which contains the down payment amounts.

b. Click **Conditional Formatting** in the Styles group, point to **Data Bars**, and then select **Purple Data Bar** in the *Gradient Fill* section. Scroll through the list, and then save the workbook.

   Excel displays data bars in each cell. The larger bar widths help Ryan identify quickly the largest down payments. However, the largest down payments are identical to the original amounts when the customers pay in full. This result illustrates that you should not accept the results at face value. Doing so would provide you with an inaccurate analysis.

STEP 4 ▶ CREATE A NEW RULE

Ryan's next request is to analyze the amounts owed by Prescott's customers. In particular, he wants to know how many customers owe more than $5,000. To do this, you realize you need to create a custom rule that evaluates both the Sales Rep Last Name column and the Owed column. Refer to Figure 4.48 as you complete Step 4.

FIGURE 4.48 Custom Rule
Created ➤

a. Select the **range J6:J75**, which contains the amounts owed.

b. Click **Conditional Formatting** in the Styles group, and then select **New Rule**.

The New Formatting Rule dialog box opens.

c. Select **Use a formula to determine which cells to format**.

d. Type **=AND(D6="Prescott",J6>=5000)** in the **Format values where this formula is true box**.

Because you are comparing the contents of cell D6 to text, you must enclose the text within quotation marks.

e. Click **Format** to open the Format Cells dialog box.

f. Click the **Font tab**, if necessary, and then click **Bold** in the **Font style list**. Click the **Border tab**, click the **Color arrow**, select **Purple**, and then click **Outline**. Click the **Fill tab**, click the **lightest purple background color** (the eighth color on the first row below the first horizontal line), and then click **OK**. Look at Figure 4.48 to compare your new rule.

The figure shows the Edit Formatting Rule dialog box, but the options are similar to the New Formatting Rule dialog box.

g. Click **OK** in New Formatting Rule dialog box, and then scroll through the list to see which amounts owed are greater than $5,000 for Prescott only. Save the workbook.

STEP 5 ▸ FILTER BY RULE

Ryan commented that it is difficult to see which of Prescott's transactions were greater than $5,000 without scrolling. To help Ryan review the Owed column where you applied a formula-based conditional format, you will filter that column by the fill color. Refer to Figure 4.49 as you complete Step 5.

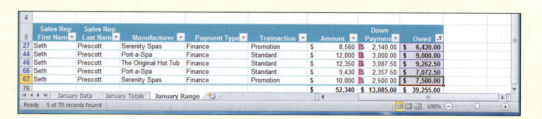

FIGURE 4.49 Owed Column Filtered by Fill Color ➤

a. Deselect the range by clicking inside the dataset. Click **Sort & Filter** in the Editing group, and then select **Filter**.

Filter arrows display for the column headings.

b. Click the **Owed filter arrow**, point to **Filter by Color**, and then select the **light purple fill color**.

Excel filters the range to display records where the fill color is lavender. Now it is easy to see that Prescott sold five spas where the customers owe more than $5,000.

c. Save and close the workbook, and submit based on your instructor's directions.

After reading this chapter, you have accomplished the following objectives:

1. **Freeze rows and columns.** To prevent labels from scrolling offscreen, freeze rows or columns. The Freeze Panes setting freezes the row(s) above and the column(s) to the left of the active cell. When you scroll, those rows and columns remain onscreen so that you know what type of data is in each row or column. You can use Unfreeze Panes to clear the frozen rows and columns.

2. **Print large datasets.** Display the data in Page Break Preview to see the automatic page breaks. Dashed blue lines indicate automatic page breaks. You can insert manual page breaks, indicated by solid blue lines. If you do not want to print an entire worksheet, select a range and set a print area. Dotted lines surround the print area onscreen. When a dataset will print on several pages, you can control the sequence in which the pages will print.

3. **Understand table design.** A table is a structured range that contains related data. Tables have several benefits over regular ranges, such as keeping headings onscreen as you scroll. Each table column is a field. The column headings, called *field names*, appear on the first row of a table. Each row is a complete set of data for one record. You should plan a table. For example, create unique field names on the first row of the table, and enter data immediately below the field names, avoiding blank rows.

4. **Create a table.** You can create a table from existing structured data. Excel applies the Table Style Medium 9 format and assigns a default name, such as Table1, to the table. When the active cell is within a table, the Table Tools display with the Design tab. You can insert and delete table rows and columns and remove duplicate records in your table.

5. **Apply a table style.** Table styles control the fill color of the header row and records within the table. To further customize the formatting, click options, such as First Column or Total Row in the Table Style Options group.

6. **Sort data.** The data in a table are often easier to understand and work with if they are in some meaningful order. Sorting arranges records in a table by the value of one or more fields within the table. You can sort text in alphabetical or reverse alphabetical order, values from smallest to largest or largest to smallest, and dates from oldest to newest or newest to oldest. To sort a single field, click the filter arrow and select the sort method from the list. To sort multiple fields, open the Sort dialog box and add column levels and sort orders. You can create a custom sort for unique data.

7. **Filter data.** Filtering is the process of specifying conditions for displaying records in a table. Only records that meet those conditions display; the other records are hidden until you clear the filters. You can apply text, value, and date filters based on the data in a particular field.

8. **Use structured references and a total row.** A structured reference uses field names instead of cell references, such as =[Amount]-[Down Payment]. Field names must appear in brackets within the formula. When you press Enter, Excel copies the formula down the column. You can display a total row after the last record. Excel sums the values in the last column automatically or counts the number of text entries. You can add totals to other columns, and you can select a different function, such as Average.

9. **Apply conditional formatting.** Conditional formatting applies special formatting to cells that contain values that meet set conditions. The five major conditional formatting categories are Highlight Cells Rules, Top/Bottom Rules, Data Bars, Color Scales, and Icon Sets. Data bars display horizontal bars that compare values within the selected range. The larger the value, the wider the horizontal bar. Color scales indicate values that occur within particular ranges. Icon sets display icons representing a number's relative value compared to other numbers in the range. When you no longer need conditional formatting, you can clear it for the selected range or entire worksheet.

10. **Create a new rule.** You can create conditional format rules. The New Formatting Rule dialog box enables you to select a rule type. Based on the type you select, the *Edit the Rule Description* section changes to provide specific options for defining your rule. You can create rules based on formulas to set conditions based on content in multiple columns. Use the Conditional Formatting Rules Manager dialog box to edit and delete rules.

11. **Sort and filter using conditional formatting.** After you apply conditional formatting, you can sort or filter a column based on its formats. Use Sort by Color to select a sort sequence, or select Filter by Color to filter out records that do not meet the color condition you specify.

KEY TERMS

Color scale **p.268**	Icon set **p.268**	Structured reference **p.254**
Conditional formatting **p.265**	Page break **p.232**	SUBTOTAL function **p.255**
Data bar **p.267**	Print area **p.233**	Table **p.240**
Field **p.240**	Print order **p.234**	Table style **p.243**
Filtering **p.251**	Record **p.240**	Total row **p.255**
Freezing **p.231**	Sorting **p.249**	

1. You have a large dataset that will print on several pages. You want to ensure that related records print on the same page with column and row labels visible and that confidential information is not printed. You should apply all of the following page setup options except which one to accomplish this?

   (a) Set a print area.
   (b) Print titles.
   (c) Adjust page breaks.
   (d) Change the print page order.

2. You are working with a large worksheet. Your row headings are in column A. Which command(s) should be used to see the row headings and the distant information in columns X, Y, and Z?

   (a) Freeze Panes command
   (b) Hide Rows command
   (c) New Window command and cascade the windows
   (d) Split Rows command

3. Which statement is not a recommended guideline for planning a table in Excel?

   (a) Avoid naming two fields with the same name.
   (b) Ensure no blank columns separate data columns within the table.
   (c) Leave one blank row between records in the table.
   (d) Include field names on the first row of the table.

4. You have a list of all the employees in your organization. The list contains employee name, office, title, and salary. You want to list all employees in each office branch. The branches should be listed alphabetically, with the employee earning the highest salary listed first in each office. Which is true of your sort order?

   (a) Branch office is the primary sort and should be in A to Z order.
   (b) Salary is the primary sort and should be from highest to lowest.
   (c) Salary is the primary sort and should be from lowest to highest.
   (d) Branch office is the primary sort and should be in Z to A order.

5. You suspect a table has several identical records. What should you do?

   (a) Do nothing; a logical reason probably exists to keep identical records.
   (b) Use the Remove Duplicates command.

   (c) Look at each row yourself, and manually delete duplicate records.
   (d) Find the duplicate records and change some of the data to be different.

6. Which check box in the Table Style Options group enables you to apply different formatting to the records in a table?

   (a) Header Row
   (b) Banded Rows
   (c) Banded Columns
   (d) Total Row

7. Which date filter option enables you to specify criteria for selecting a range of dates, such as between 3/15/2012 and 7/15/2012?

   (a) Equals
   (b) Before
   (c) All Dates in the Period
   (d) Between

8. You want to display a total row that identifies the oldest date in a field in your table. What function do you select from the list?

   (a) Max
   (b) Sum
   (c) Min
   (d) Count

9. What type of conditional formatting displays horizontal colors in which the width of the bar indicates relative size compared to other values in the selected range?

   (a) Color Scales
   (b) Icon Sets
   (c) Data Bars
   (d) Sparklines

10. When you select the _____ rule type, the New Formatting Rule dialog box does not show the Format button.

    (a) Format all cells based on their values
    (b) Format only cells that contain
    (c) Use a formula to determine which cells to format
    (d) Format only unique or duplicate values

1 Fiesta® Collection

Your Aunt Laura has been collecting Fiesta dinnerware, a popular brand from The Homer Laughlin China Company, since it was reintroduced in 1986. Her collection has grown, and she enlisted you to help her maintain a list. So far, you and Aunt Laura have entered data by color, item number, and item. In addition, you researched current replacement costs from Homer Laughlin's Web site (www.fiestafactorydirect.com); Replacements, Ltd. (www.replacements.com); and eBay (www.ebay.com). Now you need to apply techniques to manage the list, convert it to a table, and then apply table features. This exercise follows the same set of skills as used in Hands-On Exercises 1, 2, and 3 in the chapter. Refer to Figure 4.50 as you complete this exercise.

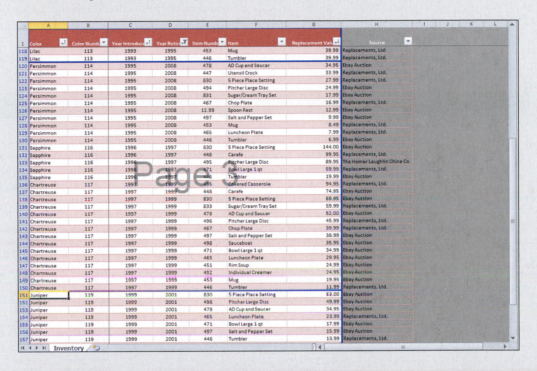

FIGURE 4.50 Fiesta® Collection ➤

a. Open *e04p1fiesta* and save it as **e04p1fiesta_LastnameFirstname**.

b. Click **cell C2**, click the **View tab**, click **Freeze Panes** in the Window group, and then select **Freeze Panes**.

c. Press **Ctrl+End** to go to the last data cell. Note that the frozen rows and column headings remain onscreen. Press **Ctrl+Home** to go back to **cell C2**.

d. Click the **Insert tab**, click **Table** in the Tables group, and then click **OK** in the Create Table dialog box.

e. Click the **More button** in the Table Styles group, and then click **Table Style Medium 3**.

f. Click **Remove Duplicates** in the Tools group, click **Select All** to ensure all columns are selected, and then click **OK**. Click **OK** in the message box that informs you that 12 duplicate values were found and removed.

g. Click within the table. Click the **Data tab**, and then click **Sort** in the Sort & Filter group. Do the following in the Sort dialog box:
   - Click the **Sort by arrow**, and then select **Year Introduced**.
   - Click **Add Level**, click the **Then by arrow**, and then select **Color**.
   - Click **Add Level**, click the **Then by arrow**, select **Replacement Value**, click the **Order arrow**, and then select **Largest to Smallest**. Click **OK**.

h. Click the **Year Retired filter arrow**, deselect the **(Blanks) check box**, and then click **OK** to filter out current colors and display only retired colors.

i. Click the **Design tab**, and then click **Total Row** in the Table Style Options group. Scroll down to the total row on row 316, click the **Source total cell** (which contains a count), click the **Source total arrow**, and then select **None**. Click **cell G6**, the Replacement Value total cell, click the **Replacement Value total arrow**, and then select **Sum**.

j. Prepare the worksheet in case your Aunt Laura wants a printout by doing the following:
- Click the **Page Layout tab**, click **Orientation** in the Page Setup group, and then select **Landscape**.
- Click **Print Titles**, click the **Rows to repeat at top collapse button**, click the **row 1 header**, and then click the **expand button**. Click **OK**.
- Select **cells A1:G316**. Click **Print Area**, and then select **Set Print Area**.
- Click the **View tab**, and then click **Page Break Preview**. If the message box appears, click **OK**.

k. Click **cell A89**, click the **Page Layout tab**, click **Breaks** in the Page Setup group, and then select **Insert Page Break** to insert a page break so that the Periwinkle Blue item on row 89 appears after the page break, along with the other Periwinkle Blue items.

l. Adapt step k to insert a page break before **cell A120** to move Persimmon to the top of a page. Insert another page break before **cell A151** to move Juniper to the top of a page.

m. Create a footer with your name on the left side, the date code in the center, and the file name code on the right side.

n. Save and close the workbook, and submit based on your instructor's directions.

2 Salary Data

As the Human Resources Manager, you maintain employee salary data. You exported data from the corporate database into an Excel workbook. You want to convert the data to a table. You will use structured references to calculate raises and new salaries. Finally, you want to display a total row to show the total salaries. This exercise follows the same set of skills as used in Hands-On Exercises 1, 2, and 3 in the chapter. Refer to Figure 4.51 as you complete this exercise.

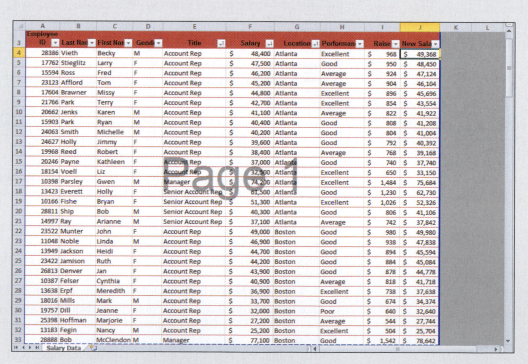

FIGURE 4.51 Salary Data ➤

a. Open *e04p2salary* and save it as **e04p2salary_LastnameFirstname**.

b. Click in the dataset. Click the **Insert tab**, click **Table** in the Tables group, and then click **OK**.

c. Click the **More button** in the Table Styles group, and then click **Table Style Light 10**.

d. Click the **Data tab**, click **Sort** in the Sort & Filter group, and then do the following in the Sort dialog box:
- Click the **Sort by arrow**, and then select **Location**.
- Click **Add Level**, click the **Then by arrow**, and then select **Title**.

- Click **Add Level**, click the **Then by arrow**, select **Salary**, click the **Order arrow**, and then select **Largest to Smallest**. Then click **OK**.

e. Click **cell I3**, type **Raise**, and then press **Tab**. Type **New Salary** in **cell J3**, and then press **Enter**.

f. Click **cell I4**, type =[and then double-click **Salary** from the list. Type]*$I$1 and press **Enter**.

g. Click **cell J4**, type =[Salary]+[Raise], and then press **Enter**.

h. Format the last two columns with **Accounting Number Format** with no decimal places.

i. Click the **Design tab**, and then click **Total Row** in the Table Style Options group. Scroll to the bottom of the table, click the **Raise total cell** on row 159, click the **Raise total row arrow**, and then select **Sum**. Click the **Salary total cell** on row 159, click the **Salary total row arrow**, and then select **Sum**.

j. Prepare the worksheet to be printed by doing the following:
- Click the **Page Layout tab**, and then set **landscape orientation**. Adjust column widths so that the data fits on one page, wrap text, and center align field names.
- Click **Print Titles**, click the **Rows to repeat at top collapse button**, click **row 3**, click the **expand button**, and then click **OK**.
- Click the **View tab**, and then click **Page Break Preview**. If a message box appears, click **OK**.

k. Drag the second page break to be between rows 58 and 59. Move the third page break to be between rows 81 and 82. Move the fourth page break to be between rows 110 and 111. Move the last page break to be between rows 139 and 140.

l. Create a footer with your name on the left side, the date code in the center, and the file name code on the right side.

m. Save and close the workbook, and submit based on your instructor's directions.

3 Dentist Association Donation List

The Midwest Regional Dentist Association is planning its annual meeting in Lincoln, Nebraska, this spring. Several members donated items for door prizes at the closing general session. You need to organize the list of donations and format it to highlight particular data for your supervisor, who is on the conference board of directors. This exercise follows the same set of skills as used in Hands-On Exercises 2, 3, and 4 in the chapter. Refer to Figure 4.52 as you complete this exercise.

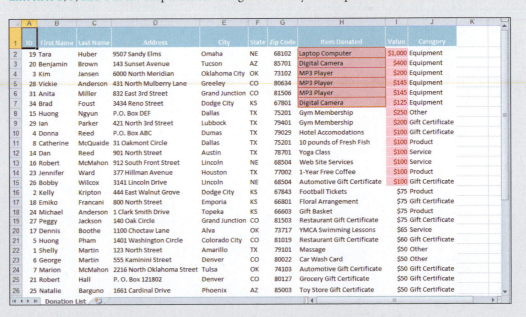

FIGURE 4.52 Donation List ➤

a. Open *e04p3donate* and save it as **e04p3donate_LastnameFirstname**.

b. Click the **Design tab**, click **Remove Duplicates** in the Tools group, and then click **OK**. Click **OK** in the message box that tells you that Excel removed three duplicate records.

c. Click **Convert to Range** in the Tools group, and then click **Yes** in the message box.

d. Select the **range A2:J35**, click the **Home tab**, click the **Fill Color arrow** in the Font group, and then select **No Fill** to remove the table fill colors.

e. Select the **range I2:I35**. Click **Conditional Formatting** in the Styles group, point to **Highlight Cells Rules**, and then select **Greater Than**. Type **99** in the **Format cells that are GREATER THAN box**, and then click **OK**.

f. Select **cells H2:H35**. Create a custom conditional format by doing the following:
- Click **Conditional Formatting** in the Styles group, and then select **New Rule**.
- Click **Use a formula to determine which cells to format**.
- Type =(J2="**Equipment**") in the **Format values where this formula is true box**. The basic condition is testing to see if the contents of cell J2 equal the word *Equipment*. You type *Equipment* in quotation marks since you are comparing text instead of a value.
- Click **Format**, click the **Fill tab** if necessary, and then click **Red, Accent 2, Lighter 60%** (sixth background color on the second row below the first horizontal line).
- Click the **Border tab**, click the **Color arrow**, click **Dark Red**, and then click **Outline**.
- Click **OK** in each dialog box.

g. Click anywhere in the table to deselect the range. Click **Sort & Filter** in the Editing group, and then select **Custom Sort**. The dialog box may contain existing sort conditions for the State and City fields, which you will replace. Set the following sort conditions:
- Click the **Sort by arrow**, and then select **Item Donated**. Click the **Sort On arrow**, and then select **Cell Color**. Click the **Order arrow**, and then select the **RGB(242, 220, 219)** or **RGB(230, 184, 183) fill color**. The fill color displays for the Order.
- Click the **Then by arrow**, and then select **Value**. Click the **Order arrow**, and then select **Largest to Smallest**.
- Click **OK**.

h. Select **landscape orientation**, set appropriate margins, and adjust column widths so that all the data will print on one page. Do not decrease the scaling.

i. Create a footer with your name on the left side, the sheet name code in the center, and the file name code on the right side.

j. Save and close the workbook, and submit based on your instructor's directions.

MID-LEVEL EXERCISES

1 University Band Member List

You are the assistant to the band director at Mountain State University. The secretary created a list of band members, which you need to prepare to print. In addition, you want to convert the data to a table, manipulate the data, and meet with the band director to discuss the roster and ensure you have ample coverage of all instruments, chair position, and classification. For example, if 75% of flute players are 2nd chair, you might want to reassign some flute players to 1st or 3rd chair. Or if all of your baritone players are seniors, you might need to recruit some freshmen baritone players.

a. Open *e04m1band* and save it as **e04m1band_LastnameFirstname**.

b. Freeze the panes so that the column headings and the student IDs, last names, and first names do not scroll offscreen.

 c. Convert the data to a table, and then name the table **BandRoster**.

d. Apply **Table Style Medium 7** to the table. Use Format Painter to copy the heading formats to the Solo Rating heading, if needed.

 e. Sort the table by Instrument, then Chair, and then Class. Create a custom sort order for Class so that it appears in this sequence: Senior, Junior, Sophomore, and Freshman.

f. Remove duplicate records from the table. Excel should find and remove two duplicate records.

g. Add a total row to determine the average scholarship amount per student. Remove any other totals that appear. Change the row heading in **cell A75** to **Average**.

h. Copy the Band Members worksheet, and then place the copied worksheet to the right of the original worksheet. Rename the duplicate worksheet **Filtered Seniors**.

i. Filter the copied table to show only seniors who are 1st or 2nd chair and were awarded a scholarship of at least $4,750 or more. The status bar indicates 10 of 73 records found.

j. Adjust orientation, column widths, margins, row height, and wrap text so that the filtered data will fit on one page.

k. Display the Band Members worksheet in Page Break Preview.
   - Select **landscape orientation**. Adjust the page breaks so that the Instrument column will print on the same pages as the Chair, Class, and Scholarship columns.
   - Repeat the column headings and student ID, last name, and first name on printouts. Adjust the widths of the last five columns as needed, and increase the height of the first row. Do not change the margins or orientation.
   - Set the print range to print all columns and rows except the Solo Rating column.
   - Change the print page order to print horizontally and then down.

l. Create a footer with your name on the left side, the sheet name code in the center, and the file name code on the right side of each worksheet.

m. Check the Band Members worksheet in Print Preview to ensure that it can print on six pages.

n. Save and close the workbook, and submit based on your instructor's directions.

2 Credit Card Expenses

You started recording every credit card transaction so that you can analyze your monthly expenses. You used an Excel worksheet to track dates, places, categories, and amounts. Because you are a consultant who travels periodically, you also have business expenses. You included a column to indicate the business-related transactions. You are now ready to analyze the data. Refer to Figure 4.53 as you complete this exercise.

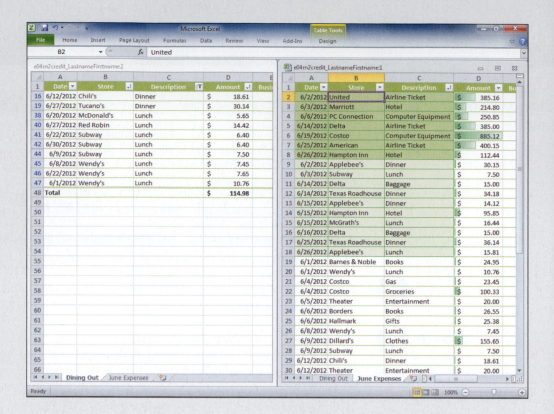

FIGURE 4.53 Credit Card Analysis ➤

a. Open *e04m2credit* and save it as **e04m2credit_LastnameFirstname**.

b. Make sure the Dining Out worksheet is active. Convert the data to a table, and then apply **Table Style Light 11**.

c. Sort the table by the description in alphabetical order, sort the store in alphabetical order, and then sort by amount from smallest to largest in that sequence.

d. Filter the records to show personal (i.e., non-business) lunches and dinner expenses. Add a total row to sum the amounts but do not include other totals.

e. Click the **June Expenses worksheet tab**, and then apply the **Green Data Bar** in the *Gradient Fill* section setting to the Amount column.

f. Create a conditional formatting rule with these specifications:

- Applies to the **range A2:C47**.
- Uses a formula to determine which cells to format based on amounts of $100 or more *and* that are classified as business expenses. Because this conditional formatting applies to several columns (A, B, and C), you must use mixed cell references in the formula.
- Formats data with a **Medium Green fill color** and a **Green line border** using the **Outline preset border style**.

g. Create a conditional formatting rule with these specifications:

- Applies to the **range A2:C47**.
- Uses a formula to determine which cells to format based on amounts less than $100 *and* that are classified as business expenses. Because this conditional formatting applies to several columns (A, B, and C), you must use mixed cell references in the formula.
- Formats data with a **Light Green fill color** and a **Green line border** using the **Outline preset border style**.

h. Create a custom color sort for the Description column with these specifications:

- Sorts on cell color.
- Displays the **Medium Green fill color** on Top as the primary sort.
- Displays the **Light Green fill color** on Top as the secondary sort.

i. Create a footer with your name on the left side, the sheet name code in the center, and the file name code on the right side on each worksheet.

j. Save and close the workbook, and submit based on your instructor's directions.

You work for a gallery that is an authorized Greenwich Workshop fine art dealer (www. greenwichworkshop.com). Customers in your area are especially fond of James C. Christensen's art. Although customers can visit the Web site to see images and details about his work, they have requested a list of all his artwork. Your assistant prepared a list of artwork: art, type, edition size, release date, and issue price. In addition, you included a column to identify what pieces are sold out at the publisher, indicating the rare, hard-to-obtain artwork that is available on the secondary market. You now want to convert the data to a table so that you can provide information to your customers.

a. Open *e04m3fineart* and save it as **e04m3fineart_LastnameFirstname**.

b. Convert the data to a table, and then apply **Table Style Medium 5**.

c. Add a row (below the The Yellow Rose record) for this missing piece of art: **The Yellow Rose, Masterwork Canvas Edition**, **50** edition size, **May 2009** release date, **$895** issue price. Enter **Yes** to indicate the piece is sold out.

d. Sort the table by type in alphabetical order and then by release date from newest to oldest.

e. Add a total row that shows the largest edition size and the most expensive issue price. Delete the Total label in **cell A173**. Add a descriptive label in **cell C173** to reflect the content on the total row.

f. Create a custom conditional format for the Issue Price column with these specifications:
- 4 Traffic Lights icon set (Black, Red, Yellow, Green)
- Red icon when the number is greater than 1000
- Yellow icon when the number is less than or equal to 1000 and greater than 500
- Green icon when the number is less than or equal to 500 and greater than 250
- Black icon when the number is less than or equal to 250.

g. Filter the table by the Green Traffic Light conditional formatting icon.

h. Set the print area to print the **range C1:H173**, select the **first row to repeat at the top of each printout**, set **1″** top and bottom margins, set **0.3″** left and right margins, and then select **landscape orientation**.

i. Wrap text and horizontally center column labels, and then adjust column widths and row heights as needed.

j. Adjust the page break so that at least five Limited Edition Canvas records print on the second page.

k. Create a footer with your name on the left side, the sheet name code in the center, and the file name code on the right side.

l. Save and close the workbook, and submit based on your instructor's directions.

CAPSTONE EXERCISE

You just got an internship at Mountain View Realty, a real estate firm that focuses on the North Utah County area. The previous intern developed a spreadsheet listing houses listed and sold during the past several months. She included addresses, location, list price, selling price, listing date, and date sold. You need to convert the data to a table and manipulate the table. You will manage the large worksheet, prepare the worksheet for printing, sort and filter the table, include calculations, and format the table.

Prepare the Large Worksheet as a Table

You need to freeze the panes so that labels remain onscreen. You also want to convert the data to a table so that you can apply table options.

a. Open the *e04c1houses* workbook and save it as **e04c1houses_LastnameFirstname**.

b. Freeze the first row on the Sales Data worksheet.

c. Convert the data to a table, and then apply the **Table Style Medium 17**.

d. Remove duplicate records.

Add Calculated Fields and a Total Row

The office manager asked you to insert a column to display the percent of list price. The formula finds the sale price percentage of the list price. For example, if a house was listed at $100,000 and sells for $75,000, the percentage of list price is 75%. In some cases, the percentage is more than 100%. This happens when a bidding war occurs, and buyers increase their offers, which results in the seller getting more than the list price.

a. Insert a new field to the right of the Selling Price field. Name the new field **Percent of List Price**.

b. Create a formula with structured references to calculate the percent of the list price.

c. Format the column with **Percent Style** with one decimal place.

d. Insert a new field to the right of the Sale Date field. Name the new field **Days on Market**.

e. Create a formula with structured references to calculate the number of days on the market. If the result displays in a date format, apply the **General number format** to the average.

f. Add a total row to display the average percent of list price and average number of days on market. Format the average number of days on market as a whole number. Use an appropriate label for the total row.

Sort and Print the Table

To help the office manager compare house sales by city, you will sort the data. Then, you will prepare the large table to print.

a. Sort the table by city in alphabetical order, and add a second level to sort by days on market with the houses on the market the longest at the top within each city.

b. Adjust column widths so that the data is one page across (three pages total), and then wrap the column headings as needed.

c. Repeat the column headings on all pages.

d. Display the table in Page Break Preview.

e. Change page breaks so that city data does not span between pages, and then change back to Normal view.

f. Add a footer with your name on the left side, the sheet name code in the center, and the file name code on the right side.

Copy and Filter the Data

The office manager needs to focus on houses that took longer than 30 days to sell within 3 cities. To keep the original data intact for the agents, you will copy the table data to a new sheet and use that sheet to display the filtered data.

a. Copy the Sales Data worksheet, and then place the duplicate worksheet to the right of the original worksheet tab. Convert the table to a range of data, and delete the average row.

b. Rename the duplicate worksheet **Filtered Data**.

c. Display the filter arrows for the data.

d. Filter the data to display the cities of *Alpine*, *Cedar Hills*, and *Eagle Mountain*.

e. Filter the data to display records for houses that were on the market 30 days or more.

Apply Conditional Formatting

To highlight housing sales to illustrate trends, you will apply conditional formatting. Since data are sorted by city, you will use an icon set to color-code the number of days on market. You will also apply a data bar conditional formatting to the sale prices to help the office manager visualize the difference among the sales.

a. Apply the **3 Arrows (Colored) icon set** to the days on market values.

b. Apply the **Light Blue Data Bar conditional formatting** in the *Gradient Fill* section to the selling prices.

c. Create a new conditional format that applies **Yellow fill** and **bold font** to values that contain 95% or higher for the Percent of List Price column.

d. Edit the conditional format you created so that it formats values 98% or higher.

Finalize the Workbook

You are ready to finalize the workbook by adding a footer to the new worksheet and saving the final workbook.

a. Add a footer with your name on the left side, the sheet name code in the center, and the file name code on the right side.

b. Remove all page breaks in the Filtered Data worksheet.

c. Select **landscape orientation**, and then set appropriate margins so that the data will print on one page.

d. Save and close the workbook, and submit based on your instructor's directions.

Doctor Search

You just moved to Florida with your family and are searching for doctors who can meet your family's medical needs. You obtained a list of more than 150 board-certified physicians from the state licensing agency. Open *e04b1doctors* and save it as **e04b1doctors_LastnameFirstname**. Freeze the panes to keep the column labels and IDs from scrolling offscreen. Convert the data to a table, and apply an appropriate table style. Filter the table to show only those who practice Cardiology, Pediatrics, and Internal Medicine and who are accepting new patients in Fort Lauderdale. Sort the filtered records by specialty, last name, and then first name. Set a print area to include all columns except the ID and New Patient columns. Apply a conditional format for dates after 1/1/2008 with a custom format of an Orange fill and a White font. Create a footer with your name, the sheet name code, and the file name code. Save and close the workbook, and submit based on your instructor's directions.

Automobile Car Comparisons

You want to research various car models. Choose a category, such as sedan. Use the Internet to research at least 40 new vehicles. Start a new workbook and save it as **e04b2cars_LastnameFirstname**. Create an input area for a down payment of $5,000, APR, number of payment periods, and number of payments per year (12). Create a source area to list the URL of the Web site you used and the date you retrieved the information. Design the worksheet to list the make, model, year, transmission (automatic or manual), cylinders, liters, horsepower (HP), city miles per gallon (MPG), highway MPG, and manufacturer's suggested retail price. If you can't find the mpg for a particular vehicle, leave those cells blank. Format columns appropriately. Find information for at least five different makes. Include a few similar models, such as a Nissan Altima 2.5 and a Nissan Altima 3.5. Use the base prices. Freeze panes as necessary. Convert the data to a table and apply a table style of your choice. Sort by transmission, then by HP with the largest first, then by make, and finally by model. Add a new calculated column and use structured references to calculate the estimated monthly payment given the input cells. Add a total row to calculate the average HP, MPG, MSRP, and monthly payment. Apply a conditional format to apply a custom fill and font color for the five most expensive vehicles in the sorted list. Apply an icon set to the highway MPG values. On another worksheet, answer these questions: (1) What are the averages? (2) What are the averages for only automatic transmissions with V6 engines? (3) Which vehicle(s) had the highest highway MPG of all the vehicles? and (4) What is the mpg? Filter the Hwy MPG column by one icon color. Prepare both worksheets to print using appropriate page setup options. Create a footer with your name, the sheet name code, and the file name code. Save and close the workbook, and submit based on your instructor's directions.

U.S. Population

A colleague at an advertising firm downloaded U.S. population information from the government Web site. In the process of creating tables, he made some errors and needs your help. Open *e04b3populate* and save it as **e04b3populate_LastnameFirstname**. As you find the errors, document them on the Errors worksheet and make the corrections. Your documentation should include these columns: Error Number, Location, Problem, and Solution. Both tables in the U.S. Population worksheet should show grand total populations per year. The state table should be sorted by region and then by state. Your colleague wants to emphasize the top 15% state populations for the most recent year in the state table. The last column should show percentage changes from year to year, such as 0.6%. Your colleague wants to print only the state data. Select the sorted data population for one region at a time to compare to the regional totals in the first table to cross-check the totals. For example, when you select the July 1, 2008, Midwest values in the second table, the status bar should display the same value as shown for the Midwest July 1, 2008, values in the first table. Create a footer with your name, the sheet name code, and the file name code. Save and close the workbook, and submit based on your instructor's directions.

GLOSSARY

100% stacked column chart A chart type that places (stacks) data in one column per category, with each column having the same height of 100%.

3-D chart A chart that contains a third dimension to each data series, creating a distorted perspective of the data.

Absolute cell reference A designation that provides a permanent reference to a specific cell. When you copy a formula containing an absolute cell reference, the cell reference in the copied formula does not change, regardless of where you copy the formula. An absolute cell reference appears with a dollar sign before both the column letter and row number, such as $B$5.

Access A database program that is included in Microsoft Office.

Active cell The current cell in a worksheet. It is indicated by a dark border onscreen.

Area chart A chart type that emphasizes magnitude of changes over time by filling in the space between lines with a color.

Argument A variable or constant input, such as a cell reference or value, needed to complete a function. The entire group of arguments for a function is enclosed within parentheses.

Auto fill A feature that enables you to copy the contents of a cell or a range of cells or to continue a sequence by dragging the fill handle over an adjacent cell or range of cells.

AVERAGE function A predefined formula that calculates the arithmetic mean, or average, of values in a range.

Axis title A label that describes either the category axis or the value axis.

Backstage view Display that includes commands related to common file activities and that provides information on an open file.

Backup A copy of a file, usually on another storage medium.

Bar chart A chart type that compares values across categories using horizontal bars. In a bar chart, the horizontal axis displays values, and the vertical axis displays categories.

Border A line that surrounds a paragraph, a page, a table, or an image in a document, or that surrounds a cell or range of cells in a worksheet.

Breakpoint The lowest value for a specific category or series in a lookup table.

Bubble chart A chart type that shows relationships among three values by using bubbles to show a third dimension.

Category axis The chart element that displays descriptive group names or labels, such as college names or cities, to identify data.

Category label Text that describes a collection of data points in a chart.

Cell The intersection of a column or row in a worksheet or table.

Cell address The unique identifier of a cell, starting with the column letter and then the row number, such as A9.

Chart A visual representation of numerical data that compares data and helps reveal trends or patterns to help people make informed decisions.

Chart area A boundary that contains the entire chart and all of its elements, including the plot area, titles, legends, and labels.

Chart sheet A sheet within a workbook that contains a single chart and no spreadsheet data.

Chart title The label that describes the entire chart.

Circular reference A situation that occurs when a formula contains a direct or an indirect reference to the cell containing the formula.

Clip art An electronic illustration that can be inserted into an Office project.

Clipboard An Office feature that temporarily holds selections that have been cut or copied.

Clustered column chart A type of chart that groups or clusters similar data into columns to compare values across categories.

Color scale A conditional format that displays a particular color based on the relative value of the cell contents to other selected cells.

Column chart A type of chart that displays data vertically in columns to compare values across different categories.

Column index number The number of the column in the lookup table that contains the return values.

Column width The horizontal measurement of a column in a table or a worksheet. In Excel, it is measured by the number of characters or pixels.

Command A button or area within a group that you click to perform tasks.

Conditional formatting A set of rules that apply special formatting to highlight or emphasize cells that meet specific conditions.

Contextual tab A Ribbon tab that displays when an object, such as a picture or clip art, is selected.

Copy Duplicates a selection from the original location and places the copy in the Office Clipboard.

COUNT function A predefined formula that tallies the number of cells in a range that contain values you can use in calculations, such as numerical and date data, but excludes blank cells or text entries from the tally.

COUNTA function A predefined formula that tallies the number of cells in a range that are not blank; that is, cells that contain data whether a value, text, or a formula.

COUNTBLANK function A predefined formula that tallies the number of cells in a range that are blank.

Cut Removes a selection from the original location and places it in the Office Clipboard.

Data bar A conditional format that displays horizontal gradient or solid fill indicating the cell's relative value compared to other selected cells.

Data label A descriptive label that shows the exact value of the data points on the value axis.

Data point A numeric value that describes a single value on a chart.

Data series A group of related data points that appear in row(s) or column(s) in the worksheet.

Default A setting that is in place unless you specify otherwise.

Dialog box A window that opens when you are accomplishing a task that enables you to make selections or indicate settings beyond those provided on the Ribbon.

Dialog Box Launcher An icon in Ribbon groups that you can click to open a related dialog box.

Doughnut chart A chart type that displays values as percentages of the whole but may contain more than one data series.

Enhanced ScreenTip Provides a brief summary of a command when you place the mouse pointer on the command button.

Excel Software included in Microsoft Office that specializes in organizing data in worksheet form.

Exploded pie chart A chart type in which one or more pie slices are separated from the rest of the pie chart.

Field The smallest data element contained in a table, such as first name, last name, address, and phone number.

File A document or item of information that you create with software and to which you give a name.

Fill color The background color that appears behind data in a cell.

Fill handle A small black square at the bottom-right corner of a cell used to copy cell contents or text or number patterns to adjacent cells.

Filtering The process of specifying conditions to display only those records that meet the conditions.

Find Locates a word or phrase that you indicate in a document.

Folder A named storage location where you can save files.

Font A complete set of characters—upper- and lowercase letters, numbers, punctuation marks, and special symbols with the same design that includes size, spacing, and shape.

Format Painter A Clipboard group command that copies the formatting of text from one location to another.

Formula A combination of cell references, operators, values, and/or functions used to perform a calculation.

Formula AutoComplete A feature that displays a list of functions and defined names that match letters as you type a formula.

Formula Bar An element in Excel that appears below the Ribbon and to the right of the Insert command that shows the contents of the active cell so that you edit the text, value, date, formula, or function.

Freezing The process of keeping rows and/or columns visible onscreen at all times even when you scroll through a large dataset.

Function A predefined computation that simplifies creating a complex calculation and produces a result based on inputs known as arguments.

Function ScreenTip A small pop-up description that displays the arguments for a function as you enter it.

Gallery A set of selections that appears when you click a More button, or in some cases when you click a command, in a Ribbon group.

Gridline A horizontal or vertical line that extends from the horizontal or vertical axis through the plot area.

Group A subset of a tab that organizes similar tasks together.

HLOOKUP function A predefined formula that looks up a value in a horizontal lookup table where the first row contains the values to compare with the lookup value.

Horizontal alignment The placement of data or text between the left and right margins in a document, or cell margins in a spreadsheet.

Icon set A conditional format that displays an icon representing a value in the top third, quarter, or fifth based on values in the selected range.

IF function A predefined logical formula that evaluates a condition and returns one value if the condition is true and a different value if the condition is false.

Input area A range of cells to enter values for variables or assumptions that will be used in formulas within a workbook.

Key Tip The letter or number that displays over features on the Ribbon and Quick Access Toolbar.

Landscape Page or worksheet that is wider than it is tall.

Legend A key that identifies the color, gradient, picture, texture, or pattern assigned to each data series in a chart.

Library An organization method that collects files from different locations and displays them as one unit.

Line chart A chart type that displays lines connecting data points to show trends over equal time periods, such as months, quarters, years, or decades.

Live Preview An Office feature that provides a preview of the results of a selection when you point to an option in a list.

Logical test An expression that evaluates to true or false.

Lookup table A range that contains data for the basis of the lookup and data to be retrieved.

Lookup value The cell reference of the cell that contains the value to look up within a lookup table.

Margin The blank space around the sides, top, and bottom of a document or worksheet.

MAX function A predefined formula that finds the highest value in a range.

MEDIAN function A predefined formula that finds the midpoint value, which is the value that one-half of the population is above or below.

Microsoft Office A productivity software suite that includes word processing, spreadsheet, presentation, and database software components.

MIN function A predefined formula that finds the lowest value in a range.

Mini toolbar An Office feature that provides access to common formatting commands when text is selected.

Mixed cell reference A designation that combines an absolute cell reference with a relative cell reference. When you copy a formula containing a mixed cell reference, either the column letter or the row number that has the absolute reference remains fixed, whereas the other part of the cell reference that is relative changes in the copied formula. A mixed cell reference appears with the $ symbol before either the column letter or row number, such as $B5 or B$5.

Multiple data series Two or more sets of data, such as the values for Chicago, New York, and Los Angeles sales for 2010, 2011, and 2012.

Name Box An element in Excel that identifies the address or range name of the active cell in a worksheet.

Navigation Pane Located on the left side of the Windows Explorer window, providing access to Favorites, Libraries, Homegroup, Computer, and Network areas.

Nested function A function that contains another function embedded inside one or more of its arguments.

Nonadjacent range A collection of multiple ranges that are not positioned in a contiguous cluster in an Excel worksheet.

NOW function A predefined formula that uses the computer's clock to display the current date and time in a cell.

Nper The number of payment periods over the life of the loan.

Order of precedence A rule that controls the sequence in which arithmetic operations are performed.

Output area A range of cells that contains the results of manipulating values in an input area.

Page break An indication where data will start on another printed page. The software inserts automatic page breaks based on data, margins, and paper size. Users can insert additional page breaks.

Paste Places a cut or copied item in another location.

Picture A graphic file that is retrieved from the Internet, a disk, or CD and placed in an Office project.

Pie chart A chart type that shows each data point in proportion to the whole data series as a slice in a circular pie.

Plot area The region containing the graphical representation of the values in the data series.

PMT function A predefined formula that calculates the periodic payment for a loan with a fixed interest rate and fixed term.

Pointing The process of using the mouse pointer to select cells while building a formula. Also known as *semi-selection*.

Portrait Page or worksheet that is taller than it is wide.

PowerPoint A Microsoft Office software component that enables you to prepare slideshow presentations for audiences.

Print area The range of cells within a worksheet that will print.

Print order The sequence in which the pages are printed.

Pv The present value of the loan or an annuity.

Quick Access Toolbar Provides one-click access to commonly used commands.

Radar chart A chart type that compares aggregate values of three or more variables represented on axes starting from the same point.

Range A group of adjacent or contiguous cells in an Excel worksheet.

Range name A word or string of characters assigned to one or more cells. It can be up to 255 letters, characters, or numbers, starting with a letter.

Rate The periodic interest rate; the percentage of interest paid for each payment period.

Record A group of related fields, representing one entity, such as data for one person, place, event, or concept.

Relative cell reference A designation that indicates a cell's relative location within the worksheet using the column letter and row number, such as B5. When a formula containing a relative cell reference is copied, the cell references in the copied formula change relative to the position of the copied formula.

Replace Finds text and replaces it with a word or phrase that you indicate.

Ribbon The long bar of tabs, groups, and commands located just beneath the Title bar.

Row height The vertical measurement of a row in a table or a worksheet.

Semi-selection The process of using the mouse pointer to select cells while building a formula. Also known as *pointing*.

Sheet tab A visual item in Excel that looks like a folder tab that displays the name of a worksheet, such as *Sheet1* or *June Sales*.

Shortcut A link, or pointer, to a program or computer resource.

Sizing handles A series of faint dots on the outside border of a selected chart; enables you to adjust the size of the chart.

Sorting Listing records or text in a specific sequence, such as alphabetically by last name.

Sparkline A small line, column, or win/loss chart contained in a single cell.

Spreadsheet An electronic file that contains a grid of columns and rows to organize related data and to display results of calculations.

Spreadsheet program A computer application, such as Microsoft Excel, that people use to create and modify spreadsheets.

Stacked column chart A chart type that places stacks of data in segments on top of each other in one column, with each category in the data series represented by a different color.

Status bar The horizontal bar located at the bottom of an Office application containing information relative to the open file.

Stock chart A chart type that shows fluctuations in stock changes.

Structured reference A tag or use of a table element, such as a column heading, as a reference in a formula.

Subfolder A folder that is housed within another folder.

SUBTOTAL function A predefined formula that calculates an aggregate value, such as totals, for values in a range or database.

SUM function A predefined formula that calculates the total of values contained in two or more cells.

Surface chart A chart type that displays trends using two dimensions on a continuous curve.

Syntax The rules that dictate the structure and components required to perform the necessary calculations in an equation or evaluate expressions.

Tab Ribbon area that contains groups of related tasks.

Table Organizes information in a series of records (rows), with each record made up of a number of fields (columns).

Table array The range that contains the body of the lookup table, excluding column headings. The first column must be in ascending order to find a value in a range, or it can be in any order to look up an exact value.

Table style The rules that control the fill color of the header row, columns, and records in a table.

Template A predesigned file that incorporates formatting elements, such as a theme and layouts, and may include content that can be modified.

Text One or more letters, numbers, symbols, and/or spaces often used as a label in a worksheet.

Title bar A horizontal bar that appears at the top of each open window. The title bar contains the current file name, Office application, and control buttons.

TODAY function A predefined formula that displays the current date in a cell.

Toggle Commands such as bold and italic that enable you to switch from one setting to another.

Total row A table row that appears below the last row of records in an Excel table, or in Datasheet view of a table or query, and displays summary or aggregate statistics.

Trendline A line that depicts trends or helps forecast future data.

User interface A collection of onscreen components that facilitates communication between the software and the user.

Value A number that represents a quantity or an amount.

Value axis The chart element that displays incremental numbers to identify approximate values, such as dollars or units, of data points in the chart.

Vertical alignment The position of data between the top and bottom cell margins.

View The way a file appears onscreen.

VLOOKUP function A predefined formula that looks up a value and returns a related result from the lookup table.

Windows Explorer A Windows component that can be used to create and manage folders.

Word A word processing program that is included in Microsoft Office.

Workbook A collection of one or more related worksheets contained within a single file.

Worksheet A single spreadsheet that typically contains labels, values, formulas, functions, and graphical representations of data.

Wrap text A formatting option that enables a label to appear on multiple lines within the current cell.

X Y (scatter) chart A chart type that shows a relationship between two variables using their X and Y coordinates. Excel plots one variable on the horizontal X-axis and the other variable on the vertical Y-axis. Scatter charts are often used to represent data in educational, scientific, and medical experiments.

X-axis A horizontal border that provides a frame of reference for measuring data horizontally on a chart.

Y-axis A vertical border that provides a frame of reference for measuring data vertically on a chart.

Zoom slider Enables you to increase or decrease the size of file contents onscreen.

INDEX